Dave Stamboulis was born in 1962 in Athens, Greece, grew up in Berkeley, California, and has called Japan, Nepal, the United Kingdom, and the isle of Crete home at various times. He has taught English as a second language overseas, been a bicycle tour guide, instructed mountaineering, and picked organic strawberries for a living, amongst other things.

Dave now divides his time between Bellingham, Washington and Thailand, freelance writing between adventure travel stints. Stamboulis has travelled extensively, from Asia to Africa to Latin America, predominantly via self-propelled transport, and reckons he will never stop doing so, as long as there is an adventure to be had, and a story to be told.

Published by Sanuk Press, Bellingham, Washington, U.S.A.

Edited by Curtis Foreman
Maps and Cover Design by Sombat Somkiatcharoen

All photographs in this book taken by the author

Cover photo: Odysseus and friend, on the road to Tibet; Gansu, China
Back Jacket: Mount Everest and Nuptse, Nepal; bicycle sunsets from heaven; Swayambunath Stupa, Kathmandu, Nepal; author in Ilhara Valley, Cappadocia, Turkey

Lyrics from 'Wherever I May Roam," written by James Hetfield and Lars Ulrich, courtesy of Creeping Death Music, © 1991, All Rights Reserved.

Publisher's Cataloging-in-Publication:

    Stamboulis, Dave.
        Odysseus' last stand : the chronicles of a bicycle
    nomad / Dave Stamboulis.
        p. cm.
        LCCN 2004096483
        ISBN 0-9760134-5-2

        1. Stamboulis, Dave--Travel. 2. Cyclists--Biography.
    3. Bicycle touring. 4. Voyages around the world.
    I. Title.

    GV1051.S68A3 2005   796.6'092
                QBI04-200395

Printed in Thailand

To contact the author or see more photos of the journey, go to
www.odysseuslaststand.com

10 9 8 7 6 5 4 3 2 1

For all the providers of tea on the high roads of Asia

Odysseus' Last Stand
The Chronicles of a Bicycle Nomad

Dave Stamboulis

SANUK PRESS

CONTENTS

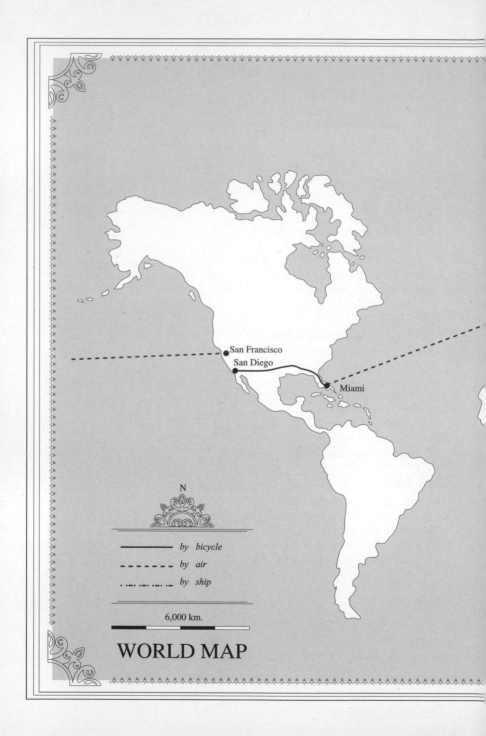

San Francisco
San Diego
Miami

N

——————— by bicycle

- - - - - - - by air

-·-··-··-··-· by ship

6,000 km.

WORLD MAP

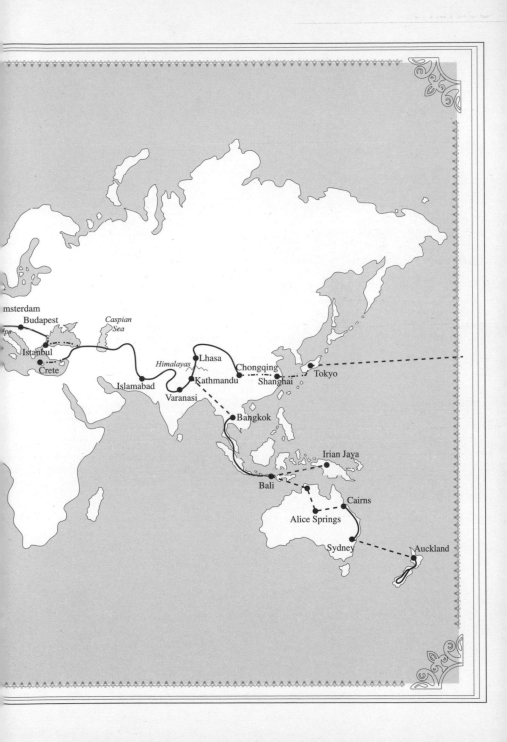

Prologue

There are basically two types of men in the world. Those who stay at home, and those who don't.

Kipling

The sole cause of man's unhappiness is that he does not know how to stay quietly in his own room.

Blaise Pascal

I n the fall of 1992 I began a bicycle trip around the world. From my home in New Mexico, I made a tune-up ride to my family home in California, then caught a flight across the Pacific Ocean to Japan. This was only the beginning.

I had only two real goals in mind at the start of this adventure: to visit India and the Himalayas, and to cover the 40,000 odd kilometers one would traverse if following a straight line around the circumference of the equator.

I had a fair amount of travel experience, a stint of bicycle touring under my belt, and a meager amount of savings—but I had little idea of how I would proceed to follow my dreams. I was sure of one thing, though. I wanted an adventure. I figured that an irrevocable change was coming to the mysterious world of foreign travel, of exotic lands, of princes and princesses, of unexplored castles and ruins. Guidebooks, air access, and visas to hidden kingdoms were becoming commonplace. The ends of the earth were no longer a myth passed down by a grandparent, but a package tour that included a rental car.

In San Francisco, where I had grown up, adventure travel was becoming a fad. Anyone with the time and money could now raft a wild rapid in the Amazon, climb a Himalayan peak, or mountain bike along tracks in the Alps. I felt sure that with all this exotic tourism taking place, indigenous cultures weren't long for the earth. The world's sleepy hamlets and island villages were headed for changes that I wasn't sure I wanted to witness.

I also knew that I was changing. Ten years forward might find me married, settled down, or in a career that might not be so easy to leave. My health might deteriorate, the world might go to war, and there were a million things that might be markedly different, rendering such a journey impossible.

Although I knew I would always be a traveller, I wanted to experience one great adventure, one I would remember for the rest of my days, one I could tell grandchildren and take to my grave. I wanted one last stand.

My companion in this endeavor was to be a Trek Single-Track mountain bike, a solidly built piece of metal that I had bought from a friend. I christened the bike Odysseus, after the hero of Homer's epic, a man who roamed every inch of the Mediterranean fighting monsters, saving maidens, and having one adventure on top of another.

Odysseus longed to return to his homeland, but constantly found himself in situations which prevented this; when he did finally return, he no longer recognized the place he had left, having become an eternal captive to a life at sea. Half Greek myself, I identified with Odysseus and his journeys, and the thought did cross my mind that perhaps I too would one day become adrift at sea, unable to return home, but I shrugged off such notions and set out for my sojourn.

If I had known that it would take me seven years to return home, I might not have gone. Then again, we never really know how our dreams and expectations will turn out in real life; nor are we ever truly prepared to deal with them when they take shape in front of us.

What follows is the story of my travels. Bits, pieces, and ideas gleaned from the road. Faces and places, mostly remembered from the copious notes I copied in the set of fifteen journals that accompanied me during my journey. Characters and impressions gathered along a timeline that started in Japan and ended across the Pacific, in the United States, seven years later.

Like any other traveller, I suffer from the disease of stereotyping. In order to bring some sense to our own worldview, humans label, judge, and create boxes for other people and cultures to fit into. I lay no claim to being any kind of an expert on world politics, on historical or archaeological doctrine; nor do I have a plan that will solve hunger, strife, or other ills. I do, however, have a set of keen eyes, two open ears, and a pen eager to record the tales of others, and I hope to show, perhaps, that somewhere and somehow in this great wide world, we are—more or less—all the same.

The world that I experienced on this journey was mine and mine alone, the reality I lived the same. I hope the reader will take my stories for what they are: encounters on the road of life, with no hidden meanings. More importantly, I hope he or she can garner a laugh or two from my musings and perhaps learn something new. Finally, I hope that my story will plant in the minds of all who read it the seeds of inspiration for their own journeys and explorations, in whatever form those travels may take.

Part One

Far East:
Travels in Asia

He who travels far will often see things far removed from what he believed was Truth. When he talks about it in the fields at home, he is often accused of lying, for the obdurate people will not believe what they do not see and distinctly feel. Inexperience, I believe, will give little credence to my song.

Herman Hesse, *A Journey to the East*

Travel is fatal to prejudice, bigotry, and narrow-mindedness, and many of our people need it sorely on these accounts. Broad, wholesome, charitable views of men and things cannot be acquired by vegetating in one little corner of the earth all one's lifetime.

Mark Twain

Chapter One
Beginnings

Whenever I see an adult on a bicycle, I have hope for the human race.

H.G. Wells

Peculiar travel suggestions are dancing lessons from God.

Kurt Vonnegut

"**B**icycle around the world?!"
"Are you nuts?"
"You must be plumb out of your mind."
"You'll be killed."
"It's too dangerous."
"What about settling down and getting married?"
"How will you afford it?"

My mother, fortunately, asked none of these questions, nor any of the others that I was to hear in abundance in the coming weeks and years. She had become accustomed to expecting the unusual from me. Her gene for wanderlust had been passed down, and she accepted my journeys with pride and excitement, if with the usual worrying and sadness over separation that mothers feel whenever their offspring leave the nest.

She had met my father in Greece while journeying through Europe, and had always been a lover of things foreign and mysterious, of charming side streets and hidden alleys, of the new and novel.

One of my mother's often-told stories was that of our journey to the New World. Leaving Greece when I was two years old, we sailed for New York on a packed freighter in tumultuous seas. Halfway across the Atlantic, everyone on board was in the prone position, moaning, retching, and dizzy, praying fervently to their gods to help them through the night. I, on the other hand, was busy playing on deck, despite my mother's entreaties to abandon my crawling for more restive pastures.

Many years later, although I had not made any pilgrimages to exotic places or even taken more than a normal share of family vacations, my best friend gave me a birthday card with the Chinese character for "wanderer" drawn upon it. So, perhaps it was in the cards all along.

Upon completing school, I spent three years wandering through Europe, the Soviet Union, and North Africa, mostly on foot. I had a very strong desire, for no clear reason, to get to India. I also decided that I would get there on foot, an idea that I abandoned somewhere in the mountains in Crete.

I did this partly due to the satisfaction I felt with the journey as it was at the time, partly because I had fallen in love, and mostly because I realized that walking to India might take up most of the rest of my life. I could think of a few other things that I wanted to do.

So I returned home and got involved in taking children to the mountains, sharing with them my love of walking. The walking grew to include bicycling, which I found to be a perfect medium for travel. I could travel long distances in one day, yet the pace was slow enough to keep me in contact with the landscape and its inhabitants. The bicycle had a simple design, was fairly easy and economical to maintain, and could hold more gear than a backpack without putting any strain on a rider's back.

The trips with kids expanded to include trips with adults, and I went on to lead several small tours, something I enjoyed immensely. As with walking, something about the self-sufficiency of cycling appealed to me. All the necessary gear was packed in four bike bags, and the distance covered in a day was entirely dependent on one's own muscular and cardiovascular power—not on a motor or a fossil fuel.

The intensity of life on a bicycle was also something I found most alluring. There was, of course, the physical challenge of pushing one's body to certain limits. Climbing a mountain pass, or breaking a personal distance record, produced considerable endorphin levels. The environment was also consistently providing challenges. Rarely was the weather perfect; it was often baking hot, rainy, misty, drizzling, dusty, cold, freezing, or—worst of all—windy. Cycling through these different conditions increased the intensity factor twofold.

Even more dramatic than the weather were the experiences with people. With a group of people cycling together, day in, day out, there were no diversions like jobs, classes, or other friends. When it rained, everyone got wet; when the grades steepened, everyone sweated; and when the conditions and surroundings made people testy, there wasn't really anywhere to go blow off steam—except at each other.

Obviously, this made for some rough moments, but it also created some deep bonds and true understanding. To this day, people I have toured with know me better than some of my oldest friends, and perhaps as well as my family.

People interact with cyclists because cyclists are not threatening. Few folks have ever been attacked by someone riding a loaded contraption weighing over seventy pounds. It isn't too convenient a getaway vehicle. So a cyclist is likely to be approached by strangers, and to come to see strangers as friendly and benign.

Travellers behave differently than people who stay in one place. Nobody knows a traveller's history or baggage, so the traveller can invent any personality he or she chooses. Also, because meetings are often so brief, with little or no chance of ever seeing the other again, there isn't much time to beat around the bush. Romances happen quickly when people travel because there is no time to lose.

This type of lifestyle is not for many people. Much of society is built on predictability, stability, consistency, and minimal intensity. However, if it is in one's blood, there really is no other way to go.

After leading a cycling trip across the United States for three months, I thought I would look forward to settling down. I found myself doing precisely the opposite. I had trouble sleeping indoors and missed being constantly out in the wind and sun. When I went downtown, strangers didn't come up to chat. No one asked where I was going or how I was doing. I found it strange to be taken for granted most of the time; my friends knew they would see me in a week or a month, so it didn't matter if we got together this weekend or next. The woman I was dating was thrilled to see me every other weekend, while I was tearing my hair out over not spending twenty-four hours a day with her.

I spent my free time perusing maps of every continent except the one I lived on. A good friend of mine was moving to New Zealand and I bought his bicycle, a mountain bike with a heavy frame and fat tires. I decorated it with Charlie Chaplin stickers, a Tibetan bell, and decals reading "Divorce Your Car" and "Peace on Dirt."

It hit me that there was another bike tour left. It was the one which had been inside me some years before when I descended off of the Cretan mountain. This time, I wouldn't stop after I had ridden across the country. This time, I would start at the ocean and stop when I arrived back at the same ocean. I would draw some sort of line, like the equator, and follow it around the globe.

I had long dreamed of going to the Himalayas, and of sitting beside the Ganges in India, but I had no plan for how to get there. These places were so many thousands of kilometers away that planning to ride there seemed rather unrealistic. Instead, I focused on what lay directly in front of me—the Pacific Ocean—and the first land I would come to after crossing it: Japan.

I wasn't completely ignorant when it came to the Land of the Rising Sun. I had grown up with Japanese culture around me. Many of my schoolmates were Japanese-American; I had eaten *sashimi*; I knew how to use chopsticks; I had heard about *sumo*, *taiko* drumming, flower arrangement, and tea ceremony. I had read Mishima and Lady Murasaki, and I loved the films of Kurosawa. And I had a deep interest in Zen Buddhism, particular to Japan, and its very practical and down-to-earth approach to daily living.

Two of my best friends from school had ended up in Japan. Both were earning small fortunes teaching English, and both had married Japanese women. I used to joke with them that if I reached my mid-thirties and was unmarried and without cash, I would move to Japan, but it had always been a joke and nothing more.

However, as I started planning for my journey, I realized that the first country I would reach upon crossing the ocean was expensive—and that I had minimal savings.

Searching for ideas, I came across a book called *The National Parks of Japan*. It was to chart my course, and would eventually change my life. I had always imagined Japan as a place of skyscrapers and concrete, of businessmen in suits who did nothing but work, of all the latest and greatest in technology. Yet the book showed nothing like that. It pointed out that ninety percent of Japan is made up of uninhabitable mountains, and that most people therefore live on the very densely populated plains. Here before me were huge granite spires, deep cedar forests, snowy ridges, and sleepy towns snuggled into the base of the mountains.

One range in particular caught my fancy: the Northern Alps. Alps? In Japan? Yes, indeed. The center of the main island of Honshu is composed of three very large ranges, which run west to east. The *Kita* (north), *Chuo* (central), and *Minami* (south) Alps are so named because of their resemblance to the European Alps, although in Japanese pronunciation, they come out as *"a-ru-psu."* Japan has twenty peaks higher than 3000 meters in elevation; nineteen are within the Japanese Alps. Number twenty is Mount Fuji.

Although I knew I didn't have enough savings to come close to getting around the world, I refused to think about working in places like Tokyo or Osaka, which I imagined to be big, polluted, impersonal cities. There was no way I was going to trade my quiet space in the mountains of New Mexico for hard cash. I had figured that I would deal with work and money when the situation presented itself. Yet here was a place I could imagine myself living.

The Northern Alps were the highest, snowiest, and most serrated ridges and peaks in the country, referred to as "The Roof of Japan." Yet they lay only a few hours from Tokyo, and soon I was picturing myself living at the feet of these snowy giants. I bought detailed maps, studied the topography of Central Honshu, and marked off several small cities smack in the middle of the mountains, figuring that these places would have English schools where I might find work. Then, excited by all the prospects ahead, I picked up a phrase book and dictionary and went to a sushi bar for lunch.

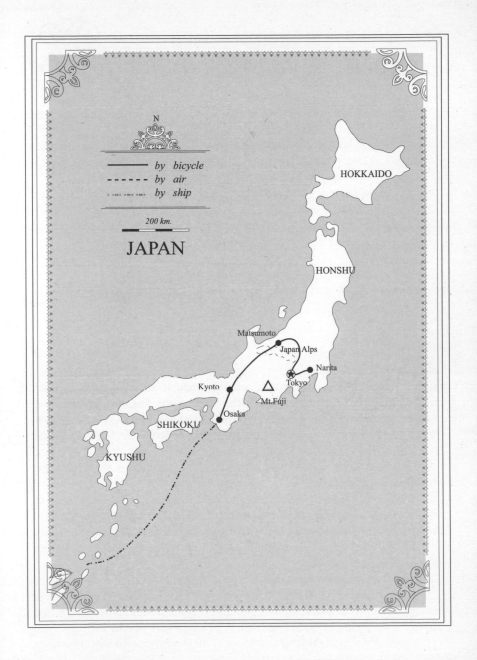

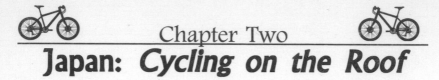

Chapter Two
Japan: *Cycling on the Roof*

> *The body's existence is like a bubble. Might*
> *as well accept what happens. Events and hopes*
> *seldom agree, but he who can step back doesn't worry.*
> *We blossom and fade like flowers; gather and part*
> *like clouds. Worldly thoughts I forgot long ago.*
> *Relaxing all day on a peak.*

> Stonehouse (Taoist Poet)

> *A good traveller is one who does not know*
> *where he is going to, and a perfect traveller does not*
> *know where he came from.*

> Lin Yu Tang

The chubby Japanese waitress with ruddy cheeks keeps giving me furtive glances. Here is this dirty, sweating foreigner, who has disembarked from an overloaded bicycle and proceeded to order and devour three times the amount of food an average customer might eat. She is waiting for the right moment to give me the bill, and thinks this will be it, but now I am laughing uproariously, sitting by myself at a corner table.

I have stopped at a Chinese restaurant in a small ski resort town in the Japanese Alps, after a crazy week of hard pedalling through some of the steepest terrain I have ever encountered. I am laughing because my fortune cookie has proclaimed, "You will make many changes before settling satisfactorily."

What an understatement.

Japan thus far has been a country of extremes, where nothing ever fits expectations or explanations. Several days before, I had been invited to stay with Ryuto Shiraishi and his wife in the city of Maebashi. Ryuto is the local Prefectural Mountain Association leader, and upon hearing of my love of mountains and hot springs, he told me to reroute my planned course into the Japan Alps through an area that would offer remote springs and scenic cycling.

So a few days later, I am on my bicycle, heading up a precipitous canyon which leads me through quaint, misty, green villages, past old wooden homes with black tiled roofs. Everywhere I stop here, people give me huge apples, as it is the harvest season, and cans of cold coffee.

Prices here are high. An apple costs over a dollar, a coffee from three to five, and a melon twenty-five! However, there are deals to be had. The Japanese do not, it seems, want to eat the ends of loaves of bread, which they use for crumbs or chickenfeed. These end pieces are called *pan no mimi* ("bread ears") and the good news is that for about twenty cents, one can buy an entire bag of these ends.

Sometimes the bakery even gives them away for free, and later on during my stay in Japan, when the staff at my local bakery would spot me coming, they would smile and get out a bag from under the counter, whispering to one another as I walked in the door, "*Pan no mimi gaijin desu!*" ("It's the bread ears foreigner!")

The mountain road narrows and climbs beside a river, and at dusk I reach Shiriake Onsen (Roasting Hip Hot Spring), as promised by Mr. Shiraishi. It is one of the best natural hot pools in Japan. The river here has been dammed off, and wide gravel beaches flank a large, deep bathing area of 104 degree mineral water. I strip off and plunge in, letting the heat and sulfur penetrate every muscle and joint, exalted after a hard day's ride.

After soaking to contentment, I towel off, pitch my tent next to the river, and before I can do anything else, am promptly invited to dinner by a group of ten young ladies here on a weekend escape. They are having a huge fish barbecue and they encourage me to eat without hesitation. As I focus on putting away protein, they "ooh!" and "ahh!" over my bike and the size of my calves, and they giggle in unison every time I ask them a question. They tell me that my use of chopsticks is extremely proficient, as well as my Japanese. Neither observation is even remotely close to the truth. They also say that I look like Harrison Ford, which is even more farfetched.

At ten p.m., absolutely sated, dizzy from several carafes of *sake* and *shochu* (rice whiskey), and after flirting with the ladies in the hot springs, I think that Japan just might be heaven on earth.

In the morning, after more flattery and an invitation to breakfast, I get on the road and begin a tremendously steep climb into the mountains. There are eleven-percent grades, hairpin turns, and rivers of water flowing down the road. The sky begins to cloud up, the temperature drops, and within an hour the wind begins to howl. A sign tells me that a pass is only twelve kilometers ahead, so I don't pay much attention to the weather, and keep on pedalling.

Shortly, side gusts threaten to throw me from my saddle, and after thirty minutes I am in a raging blizzard. Blinding snow hammers at me from all sides, temperatures are below freezing, and the winds roar up around sixty kilometers an hour. Although Odysseus is loaded with seventy pounds of gear, four saddlebags, and a backpack across the rear rack, I am still being tossed sideways by the wind, and soon I can no longer ride, so I begin to walk my bike. Shortly afterwards, even this is no longer possible. I stop in a pullout and pull on all the clothing I have: polypropylene, fleece, storm parka, gloves, wool hat, wool socks, and tights.

Quite a few cars have pulled into the parking lot, as they can no longer see to drive, and I assume that I will soon be invited into a back seat, to warmth, comfort, and probably a can of coffee and a snack. But this never happens. People stare at me through their windows as if I am an alien or a trapped animal. I start to wonder what will happen if the snow continues like this. Will I be able to pitch my tent with the winds roaring like they are? Last night I was treated like a monarch, and today I am lowlier than a serf. People continue to gape at me from safety behind glass, and I wonder if they can tell that I am becoming hypothermic. I wonder how they would react if I began to lose consciousness, and I figure they would probably stare even harder. After last night's hospitality, I am shocked by their coldness and real lack of concern.

Most fortunately, the storm abates after thirty minutes, and I push my bike the last kilometers up to the Shirane Pass, where there is a souvenir shop and a noodle stand. I sit by a heater and gulp down several bowls of steaming hot noodles, swearing they are the best thing I have ever eaten. My hands and feet begin to regain feeling. The folks around me try to make small talk, chatting on about how cold it is outside, as if I didn't know. I wonder if any of them were sitting in those cars at the side of the road.

Back in my Chinese restaurant, I pay my bill to the bemused waitress, then cycle another ten kilometers up a very steep road to the base of

Mount Shirouma (White Horse Mountain), where I have planned to camp and do some hiking. Behind a mountaineer's lodge, a large parking lot overlooks a rushing river and magnificent forests of cedar, birch, and Japanese maples. I pitch my tent in a corner of the lot, wash my sweat-drenched clothing, brew a cup of tea, and begin a hike into the forest. As I leave the parking lot, a shabbily dressed fellow stares at me; he makes me uncomfortable, but I shrug the feeling off. After all, this is Japan, the safest place in the world.

Several hours later, I am soaking my sore muscles in the 108 degree mineral water of yet another hot spring pool, staring out at the sea of autumn colors in the valley below. Fiery red Japanese maples are the centerpieces. I am alone, save for one other hiker who stops in for a quick dip, then leaves me to my solitude.

I lie back and marvel. I came on this journey in search of perfect moments like these. When I woke up this morning, I had no idea that I would be in this magical place come afternoon. I don't know where I will end up tomorrow, whom I will meet, or what lessons I will learn. Such are the fantasies of travel. I linger long, and finally, not wanting to be caught by darkness, dress and begin my descent, in the glowing late afternoon light.

I reach the parking lot shortly before dark and a wave of shock rips through my body. My tent is no longer perched on the precipice at the other side of the lot. It's gone!

My bike is still there, locked to a tree, but the tent is nowhere to be seen. I search frantically around the empty parking lot and peer over the cliff face at its edge. There is nothing but bushes, trees, and the whitewater below.

I dash to the lodge and in a panicked voice try to explain what has happened. "My *tento, tento*," I yell. "Somebody stole it! *Dorobo, dorobo!*"("Thief!")

The owner calls some younger staff over, hoping that one of them speaks some English. After they confer for several minutes, one of the group musters up the courage to speak to me.

"Yuru tento," he slowly announces, "coming hericopteru, maybe tento away browing."

I am in no mood to put my three months of Japanese study to practice, but I try to decipher what the guy has said, and slowly it dawns on me.

"You mean to say that a helicopter landed in the parking lot, and blew my tent away," I respond in disbelief.

My translator nods sheepishly.

"But that makes no sense," I reply. I point out that the tent was full of heavy gear, and that my clothes, which were drying on a rock beside the tent, are still there.

"Besides," I continue, "I saw a very suspicious fellow on my way out of the parking lot. I hate to say it, but I think I have been robbed."

In the twilight, the entire staff troops out to my camp spot, looking for clues, but we find nothing. It is dark and cold, and there is not much we can do, so I return to the lodge, pay seventy-five dollars for a futon and tiny plate of rice, fish, and pickles, and lie down feeling miserable.

My tent is gone, with all my camping and cold weather gear. At this time of year in Japan, one needs every piece of it—not to mention that at seventy-five bucks a pop for accommodation (in a spartan mountain hut, not a hotel), most of my precious savings will be eaten up in no time. Additionally, the one suit that I own is gone; I had carted it along with the intention of finding a teaching job in Japan.

I know that it is useless to ponder my misfortune any further until morning. I resolve that my journey is probably over, just as soon as it had begun, and I start making plans to call an airline for a ticket home.

The next morning, the police arrive as I am spooning the last bit of raw egg and rice into my mouth. (This culinary delicacy was included in my overnight fee.) The inspector is orderly and businesslike, and he spends an hour taking down the details of what I am missing. He asks for the measurements of my tent, the waist and cuff size of my suit, and the number of pockets in my fleece jacket. I try to describe the strange-looking fellow I saw the day before, but the inspector is more interested in recording the sizes, shapes, and colors of my various items.

After the inspector has scribbled various notes, he accompanies the staff and me on a reconnaissance mission. I end up at the river with the lodge manager, and we both gaze out at the raging water. Reading my thoughts, the manager says, "*Kawai so, ne?*" ("It's a pity, isn't it?") It's as if we both can see my tent, and my dreams of world travel, sailing down the river to a land of no return.

From above us, there is a shout and a lot of commotion, and we race back up to the parking lot to find the inspector clinging to a set of roots at the top of the cliff. He is sweating profusely, covered in dust, and out of breath, yet he beams proudly at me, and I see that he is dragging my tent behind him! It had fallen and disappeared in a thicket of brambles, and this man has conjured it up and hauled it back over the edge.

Huffing and puffing, the inspector dusts himself off, shakes my hand, makes some final notes, bows to us all, and departs.

I offer multiple thanks to the lodge staff—as well as profuse apologies over my accusations of theft—then sit back and try to figure out how the tent blew away while my t-shirts and socks did not.

All is okay, except that two of the tent poles are broken. The lodge staff tell me about an outdoor shop in the city of Matsumoto, about fifty kilometers away, which should be able to repair or replace the poles. I load my gear and say goodbye and thank you once again to the staff, who line up and bow repeatedly in unison. Then I head off down the road, my spirits buoyed by the turn of events.

A day later, I am in Matsumoto, a lovely city set in a basin and surrounded by mountain peaks in an area known as "the Roof of Japan." On one side of the city rise the highest peaks of Japan's Northern Alps, with such evocative names as *Yarigatake* (Spear Peak), *Chogatake* (Butterfly Peak), and *Washibadake* (Eagle Peak). All are around 3000 meters in height, towering several thousand meters above the city, and all are deep in snow at this point in mid-fall. On the other side of the valley rises a 2000-meter highland plateau called *Utskushigaharakogen* (Beautiful Highlands), home to abundant hot spring waters.

Matsumoto is home to an old castle, built by the samurai lord Ishikawa in the late 1500's. With its slanted roof of black tiles, its red bridges, and its long moat surrounded by cherry trees, the castle is the main attraction of the city.

I have no trouble finding Ishii Sports, a sleek, high-tech outdoor shop which promises to have my poles repaired in several days. I spend my free time wandering about the city sampling the local specialties (in descending order of taste: buckwheat noodles, fried grasshoppers, and raw horsemeat) and I make camp in the local cemetery.

Japanese cemeteries are ideal camping spots; they are clean, well maintained, completely safe, and quiet—no one visits at night, due to fear of ghosts. If a camper were famished, he or she might be tempted by the fruit, cakes, and other goodies left as offerings throughout the tombs and shrines.

On my third night in Matsumoto it pours for six hours. Without my tent, I can only lay in a huge puddle, unable to leave the relative warmth of my soaked sleeping bag. Come morning, I feel like a sponge and check into the Nishiya *minshuku*.

A *minshuku* is the equivalent of a bed and breakfast, a family style inn with traditional Japanese *tatami* (bamboo mat) rooms and excellent home cooking. Upon arrival, one is served tea, then proceeds to take a leisurely bath, dons a *yukata* (robe), and relaxes until a scrumptious dinner is served.

Foreigners are often greeted with reservation in these places, owing to the often-correct belief that foreigners know nothing about Japanese customs. Most visitors do know the rule about removing shoes before entering homes or inns; however, other rules can be quite confusing.

One rule is that different slippers are to be worn in different parts of a house. For example, there are room slippers and then there are toilet slippers. Wandering through the *minshuku*, I forget that the toilet slippers are still on my feet, not realizing why the other guests are staring at me until I have returned to my room and discovered my mistake. Shame-faced, I tiptoe back down the hallway to make an exchange.

Bath etiquette is also tricky. In Japan, the tub of hot water is meant for many people to enjoy; one soaps up and rinses off outside the tub before climbing in to relax. On my first foray, I make the error of cleaning myself in the tub, then commit the cardinal sin of draining the tub when I am done, which leads the staff of the *minshuku* to ignore me completely for the rest of my stay.

I will be prepared against such blunders the second time round, but even as I prepare to leave, I see that my soaked bike panniers have stained the *tatami* mat floors. Flushed deep with embarrassment, I sneak out in the early hours of the morning.

By late afternoon, the rains have started again. I linger in a ramen shop for two hours slurping something called *tanuki* (raccoon) ramen—which fortunately does not contain any raccoon—then go to the train station. Matsumoto station is dry, with restrooms, noodle shops, sushi bars, and newsstands. A loudspeaker announcement screams, *"Matsumoooooooto, Matsumoooooooto, Matsumoooooooto desu,"* to greet every incoming train. Throngs of skiers, alpinists, and nature lovers tumble wearily out of trains from Tokyo, Osaka, Nagoya, and other metropolises.

I spend several hours in the relative comforts of the station, watching a group of junior high school girls in their matching uniforms giggling over the contents of their animated *manga* magazines. These include pictures of women in compromising positions with horses, and also a superhero-like character who soars over the streets of Tokyo, relieving himself as he flies. The girls show me both of these unabashedly, as if they were something one might see every day.

At six, I return to the outdoor shop to collect my poles, only to learn that they won't be ready for two more days. Dismally, I retrace my steps through the flooded streets to the station, where the girls have been replaced by businessmen who practice imaginary golf swings as they wait for their train.

At nine it is still raining, and I make several resolutions. One: I will not return to the cemetery to sleep. Two: I will not pay for the *minshuku* (I probably wouldn't be welcomed back anyway). I sit, pace, check on my bike every half an hour or so, and sit some more.

As I sit, it hits me that I might find myself in this position a lot in the coming years. Here I am in the middle of Japan, in a town where I know no one, with no place to go and no money to make myself comfortable. I feel lonely, bored, and quite miserable. Yet this is just the beginning. If I want to ride my bicycle around the world, I will probably be in situations like this thousands of times. Then again, during the tent incident a week earlier I had been ready to cash the whole trip in. I resolve to stay in the train station until the rain stops, whenever that might be.

At ten, I check on my bike again as an excuse to stretch my legs and escape the chain-smoking imaginary golf pros. As I bend over my panniers to take out my toothbrush, I notice a man standing close to me and staring. He is a *salaryman*, one of Japan's famed overworked millions, a man who gives his life to his company. His eyes are bloodshot, his hair disheveled, his teeth stained, and he reeks of alcohol.

He continues to stare, then points a finger at me and slurs out in broken English, "You know, when I was young man, twenty-five years ago, I rode my bicycle from Hokkaido to Tokyo. Very good times and I know exactly how you feel. You are now coming with me."

We stare at each other and he lurches toward the street, ordering me to follow. In no position to refuse, I do so. Twenty minutes later, I am seated in the warm, dry living room of Kazuhiro Suzuki, being served warm *sake* by his kind wife, and being gaped at by his cute young daughter.

Suzuki runs a small trading company, which consumes his life. He rises at four-thirty and is at his desk by six. Around five p.m., the *sake* bottle comes out and Suzuki and his co-workers begin the transition from business to pleasure. At around nine, he makes his way to the local bathhouse, where he soaks for an hour; then he returns home, where his wife greets him with a cup of tea and snack. He watches the news, tumbles into bed, and arises six hours later to do the same thing again. And again.

Over the next few months I met dozens of men exactly like Suzuki, entrenched in a grinding routine that seemed to sap them of all strength and energy, yet one to which they remained dutifully committed. I had seen overworked people back home, but the level of it here was astounding. The *salarymen* I met often had little communication with their wives and children, yet they claimed that every minute spent at work was solely for the family's benefit. A more reasonable middle ground was not an option. The longer I remained in Japan, the more I saw and understood the focus on responsibility and commitment that drives Japan's economic miracle.

The concepts of *giri* (obligation) and fate were usually expressed in Japanese with the words *"shokatta ga nai."* (Literally, "There is nothing that can be done.") These concepts were integral parts of Japanese life, in total contrast to my own culture's attitude, which decreed, "If you don't like it, change it—or leave."

Here, one accepted things for what they were, even if they often seemed a burden. Perhaps the kindness of a fellow like Suzuki was based on a memory, a fantasy long past, that in sharing in my journey he could find some small escape.

Hours later, introductions made, bath readied, far too much *sake* drunk, I sprawl on my futon next to Suzuki, who snores away in a deep stupor, and ponder my change in fortune. In years to come, I would learn to expect situations like these when I needed them, to teach me, guide me, and assist me on my journey. As one event led to another, I would begin to see the connectedness between all things, the impossibility of separate events or choices. A week ago, my tent poles broke, which brought me to Matsumoto. Now the poles were not yet ready, and that brought Mr. Suzuki into my life. In the weeks and months to come, dozens of other events would completely change my life, and all because a helicopter had blown my tent over a cliff.

Soon afterwards, I find myself living in Matsumoto. Upon hearing that I like the city so much and find its inhabitants so friendly, Mr. Suzuki proceeds to introduce me to various people who all take an immediate interest in my welfare. Due to the high cost of living in Japan, I insist that I must find work; immediately, all my new colleagues ask all of their friends if they need an English teacher.

My first students are the Minemuras, a young couple who are to become my very close friends in the coming months. Koichi, the husband, is an animated, stocky fellow with little interest in studying. Mikiko, his wife, is fluent and doesn't need much instruction, but she comes along to help Koichi with translation and to enjoy our evenings together. I realize that they are both probably just doing a favor for Koichi's sister Sayaka, who introduced us, and who is concerned about my staying and finding work.

Our first English lesson, for which I am paid fifty dollars an hour, goes something like this: we go to an elegant *sashimi* restaurant and put away over a hundred dollars' worth of exquisite fresh raw fish, ranging from eel to octopus to salmon eggs. Following this, we head to a beer bar and get sloshed. With Miki translating, Koichi asks me which sports I like, what foods I eat, and how I rate American women; he also tells me about his passion for collecting aquarium fish. I don't teach one grammar point or correct any pronunciation, and the only English Koichi speaks is the frequent "Cheers!" as we raise our glasses.

For our next lesson, Koichi insists that we go to a Philippine bar. I have heard stories of ethnic bars in Japan, reputed to be brothels and seedy strip joints full of bonded slave girls. The bar we visit could not be further from this description—at least on the surface. We enter the smoky chambers and are surrounded immediately by several young and smiling hostesses, who seat us and bring a bottle of whisky to our table. I will learn later that Koichi paid 500 dollars for this bottle.

We sip our whisky while the hostesses massage our hands, fill our glasses, and tell us how handsome we are. They then lead us to the jukebox to sing karaoke songs in duet. The only English songs available are classics by the Beatles, Elvis Presley, and Tony Bennett; after several months of bar invitations, I will become proficient at singing "Imagine" and "I Left My Heart in San Francisco."

At two a.m., we leave and head for a ramen shop to eat. We find a "Korean" ramen shop, where Korean hostesses make sure we wipe our chins after slurping noodles. Once we have finished, of course, we go to the karaoke box for the obligatory sing-along. I think I am seeing things when Koichi pays 400 dollars for the four bowls of noodles we have eaten, and I ask Miki to make sure I have not lost my mind. She checks with him, turns to me, and shrugs her shoulders with a smile that seems to say, "What can I do?"

The Minemuras certainly aren't wealthy by Japanese standards, although they are definitely overgenerous. As we leave the bar, I think about the phrase, "Money grows on trees," and how that tree seems to flourish in Japan.

Several months later, I have a full-time teaching job, a nice apartment, and a very settled life. I am working hard and saving much of my salary in preparation for continuing my journey.

One evening, as I finish my last class and am packing up for the evening, a very pretty and petite woman walks into my schoolroom. Her name is Hitomi Sumita, and she is interested in language lessons. She has sparkling dark eyes, thick black hair, a mirthful and infectious laugh, and a wide smile. Her English is more than decent, and she speaks it as though she is more Italian than Japanese, expressing herself with body language, waving hands in the air, and moving to and fro.

The word *genki* in Japanese is often translated as "healthy," but the words "vivacious" and "animated" do a much better job. Hitomi is all these things and more. Less than five feet tall, yet not nearly as demure as so many other Japanese women I have met, she bubbles with energy and radiates enthusiasm. We go cross-country skiing, ending up on steep terrain where she falls countless times but never quits laughing or having fun. We climb mountains together, another new experience for her. On our first trip we find ourselves stuck in darkness on a narrow ledge; Hitomi, instead of panicking, cooks up a big soup and marvels at the stars that light up the nearby peaks. I am absolutely charmed.

She joins one of my classes and we begin to spend a lot of time together, going to cafés, films, and parties. On long walks together, we talk about our lives. Although, as a foreign male, I am a big fish in a small pond—and although Japanese women are the most beautiful women who have ever given me any attention—I have resolved to avoid serious involvement with anyone, because of my cycling plans.

One moonlit winter evening, Hitomi and I visit a hot spring in the mountains above Matsumoto, and we are soon kissing passionately in the hot pools, surrounded by snow, ice, and the stillness of winter. With great sadness, I realize that the time has come to break it to Hitomi....

"You are an absolute sweetheart," I tell her, "but you have to know how committed I am to my plan. I have to ride my bicycle around the world, and the only way for us to be together is if you want to join me."

I look at her sadly and continue, "Since this is so farfetched, it is probably better if we don't get any more involved than this, as there will only be pain for us both in the end."

Hitomi smiles and remarks, "Bike around the world...hmmm...sounds like it would be pretty interesting. I wouldn't mind doing something like that."

We spend the next months laughing, loving, and occasionally planning the logistics of the journey: how much time and money it will take, what type of gear we will need, and how much training will be necessary. Hitomi has never toured on a bike, travelled in the developing world, or spent much time living outdoors, and her savings are not as abundant as mine. Yet as the Chinese Taoist philosopher Lao Tzu once said, "The journey of one thousand miles begins with one step." Soon Hitomi has a bicycle and panniers, and she begins to train with me every weekend. Several months later, she sells her car, begins commuting to work by bike, and tutors private students in English after work in order to save for the trip.

By the following summer, we are focused on our plans. We teach, save our yen, climb mountains and cycle every weekend, read guide-books, and lay in each other's arms dreaming of the strange places and adventures that await us.

One hitch remains—Hitomi hasn't told her parents about us or our plans. They are traditional rice farmers from a small island in the Japan Sea. Hitomi tells me not to worry, and that she will handle it, but I have my doubts. Also, in order for us to remain living together, in either of our respective countries, we must be legally married, something that does not particularly interest either of us. And in Japan, marriage is a pretty big and expensive deal.

Hitomi drops a series of surprises on her family, the first of which goes something like this: "Hello, Mom and Dad. You, uh, remember Dave, who visited us last spring? Well, uh, he and I are going to get married."

This one takes a few weeks to clear, but does eventually, buoyed by the fact that Hitomi is far past "Christmas Cake." In Japan, there is a saying that a woman is like a *Kurisimasu Kekki*. At twenty-four or twenty-five she is just right; at twenty-seven she is still edible; after this, forget it. The words "mature," "wise," and "experienced" don't count for much here, replaced by "stale" and "old."

The next visit with Mom and Dad goes along the lines of, "So we are going to go on a little trip."

"Oh?" they reply. "How sweet. A honeymoon. You can use some of the money you saved by not wanting a formal wedding. Where will you go?"

"Actually, our trip is going to take a while, and we'll be visiting several places."

It isn't pretty, but it works. We set our departure date for the following spring.

A month from departure, we are feeling pretty confident. We've been training every weekend. All our gear is ready: tent, stove, clothing, bike parts, tools, cameras, guidebooks, phrasebooks, journals, maps, and first aid kits. We have been inoculated against typhoid, hepatitis, rabies, Japanese encephalitis, and anything that might bite, and we have converted all our savings into U.S. traveller's checks.

We have mapped out a tentative route, by which we will sail to Shanghai from Osaka, then cycle across China and Tibet and make our way over the Himalayas into Nepal, hopefully by October. From Nepal, we plan to travel through Southeast Asia, then to New Zealand and Australia before returning to Asia. We then plan to head to Europe, although the land borders to Myanmar (Burma) are closed, and we will have to fly over it.

Everything is planned so that we will avoid monsoons, hot seasons, and winters wherever possible. The only thing we don't know is whether the Chinese will allow us to bring our bicycles into China! The country has only recently opened up to individual travellers, and many areas that we wish to visit are still "closed." When we call travel agents, information bureaus, or the Chinese embassy, we cannot tell them that we plan to cycle to Tibet; supposedly, we cannot visit Tibet unless on an organized tour.

We have also heard that it may be illegal to bring a bicycle into China, and we cannot find a source to confirm whether or not this is true.

As the day of departure draws near, we clean out the apartment, send boxes to Hitomi's parents for storage, do interviews with local newspapers, and enjoy our last views of the Alps. We each have about fifty pounds of gear on our bicycles, and although we don't say anything, we silently wonder how in the world we will be able to ride with so much stuff.

On our last night we cycle to a nearby campground, where a group of friends have assembled to say goodbye and see us off. We eat, drink, and talk half the night. As I glance over at Hitomi, I see a trace of nervousness behind the wonder in her eyes. Looking back now, I don't think we had any idea what we were getting ourselves into—or how much our lives would change in the coming years.

Loaded down like a pair of overworked mules, we begin the long crawl up *Nomugi-toge*, the pass which separates the Alps from the Kansai plains. It is our first full day of cycling, and we struggle to steer our bikes with their heavy loads. One rather bizarre reason we are carting so much is that we are hauling several unexpected kilos in money!

In this land of the money tree, there is a tradition called *senbetsu*, "going-away money." Anyone leaving on a first trip or a big journey receives this money as a present to assist in the adventure. Completely unaware of this, I had spent the last two weeks watching open-mouthed as friends, students, and all of Hitomi's relatives gave us small envelopes. These usually contained a 10,000 yen note, equivalent to 100 dollars. The notes began to add up, and we decided we would celebrate when we got to Kyoto by staying in a nice *minshuku* or eating in a fancy restaurant.

As we strain up the switchbacks toward the pass, rivulets of sweat cascading from every pore, a car drives by and pulls over. It is Miki and Koichi, and Miki leans out the window to say, "We forgot to give you something; a little present from Koichi's dad."

I know what is inside, and absolutely refuse. I already owe these two the world for all the kindness they have done me, and I do not want to be given money. I thrust the packet back at her.

Miki smiles and will not take it. "It's okay, really," she insists. "You two are about to live something people spend their whole lives dreaming about. Besides, you've inspired us enough that we will come and visit you when you reach Australia! *Kyo tsukete*, be careful, and take care of each other." They smile again, we hug, and they drive off, leaving us to tackle the pass.

Several hours later, exhausted and bent over double, we reach *Nomugi-toge*, where it is raining and cold. There are no views, but we stop to eat, too tired to go on. An old man does a double take and almost falls off a bench as he watches me devour a carrot. In Japan, carrots are generally not eaten raw, and this fellow looks at me as if I am a rabbit. He mutters to his friend something about *henna gaijin*, "strange foreigner," but after all this time in Japan I am used to such remarks.

Despite the cold, we have no trouble staying warm, thanks to our winter clothing and the hot drink machine on the top of the pass. In Japan, the ubiquitous vending machine can be found in almost every nook, cranny, and ravine imaginable, and atop every summit as well. From early fall to late spring, the coffee, tea, and other drinks inside are hot; in summer, they become cold. Also available in these machines are panties, X-rated videos and magazines, condoms, and toothbrushes, as if these items would be indispensable in the rain at 2000 meters.

We descend along the Hida River, leaving behind us the pretty rural valleys filled with blossoming peach, plum, apple, and cherry trees, and enter the huge city of Gifu. It is late, and we are soaked and can't find a park to camp in. A woman directs us to a spot under a freeway overpass, where we pitch our tent. Elsewhere in the world, this type of spot might be a prime place for getting mugged, but in Japan it is a safe and dry piece of ground. There is a *sento* (bathhouse) around the corner, and in the morning a woman comes out of a nearby house with coffee for us. Over the next week, we will be given bread, ham, beer, coffee, whiskey, plum wine, *sake*, spareribs, dried fish, seaweed, and several rolls of slide film.

A few days later, as the rain continues, we reach Kyoto, the ancient capital and heart of Japan. Neither of us is terribly impressed, as for the most part modern Kyoto is a big, ugly city. We navigate through concrete, pollution, and traffic, and are splashed by passing trucks.

One tranquil spot is *Ryoanji*, a famed Zen rock garden removed from the bustle and noise of the city. The sand here has been meticulously raked and sculpted around rocks, carefully placed to suggest mountains, islands, or clouds. The empty space creates form, the sand's presence illuminates the rocks, and the rocks reveal the sand. I am reminded of the Taoist Lao Tzu, who mused, "A wheel is not created by the spokes, but by the space between the spokes."

This sense of interconnectedness is apparent on our journey, and applies to our goals and everyday realities. Hitomi and I left Matsumoto focused on reaching Kyoto, where we could rest and enjoy being tourists. The road to Kyoto was a series of kilometers, broken into numbers of days needed to get from A to B. However, what actually occurred on those days was a series of unexpected and very pleasant surprises: receiving presents and words of encouragement from people we met; stopping to picnic under a flowering persimmon tree in the countryside; chatting with a farmer about his rice crop; spending a quiet moment in the tent, writing in journals and studying maps as the rain fell softly outside. The space between the spokes, composing the wheel.

It is seventy kilometers from Kyoto to Osaka, mostly through polluted industrial wasteland, but the ride turns quite pleasant as we pick up a bicycle path along the Yodogawa River for most of the way. We ride in silence, Hitomi perhaps reflecting on the fact that it is her last day in Japan; as for myself, I do a lot of worrying over meeting her parents.

Hitomi's parents are meeting us in Osaka to wish us well and see us off on the ferry for Shanghai in the morning. They have booked a room for all of us in a nice hotel, and I am nervous; despite the good will, Dad definitely wants to make sure that I know what I am getting us into—and he wants to be assured that I will be taking good care of his daughter. My belief that she is quite capable of taking good care of herself is rather irrelevant here.

As we head into sprawling Osaka along the riverside path, I come around a bend and notice that Hitomi is no longer behind me. I stop, wait about fifteen minutes, then backtrack, with no luck. Panicking, I ride back the way we came at top speed, then turn around and go forward doing the same thing. After I ride in circles for the next half hour, it sinks in that she has vanished.

I have no idea where she is, and all I can do is make my way to the hotel, hoping we will meet there.

At the Tokyu Inn, there is still no sign of Hitomi. With puzzled expressions the staff look at me, a dirty and overheated bicyclist who does indeed have a reservation in this fancy place.

I guzzle a beer, then collapse on the bed, and am awakened half an hour later by the phone ringing. It is Mr. Sumita.

"Hello," he says, "this is Mr. Sumita. We've just arrived, and are in the lobby. Are the two of you fine? Can I speak with Hitomi?"

Dazed, I mutter in passable Japanese, "Uh, she's not here. Actually, I don't know where she is." Yes, I think to myself, we haven't even made it out of Japan and we are already lost.

Fortunately, Hitomi shows up twenty minutes later, dissipating our anxieties. It turns out that she ended up at the ferry terminal (how we were separated remains a mystery to both of us), where she stored her bike, and took a bus back into the city.

Our last meal in Japan is an enormous feast. We visit a restaurant

that caters to sumo wrestlers, and are served *chanko nabe*, which is a large
barbecue pot placed at our table along with heaping platters of meat,
fish, vegetables, and seasonings. The pot is kept full and cooking throughout the evening. After our first 500 kilometers on the road, it isn't too
difficult to imitate *sumo* appetites, and we go to bed gorged—and excited
over our impending departure to China.

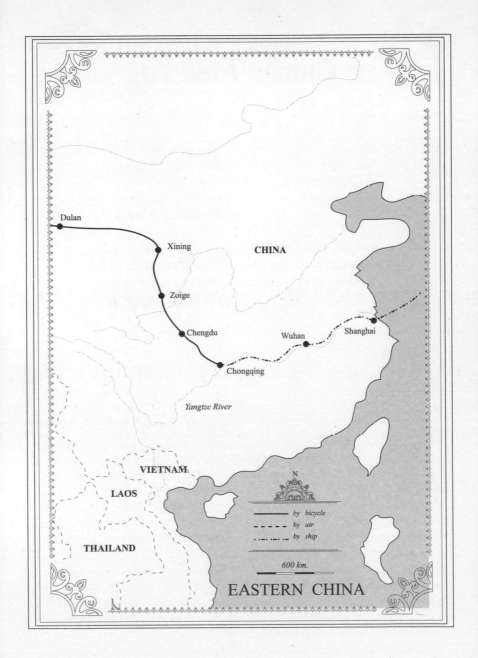

Dulan

Xining

Zoige

Chengdu

CHINA

Wuhan

Shanghai

Chongqing

Yangtze River

VIETNAM

LAOS

THAILAND

N

——— by bicycle
- - - - by air
—·—·— by ship

600 km.

EASTERN CHINA

Chapter Three
China: *Mei Yo*

Do not take the Buddha for the Ultimate.
As I look at him, he is still like the hole in the privy.

Lin Chi (Rinzai Master)

Either I am a traveller in ancient times,
and faced with a prodigious spectacle which would
be almost entirely unintelligible to me and might,
indeed, provoke me to mockery or disgust; or I am a
traveller of our own day, hastening in search of a
vanished reality. In either case I am the loser.

Claude Levi-Strauss

After a very smooth and luxurious forty-eight hour sail aboard the sleek, efficiently run Hino-Maru, we approach the harbor of Shanghai. The Japanese staff aboard the boat still cannot tell us whether we will be able to bring our bicycles into China, and as we look out at the famous Bund, where old British colonial buildings line the waterfront, we cross our fingers and make small prayers.

The immigration hall is a scene of utter bedlam. People scream and yell at one another, soldiers of the People's Liberation Army give orders, and hordes of Chinese haul caseloads of stereos, cameras, and televisions from the duty free shops into the sea of people and possessions.

A guard glances at our six-month business visas, stamps them, and points us toward a set of double doors.

I had expected to be surrounded by squadrons of bicycles in China, but we are greeted instead with a cacophony of screeching horns, sirens, and squealing brakes. Millions of trucks, buses, and taxis belch diesel and black soot. Overwhelmed, we approach a man and ask directions to our hotel; he points at my nose and laughs hysterically. Foreigners in China have been referred to as "big-nosed hairy devils" in the past, and it appears that in this regard, the Middle Kingdom hasn't changed one bit.

We eventually track down the Pujiang Hotel, which is quite typical of the hotels we will frequent in China. The lobby is sculpted in marble, with huge chandeliers and sparkling floors. Well-groomed staff run to and fro with teapots, towels, and trays of food. At six dollars a night, I figure we are going to be in the lap of luxury for a pittance, but past the reception we find corridors with blackened walls and ceilings covered in spider webs. Cockroaches scurry across the dirty floors, and the rooms resemble prison quarters. The beds are lumpy and the sheets smell of a history of truck drivers, hookers, and unwashed visitors. The toilets are a trip back into Chinese history, as they look like they have not been cleaned in many a dynasty.

"Key" ladies sit on each floor. Their job is to let people into their rooms, but they seem to have been placed there to report the activities of the foreign devils. They sit complacently, appearing to be nodding off, only to peep into rooms moments later when we undress or use the bathrooms.

Famished, we head into the streets to find food, which isn't much of a problem, as there are street vendors everywhere selling all sorts of dumplings, soups, and noodle dishes. What is a problem is communicating with them. Our attempts at Chinese are met with derision and jeering. Whenever we attempt something from our Chinese phrasebook, people point in our faces and laugh; when we try pantomiming, they laugh even harder.

Many of the teahouses and grand old homes in the French and English Quarters are being torn down and replaced with high-rises. In fact, much of Shanghai appears to be under construction, and the noise of drills, cranes, and cement mixers only adds to the chaos in the streets. Consulting a map, we realize that it will take several horrid days to escape this madness, and we decide to take a ferry up the Yangtze River to avoid some of the congestion and escape into the Chinese countryside.

At the ferry terminal, I find one phrase of Chinese that is easily understood; some months later, I will swear that they are the only words one needs for travel in the country. It is *mei yo*, which means "there isn't."

Asking for things is actually quite simple in Chinese. One just points at an object and asks, *"Yo mei yo?"* ("Is there any?") The answer will invariably be *"mei yo."* As Hitomi and I will soon discover, sullen refusal is the usual response when one asks for a hotel room, goods in a department store, or even for stamps in the post office. This is the bane of a society in which the government assigns jobs; there is no unemployment, nor is there any incentive to give service. At the ferry terminal, when I show the clerk my phrasebook to ask for boat tickets, I am met with an angry glare.

Fortunately, an elderly man named Lee asks in English if he can be of help. He waxes nostalgic about the British days of Shanghai, "when you didn't have to fight your way through animals like these to get on a boat." To illustrate, he gestures at the throngs of people in the long queues around us.

After much argument and several *mei yo*'s, Lee emerges triumphant from the Special Foreigner's Window where we have been sent, clutching two tickets for the following morning. Thanking him, we rush back to the hotel to pack.

A few days later, we are happily ensconced in a comfortable eight-person berth cabin and are sailing very slowly up the Chiang Jiang, known in the West as the Yangtze. The Yangtze is the world's third-longest river after the Nile and the Amazon. We plan to follow it, by ferry and then by bicycle, all the way to its source in Quinghai Province in the west of China.

The Yangtze has been portrayed in many Taoist paintings, murals, and water colors as a romantic and mysterious river with mighty gorges, forested shores, and rocky cliffs looming in the mist, but the modern-day version appears a far cry from this. In its eastern reaches, the river runs through countless industrial sprawls, where factories belch huge plumes of black smoke into the heavy, sultry air. The Yangtze also appears to be on its way to becoming the world's largest garbage dump.

On the morning of our second day on the ship, I am very impressed to see several cleaning women march into our cabin, exhorting us to rise and shine as they merrily sweep the room. They fill large cardboard boxes with dust, debris, and empty Tsingtao beer bottles. I pause from writing in my journal to watch their efforts, then look on in horror as they nonchalantly dump the boxes and all their contents over the railings into the murky waters below. This goes on in every room, every day, and presumably on every boat plying up and down the river.

The same disaster takes place down in the canteen, where skinny chain-smoking men dole ladles of fatty pork or beef into Styrofoam cartons. Three times a day, several hundred people wolf down their oily rations, then toss all the cartons—and the beer bottles that go with them—into the free-flowing sewage system below us.

The toilets on the ship consist of a long single corridor of water, with stalls separated by a concrete wall. The common river runs underneath all of the squatting stations, then continues from the last stall to the edge of the boat, where its contents merge into the mighty Yangtze.

But to say that we are on a ship of horrors would be misleading, as there are actually many things to make our passage rewarding. Downstairs, there is a movie theatre, a large room filled with lawn chairs. Films screen throughout the day. I ask Hitomi to read the Chinese characters in the hope that something decent is showing, but she cannot make head nor tail of the offerings.

One of our cabin mates continuously informs us that the films of Sho Ne Ga will be screening in the afternoon, and when we profess no knowledge of this person he looks at us in dismay, wondering what kind of illiterates we are.

"Sho Ne Ga," he says, "he most of famous America." We soon learn that the character in question is Arnold Schwarznegger.

We leave the ferry the following morning, disembarking at Chongqing, and our first day of full cycling in the Middle Kingdom is the hardest I've ever spent in a bicycle saddle. Chongqing is horrible, over twenty kilometers of smoggy streets packed with screeching, belching trucks. We find almost no signs to navigate by, even if they are in Chinese. Every building is a factory or a bombed-out hovel. There isn't a single space without people, and the Chinese have devised over a thousand horrid ways to shriek, "Hello!" at us as we bike along.

Once we leave the city, the scenery gets better, but the horn-blowing, dust-kicking rust buckets passing us never cease. The heat, dust, noise, and pollution are eleven on a scale of ten, and the road is crap too, all mud pits, gravel, rocks, and potholes. Half the humanity passing us scream out of their windows while blasting their air horns. Even in the countryside, people continue to pour out of every crevice in the land, every inch of which is completely cultivated. Camping out here would be totally out of the question.

It is madness, sheer madness!

Before we left Japan, a good friend who had travelled widely gave me his opinions on China. "All I could think of in China," he mused, "was how lucky I was not to be born there." I thought his opinion was extreme and rather intolerant. Yet after a week in China, I feel exactly the same way.

Shell-shocked, we roll into the small town of Hechuan as the sun goes down, over ten hours and ninety-five kilometers from Chongqing. Even tiny villages in China seem to have over a million inhabitants. A friendly young man on a bike escorts us to the Hechuan Binguan Hotel, where for twenty yuan (two and a half dollars) we are given a double room with a television, shower, and a toilet that looks like it was last used by Ghengis Khan.

Locals are very friendly, but stare as if we are from Mars. I don't think any foreigners have ever come through this place. Hordes follow us from our room out to a small restaurant, and the manager has to put us in a private banquet room upstairs as hundreds press into the downstairs and up against the glass outside to get a peek at the circus.

We proceed to dig into a huge feast, but there is no telling what we have eaten. I assume that the hot Szechuan peppercorns, which taste like laundry detergent, will kill any amoebas or other bugs in the very unidentifiable pieces of flesh we have consumed. Completely sated, we return to our room looking forward to a long quiet evening. The karaoke bar downstairs gets going at around midnight and blares long and hard into the wee hours of the morning.

The road to Chengdu does not improve in the slightest, and is a maze of potholes, boulders, washboard, and red dust. Yet for all our miseries, we fare better than those in buses and trucks. At least we can swerve around the potholes and control our speed over the bumps and ruts. Buses pass us with women puking out of the windows, adding yet another obstacle for us to maneuver around. Stopped vehicles are to be avoided at all costs, as in addition to the vomiting, people spit and throw all their garbage from the windows. Public spitting is rampant in China, indoors and out; we have gotten used to being woken up in our hotel rooms every morning by the sound of neighbors clearing their throats of phlegm. Unlike in Japan, where everyone tries to be polite and quiet, in China there seems to be a premium on making as much noise as is humanly possible.

As we approach Chengdu, the traffic picks up in noise and volume. Our days of hardship inure us to what now surrounds us daily, and I find myself enjoying the ride immeasurably. Much of this has to do with the continuous passage of photogenic scenes on the road. A family of five passes on a small motorcycle, small daughter on the driver's lap, son behind him, wife seated sideways behind the son with another boy on her lap. Another motorcycle passes, the rider transporting three huge dead pigs which he has draped across the back of his bike. We keep pace with a pedicab on which a man is transporting a sofa, with an old man snoozing away on the sofa. We gape as hard at all these characters as they do at us.

We stay at the Traffic hotel, where we meet several travellers from Tibet and even hear of some other bicyclists. It seems that the road west to Tibet is completely off-limits to foreigners. There are major checkpoints on bridges across deep rivers; the only way to get to Lhasa will be to cycle at night and avoid towns altogether. We decide that this would be suicidal, especially given what we have seen and ridden on thus far, so we decide to take a more circuitous northerly route via Gansu and Quinghai provinces, then over the Tian Shan mountains south into Tibet.

North of Chengdu, the mountains begin to rise up and the humid valley gives way to cool pine forests. The roads remain atrocious, and we come across a truck stuck in a chest-deep pool of mud with more than fifty people trying to haul it out of the bog.

Despite the road conditions, we are enjoying ourselves. The scenery is beautiful and the air is fresh and cool. Best of all, the people here are far less obnoxious than elsewhere. In the town of Songpan, colorful Tibetan ladies with turquoise amulets mix with old Moslem men in skullcaps and Chinese students. All are singing the latest pop hits, which blare from radios in the teahouses at top volume.

This area of China is on the edge of the Tibetan grasslands and plateau. It was once part of Tibet, and much of the population here is Tibetan. The area also supports a large Chinese Moslem community. We meet two old men, Gong and Ma, who want to take us on horseback to their village in the mountains, and we spend the afternoon with them at the local market watching people haggle over yak hair brooms, daggers, and lynx pelts.

I buy a kilo of yak butter, mistaking it for cheese, and Gong gives me my first taste of *tsampa*, the roasted barley flour on which highland Tibetans survive. Mixed with rancid yak butter tea, the *tsampa* tastes a bit like raw cookie dough. It is definitely edible, but not something one would want to eat a whole bowl of. Ma urges us to chase down the lot with cups of local 120 proof white alcohol, and after several cups we are joining in the raucous singing along with the radio like everyone else.

A day later, we are on our way to the Tibetan plateau, climbing a logging road beside a gurgling river. There is absolutely no traffic. It is as if we are in another country. The incline is gradual but unrelenting, and at around 3400 meters, Hitomi is very short of breath. We stop and camp under our second full moon of the trip, disturbed only by an elderly Tibetan woman who is herding several yaks. She pauses to inspect our tent, mutters to herself, smiles, and moves on. We brew up yak butter tea and *tsampa*, of which we are becoming quite fond, and fall asleep easily.

Bike travel, we are discovering, brings tremendous changes quickly. On one day we are surrounded by urban grit and din; on the next we sleep in a silent field of barley under a harvest moon. The following morning it is raining, and ten minutes after starting out we both have flat tires. We grumble over the time spent fixing them, soaking with sweat inside our raingear, and continue to go uphill. By eleven, Hitomi has had three flats. The road is made up of steep curves and both of us are gasping for air. We are at 3500 meters, travelling like snails, and I wonder what it will be like to cycle at over 5000.

Just when we feel as if we can't ride any further, the climbing ends. We come around a final turn and arrive on the edge of the great Tibetan grasslands, a flat plateau, desolate and endless as far as the eye can see. There is a lonely police outpost here, and the two fellows manning it order us in for tea. We sit by a roaring fire drinking endless cups of tea with lychees. The two policemen encourage us to join them in singing the same pop song we heard everyone singing in Songpan, and for that matter, in Chengdu, Shanghai, and every hamlet in between.

Outside the wind is roaring, with no trees, mountains, or side valleys to buffer it. Fortunately, it is at our backs, and we sail along at twenty kilometers an hour without even having to pedal. The only signs of civilization out here are large yurts, octagonal tents made of wooden poles and covered in sheepskin. Tibetans with crimson cheeks and sunblackened skin come running out as we cycle past, beckoning us in for tea. I am amazed that they exist in such a remote place, where nothing grows except barley, flowers, and the grass on which the yaks feast voraciously.

We let the wind blow us along, and finally make camp on a patch of grassland next to a snaking stream just before the first drops of a big rainstorm begin to fall. As my head hits the pillow, I ask Hitomi if she thinks that the people up here ever receive any mail.

The rain continues throughout the night and morning, which makes riding difficult. The soft road shoulder, on which we cycle to avoid the rutted, washboard road, has turned to quicksand.

Weary, we roll into Zoige, a dusty frontier town straight out of a Chinese cowboy movie. Tiny shacks which serve as cinemas blast out the latest kung fu movies; we can hear the grunts and blood-curdling screams from several kilometers out of town. Cowboys from the Kham region of Tibet swagger along the dusty streets, their braided hair tied around their heads. Next to them walk crimson-robed monks, and women with braids down to their multi-colored aprons. Characters with sheep-skin robes and matted hair roam the bazaar buying fresh yogurt, clothing, and Buddhist scriptures and prayer flags.

The teahouses here continue in the local tradition of serving sweet tea. Hitomi and I visit one and are given packets containing tea, dried apricots, lychees, and other fruit, as well as big chunks of rock sugar. We empty the packets into a cup, which is continuously refilled with water. At first, the tea is overpoweringly sweet due to all the rock sugar, but the more we drink, the more it mellows, and on a rainy afternoon there isn't a better way to pass the time.

We are joined in the teahouse by Yoel, an Israeli we met back in Songpan, as well as an entourage of monks who wish to communicate with us. One of them asks me for a Dalai Lama picture, forbidden by the Chinese but prized ever so highly by the Tibetans. The same fellow also asks if he can have my beard, as he laments his inability to grow one.

Another monk, hacking away on his cigarettes, merely rolls his eyes when we tell him that we didn't think monks were allowed to smoke. When we refuse his offer of tobacco, he tells us that we are like the Dalai Lama for having such resistance.

Yoel recommends a hotel which supposedly has hot showers and toilets with at least some semblance of decency. As the *tsampa* has not been agreeing with our digestive systems, we would like a little more comfort for our hourly runs. In our hotel, the mens' toilet turns out to be a cave-like affair, with walls that appear to have been used as toilet paper over the years. The floor is made of wooden boards with small rectangular holes cut out at intervals of about a meter. Most of the visitors to the toilet seem to have missed the mark, and the floorboards are covered with stools in various stages of decomposition, color, and texture. In addition to smelling the foul odor, one must share the cramped quarters with five others, as the toilet is perpetually packed. I get the impression that people in China spend a lot of time in the toilet, and that most of them have diarrhea.

Hitomi has similar reports from her outhouse, so we try to move to Yoel's Hotel. No one is at the front desk, so I wander through the corridors to inspect the premises and find the proprietor. The rooms, almost all of which are empty, appear clean. There are even private bathrooms, which look like they have been cleaned at least within some time in recent memory.

Returning to the front desk, I see that Hitomi has tracked down a member of the staff. We ask, in our now decent Chinese, *"Fanzhien yo mei yo?"* ("Is there a room?") The reply, of course, is *"Mei yo."*

"But there is a room," I protest. "I've just seen dozens of empty rooms."

"Mei yo." The clerk stands firm.

"Yo, yo, yo, yo, yo," I counter, mimicking him in frustration.

The clerk stares back, purses his lips, then begins to grin slightly. I think I sense the tension breaking. He spits on the floor, looks at Hitomi, then at me, and *mei yo*'s us until we exit the foyer. This being China, there is nothing we can do. We go for a cup of tea and a spinach dumpling, and come back an hour later to leave a message for Yoel that we haven't been able to get a room. Another clerk is working at the reception.

I ask him if there is a room, and he beams at me and says, *"Yo, yo!"*

About 100 kilometers from Zoige lies the small village and monastic community of Langamusi, also known as Lamasu. The village is snuggled into the end of a valley amid towering peaks, green hills, and red rocks, and is reminiscent of the southwestern U.S.A.

The population of Lamasu is almost entirely Tibetan, the rest being Moslem Han, and the activities of the village revolve around the large monastery at the center of town. The monastery is part of the *Gelugpa*, or Yellow Hat sect of Tibetan Buddhism, and as we walk by, playful young monks run out to greet us in their maroon robes and curved yellow hats. They dance, sing, and pose for pictures until one of their elders appears to chastise them. It is comforting to know that everywhere in the world, kids will be kids.

The monks spend their days studying Buddhism, meditating, working in the fields, and performing various daily rituals. Every morning they have a long debate session, in which they pair up and take turns posing challenging questions about the nature of things. The debates are most comical, as whenever a question is answered insufficiently or too slowly, the questioner claps his hands and points in the face of the answering party, all in one big swoop, crying out in merriment.

The monks also spend time blowing huge horns like the ones played in the Alps of Switzerland. The tones from the horns are supposed to be the closest sound to the voiced "Om," a tone so basic and pure that it is used in meditation to create breakthroughs into understanding the human spirit. I think it sounds a lot like someone farting.

On a hill high above the monastery is a burial site. In contrast to our tradition of putting the dead into the earth, the Tibetans believe in returning the dead to the air and land of which they are a part. They carry out a practice called sky burial, in which the dead are hacked to small bits, mixed with *tsampa*, and left out for the vultures to carry away. It makes a lot of sense, certainly in terms of recycling and economics.

However, the burial site above Lamasu seems to be missing a few steps. There are skeletons on the ridge, still dressed in their faded clothing, torn and battered by the elements. Yet they are not hacked to bits, nor do they show any sign of being hauled away by the vultures. The only vultures we come across are two Chinese men stuffing clothes, jewelry, and gold teeth into sacks they carry. They flee as they see us approaching, and I shake my head in disbelief. I have heard stories of people being stoned to death in Tibet for disturbing sky burials, and I can imagine the punishment for these two grave robbers if they are caught. Their sacrilege toward Tibetan beliefs and culture is truly shameful.

The following days of bicycling are tough. We ride into strong winds on rutted and rocky roads. I suffer from diarrhea, which makes for sleepless nights and subsequent exhaustion. Villages throughout the region are nondescript collections of shabby mud-brick houses, and most of the inhabitants wander aimlessly, dressed in filthy rags. Children fling stones at us and huge mastiffs come roaring after our heels.

The obstacles we face on the road often create tension between us, and it is easy to take out daily frustrations on each other, especially in the middle of nowhere. After a day of screaming kids and rutted roads, sometimes the smallest thing makes us snap at each other, and for the first time since we have been married, we have some serious spats.

Fortunately, for all the rough spots, there are moments that diffuse any tension and make it all worthwhile. After a day of harassment and hassle, we wander into a Moslem restaurant in a small village, where seven brothers merrily chop homemade noodles in the tiny kitchen. We are served hearty, delicious noodle soup, and one of the brothers strolls up to us, puts out his hand, and proudly announces, "Hello, your name is China!"

Seeing us grinning, he continues, "Good morning, fuck you," beaming all the while. Tired and cranky, we laugh until we are both crying deliriously.

We have entered Quinghai Province, and the landscape has completely changed. Gone are the green hills and grasslands, replaced with land that has turned blood-orange. Large mountains, ranging in color from orange to red to brown, surround tidy, well-irrigated villages, oases in a desert of dry tones. A screeching descent finally comes to a halt after three wonderful—if jarring—hours, when we reach the Yellow River, which flows through red and yellow canyons much like the Grand Canyon back home.

Two towns we pass through, Xinhua and Hualong, appear much more prosperous than their counterparts back in Gansu, and are full of bustling markets selling the sweetest melons I have ever tasted. Hitomi and I gorge ourselves on crenshaw melons, honeydew, watermelon, cantaloupe, casaba, and the ultra-sweet hami melon.

Hotels in this region also prove more regal. Rooms are clean, as are the bathrooms. There are TVs in every room, and we are treated to the spectacle of watching the NBA finals between the Orlando Magic and Houston Rockets in Chinese. And the beds are firm, solid, and comfortable, a far cry from the lumpy springs we have suffered with for the past several weeks.

Our only complaint here is with the police. The area has just opened to foreigners, and travelling by bike, we figure that we just might be the first foreign devils the locals have ever seen. Our arrival in any town brings out the mobs, which scrutinize our every move and seem endlessly fascinated with the toe clip straps on our bikes.

Our presence is quickly reported to the *Gong An*, or Public Security Bureau, and someone is usually at our door in minutes to see what all the fuss is about. Here in Hualong, the Chief Inspector seems like a friendly enough chap, but he has a very engaged discussion with the hotel staff, then sends for the local village teacher (who knows less English than I do Chinese) to act as an interpreter.

The Inspector demands a marriage certificate before he will allow Hitomi and I to remain in the same room. At first, I think, he is horrified to find a foreign devil with a local woman, but after learning that the oriental lady in my bed is also a foreign devil, he eases up. We do have a marriage certificate, as we knew we might need one in countries like Pakistan where unmarried couples may not inhabit the same quarters. The only problem is that the Chief cannot read the marriage certificate, as it is in Japanese.

We manage to squirm out of the predicament when I remember that my passport has a Japanese marriage visa stamped in it. I show him the word "marriage," written in English, which he looks up in my Chinese-English dictionary, and he seems satisfied.

Yet then we have another problem. We are from different countries. How is it possible that we can be married? This charade goes on for half an hour, with the chief holding up our separate passports in each hand, exclaiming, "This one green, this one blue! Together no possible!"

At this point I am weary and disgusted with the whole affair. I rise, take the passports from him, stand in the center of the room, and announce, "In *Mei Guo* (America), one green, one blue, okay," giving a big grin and thumbs-up. We are shortly thereafter allowed to go to sleep.

Throughout every little village in Gansu and Quinghai Province, the only food that is consistently available is noodle soup, with a side dish of stir-fried egg and tomatoes. So it is with great relief that we reach the provincial capital of Xining, which is basically a gigantic outdoor food stall, dominated by the West Gate Market.

The West Gate Market puts to shame any outdoor food conglomeration we have seen thus far. Lanes, aisles, and alleyways teem with hawkers, vendors, and stalls. Within an hour, we have munched our way through dried apricots, fine chocolate (normally an oxymoron in China), steamed potatoes, sweet yogurt, whole wheat rolls, butter toffee peanuts, apples, and a delicious steaming dish of vegetables and stewed meat which the vendor calls *mishi mishi*. We avoid the tables serving noodles and fried eggs with tomatoes.

Besides the food and other shopping stalls in the markets, there are also entertainers. Men with trained monkeys do tricks, acrobats perform, and people sing verses from the Koran. We see Tibetans, Hui Moslems, Han Chinese, Mongols, and Kazakhs, and we feel as though we are at some crossroads on one of the great trade routes of the world. We also see beggars for the first time in China.

After our stint at the ends of the earth, we can only gawk, like peasants in the city for the first time, at all of the color, variety, and hubbub.

Reluctantly, we leave Xining and cross the Southern Quinghai Mountains back into rural China. Villages are again very poor, and our accommodations match the surroundings: surly staff, filthy rooms, and lumpy beds. At one inn, the maids barge into our room at seven a.m. and tell us it is time to get out.

I have learned to say, "Do you have any sweet and sour fish?" in Chinese, and I am becoming a whiz with the numbers. It helps that every time we bicycle by a school, the kids are in the courtyard doing calisthenics, shouting as they go.

"Yi! Ar! San! Su! Wu! Liu! Chee! Ba!

"Yi! Ar! San! Su! Wu! Liu! Chee! Ba!"

Unfortunately, the kids never go past eight, which is rather limiting, but I like the counting so much, I begin to use it as a mantra when climbing hills.

We ride along the shores of Quinghai Lake, the largest in China. The lake is bathed in a rather surreal blue light. This is the beginning of the Quaidam Basin, a vast, barren salt flat on the south side of the Tian Shan Mountains. There is almost no traffic, and the road is decent and flat for a change. We make good time, stopping only for a scrumptious fish meal at the Electric River Taste Restaurant.

The further west we travel, the more desolate the land appears. No plants grow out here, and we don't see any signs of life, just baked earth and brown mountains. After several days, I spot huge vultures perched on nearby ridges, which I take as an ominous sign.

The sky turns hazy, and it begins to snow. We struggle along at the grand speed of ten kilometers an hour, fighting the wind and trying to concentrate on the kilometer markers, the only things standing in this desolate outpost. I am normally stronger than Hitomi in these conditions, but today I lag far behind her, and have to stop and rest every few kilometers.

By mid-afternoon, I am too weary to continue, and when the village marked on our map turns out to be a river, with not a single dwelling in sight, we call it quits for the day. I collapse into the tent, burning with fever, muscle aches, and diarrhea. Within two hours my temperature has risen to 102, and I am quite dizzy. Hitomi feeds me liquids and aspirin, worrying about what to do. This is one of those moments we may have planned for, but have not dealt with until now. We are in the wilds of China, cold and wet, too ill to get on bicycles, separated from the elements by only the thin wall of our tent. Hitomi snuggles close to me, trying to draw some of her sleeping bag around mine. I shiver deliriously and try to find solace in sleep.

By morning, my fever has gone down slightly, but I am still feeling horrendous. Conditions outside remain wet, cold, and extremely windy. Not wanting to remain in this desolate place, I force myself to get up, and we slowly pack up and continue on, hoping to reach the settlement of Dulan, about seventy kilometers away. I have no appetite and am extremely weak, and it takes every bit of strength I have to keep up with Hitomi, who leads us through the stark hills and barren, windswept land. This is one of those days when I ask myself why we are doing this. At this moment, I can find no answer.

By evening, we reach Dulan, a dusty and sprawling town. All I can think of is a bed. The Bus Station Hotel is the only lodging in town, run by a friendly man in a fur cap, who appears happy to see us and gives us room keys without any hassle. Our room is better than others we have seen, and we even have a welcome mat outside the door. Unfortunately, there is a human turd smack in the middle of the mat, and this is our welcome to Dulan.

This welcome is soon explained when I go to visit the bathroom. The hotel bathroom serves the entire town and is truly the worst I have ever encountered in my life. Actually, it isn't that the bathroom itself is so bad, but that one cannot even reach the bathroom. A minefield of crap surrounds the building, as if someone has planted a scat garden. One can barely take a step without encountering poop; it seems that locals go as far as they can, then add to the collection wherever they may be. It is so revolting that when Hitomi returns from witnessing all this, we burst out laughing for twenty minutes, nicknaming the place *Unchimura*, Japanese for Shitsville.

Still extremely weak, I go to bed early and sleep a few hours, only to be awakened in the middle of the night by a dog which proceeds to howl all night. Sometime around four a.m. I drift off and dream of being chased by dogs across the Tibetan Plateau, feeling sicker and weaker as they approach. I wake in a sweat and discover that I have soiled the bed and myself, and I am too weak to move.

I moan and tell Hitomi what I have done, and she goes to the tap to get me a bowl of water to clean up with. The tap has nothing in it but a trickle, which turns into a couple of droplets, and that is all.

Opening the door to find water, Hitomi discovers that it has rained all night, and that the minefields of *Unchimura* have turned into a huge bog of nightsoil.

Using an old towel to help me clean off, Hitomi makes me more comfortable, then takes my soiled clothes out to wash. She opens the door, looks out over the rivers of excrement outside our door, looks at me, and shrugging her shoulders, tosses the whole lot out into the rain.

We stay four days in this hellhole, as I remain too weak to do anything except find somewhere outside to go to the bathroom. The unsanitary conditions have me worried, and I fear I will get something far more serious than what I already have if we stay much longer.

Hitomi goes off to explore the town, buy food, and write letters. I stay in bed, plowing through books we have carted with us, in three days finishing George Orwell's *Nineteen Eighty Four*, Barbara Kingsolver's *Animal Dreams*, and Pico Iyer's *Video Nights in Kathmandu*. When I emerge to eat for the first time in days, I feel as if I have been out of China for ages, away from the staring squads, filth, and squalor.

After four days, I still have a bad stomach ache and am feeling pretty weak, but I have seen enough of Dulan to last a lifetime. We do a short day's ride to the village of Xiarte, where we find a small inn with comfortable old armchairs and, for once, a clean toilet. We are now about three days from Golmud, the last major town before Tibet.

Before we reach Golmud, we must cross the most barren stretch of the Quaidam Basin. According to our map, there will be no water for the next 100 kilometers, and the next village is 160 kilometers away. We set out early, determined to reach the river by the end of the day.

The wind shifts in our favor, and we leave Xiarte at thirty kilometers an hour, sailing past sand dunes and salt flats. Blowing along in the big wind, I forget the troubles of the last few days. My stomach feels stronger, and even the drab and parched surroundings don't appear so stark.

By early afternoon we have covered eighty kilometers. During a lunch break in a dry riverbed, I suggest to Hitomi that we might make the next village today. She is immediately opposed to the idea—thus far on our journey, we have not yet cracked 100 kilometers in a day. She does agree to consider the idea, and we push on to the river.

The river is as big as our map indicates, but looks like chocolate-brown sludge and is none too inviting for either drinking or cooking. There is also absolutely no shade anywhere, and the desert is baking under the afternoon sun. I again vote to go on. It is four o'clock, we are averaging just under twenty kilometers an hour, and we have roughly another sixty-five to go. Another glance at the boiling and murky river is enough to convince Hitomi, and we set off.

In less than an hour, the wind shifts, quickly cutting into our sides, then directly into our faces. We manage the first thirty kilometers without many problems, stopping to eat and consuming most of our remaining water. It is five-thirty, and we are still pretty strong. Yet the winds don't stop, and now begin to howl with fury. We are forced to ride at seven kilometers an hour in our lowest gears, despite the flat terrain.

Ten kilometers from Nomhon, the dot of a village on our map, it grows dark and stormy, and we are too weary to ride any more. Hitomi stops and cries inconsolably by the side of the road and says she can't go on. I am close to this point myself, but I face the hard facts. We have no water, no food, and appear to be just in front of some sort of dust storm. We are dehydrated and will not be able to drink for the next ten to fifteen hours. There are no cars out here, and few options. I urge Hitomi to find some inner strength. But she can no longer can hear me, and has slipped into a world of exhaustion, in which her body and mind no longer want to respond.

I am frightened and bewildered. I don't know what to do, but I do know that standing around is not going to help us in any possible way. In confusion, I end up losing my temper, throwing my bike off into the desert, ripping the tent out of our packs, and starting to assemble it, while screaming curses at Hitomi, the winds, and this godforsaken land.

Somehow, my responses wake Hitomi. She snaps out of her catatonic state and says quietly and determinedly, "Let's go on."

The next two hours are absolute, sheer hell. We ride in a total daze of pain, crawling along at five kilometers an hour, our legs revolving only out of habit, with sand blowing into our parched mouths. In the distance, we can see the tiny lights of Nomhon, but they appear almost as a mirage as we move through the gale.

My body feels as if it has been run over by a truck. My lips are swollen, and a veil seems to separate the thoughts that stumble through my mind from the rest of my beaten and weary outer core. I tell my legs to keep spinning, and I count to eight in Chinese over and over, trying to take away the pain and forget the conditions around me. Somewhere next to me, in her own way, Hitomi deals with her own demons. Just as a lightning storm violently strikes the desert, we reach Nomhon. It is nine-thirty, and we have cycled 160 kilometers in twelve hours.

The village consists of about five mud brick dwellings. They appear deserted, but out of the dark, a man rushes into the road as if he has been waiting for us. He screams in Chinese, "Restaurant! Restaurant!" and directs us into a courtyard where we park our bikes. We collapse into a tiny room with one table, three chairs, and a small kitchen, Nomhon's only eatery.

We sit like zombies, unable to speak or move, while our proprietor asks us animatedly if we would like chicken, fish, or duck. Neither of us can conceive of eating at this point, and we point weakly at cans of *Jian Li Bao*, a Chinese soft drink for athletes which claims to restore electrolytes.

After guzzling three cans each and a pot of tea, while our host looks on in amazement, we feel well enough to order noodle soup and our favorite, stir-fried egg and tomatoes. The owner orders a young cook into action, then tells us proudly that he is studying English. He whips a cassette player from a closet and plunks in a tape, which he turns on full-blast. The tape is a monologue of random English words, with no sense, order, or reason.

"Murder, we, supper, fall down, magazine, enchantment," the speaker drones. "Permit, advance, here, bloodshed, cup, fortitude."

Hitomi and I look at each other, dazed and exhausted, and begin to laugh, slowly at first and then hysterically. The whole scene, the whole day, are something out of a Fellini movie.

For two hours we slurp noodles and swallow pots of tea to rehydrate our depleted systems. The kind owner takes us across the street to lodgings, and shows us our room. The dirty earthen floor is full of cracks, clothing is strewn everywhere, and the bed in the middle of it all resembles a badly molded lump of clay. Two dogs sit at attention outside our window, howling at our bikes, which are chained up just beyond their reach.

But tonight, the conditions don't matter. We are in a magical dreamland seconds after hitting the pillow, the sufferings of the past hours blown off into the Quaidam Basin with the sand, carried by the shrieking and moaning gale.

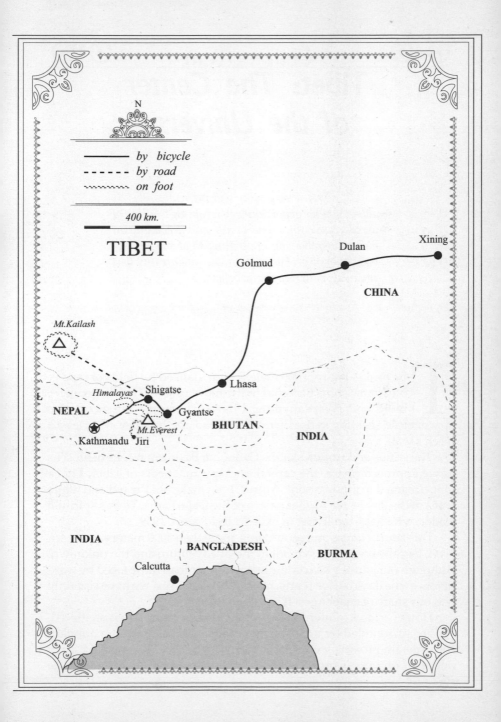

Chapter Four
Tibet: *The Center of the Universe*

> *Travel magnifies and intensifies life. It*
> *allows you the opportunity to recapture a feeling of*
> *wonder, innocence, and youth; and depending on*
> *how vulnerable you are willing to become, it can*
> *also deliver a profound experience of unreality that*
> *can rattle your most basic beliefs.*
>
> Eric Hansen, *The Traveler*

The peaks, nearly 7000 meters high, flanked by fields of rape blossoms, shine like gold in the midday sun. They are enormous and dwarf anything I have ever seen. The mountains appear close, seeming to rise up from the roadside, but they are at least a week's walk away.

The winds and troubles of the Quinghai Basin are weeks behind us as we approach Lhasa, the capital and spiritual heart of Tibet. I have long dreamed of this moment. Ahead, I can make out the red and white walls of the Potala, the former palace of the Dalai Lama, Tibet's spiritual leader, who has been living in exile in India since 1959.

This land of lamas and mountains, more than 3000 meters above sea level, has always been a symbol to me of adventure and the unknown. Although our journey has certainly been easier than those faced by wanderers in the days before roads, maps, and Gore-Tex, we have certainly had our share of challenges. It is a thrill to be here.

However, as we enter Lhasa, our state of enchantment is shattered. We are surrounded by ugly concrete housing blocks and the rampant construction projects we thought we had left back in China. Military police sit on every corner; soldiers with rifles stand guard along the sprawling boulevards.

It is as if we are in the wrong country, and in some ways, we are. Tibet has been occupied by China since 1959. The Dalai Lama's attempts at reconciliation have failed, even those asking not for independence, but for provisions which will help preserve Tibetan culture and religion. Tibetans are not even allowed to own pictures of the Dalai Lama. Monasteries are watched closely, and jailings and torture are common for those who show any opposition to Chinese rule.

Lhasa has been heavily populated with Han Chinese, who are given special incentives to relocate here, such as exemptions from the "one family, one child" policy, or extra "hardship" pay for posting out to the frontier. University education is in Chinese, and subsequently any advancement—financial, educational, or otherwise—is based on being part of the Chinese world, not the Tibetan one. As we ride past the blaring kung fu movie houses and spitting soldiers, it is as if we are back in Shanghai.

Fortunately, not all of Lhasa is lost. On the east side of the Potala is the Tibetan side of town, which stands in extreme contrast to its Chinese counterpart. Orderly streets with segregated bicycle and pedestrian lanes are flanked by simple two-story houses and apartments with brightly painted shutters, and colorful pots of flowers adorn every windowsill. The streets are clean, people don't spit, and everybody is smiling.

Pilgrims wander through the nearby Barkhor, the area that surrounds the Jokhang Palace. It is the spiritual heart of Lhasa, and the most worshipped Buddhist spot in Tibet. The pilgrims twirl small prayer wheels and recite mantras as they walk. Their route around the Jokhang is clockwise, although believers in the Tibetan *Bon* religion perform their perambulations counterclockwise. Larger, fixed prayer wheels adorn many areas of the Barkhor, and Tibetans stop to spin each one as they go past, hoping that their wishes and messages will be carried out into the world.

The *koras*, as the perambulations are called, seem to serve both a spiritual purpose and a social function, and I watch families greet each other, exchange pleasantries, and plan get-togethers. Pilgrims also throng together in front of the Jokhang Palace and spend much time prostrating themselves in front of the main entrance. Their prostrations remind me of the Sun Salutations I perform as part of my yoga routine.

Conditions may be difficult for the Tibetans, but they are some of the most congenial and gentle people I have ever encountered. Almost everyone we meet on the streets is smiling, and most people go out of their way to approach us and wish us "*tashi delay*," the usual greeting among

Tibetans. Another form of greeting is to stick out one's tongue as far as possible, opening the mouth wide; I figure that any culture in which the adults can remain so childlike and playful is one I am most happy to be in.

Although there are more foreigners here than in China, the Tibetans remain inquisitive toward us. People often approach and pantomime questions about our clothing and gear, or discreetly appeal for a photo of the Dalai Lama. Whereas in the rest of China, people would yank on my beard and leg hairs to see if they were real, people here ask shyly if they can stroke my beard. The women wink and coo softly after doing so, while the men often mime their inability to grow facial hair and stick out their lower lip in a joking pout.

We take a room at the Yak Hotel, where a large Tibetan tent shades the courtyard from the harsh sun. Lhasa lies at an altitude of 3600 meters and has no humidity; in the middle of the day, one understands why the Tibetans' skin is so dark.

Travellers are sprawled out in the courtyard, drinking tea, catching up on travel journals, and making plans. We share a room with two Koreans, one of whom tells us how he wore a Mao suit and never spoke in order to sneak on a Chinese bus to get here.

My stomach is still plaguing me, and I am convinced I have some sort of a parasite, so I head to the People's Hospital for a stool test. I show the Chinese doctor the character for "parasites" in my phrasebook, and she gives me a small scrap of torn and dirty paper. I stare at it until I realize that this is to be the vessel on which I am to collect my specimen.

It is a ten-minute walk to find the single toilet that serves the monolithic hospital. It is as filthy as most of the toilets I have seen in the past months, if not more so. As usual, there is a single river of water flowing through each stall, and since there is little water flowing in this one, the stalls are backed up with mounds of crap. I try to figure out how I can keep mine separated from all the others and get an honest sample.

As I return through the corridors, everyone pauses to examine my little scrap of excrement, foreign feces being a novelty in these parts. Back in the office, the doctor puts a tiny sample on a slide and throws the rest in the corner of the room, where there are other torn scraps of brown paper and various stool segments covered with flies. She puts the slide under a microscope, studies it carefully, and then looks at me long and hard. With a wide grin, she puts both of her thumbs up and screams,

"Okay!"

I return to the front desk, pay my twenty-two yuan, and go back to the hotel, where I promptly have diarrhea.

Mount Kailash, in the west of Tibet, is one of the least accessible places on the planet. It is a solitary, snow-dusted giant rising out of the Tibetan plains, considered to be the spiritual center of the universe by Buddhists, Hindus, Jains, and followers of the Tibetan Bon religion. A pilgrimage to the holy mountain, followed by a *kora* (a perambulation around the holy object), is believed to redeem one's past transgressions and give merit for lifetimes yet to come.

It takes a minimum of a week to travel from Lhasa to Kailash, if all goes well. There are no gas stations, very few settlements, and outside of *tsampa*, little is available in the way of provisions. To the south of Kailash lie the Himalayas, and the nearest settlement on the Nepal side is a three-week walk away. To the west, a nearly impassable "road" crosses Xinjiang Province, skirting the north side of K2 and the Karakoram Mountain Range before ending in Pakistan, over 2000 kilometers away. And to the north lies the Chiangtang, the vast, empty Tibetan plateau. At an altitude of over 5000 meters, the Chiangtang is a place without roads, thousands and thousands of kilometers of open and empty space inhabited only by the Tibetan antelope.

When I see a notice on the bulletin board in the Yak Hotel asking for "partners for an adventure to Mount Kailash," I run to our room and ask Hitomi if she feels like taking a break from bicycling.

Within days, we have a contingent of Japanese travellers, led by a woman named Masako and three young guys. There is also a Danish couple, Brian and Gita; an Australian named Spencer, who plans to sit at the base of Kailash and play the dijeridoo he has carried from Australia; and Jamie Carr, an Englishman who guides cycling and climbing trips in Nepal. Jamie is bringing his bike to Kailash, and plans to ride around the mountain.

We hire a Chinese truck and agree to travel with another group, who are taking a Landcruiser. They will pay more, but we will all have the security of two vehicles in case anything goes wrong. There are two Japanese travellers in the Landcruiser: Chiaki is a photographer for the Tibet Foundation and Dalai Lama Support Group in Japan, and Sachiko is a veteran traveller to Tibet and a student of Buddhism. Also in the jeep are Madeleine, a Quebecois en route to Bhutan, and her friend Carol, an English teacher from New York with flaming red hair and a Brooklynese accent to match.

Hitomi and I find it a difficult adjustment to deal with the group dynamics of such a large party of strangers, and the difficulties of preparing for the trip give us some warning of what is to come in the wilds of Tibet. We buy a month's supply of food in the Lhasa markets, stocking up on rice, noodles, oatmeal, *tsampa*, tea, kerosene, chocolate, and other essentials, and we check that everyone has the gear necessary to deal with the altitude and cold we will be facing. The Westerners, who seem strapped for cash, do not want to be part of the group purchases, preferring to buy their own. This is okay by the rest of us, but when I see how small their bags of provisions are, I begin to wonder.

After days of haggling over details, we finally have all the permits and provisions we will need. We are introduced to our truck driver, Tsering; his sidekick Ruri; and Lobsang, who is to act as our interpreter and liaison officer. We stuff the back of our sturdy Dong Feng truck with food, water, gear, and five barrels of gasoline, then begin along the route which will lead us to the mountain.

Two roads lead from Lhasa to Kailash. According to Lobsang, the southern route is shorter and clearer, but is often flooded at this time of year. The northern route is through barren salt flats on the edge of the Chiangtang, and can be difficult to find. We opt for the southern route, and figure we will reach Kailash in a week. Weary of all the planning, Hitomi and I go to sleep, ready to pitch our tent out in the Tibetan wilds and enjoy the scenery and space.

Our first day out of Lhasa gives us a taste of the pleasures to be had on a journey to Mount Kailash. The road out of Lhasa initially follows the "Friendship Highway," a dusty, bumpy set of ruts which connect Tibet and Nepal. Dust pours into the back of the truck and covers everything; we look like a gang of dirty bank robbers, everyone wrapped in head coverings with bandanas over our mouths. Our packing job falls to pieces immediately, with sacks flying all over the truck and spilling their contents. Finding anything, such as supplies for lunch, takes up a tremendous amount of time and energy.

As we cannot see what is in front of us, we have no idea that Tsering has gotten lost. Backtracking, it is not until two a.m. that we arrive in the town of Lhatze, where the main road turns off, and we head on into the wilds. Spencer has horrible diarrhea and thinks he has giardia; Brian is nauseous and vomiting; and Hitomi is not feeling great. Carol and Madeleine, in the Landcruiser, inform us that their driver is an idiot and hasn't a clue in the world where we are headed. We huddle together in the back of the truck and try to sleep.

The following morning, we are again covered from head to toe in dust. Covering the back of the truck stops it from pouring in, but is an even less agreeable option, as the overwhelming fumes from the leaky gas containers cause headaches. Everyone stakes out a position offering some semblance of comfort, but every five minutes we hit a large bump or pothole and are avalanched by falling bags of rice and shifting bodies. Our only break in the day comes when we happen upon an ice-cold lake. We all strip off and jump in, refreshed and revitalized for all of the next twenty minutes, after which we are again engulfed in Tibetan sands.

Sometime around eleven at night, the truck rumbles to a halt, and we tumble out to discover that both vehicles are stuck in quicksand. The drivers are unwilling to do anything about it, as it is snowing and pitch dark outside. We pile our bodies in the back of the truck like sardines in a can, and have a very restless night of sleep.

Come light, Tsering has managed to free our truck, and haul out the Landcruiser as well, but he has damaged an engine part and the truck can no longer run. The group spends an hour mulling over this latest catastrophe, and decides that the jeep will go back to Lhatze and search for a spare part. It is actually quite nice to be stuck, as we have our first chance to sit and watch the scenery without being jarred about. We sit and talk in hushed voices as Spencer's dijeridoo drones out across the high plains.

Everyone is here for his or her own reasons. Spencer buys clothing and jewels in India to sell at fairs back home in Australia. His wife is pregnant, and he figures this might be their last journey to India for the next few years, so he wants this trip to be to some special place. Jamie is toying with the idea of putting together a cycling trip out here for his adventure travel company, but what he has seen thus far isn't promising, even for hardcore bicyclists. Sachiko and Chiaki are in love with Tibetan culture, and they wish to take part in the great Tibetan ritual of the pilgrimage to Kailash. Matsuda loves nature, mountains, and adventure. He works in a mountain hut in Japan, and he laughs when I tell him of my adventures in the Japan Alps. My tent going over the cliff now seems like a long lost story from my childhood. Masako is engaged to be married and her fiancé is not a traveller, so she figured she had better take this opportunity to make a crazy and difficult journey while she could. Kuwahara and Akama, the other two Japanese travellers, don't say much, though Kuwahara informs us at every meal that he is fine to only eat instant ramen.

By nightfall, the Landcruiser returns with Carol, Madeleine, and a spare part for the truck. They have nicknamed their driver Bozo, and they tell us that he has almost crashed twice. It turns out that he got his driver's license two weeks ago and has never driven anywhere outside Lhasa in his brief career.

Bozo lives up to his reputation, as shortly after Tsering installs the new part, he runs over the old part, which has been left in the road; he then proceeds to veer straight into a mud hole, and the Landcruiser becomes stuck for the night. We pile back into the truck and go to sleep grumbling and laughing at the same time over the absurdity of it all.

It snows all night, and I awake with diarrhea, rushing out into the frozen morning to relieve myself. The remote and rugged landscape of Tibet continues to amaze. Mammoth mountains and brown land seem to go on into eternity.

We make decent progress on this, our fourth day out of Lhasa. There are no breakdowns or other calamities. At all major river crossings, Tsering now drives both the truck and Landcruiser across, swimming back to the other side after safely delivering the first vehicle, and saving Bozo the embarrassment of further blunders.

At every stop, Madeleine approaches me and complains that the Japanese never speak up about their driver's mistakes or voice an opinion when it comes to making decisions. I learn from Hitomi that Sachiko and Chiaki have approached her, griping that the Westerners are rude and insensitive, and that they make decisions without ever consulting them. I am becoming annoyed with Kuwahara and Akama, who are unwilling to help with cooking or cleaning, and I am unhappy that Masako and Hitomi seem to do an extra share without complaining. Brian and Gita appear to be helping themselves to various snacks from our provisions without asking. It is a study in psychology to watch these minor things get blown out of proportion, here in these harsh conditions without walls or spaces to buffer our human foibles. Hitomi and I manage to create a little distance by setting up our tent next to a stream far from the truck, and we have a quiet meal in front of a magnificent sunset, by ourselves.

As we proceed, it is as if we are descending into Dante's Inferno, as the conditions continue to deteriorate. It rains again all night, and wet tents and sleeping bags fill the back of the truck. We all smell of gasoline and are covered in grime. Most of us have diarrhea, and the rest have splitting headaches, brought on by the jarring road and the altitude, which is now at over 5000 meters. I think to myself that we will all become deranged if this continues.

We pass a small settlement of *yurts* made from yak bones and pelts. A few families of *drogpas* (nomads) pass the summer here, herding their yaks and staring at the sky. The track we have been following disintegrates completely into a quagmire of wet sand, and we alternate between short spurts of driving and long stops during which we discuss whether we should trust the set of tire tracks we are following. The drivers have no maps, and they appear as befuddled as we are, but Lobsang informs us not to worry. He says, "Ve are going za right way, ya?" and climbs back into the heated comfort of the cab.

By six p.m. we discover that we are on track, as we arrive at the first of two major river crossings, as foretold by our travel agents. Bozo, eager to show that his lack of mistakes in the past twenty-four hours is a true sign of progress, lurches the Landcruiser at full speed into the swiftly flowing water, and makes it about halfway across before the engine dies and the vehicle begins to sink. We watch in disbelief as the windows are rolled down. Madeleine and Carol bail water from inside with their coffee mugs, while Chiaki and Sachiko yell hysterically in the back seat. In the truck, we are too busy laughing and whipping out cameras out for this epic photo opportunity to notice that our own attempt to cross is failing. The truck grinds to a halt seconds later, about a third of the way across.

It takes a few minutes to dawn on us that we are stuck in the middle of a river. We haul out our gear and jump into the cold water, which is fortunately only waist to chest deep, although almost up to Hitomi's neck. It takes several trips to bring sleeping bags, tents, stoves, food, and other provisions to safety; this done, the group spends half an hour in an amusing attempt to haul the Landcruiser out of the river. On our fifth try we are successful, sixteen frantically tugging bodies being the magic number. However, the truck remains steadfast, and Tsering can only tether it to a boulder on the opposite shore in hopes that it won't drift away during the night.

In the excitement, Madeleine, Carol, Matsuda, and all the Tibetans end up on the other side of the river, while the rest of us remain with the Landcruiser. Half of our provisions are in the truck, so we pool together a meal and again laugh at the mess we are in. Brian whips out a guitar to sing songs under the first clear sky in days.

Some hours later I open my eyes to see a young girl with a mischievous grin peering into our tent. The first light has brought out a family, who live along the banks of this river. They are dressed in sheepskin robes that look like they have never been washed, and they smell of rancid yak butter and smoke. The father is about four foot seven, with beautiful lines etched throughout his leathery face, and he smiles perpetually, revealing his one and only tooth. He twirls a prayer wheel nonstop, and spends most of his time chanting and talking to himself.

His wife is a total contrast. She is very tall, with hair down her backside neatly woven into two long braids. In addition to her sheepskin robe, she wears a pair of shiny green Chinese Army tennis shoes and a huge pair of bifocals which do not fit her face. She holds tightly to her youngest daughter, who is around two years old, and looks to her oldest child, the one peering into our tent, for some explanation of how these aliens have landed at her doorstep.

In the course of the next hours, the ice is broken between all of us. The Tibetans marvel as we fire up our cookstoves to brew them tea and coffee; Brian whips up a breakfast of pancakes and honey, which thrills them to no end. Their fascination with the food, however, is surpassed by their wonder over our gear, from tents to sleeping bags, pads, water filters, and altimeters. Chiaki, who speaks a bit of Tibetan, informs us that they think we are a type of *drogpa* without yaks. Hitomi teaches Pemba, the older girl, how to set up the tent, use her camera, and filter water, and she gains a friend for life in the process. In the meantime, Spencer has the rest of the crowd spellbound as he starts up on his dijeridoo, and soon everyone is laughing and dancing.

Our hospitality is returned immediately, as we are invited to the family's nearby home, a simple adobe hut in a compound surrounded by a mud wall. They ply us with delicious fresh yogurt from their few goats, and with the standard yak butter tea and *tsampa*. The hut is a basic two-room earthen dwelling, clean and cozy, warmed by a fire, with several thick Tibetan rugs to sit on. There are several pictures of the Dalai Lama and the Panchen Lama on the mantle, as well as an old black-and-white photo of great-grandparents. Where they procured any of these items, I have no idea. We add to the Dalai Lama photo collection, which pleases the father to no end, and spend the rest of the afternoon teaching each other songs and relaxing by the warm fire.

Back at the river, a passing vehicle has pulled the truck out, but it remains on the opposite bank. Additionally, the engine needs work, so by mid afternoon, it is apparent that we are not going anywhere. The space, scenery, and chance to dry out gear and recuperate bodies is well received by all at first, but as time passes, the group begins to splinter quite severely.

The following morning, Tsering announces that he will not risk crossing the river again without another truck here to help pull us across. Of course, not a single vehicle arrives in the next ten hours, and everyone is starting to become very antsy, something akin to "cabin fever" except that there are no cabins out here. It comes out in translation that none of the drivers have ever been here before, that they do not know the way, and that most of what the travel agency told us was a pack of lies. Carol gets into a fistfight with Lobsang, and Tsering stomps off into the countryside. The Tibetans all want to turn around and go back.

Meanwhile, on our side of the river, several folks are out of food, and want to go back to Lhatze. We are forced to give away many of our dwindling supplies to prevent a total mutiny. The food arrangements have completely broken down due to our positions on opposite sides of the river, and whenever one group goes to the truck to pick up rice, carrots, tomatoes, or hot chocolate, they often find that the other group has already depleted the supply.

Jamie decides to strike out on his own, and with a tinge of envy, we watch him pump his mountain bike slowly through the packed sand tracks into the distance. Other members of the group discuss going back to Lhatze, calling the travel agency and asking for a permit extension, and then trying to take the northern road, but I manage to convince them that Kailash will be over two weeks away via this route, whereas from here, we are only one day away, if only we can get across the river. The afternoon seems to stretch on forever, and even our local family doesn't show up, as we have become old news by now. Evening brings an electrical storm and snow on the nearby hills, and a surreal golden light bathes the land. As I sit sipping tea, I realize that the rigors of reaching Kailash are turning out exactly as I had assumed they would.

Midnight brings the din of engines to the river, and we stumble out of our sleeping bags to hail two trucks which have arrived. The drivers inform us that there is a seventy-kilometer detour which will allow us to cross the river unaided, as they do not want to jeopardize their own engines trying to tow us across. Thus, at first light we break camp, haul everything back across the water, and are soon following a track downstream. I wonder why the drivers never asked about this one.

We pass through a tiny settlement called Horpa, which, incredibly, has a small shop. We file in and buy most of the provisions available. A can of pineapple, dated from 1980, proves absolutely delicious.

Ignoring our sightings of an obvious track, the drivers proceed to get wedged in on the side of a hill, then on a sand spit. We eventually break free and find the right place to cross the river. Carol and Lobsang have another punchout, and then make up. Madeleine goes ballistic, ranting vehemently at the Japanese for no apparent reason. Matsuda has a high fever and lays comatose, wrapped in a blanket; Masako, usually the iron woman of the group, is also weak, yet somehow we proceed.

At the second major river we meet up with Jamie again. He is happy to see us, as biking through sand has been demoralizing. We also agree to give a ride to two Tibetan pilgrims on their way to Kailash. They seem to bring us good luck: we power both vehicles across the water and surge on, now less than 100 kilometers from the magical mountain.

We chug over a 5200 meter pass and are greeted by a panorama of red earth, rock outcroppings, and endless space and sky. Tibet is the most desolate, harsh, and beautiful place in the world.

Dropping to a lake, we pitch camp and a sense of electric excitement buzzes in the air. Ruri begins to pace frantically, whirling his prayer wheel like a man possessed, while Sonam, the pilgrim from eastern Tibet, sits in a field and chants verses from his Sanskrit scrolls. There are no squabbles this evening, and even Matsuda arises from his sleeping bag, to join us around the fire for soup.

It is a short ride the next morning to Darchen, the tent city at the base of Mount Kailash. Weary as we are, arrival in Kailash exceeds all our expectations. Shaped like a hat, the mighty peak towers over the plains and overlooks nearby Lake Manasarovar, a huge blue gem second only to Kailash on the Hindu pilgrimage route. Behind Manasarovar, fluted ice walls glow in the twilight. They are the Gurla Mandata, a 7700 meter set of peaks in the great Himalayan chain.

We are, if only for a moment, truly in the lap of the gods.

Darchen consists of a few enclaves of clay-walled encampments, sheltered from the winds. There are rooms for rent, a small shop selling provisions and prayer flags, and a room which bills itself as a restaurant, opening sporadically whenever its Chinese cook sees fit. There is a single-burner kerosene stove in the kitchen with a rusty wok set on it, where the cook whips up stir-fried vegetables. He charges a fair premium for the pieces of cabbage or carrots which have somehow survived the arduous journey from Lhasa in better shape than we have.

There are pilgrims here from across Tibet, some of whom have walked for months to get here. Supposedly, the purest act of pilgrimage is to prostrate oneself all the way here, but I have a hard time imagining someone prostrating themselves across thousands of kilometers in the terrain we have just crossed. Then again, the Khampas, from the area of Cham in eastern Tibet, look strong enough to accomplish such a feat. The Khampa men are all devilishly handsome, with thick shocks of black hair which they wear like the mane on a lion. They are known as the warriors of Tibet, and indeed, during the Chinese invasion of 1959 the Khampas managed to hold off the Chinese army without any modern weapons and inflict substantive damage against a heavily armed opponent. A famous Tibetan saying goes, "The best horses are from Amdo; the best religion is in Lhasa; and the best men are from Cham."

Our pilgrim, Sonam, is a Khampa, and he is most regal. He struts around with his chest puffed out, dapper in his red *chupa* robe with black sash around the waist and a pair of elegant riding boots. When it comes out in conversation that he isn't married, Sachiko and Chiaki spend a lot of time feeding him compliments, which he laps up happily between his readings of the long Sanskrit scrolls he carries with him, preparing himself for his *kora*.

And then there are the foreigners. Scores of Japanese travellers are seeking the connections to Buddhism that they feel they can no longer find in modern Japan. Professional photographers snap away, Tibet being the hottest topic in every adventure travel magazine worldwide. A few wealthy private groups have made the epic trek across the Himalayas in style, Nepalese porters carrying all their belongings.

Hitomi and I load our packs and agree to meet the group back in Darchen in four days' time, then we set out to do our *kora* and meet the holy mountain head-on. Most of the others have neither the equipment nor the energy to travel around the mountain. Carol and Madeleine, hearing that there are hot springs at Lake Manasarovar, demand that Bozo zip them over there immediately, their bodies having gone without hot water longer than they imagined humanly possible. I contemplate the Tibetan belief that washing carries away all one's happiness and memories. Up in the dry air of Tibet one really doesn't sweat much, and most people smell of the smoke from cooking fires. There is little need to bathe, nor are many inclined to do so, the temperatures being what they are and the water being permanently glacial.

The tents of Darchen become specks on the lunar landscape as we make our way out of the village and descend into the La Chu Valley, ringed by earth-toned mountain walls on one side and purple sandstone on the other. As the valley narrows, the mountains become more jagged, giant serrated ridges with the black rock face of Kailash rising behind them.

Throughout the valley there are *gompas*, tiny monastic retreats built right into the mountainsides, some of which are inhabited by one or two monks. We are always welcome in the *gompas* for yak butter tea, for which we exchange Dalai Lama photos. The monks are delightful, part jester, part sage.

In the Chuki *gompa*, we meet a middle-aged monk who speaks a fair amount of English, learned almost entirely from meetings with travellers and pilgrims from around the world. His name is Tsewang, and he spends three to four months here in meditation and prayer.

We wait out a sudden thunderstorm over several cups of tea with Tsewang, who discusses the Tibetan Buddhist belief that all of life is about preparing for death. This sounds like a rather morbid view of things at first, but Tsewang's explanation makes a lot of sense. He says that most human beings live in states of perpetual fear, and that all of our "smaller" fears—of heights, of the dark, of strangers—are actually manifestations of the primal fear of death. If we live aware of our own death, and ultimately accept it, we become truly free to live life. When we know that each moment might be our last, we become fully aware of our surroundings, our companions, our actions, and each precious and fleeting moment.

We push on for several hours and make camp above a river at the corner of the northwest face of Kailash. Our stove has serious problems at this altitude, sputtering and coughing black kerosene fumes, and it often takes three cleanings and over an hour just to boil water. We opt for muesli for dinner and snuggle in our tent, reflecting on the fact that this is our fourth full moon of the journey. We have been keeping track of time via the lunar calendar lately, which seems to make a lot of sense. Our first moon was on the Yangtze River, the second on the grasslands outside Zoige, the third in wretched Dulan, and here we are at Mount Kailash for the fourth. Hitomi and I have changed in our passage through time and places, and are increasingly relaxed and attuned to the rigors of travel. I hope that our wisdom and maturity become as seasoned as our blackened skin, thick and leathery from being outside all this time.

The stove is no longer working the following morning, but it is okay. We munch on leftover lentil curry and enjoy a leisurely stroll along flat terrain, arriving at the Drigaphuk *gompa* in less than an hour. Here the entire north face of Mount Kailash is revealed, its bulk dominating everything around it. Our driver Tsering arrives, en route to his second *kora* in two days! It will take us three days to cover the fifty-five kilometers around the mountain, carrying our loaded packs over a 5500 meter pass; Tsering, Ruri, and the other pilgrims will do three circuits in three days, carrying nothing but their Chinese suit jackets! Lobsang, being of another generation, has chosen to remain by the truck filing his nails, brushing his hair, and dreaming of his girlfriend back in Lhasa.

After lunch, we climb to the Gangtong Glacier, which hangs from Kailash's lower flanks. The wall of the north face is absolutely tremendous, and from the base of the glacier, the mountain won't even come close to fitting into my camera lens. Snowfalls cascade from the rock high above us while the glacier creaks and moans, and crevasses stretch out not far from where we stand. The traverse becomes quite dangerous from here on. Kailash is a mountain no human has summited, as it is now protected by the Chinese government due to its religious significance (one of the few religious claims supported by the Chinese). We turn around after performing our own prostrations before this mighty deity, giving thanks for our opportunity to be here.

The following morning I am ill with stomach problems again, and Hitomi nearly has to drag me out of camp and on towards the Dolma La. At 5555 meters, this is the highest point I have been in my life. The climb is fairly gradual, but though I am well acclimatized, it still takes many rest stops and much deep breathing to reach the pass. On top, we add the prayer flags we have carried to the thousands that bedeck the mountainside, the hope being that the winds will carry the prayers and wishes across the earth. Tsering and Sonam whiz past us on round three, cheerfully wishing us a happy morning as they motor along. I figure that if the Boston Marathon were a holy event, the Tibetans would win by many legs.

As we descend from the other side of the Dolma La, we come across three Tibetans prostrating themselves around the mountain. In contrast to our drivers' mad dashes, these pilgrims' perambulations will take three weeks. They move in rhythm, palms together in prayer, then fall to their knees, and finally lay flat on their stomachs. Then they rise to repeat the cycle, over and over. They wear kneepads and handpads to avoid tearing their skin, but they have nothing else besides the dirty robes they wear. I wonder to myself if they even carry any food. Their faith is astounding, something so deep I cannot come close to fathoming it—although I figure I might try a few prostrations if that would get rid of my stomach woes.

The last stretch of the trek meanders through a valley of red and brown cliffs. Kailash is no longer visible, and there are fewer pilgrims in this valley. We are forced to camp one more night, before fording the Drong River, but we do so most happily. Being out here, away from all the craziness of the group, has been a real vacation. We sit and watch the river flow, realizing that we are at the source of four of Asia's mightiest and holiest rivers. Kailash spawns the Indus, the Brahmaputra, the Sutlej, and the Karnali, which eventually leads to the Ganges. The Tibetans call Kailash *Gangrimboche*, which means "Precious Jewel of Snow;" sitting at the river's edge, watching clouds sail over the peak, I can see why.

Breakfast is a leisurely affair, the stove deciding to work again. We have tea and porridge, reluctant to vacate this magical spot. Only the rapidly rising Drong gets us to our feet, and we move onward toward Darchen. At the outskirts of the tent city, some foreigner has left a rock in the middle of the path, painted with the words, "may Tibet become a zone of peace." The rock lies on the ground in an endless expanse of land and sky, a speck in a sea of space.

Back in Darchen, little has changed. Carol and Madeleine continue to complain, Lobsang is still preening, and Kuwahara sits in his favorite corner slurping ramen noodles. Masako, however, has taken a turn for the worse. I am certain that she has come down with hepatitis A, as her fever and weakness continue, and her skin has turned the color of freshly ground turmeric. I have never seen a truly yellow-skinned person before, and it is quite alarming, especially as hepatitis A is most definitely contagious. We have at least a week of unknown horrors and trials ahead of us. I shudder as I watch Chiaki and Sachiko help Masako to the Landcruiser, where Carol and Madeleine have graciously offered their seats for the return journey. I find myself wondering how long their kindness will last when they are covered in dust and stuck in the mud somewhere.

The journey from Mount Kailash is almost as horrendous as the outbound trip. We return via the northern route, after a Tibetan guide tells us it is the more travelled road. This turns out to be true, but our drivers still manage to get lost and stuck several times. Carol ends up driving the Landcruiser at one point, tossing Bozo in the back seat and taking over even though she has not driven in twenty years. Madeleine completely loses control in a small-town restaurant, screaming at us and telling us how much she hates us all.

The truck is held up by Chinese police, and Tsering's keys are taken away on the premise that he must pay a "fine." We are able to escape after I claim that my father is the ambassador to China in Beijing; I tell the pipsqueak officer in charge that if the keys don't find their way back into the ignition, he will spend the rest of his life in this outpost. Masako continues to slip in and out of fever, but ever the iron horse, is up and will be climbing around Lhasa only days after doctors diagnose her with hepatitis and tell her to rest indefinitely. The only person who appears not to suffer is Kuwahara, who sits stoically in the worst spot in the truck, right over the wheel well, bouncing along silently and speaking only to inform us that instant ramen will be fine for supper.

Lhasa has a somber feel to it. The Chinese are preparing to celebrate "Thirty Years of the Naming of the Tibet Autonomous Region," an event for which the Prime Minister will fly in from Beijing. Preparations are underway to ensure compliance with the "celebrations." Chinese fighter planes take up space in the large square beneath the Potala; their significance is not lost on the Tibetans who come to the square to play with their children. Military police and soldiers are everywhere, truncheons in hand, making sure there are no demonstrations. Years before, monks took to the streets to protest prohibitions of their practices, and the demonstrations were filmed by foreigners and shown to the world. Security cameras are mounted all around the Barkhor and Jokhang, as well as inside the Potala. Some cameras have microphones dangling off them to eavesdrop on any conversations the Chinese may deem inappropriate.

One can sense the anger and outrage behind the smiles of the Tibetans. It comes out when they are drunk, often in fights or slurs against the Chinese, in the *momo* shops, karaoke booths, and tearooms around town. Rumor has it that all foreigners will be kicked out of Lhasa for the "festivities," and not wanting to find out, we decide it is time to get back on our bicycles. Furthermore, as it is late summer, it is imperative to get over the Himalayas. The snows will come shortly.

The first sixty kilometers out of Lhasa are level and paved, and there is a bike lane as big as the road itself. This is the route to the airport, and the Chinese have built this section to demonstrate to foreign dignitaries just how advanced and civilized they have made Tibet. Of course, once the airport road turns off, we cross the Brahmaputra and are back on rocks and dirt, bouncing along in the dust.

The Kampa La is the first of five passes through the Himalayas. It is at 4800 meters, a tiny pass by Tibetan standards, but coming from the Lhasa Valley at 3600, we can feel every meter of gain. The road is atrocious, covered in boulders and riddled with holes. Despite our six a.m. start, it is close to dusk when we approach the prayer flags at the top of the pass. Well-versed by now in Tibetan etiquette, we both prostrate ourselves and give thanks, chanting, "*la la la so*."

Below us sprawls Yamdrok Lake, a huge turquoise jewel sparkling in the day's last light. We zip down to its shores and pitch camp, too tired to cook or do much else.

We have carried all the fixings for a pancake breakfast from the market in Lhasa, planning to treat ourselves on a leisurely morning when we found the perfect camp spot. This is it. However, after mixing eggs, sugar, flour, raisins, and all the other ingredients together, we discover that the flour we have purchased is some sort of salt flour, and is completely inedible. Gloomy, we enjoy our lake view to the tune of *tsampa*, and ride on hungry.

We pass through Nagartse, a Tibetan village of prayer flags, stone houses, and howling mastiffs that chase us out of town. The road climbs steadily to the Karo La, the second major pass on the road to Nepal. The pass sits at just over 5000 meters, under the large icefall of an almost 7000 meter peak which is unnamed on our map. As always, a few Tibetans materialize atop the pass, and they gawk as we spread peanut butter on the stale Chinese *mantous* (steamed buns) we have carried since Lhasa.

It is 100 dusty kilometers to Shigatse, Tibet's second largest city, past barley fields and obnoxious kids who manage to steal our lunch from the rear carriers of our steeds. Shigatse is pleasant enough, aside from the fact that it is close to impossible for us to sleep, as every single dog in the city wakes up promptly at two in the morning, and they howl all night. We decide to stay several days.

The centerpiece of Shigatse is the Tashilumpo Monastery, the seat of the Panchen Lama. The present Panchen Lama is something of a Chinese puppet, living in Beijing; therefore, Tashilumpo is well funded and has been rebuilt with glittering gold domes that cost a fortune. At least tourism has made the Chinese realize that the monasteries are worth something, so they have spent a lot of money rebuilding what the Red Guards razed to the ground during the Cultural Revolution. The monasteries often only radiate in gold, rather than in spirit.

A long day's climb later, we struggle over the Lagpa La, at 5200 meters the highest pass yet. We huff and puff all the way, then descend into valleys surrounded by chocolate mountains and red cliffs. Strong headwinds and abysmal road conditions keep us from enjoying the view of huge snowy peaks that have appeared up ahead. Both of us are cursing in every language we know when it dawns on me that we are looking at Mount Everest for the first time.

I bellow to Hitomi to stop, and say, "Wait a minute! This is what we dreamed about back in Japan! This is what we read about in magazines, and here we are! We're cycling along next to Mount Everest on the high roads of Tibet and all we can do is complain about the road surfaces. We are in the movie!" We slow to a crawl and try to savor every bump and hole, and the exquisite scenery that envelops us.

The only settlement out here is Tingri, a small, weathered village with tremendous views of Everest and Cho Oyu, another 8000 meter giant. The appropriately named Everest View Hotel is full of climbers, hitchhikers, and several bicyclists as well. We meet two other cyclists, John and Sonja, who are also on a world tour. It turns out that Sonja is from my hometown, and even more bizarre, that we worked in the same outdoor adventure program many years before!

A feast is served for dinner, and the boisterous crowd is a change from the deserted road and silent staring kids we've had in camp for the past nights. People here live large, and exist, as Thoreau said, to suck the marrow from life.

After a few days of storytelling competitions among mountain climbers, bicyclists, and other adventure seekers, the Everest View empties out, and we head on to tackle the last major passes separating us from Nepal. We celebrate our 3000th kilometer cycled in a Chinese Army post with a meal of oily soup, with dirty, withered cabbage leaves and Spam. We swear it is one of the most delicious meals we have ever had, as we often do after a day of cycling.

Past the army camp, the road begins to climb again for the last time in Tibet, and we approach the Tang La, the final pass before the border. It is a double pass, and after the first summit the winds are too strong for us to go on, not to mention that the road is completely obscured by clouds and driving snow. We are forced to stop for the night in a lonely guesthouse, where children materialize out of thin air as soon as we have checked in; they spend the next hours climbing on each others' shoulders to peer over the curtains we have closed in our room.

Weeks ago, these children would have enraged me, but now I know there isn't anything wrong with their actions. Their world includes no concept of public versus private. Everything exists out in the open, laid bare for inspection and scrutiny by all.

At dawn, we make our way up to the last pass in a sea of mist and clouds. Sticking out of the clouds to our right is Shishangpagma, the smallest of the fourteen 8000 meter peaks. Somewhere to the left is Everest, the largest of the giants, known as Chomolongma to the Tibetans. The road weaves through a maze of *mani* walls, and we see dozens of stones inscribed with the Buddhist mantra of "*Om mani padme hum*" ("Hail to the Jewel in the Lotus"). We reach our final prayer flags in Tibet, which wave in the incessantly raging wind. Offering our last "*la la la so*," we revel in the fact that from this pass, the road will drop more than 4500 meters to the Sunkosi River in Nepal.

Our celebrations soon come to a halt, however. After an initial descent into a canyon, the road washes out, and begins to weave up and down through a twisting valley with continuously steep drops and climbs, made all the worse by persistent headwinds. We abandon all thoughts of covering 100 kilometers, and instead stay in the town of Nyalam, a dusty bazaar town full of the usual ugly Chinese concrete tenements. A sheep drive blocks the entire road and main square in town, and we avoid it by checking into the Trade Station Hotel, which has clean rooms with double windows to keep out the street noise. The short and perky desk clerk mutters, "*Zu tsing tsa, zu tsing tsa*," ("bicycle, bicycle") every time we walk past.

The road resumes its plunge where it left off, down into the first trees we have seen in months. Everything is bathed in a tropical green, there are abundant flowers, and higher humidity. Water seems to pour out of every crack and crevice in the earth's surface. After months of rarely sweating, even while climbing the giant passes, we now perspire freely in the heavy air. It feels heavenly.

The mad plunge continues into Zhangmu, a frontier town where we see bananas for the first time in months, and where moneychangers and banks make up most of the town's streetside commerce. The Chinese border post is here, and we are forced to wait a long while, as a soldier brandishing a machine gun fixes us with an unnerving stare. We are eventually called into a small office, where an official begins berating us.

"Where is your group?" he barks.

I point to Hitomi and then to myself.

"Where is your group leader?" he continues.

I sheepishly point to myself.

The official nods slowly, and then confers at length with a few of his colleagues. He leers at me and shouts, "Do you know that you are not allowed to bicycle in China?"

Surpressing a grin, I bow my head and offer apologies.

"No, we did not know this. We are sorry, and we won't do it again."

Satisfied that he has won the power struggle, he brings out his stamp pad and gives us permission to leave, striking exit stamps into our passports.

Outside the enormous gate with "Welcome to China" scrawled above it, we run into one last obstacle before leaving Tibet. The Nepali festival of Dasain, the largest of the year, will be taking place in a week, and the blood of thousands of sheep and goats is needed for sacrifices. Every car, plane, bike, and other possession will be doused in blood to ensure success and good luck in the coming year. There are not enough animals to go around, so many are brought from Tibet. Thus, we run into another massive sheep jam.

I track down the lead shepherd and ask him to move the sheep for us, but he merely laughs and asks me for money. I figure I have listened to enough shepherds in our travels across Tibet to do a decent job myself, so I plunge right into the sheep with my bicycle, shouting *"haa"* in my best shepherd impersonation. Hitomi follows close on my heels, but soon we are swallowed up by the mass of muddy hooves and stinking wool, sinking into the thick muddy bog created by the flock. I turn around to see Hitomi falling halfway over, jostled back and forth by the stubborn animals, and my only words of comfort are "hold that pose," as I struggle to get out my camera and capture our truly asinine position.

After about fifteen minutes the end is in sight, and covered in mud and sheep urine, we emerge grinning. It is eight kilometers to the Nepal border through a "no man's land," where obviously no man has ever thought about doing any maintenance on the road. This is the "Friendship Highway," so named by the Chinese, but it looks more like a riverbed. We have to walk most of it, immersed in water and mud.

As we near the huts housing Nepal Customs, a lone Chinese soldier comes out to hail me, asking if I will give him cigarettes. I look him squarely in the eye and say, *"Mei yo,"* as we haul our bikes onto the fresh tarmac and look into the welcoming smiles of the Nepali soldiers.

Chapter Five
Nepal: *Hello Pen*

*To wander over the earth; to see and never
have my fill of seeing…new land and seas, and ideas.
To see it all as though for the first time and the last
time, with a long, lingering gaze, and then to close
my eyelids and feel the riches crystallizing inside
me, calmly or tempestuously as they will, until time
has distilled them through its fine sickle into the
quintessence of all my joys and all of my griefs.
This alchemy of the heart is, I believe, a great delight.*

Nikos Kazantzakis

We are welcomed to the mountain kingdom of Nepal by a
small man, who stands by the side of the road wearing a
topi (a small, multicolored, pointed hat) and a long baggy
shirt. He stands with his hands folded together in prayer, and half steps
into the road, imploring us to stop.

"*Namaste Dai, Namaste Didi,*" he welcomes us. *Namaste* is the formal
version of *Namaskar*, which means, "I salute the God within you." It is
the traditional greeting used throughout Nepal and northern India. *Dai*
and *Didi* are "brother" and "sister," common forms of address throughout the country.

"And what is your good name, sir?" he inquires.

"My name is Dave," I reply in slow textbook English. All this travel
has taught me that my seemingly simple name can be difficult for people
from other cultures.

"What is your name?" I ask.

"Ravi," he grins, "but you are better than I."

I look at him questioningly, not knowing where this is leading.

"In Nepali, *Dev* means God," he tells me, "so surely you have been sent from the heavens." He continues, "And who is the charming *memsahib* riding along with you? I am thinking she is looking like Nepali, but Nepali lady no riding like this on bicycle, so maybe she is coming Japanese or Chinese?"

He grins some more, wags his head from side to side, and goes on with the conversation. "You know, it is the time of taking tea. Would you be so gracious as to of joining me?"

In six months in China, we have been invited for tea just twice by the Chinese. Twenty minutes across the border, we already have an offer. We park our bikes and duck into a small roadside shack, where we have our first cups of sweet and spicy chai, the national drink of Nepal. The chai is made with fresh milk and strong black Darjeeling tea leaves, boiled with cardamom seeds, cloves, cinnamon, and loads of sugar. After all the green and jasmine tea of China—and the rancid yak butter tea of Tibet—drinking this tea is like being let loose in a candy store.

Ravi is a farmer, and grows rice, millet, and enough vegetables to provide for his wife and four children. He learns English through interaction with foreign trekkers during the two short trekking seasons, when he works as a porter. He earns three to four dollars a day at this job, carrying loads of sometimes more than a hundred pounds up steep trails in a basket on his back, attached via a strap around his forehead. He has no complaints about the work, though, and in a country where the per capita income is around 150 dollars a year, the salary is not to be scoffed at.

As we sit in the teashop, people pass by and pause for brief inspections of our bicycles. Nobody stares, no one yanks on my beard, and not one person screams at us. For the next several days, we find every Nepali we meet, and the soft charm they exude, completely ingratiating.

Scenes from a Third World documentary greet us in the mountains. We pass bare-breasted women carrying water jugs on their heads, naked kids with sores on their frail bodies, and villages with thatched-roof huts. Yet in contrast with China, everything is clean, and almost everyone we meet is smiling. Water gushes everywhere from rocks, from hillsides, through villages. Each village has public water taps where people wash, bathe, and collect water. Where there are public toilets, most have clean water for washing; even better, most of the excrement has made its way into the hole and has been flushed away.

People everywhere are friendly and curious, but there are no mob scenes like we encountered in China, and everyone is a lot more respectful of our bikes, bodies, and privacy. Children with pretty faces are everywhere, and they often approach to greet us with a smile and the words "hello pen."

Western aid groups and other travellers have often made a point of bringing pens for children, thinking that they could use them for their schoolwork. Unfortunately, this hasn't really worked, as the pens are often sold and do not end up on school desks. However, it is amusing to see how "hello pen" has become a standard greeting; in one stretch of road, we pass hundreds of schoolchildren who all stop to wave and give us the salutation. Even an old man stops us here, puts his hands together in prayer, but instead of *"Namaste,"* smiles kindly and says, "hello pen."

Though Nepal is the domain of Mount Everest, most of the country is lush, green, and subtropical. We ride through narrow and precipitous valleys full of terraced rice and millet plots, which in the humid and heavy air remind me of Japan.

Many villages have health clinics, women's associations, and centers for the deaf, most of these having been created by foreign aid projects. There are also decently stocked shops with the most incredible selection of cookies I have ever seen, most of them coming from the gigantic Indian biscuit industry. We are only forty kilometers from the Chinese border, yet almost everything in the shops comes from India, rather than China. The only major exception are the green army tennis shoes that half of the population seems to wear (the other half going barefoot).

There is ice-cold Tuborg beer in tiny refrigerators in all the shops, and small stalls called *bhattis* serve *dal bhaat*, Nepal's primary meal. *Dal bhaat* consists of rice with lentil curry, along with *saag*, which is similar to spinach, and *achar*, a spicy mix of pickled vegetables.

The small guesthouses scattered through the region are simple and clean. They are run by cheerful proprietors, as often women as men, and staffed by loads of young boys who, whistling as they go, carry our panniers and bicycles up to our rooms, refusing to allow us to carry a thing.

In the mountain village of Dhulikel, the owner of the Nawaranga Guesthouse welcomes us with steaming bowls of *gurung*, thick soup made of dried greens and mountain vegetables, followed by bowls of sweet and sticky homemade custard. We discuss the impact of tourism on his village. A rash of guesthouse building and an increase in competition have nearly forced middle-class lodges to go out of business; they are undercut by new guesthouses, which charge next to nothing in their drive to pull in guests. Additionally, most tourists these days come on package tours, demanding the comforts of home, and their overnight stay is arranged through the upscale Dhulikel Lodge, which takes the lion's share of the business.

The lodge owner tells us that many tourists come here only on day trips, and because Dhulikel lies only thirty-five kilometers from Kathmandu, most can't be bothered with staying overnight. The precarious economic situation has created aggressive competition, which in turn creates more jealousies and squabbles than the village has seen before.

Kathmandu has long been a legendary destination on the Asian travel circuit. It was the goal of hippies in the 60's and 70's, travelling overland from Europe: a Shangri-La where marijuana grew wild, the people were laid back, and one could live for next to nothing in the shadow of the mighty Himalayas. The city has also been a home away from home for the mountaineering community of the world. Since the 1950's, when Maurice Herzog climbed Annapurna, and Edmund Hilary and Tenzing Norgay became the first people to summit Everest, climbers have flocked to Kathmandu in their bids to go higher, faster, and further.

More recently, Kathmandu has become a haven for travellers escaping the rigors of travel in China and India, countries with massive bureaucracies and overwhelming populations. Although Nepal is poorer than both of these countries, the mountaineering scene and big-budget tourism have combined to create a small pocket of wealth and—at least for tourists—all the amenities that come with it.

A friend of mine jokingly calls Kathmandu "San Francisco in Asia," and in some ways, he is right. A relatively small city (the Tribuvan "International" Airport resembles a cow pasture), Kathmandu is crammed with eateries, outdoor shops, and bookstores. There are Japanese sushi bars and a plethora of vegetarian restaurants, one of which has a signboard that reads, "Come enjoy lovely free space we are no meat delightful but have beer." A former Peace Corps volunteer runs a place called Mike's Breakfast, serving fresh scones, quiche, and large stacks of whole-wheat pancakes and blueberry waffles, along with strong filter coffee from Kenya. The café is housed in an art gallery, and patrons dine to the accompaniment of Bach and Chopin.

In the tourist quarter of Thamel, there are at least twenty new and used bookshops, their shelves lined with travel guides, best-selling novels, and scores of classics. In Pilgrims Bookstore, which boasts branches in Varanasi and Delhi, one can find virtually any book ever published on Buddhism, Hinduism, mountaineering, the Himalayas, yoga, and Eastern mysticism; if the book is not on the shelf, it can be ordered from the smiling clerk who wags his head from side to side and says, "for you my friend, special order only five days."

Between the restaurants, bookstores, and souvenir shops, there are the outdoor shops, which display in their windows brand name Gore-Tex parkas, backpacks, and down sleeping bags. These items sell for around a tenth of what they cost back home. My inspection of the zippers and seams reveals that the items are complete fakes, copied right down to the label.

Kathmandu also has a burgeoning nightlife. The Rum Doodle High Altitude Bar displays autographed pictures of climbing king Reinhold Messner and dozens of other celebrities who have frequented the place. At Tom and Jerry's Sports Bar, one can catch the latest football match between Manchester and Chelsea, or the NBA Finals. There are numerous reggae bars, where Bob Marley songs blare into the street, and short Nepali guys slide up to you furtively and whisper in hushed tones, "hashish, you buy hashish?"

Video parlors show pirated versions of Hollywood blockbusters, and music shops offer the entire Billboard One Hundred on copied cassettes at a dollar apiece. There are photo labs, telephone centers promising the lowest overseas rates, and newsstands selling *The International Herald Tribune, The Guardian, The New York Times, Le Monde, Der Spiegel, Time,* and the *Asahi Shinbun* and *The Daily Yomiuri* for the Japanese readers.

If all these consumer opportunities aren't enough to drain one's bank account, there are the street vendors, who sell wooden chess sets, Tibetan bowls, Nepali daggers, and Kashmiri carpets. Curiously, their most proffered item is Tiger Balm, which they hawk at outrageous prices, more than one might pay back home. A stroll down the streets of Thamel at any hour of the day brings over scores of eager young men, all repeating, "hello Tiger Balm sir."

Aside from eating, sleeping, and writing in journals, Hitomi and I spend our time wandering the streets of Kathmandu, which are filled with diverse scenes out of another time period, if not from an entirely different planet. On the eastern side of the city lies Pashtupatinath, a large temple complex and park perched on the banks of a small river which flows into the Ganges. Pashtupati, as it is called, is a holy spot, and the dead of Kathmandu are brought here for cremation. Several *ghats*, open spaces with steps just off the water, line the riverbank, and bodies are often burned here atop flaming pyres. Men in loincloths and women in saris bathe or wash clothing, while monkeys prowl stealthily nearby, looking for scraps of food or unattended belongings to steal.

After a cremation, families of the deceased gather to scatter the ashes into the water, ensuring that the soul will return to the mighty Ganges, hundreds of kilometers away in India. Several barbers have set up along the river next to the *ghats*; the sons of deceased parents shave their heads after their parents' passing, so there is quite a demand in the cutting trade.

Above the river, a small park area and temple complex houses several large phallic stone *lingams*. The *lingams* are presided over by groups of *sadhus*, men who have renounced their possessions and families to travel throughout the land, clad only in a loincloth and carrying only a bowl with which to beg food. *The sadhus* can be found at religious sites, at holy mountains and rivers, and at festivals honoring the various manifestations of the Hindu deities.

Several *sadhus* in particular ply their trade every morning around the *lingams*. They have dreadlocks down to their knees, and their faces and arms are smeared in ashes. They flash the peace sign at the camera-toting hordes, then approach with small books that list rates for a display of their mystical powers. One fellow promises to lift a very large rock on a string tied to his penis, while another will put his legs around his head and then stick his feet in his mouth. Of course, none of these feats are free, and photo sessions cost extra.

Far more exciting are the snake charmers who perform downstream from the *sadhus*. They play wooden flutes to induce their collections of cobras and other highly poisonous snakes to come writhing out of the straw baskets in which they have been coiled. The performances have a heightened sense of danger this week, as the papers have reported that snakes attacked and killed several charmers. I wonder if perhaps someone was out of tune.

North of Pashtupatinath lies Bodhinath, home to the Tibetan community of Kathmandu. Seemingly a million miles away from the *ghats*, Bodhinath houses a large *stupa* with giant eyes painted on top, which stare out at the crowds. Locals call these "the eyes of Kathmandu," and numerous *stupas* throughout the city have the same features. Tibetans here do *koras* around the stupa, spinning prayer wheels as they go, then head off to nearby snack shops to eat *momos* and drink tea or *chang*, a potent alcohol made from barley.

Much of Kathmandu is a cacophony of motorcycle engines, horns, and Hindi music blaring from all the vehicles and shops. The air is grimy, and black fumes belch from the *tempos*, three-wheeled taxis driven at suicidal speeds throughout the city. The haze usually obscures the Ganesh Himal, soaring snowy peaks which lie close to town. Hitomi and I start out enthusiastically each morning, heading off to explore some new temple or return to a favorite spot; by early afternoon we are exhausted, overwhelmed, and congested, and beat a hasty retreat to our hotel room or one of the many tea gardens.

We have grown used to being surrounded by monks drinking yak butter tea, and to seeing women in multicolored saris carrying pitchers of water on their heads. These things are far more a part of our daily lives than shopping malls and financial districts, and I no longer take pictures of the scenes that surround us. While we are supposed to be enjoying Nepal, part of me is already fantasizing about Thailand, about spicy food, fresh coconut milk, and tropical beaches.

As I pick up a bundle of mail from home, it strikes me how far removed Hitomi and I are becoming from our own cultures. Friends and family write about rush hour traffic, second mortgages, events or news we have "missed," and climbing the career ladder. There are complaints about not having enough time to spend with husbands, wives, and kids, about bills, about the lousy state of the world. All this seems meaningless as I sit in a teashop in Kathmandu, watching a butcher across the street take a break from his card game to hack off a slab of goat meat for a customer.

Hitomi and I live now in a culture with endless time; time to sit, time to drink tea, time to wait. Every stranger here makes his neighbor's business his own. Rush hour is eternal here, with cows, goats, chickens, and cycle rickshaws competing with buses, tempos, and the throng of humankind. Here, everyday life for most people is a struggle just to put enough rice on the table, yet most folks don't complain much about the state of the world.

Our only bills are for the occasional inner tube or extra spare part; our tent's only source of heat is our bodies, nestled next to each other in our sleeping bags; we spend most of twenty-four hours a day together. Our greatest concerns each day are finding a flat patch of ground for our tent, finding food and water, getting a good night's sleep, and rejoicing when the winds are in our favor. I wonder how our nomadic lifestyle will affect us in the long run, and whether or not we have reached a "point of no return."

On a more immediate note, my guidebook's description of the Everest/Gokyo region sounds fantastic.

Nepal is a country of few roads. Less than fifty years ago, travellers walked or rode horses into the Kathmandu Valley. The *maharajas* from India were borne over the grueling mountainous terrain on chairs hoisted by their servants. While there is now full road access to Kathmandu and air service to many parts of the country, most Nepalis still live in small rural villages connected by footpaths which have been used as trading routes for centuries.

Thus, the bicycle is not the ideal vehicle for exploring Nepal. We leave ours at the guesthouse, sling on our backpacks, and head for the mountains. We plan to visit the world-famous Solo Khumbu region, abode of some of the highest peaks on earth, including Mount Everest. Most people fly in, as a round trip on foot to the Everest Base Camp takes over thirty days. Ninety-six percent of all trekkers today fly into the region, leaving only four percent making the long hike through the lowlands. This figure sounds appealing to us.

To start off the trek, one must first get to the village of Jiri, several hundred kilometers east of Kathmandu. Veteran climbers of Everest often joke that the hardest part of their climb is the bus ride to Jiri. Three buses leave each day, all by six in the morning, all crammed solid, and all taking at least thirteen hours—if one is lucky.

Our luck looks to be questionable, as my wallet is pickpocketed somewhere between the ticket counter and the bus. Several rupees lighter, Hitomi and I make our way into a vehicle that looks as if it has served as a tractor and an off-road machine for most of its life. The seats are miniscule, presumably designed for people under five feet tall without legs or knees. Hitomi, at four-eleven, can manage, but my knees do not fit between my seat and the back of the one in front of me. After much cajoling, I convice the fellow beside me to let me use the aisle seat, where I can at least stick my legs out to the side.

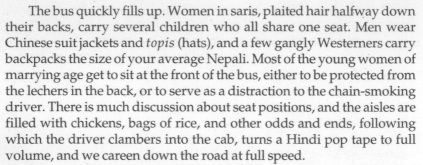

The bus quickly fills up. Women in saris, plaited hair halfway down their backs, carry several children who all share one seat. Men wear Chinese suit jackets and *topis* (hats), and a few gangly Westerners carry backpacks the size of your average Nepali. Most of the young women of marrying age get to sit at the front of the bus, either to be protected from the lechers in the back, or to serve as a distraction to the chain-smoking driver. There is much discussion about seat positions, and the aisles are filled with chickens, bags of rice, and other odds and ends, following which the driver clambers into the cab, turns a Hindi pop tape to full volume, and we careen down the road at full speed.

It is one thing to bicycle next to one of these buses, and another to ride in them. I try to sit back and enjoy the mountain scenery, but can think only about what a maniac the driver is. He roars along at full throttle, swerving around curves and narrowly missing small children who are playing in the road. A baby behind us cries incessantly, wailing into our ears; her mother vomits on the floor beside our backpacks.

It is hot and humid in the valley, and the bus makes innumerable stops to pick up passengers while we sit inside and swelter. There is no room left inside, so new passengers climb onto the roof. Soon there are between fifty and a hundred people lodged on top, clinging to the roof rack or to each other, packed as tightly as we are below.

Despite the fresh air outside, the curvy mountain roads have a brutal effect on the passengers up top, who begin throwing up en masse. Most of their offerings blow directly into the open windows below. Closing the windows is impossible, as the heat would be unbearable, not to mention that most of the windows are broken anyway. So we bounce along, our legs, knees, and shoulders crammed into each other's various joints and bones, covered in vomit. I marvel that the man next to us has a smile on his face the whole time. He is either a completely enlightened being or an absolute idiot.

We do get a respite from this ordeal, as the bus overheats and breaks down, and we get to disembark and spend two hours sitting by the side of the road. Most of the passengers go into an orange grove and proceed to strip the trees of their fruit, leaving the peels scattered all over the ground.

Having received our initiation into the rigors of Third World travel throughout China, none of this shocks either of us. We look at one another, and without saying a word, burst out laughing. The Italian tourist in the back of the bus is another story. This is undoubtedly his first time in Nepal, and he sits shell-shocked in his seat, looking rather green. He speaks only Italian, which isolates him from all conversation and the questions of curious Nepalis, and he remains frozen to his seat, gazing in horror at the situation he has gotten himself into.

After fourteen hours, we reach Jiri, at the end of the road. It is deep in the mountains, yet the road remains smooth and well paved, and Jiri looks like a very prosperous place. It has benefited from much Swiss aid and has several schools, agricultural technology projects, and hydro-power schemes—as well as the road—to show for it. Of course, the gap between appearance and reality is often wide, and as we arrive shortly after dark, the town's electricity goes out for the night.

We stumble around in the dark, trying to find headlamps in our packs, and are rescued by a young boy who encourages us to stay the night at his family's home. His name is Rajeev, and he speaks impec-cable English and decent Japanese, all learned from tourists. Rajeev takes us into a small home with bare rooms lit by candles, where his father greets us warmly and seats us around a table. Rajeev's mother, who can't be more than twenty-five years old, shuttles into the kitchen to reheat some *dal* and *chai* for us.

In the morning, after a deep and much-needed slumber, we bid adieu to the family and leave the road. It is a gorgeous day, and soon we are in the midst of rape blossoms and millet fields, all sparkling in the morning sun. Passing us on the trails are Nepalis of various castes and cultures: Thaman, Chhetri, and Sherpa, all carrying the most amazing loads. Por-ters carry cases of beer, drums of kerosene, bananas and cauliflower, and occasionally even large pieces of furniture, all on their backs, at-tached by a thin strap to their foreheads. Many walk barefoot, their wide feet and sinewy calves a striking contrast with their tiny upper bodies.

Most of the porters are men, but there are a few "Sherpanis," as they are called, hauling loads as heavy as the men. The Sherpas are Bud-dhists who inhabit the high mountain regions of Nepal, and they ap-pear to have a more equal division of labor between men and women than the lowland caste groups, who are all Hindu. The non-Sherpa women we meet on the trails here are not porters, but perform domestic work, taking care of children, cooking, cleaning, gathering wood, and working in the fields. When not portering, most of the men we meet throughout this region seem to spend much of their time drinking tea and chatting with friends.

We are greeted with cries of "Namaste" everywhere, and of course, with "hello pen" by many of the children. One young boy approaches and boldly salutes me. He tells me in an authoritative voice, "I am a student."

"Good for you," I respond. "It is a noble profession."

"Yes," he answers, "and you know, sir, a student must have a pen."

I laugh, and retort, "yes, he must, but I'm not going to give you one." He smiles back and rushes down the trail to find another victim.

We amble along a pretty river, passing women with large nose rings who smile and tell stories as they stride along. Everything along this river valley seems so lush and alive. The first village we come to is Shivalaya, a collection of small houses with tin roofs. We stop for lunch, feasting on a large plate of potatoes, vegetables, and cheese, noting that the green Italian has arrived and looks much more exuberant and energetic than he did yesterday.

Outside the inn where we are eating, a sign says, "We have two meter beds!" but this is not enough to entice us to stay. We continue, spending the afternoon climbing almost 1000 meters to a collection of lodges which straddle a ridge. Most appropriately, the settlement is named Deorali, which means "pass" in Nepali.

We emerge from a forest of rhododendrons into a sea of mist that envelops the ridge, and are greeted by a large signboard advertising one of the lodges:

WELCOME—Only guaranted with various facilities on this mountaintop lodge.

WE DON'T SAY MUCH. ONLY YOU YOURSELF QUALIFY US! We have:

1. The past present and future's various classified racial dish.

2. To escort you with various, different language musical cassette lab.

3. None competitors neighbor quiet, sound a peacePull, private, and dormitory rooms.

4. Yum yum mouth weting super famous choclet and varities.

5. The panormic view from open sun shine mini dining set varanda.

6. The hot shower renting hi trek boots also available.

MOST OF ALL WE ARE SPECIALIZE IN FIXING THE REASONABLE PRICE!"

All these amenities are too good to pass up, so we make the Deorali Lodge our home for the night. Dinner is a lovely *dal bhaat* (whether it comes from the past, present, or future, I know not), and the showers are most welcome, the lodge operating on a most practical system whereby the hot water slowly heats as the kitchen staff cook. We never come across the super famous chocolate, but the proprietress recommends her apple pie, a most suitable substitute, and I retire quite content, marveling over the juxtaposition of cultures and time warps here.

We reach the hamlet of Sete, ascending 500 meters in just under forty-five minutes and even passing several of the Sherpa guides and porters. They are quite amused by the two of us: short Hitomi and tall me, bearing large packs. Hitomi's skin is blackened from the high-altitude sunshine, and I am occasionally asked if this lady with the pack is my Sherpani!

The lodges in Sete are nowhere near as fancy as those in Deorali, and there are no billboards to welcome us. However, a friendly man who turns out to be the local schoolteacher runs a simple, homey place; he invites us in just as the usual afternoon mist begins to descend on the pass. By evening, we are joined around a smoky hearth by Claudio the Italian and his seven "*portatores*," a British couple on their way around the world, a Nepali student of Buddhism and Thangka painting, and a seventy-five year old Malaysian man, who has never done any hiking before, but says that he has little time left to do all the things that he has wondered about doing. Far away from cars and televisions, we gather at this wonderful polyglot roundtable, happily tired, sipping sweet *chai* and feeling fully how rich and colorful a tapestry this planet we call home really is.

The following morning we get an early start, hoping to get ahead of a Slovakian tour group that has shown up. The number of group tours to Nepal has increased dramatically in the past years with the rise of adventure tourism. It could be argued that the groups bring much-needed income to financially strapped places like Nepal, but the reality is that most of their dollars wind up in the hands of a foreign tour operator, or at best, in the pockets of an agency in Kathmandu. Groups pay for their food in advance and often camp, making their contribution to the local village economy negligible, while their drain of resources is the opposite. These groups clog the trails and back up service in the lodges, as they often come in from their campsites to escape the cold. They line up for showers (a group of seventeen takes from two to three hours using the bathrooms), often take up all the available seats and tables in a lodge, and overwhelm the locals. However, the "hello pen" gangs make an absolute killing.

A few days down the trail, we come around a short rise and see Mount Everest come into view, a black triangle of rock poking up behind the snowy face of Lhotse, a neighboring 8000 meter peak. Seeing Everest from this different perspective, I realize just how much terrain we have covered in this high land, and how vast the scale of everything is here. Exactly one moon before, we stood looking at the same mountain from its other side.

The trail crosses a pine forest and traverses into Ringmo, where apple orchards abound and all the teahouses have scrumptious apple pie, dried apples, and apple cider. Then we climb to the Trakshindo La, a final 3000 meter pass before the Khumbu. A defunct cheese factory marks the top of the pass, and I try to imagine what the Swiss were thinking when they put it here.

We descend into the village of Nunthala, a collection of older lodges huddled together on a track that runs through the center of town. Two young ladies approach Hitomi and me, and they ask us where our bicycles are. We look at them in amazement, then at each other, and before we can ask any questions, the older girl asks, "Don't you remember me?"

It turns out that she is Tara Sundas, a student at a school I visited in Kathmandu, where I hope to land a teaching job in the fall. Her sister, Srijana, also attends the school, which was created for Tibetan refugees and lower caste kids, who are often sponsored by trekkers or other visitors to Nepal. Both of the girls have uncanny memories, and they can recall everything we talked about during a presentation on our bicycle journey. They invite us into their home, the Thamserku Lodge, rented out by their parents, who are farmers. As elsewhere in Asia, where teachers are accorded the highest respect, we get a red carpet welcome from the family.

After we consume heaping plates of *dal*, garden vegetables, and bowls of hot soup, Tara's father brings us steaming mugs of water buffalo milk, which is extremely rich and creamy. With Tara acting as translator, the entire family gathers round us to ask questions. While the family finds Tara's translation of our bicycle tales amusing to no end, I am far more intrigued by her own story.

Tara, who is fourteen, makes the journey to and from Kathmandu at least four times a year. It takes her two days to cover the distance from

Nunthala to Jiri, a journey of about fifty kilometers over four strenuous passes; Hitomi and I took four days to make the trip. In Kathmandu, Tara has learned to speak English fluently, as her school uses English as a medium of instruction. She has her sights set on entering the university and hopes to become a doctor because there isn't one in her village. Although she enjoys the worldliness of Kathmandu, she misses her family and the slow pace of life in Nunthala.

Both she and Srijana face an uphill battle, though, for they are part of the "laborer" caste. Although the caste system has been abolished in principle, it carries on in practice throughout India and Nepal. One's caste identity cannot be hidden, as family names are based on caste. Thus Tara may not drink or wash from the same tap as a Brahman or Chhetri (priest and warrior castes), nor may she eat with them. Tradition dictates that she cannot hold certain jobs. Even if she were to become a doctor, she could not treat patients of a higher caste, which would severely limit her practice.

Without foreign sponsorship, the Sundas' could not send their daughters to a decent school. The family rents out the Thamserku Lodge, but their rental income is nominal, as the trekking season is short and visitors are few. It doesn't help that a new, upscale lodge has just opened down the path.

Tara's older brother, Kesab, wasn't able to receive an education, and now he mainly sits about, a sullen and angry young man. He helps his father in the fields, but his dreams are elsewhere, as he watches the foreign male trekkers pass through with their girlfriends in tow, appearing rich as kings. Unlike his sisters, he cannot speak with them; this alienates him even further, and given his background, his prospects appear to be dismal.

Tara's father talks with me about sending his son overseas to work. In Nepal, for a price, one can obtain a visa to Japan, Germany, or the U.S., where one can then find work illegally. In one week, a Nepali can earn the equivalent of a year's salary in Nepal. However, most people here aren't aware of the true costs. It is expensive to live in these wealthy countries, and illegal immigrants must spend their time in fear of capture and deportation. They also endure wretched conditions in the factories where they work, and they must live away from their families in an alien culture.

I caution Tara's dad about all this, as he sits nodding, and tell him that a far safer and more sensible future lies with his daughters. My observation may be a hard pill to swallow in a society where women are often seen as useful only for making babies and doing chores.

In the morning, we are draped in wreaths of marigolds and plied with mugs of buffalo milk. Promising to stay longer on our trek out, we bid the Sundas family and Nunthala adieu, and take to the trail once again.

Above Lukla and its airstrip, the trail becomes more crowded. We meet hordes of trekkers, dressed in clean, colorful, hi-tech gear, smelling of after-shave and perfume. They smell a bit better than we do, but are far less fit, and we whiz by them as stealthily as possible.

A Tibetan man shows up on his way south to India. He has just crossed the Nangpa La from Tibet, a 5000 meter pass, wearing only a suit jacket, a Mao cap, and a pair of worn tennis shoes, on his journey to reach the Dalai Lama. His lips are badly blistered, and we give him some Blistex, which he proceeds to rub all over his face, grinning and laughing uproariously. His spirit is light and large.

The high mountains begin to come into view. Kwangde, Kussum Kangru, Thamserku, Kangtega, and other snow-clad glacial giants dominate the landscape. This is Sherpa and Tibetan country. In every bend in the path are *mani* walls, *gompas*, prayer wheels, and Tibetan inscriptions reminding us that we are in the realm of the gods.

Lodges here are much more upscale and expensive, featuring carpeted rooms and extensive menus. Staff speak English, German, and French. "Hello pen," is replaced with "*Bonjour*" on the trail, and I am encouraged in each village to buy sneakers while they are still cheap. I wonder why on earth I would need an extra pair of tennis shoes up here, then realize that the vendors, in their thick accents, are actually offering Snickers bars.

Namche Bazaar is a market town, set in a bowl up against a ridge at 3300 meters. It is a haven for travellers coming from Jiri or from the high regions of the Khumbu, much like Kathmandu is for those arriving from Tibet and India. There are a variety of restaurants, souvenir shops, a telephone office, travel agents, and scores of shops renting down jackets, bags, and mountaineering equipment.

The shops here used to be noted for their abundance of cheap, high-quality gear, much of it discarded from major expeditions. Duty and weight limitations on airlines make it too expensive to cart back halfway across the world, and much equipment is procured from sponsors anyhow, so it is easier to leave it behind. In the past, Sherpas had no idea

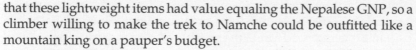

that these lightweight items had value equaling the Nepalese GNP, so a climber willing to make the trek to Namche could be outfitted like a mountain king on a pauper's budget.

Today's Sherpas know the value of the gear, and have become shrewd traders. I spend several hours chatting and sipping tea with Dorje, a shopkeeper who complains about the lack of business this year. Dorje and his father are high-altitude Sherpas. They have each summited Everest several times, and have used their expertise to earn a small fortune. Dorje now has two small children, and has decided that there is too much risk in the high mountains, so he has gotten into the retail trade, which he jokes has its own crevasses and avalanches.

Dorje goes to Colorado every year for a ski holiday, easily sponsored for a visa through his well-off climbing connections, and while there he picks up a lot of gear to take back home. When I ask him why anyone would buy a mountain stove, which sells for seventy dollars back home, for 100 here, he retorts that the same stove goes for 120 or higher in Europe, so he has plenty of customers.

Dorje tells me about the rise in material comforts in Namche over the past ten years. There is heat, electricity, television, and enough income for the kids to go to Darjeeling or Kathmandu for education, but Dorje laments that young people don't seem to respect their elders anymore, and that competition and greed seem to be driving the community. There isn't as much time for drinking tea, sitting back, and watching the kids grow up in the shadow of the mountains; all the new luxuries must be paid for. As both of us know, this scenario is being played out all over the world. I tell Dorje that perhaps the reason I am riding my bicycle is to buy a little more time.

The weekly Namche Bazaar still takes place, and anything that has survived the walk in from Jiri on someone's back is sold for a significant markup. There are cases of Snickers, cartons of cigarettes, bottles of whiskey, Chinese tennis shoes, and slabs of meat. Despite the rise in prices, items are gobbled up as if in a famine, as above Namche, prices can only rise even higher. Sherpas and lowland Nepalis spend hours bartering over biscuits, rice, ramen noodles, and bottles of Coke.

By now, Everest has become a relatively small world. We bump into several porters and guides we know, find Claudio happily sipping cappuccino with an Italian trekking group, and spend the afternoon watching the Slovakians wander in and out of the mountaineering shops, purchasing fake Gore-Tex. Mr. Chin, the old Malaysian, has arrived

looking absolutely whacked, and swearing he'll never do this again.
Around the corner, we bump into Jamie Carr, who went to Kailash with
us. Jamie is here to lead a trekking group, and we compare the luxuries of
Namche with our days back stuck in the middle of the river in Tibet.

Even better than the familiar faces are the views from the ridge above
Namche, where a sea of peaks in the high Himalayas are on display. The
summit triangle of Everest is in view, as is the Lhotse-Nuptse wall, and
the lofty vertical pinnacle of Ama Dablam, with its hanging glaciers,
glistens like a jewel in the morning sun. The peak is named after the neck
amulet worn by Sherpa women, and is considered by many to be the
most beautiful peak in the world.

At this altitude, the walking is slow going, and Hitomi and I feel
lethargic as we leave Namche. My nose runs, and Hitomi develops a
hacking cough which only gets worse as we climb higher into the cold,
dry air.

Above the monastery of Tengboche, the path turns north, up the last
valley into the base of Everest. This valley, like the high mountains, is
out of the realm of humans, and is an abode much more suitable for the
mountain gods. It is too high to grow crops, and too cold to live here
more than half a year. The lodges are not part of any community, but
rather a collection of dismal shacks, weather beaten and forlorn in the
incessantly howling wind.

Lobuche and Gorak Shep, at 4900 and 5100 meters respectively, are
two of these wastelands that mark the end of the trail. The lodges are
hopelessly overcrowded, crammed with cold and exhausted trekkers
and climbers. Most people are hacking away with deep chest coughs or
fighting sinus ailments. Many have diarrhea, and others show signs of
altitude sickness. For most people here, ourselves included, the initial
excitement is far gone. Most of us just want to make one final push to
Everest Base Camp, or to Kala Patar, a spur of the peak Pumori, where
close views of Everest can be had without climbing the mountain itself.
It is hard to imagine that this is just the start of the journey for those
planning to climb Everest.

Our lodge looks less ramshackle than those beside it, but is a poor
choice. The *Didi* in charge of the kitchen has had an argument with her
man, and has run off, leaving him bewildered and helpless. Wild-eyed,
he churns out plates of burnt, greasy hash browns for dinner, and a set
of charred, malformed pancakes for breakfast.

We move to the lodge next door and find it almost as abysmal. *Dal*

Nepal: Hello Pen

85

bhaat here resembles the soup regurgitated by the sick French group in our dorm, and costs six times what it would in Namche, not to mention that there are no seconds. The lodge is icy, as the stingy owner keeps only a tiny fire going, and he and his cronies encircle it, not allowing any intruders. The latrine brings back memories of China, a set of wooden slats out in the frigid wind, covered with putrid, yellowing bits of frozen defecations. It is indeed time to move on.

We arise at dawn, and fit toes that feel like blocks of wood into our stiff boots. I don't want to know what the temperature is. It is windy outside, but there isn't a cloud in the sky, and we race ahead of the large French group that shares our lodge, determined to have the summit of Kala Patar to ourselves for at least a few minutes.

Our breathing is labored, yet today we have no problems with the altitude. We ascend quickly and silently, passing the few others who have started out ahead of us at this frozen hour.

The mountains here are tremendous. Mammoth peaks are set against a sky of the deepest and darkest blue I have ever seen. Blocks of ice the size of houses spill off Nuptse, its towering bulk blocking out the sun. Further up, the massive Khumbu Icefall roars down from the flanks of Everest, a river of towering seracs and bottomless crevasses, which every year claim more lives than any other place on the mountain.

Everest pokes her head out of the sky. It is staggering to be at 5600 meters, higher than I have been anywhere on earth, and still have a mountain towering almost 3300 meters above me. Next to Everest, and actually more impressive, is Pumori, almost a perfect triangle of snow. Her bulk is so close that I can feel her icy breath slipping through my layers of clothing.

Ringed by peaks and the silent world of snow, I have one of those rare moments of intense clarity and awareness that the Japanese call *satori*, which translates as "enlightenment." All thoughts of past and future fall away, and for about thirty seconds, I am totally and completely in the most beautiful place on earth, feeling the wind kissing my frozen lips, bathed in a light that I thought only existed in a painting.

I feel profoundly thankful for all the events that have brought me to this spot, and I begin weeping uncontrollably, shedding tears of deep happiness. I hug Hitomi and try to put into words what I am feeling, but it is better left unspoken. There are no words to describe this, in any spoken language. I feel more at peace than I have ever felt, anywhere before.

"If I were to die right now," I tell Hitomi, "it would be perfectly okay.

No more wishes, goals, memories, or moments. Just this, these mountains, sky, us, and my breath, right here, right now."

The moment passes, the cold rips through my body, and we push on, reaching the summit of Kala Patar in an hour and a half. There is nobody else here yet, and we take photos, fold our hands in prayer, and take in the mind-boggling scenery. In this landscape, we are truly nothing but specks of dust.

"Hello sir. Buy Tiger Balm sir? Hashish sir? Something sir?"

The chaos and dust of Kathmandu actually become endearing after a time. We are back among the same *sadhus* and carpet salesmen, the beggars on the corner, the Indian banana salesman who gives me a higher price every morning, despite the fact that I speak Hindi with him and have bought bananas every morning this week at a bargained price.

It has been three weeks since we returned from the mountains, and a rather eventful time at that. After descending to Namche, Hitomi and I separated for ten days. She was tired, still coughing a lot, and wanted to go back and rest a few days in Nunthala, with Tara and Srijana. I was feeling really strong, and wanted to take an alternative route back, so I made the weeklong march out through the Arun Valley, an even steeper route than the traverse from Jiri, and one with few lodges or amenities.

Back together in Kathmandu, Hitomi and I spend the next week planning ahead. Winter is coming to Nepal, while in Southeast Asia, the "cool" season has arrived, with eighty-five to ninety degree temperatures and a hundred percent humidity, perfect for cycling! The land route to Thailand, however, is blocked by international politics. Myanmar will not allow land entry from any of its borders, and so we will have to fly into Bangkok.

The day of the flight, we pedal out to the airport, where several Immigration officials pounce on us when they see our loaded bicycles. Tribuvan Airport has no rules regarding bicycles, no requirements for boxes, turned handlebars, or removal of pedals, but we are greeted by two men who stare greedily at our steeds and rub their palms with glee, and we soon find out why. One of the men takes our panniers and bikes, and plunks them onto a large scale, watching the needle soar up to just shy of fifty kilos for my gear, plus another fifteen kilos for the bike. Hitomi's mound of equipment weighs only slightly less than this. We are informed that our luggage exceeds the allowances by over twenty kilograms, and that it will cost us 100 dollars per kilogram as excess baggage. This is over 2000 dollars—ten times the price of the plane ticket.

I argue with the official to no avail, then tell him that we cannot afford to pay this and will have to cancel our flight, which causes him to look panic-stricken. A porter, who has been watching the entire proceedings with avid interest, comes over at this point and whispers something to the official, then takes me aside.

"I help you no problem, sir, you are soon flying, sir," he advises me. He tells me that 200 dollars will rectify the whole situation.

At this point, I remember that I am in a country that was ranked in the top ten corrupt nations by a recent study, and a light goes off in my head.

"Sorry," I reply, "we don't have an extra 200 dollars to pay with. I guess we will just have to cancel our flight and do something else."

"How about 100?" the porter asks, still looking rather hopeful.

"Nope. We just can't pay that; it's half of the plane ticket."

He looks at me rather sheepishly, and says, quite crestfallen, "Fifty possible?"

I smile and say, "Let's go. The flight leaves in fifteen minutes."

Our man, now smiling widely, ushers us around a screen, where an officer sits at a desk sipping tea and yakking on a phone. The porter rambles on in Nepali with him, and then asks us for payment. This produced, the officer takes out a form in triplicate, fills in a few lines excusing our mass of baggage, and gives it a resounding whack with his stamp. We return to the baggage counter, leaving the porter and official to divide our bills. Our receipt passes muster with all the other officials, and we hand over our bikes, panniers and all, to the porter—hoping, as we walk out toward the waiting jet, that they will follow us into the airplane.

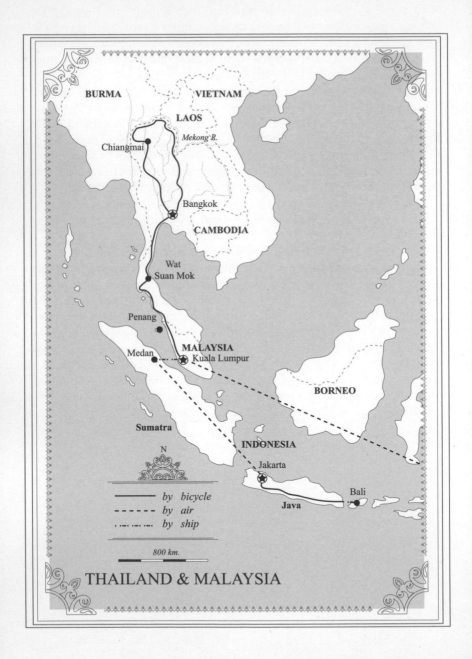

BURMA
VIETNAM
LAOS
Mekong R.
Chiangmai
Bangkok
CAMBODIA
Wat
Suan Mok
Penang
Medan
MALAYSIA
Kuala Lumpur
BORNEO
Sumatra
INDONESIA
N
Jakarta
Bali
Java

——————— *by bicycle*
- - - - - - - *by air*
–·–·–·–·– *by ship*

800 km.

THAILAND & MALAYSIA

Chapter Six
Amazing Thailand

*Life is a bridge. Cross over it. But build no
house on it.*

Indian Proverb

*It would be nice to travel if you knew where
you were going and where you would live at the end
or do we ever know, do we ever live where we live,
we're always in other places, lost, like sheep.*

Janet Frame

After three quarters of a year on the bumpy and dusty trails of China, Tibet, and Nepal, we find entry into Bangkok rather overwhelming. In Don Muang International Airport, the hub of Asia, diplomats and businesspeople from all over the planet mingle with dreadlocked backpackers, large Indian families, sheiks from various Middle East Sultanates, and tour groups from Korea and Japan.

The airport has a plethora of banks, post offices, rental car agencies, and shops. There are sparkling clean toilets—with toilet paper!—that automatically flush, and even tourist information counters, stocked with maps and travel pamphlets and staffed by grinning young Thai women. Customs and Immigration officials are courteous and efficient, entering our passport details into computers and whisking us clear in minutes. I wait to be asked for a "donation," or for someone to approach me selling something, but it doesn't happen, although a taxi driver does show up as I walk to the baggage claim.

He whispers, "Hello! Lady? You want lady?"

I wave to Hitomi, collecting panniers on the other side of a carousel, and the driver smiles at me.

"Already have lady. Maybe two lady okay?" he asks hopefully.
I shake my head.

On a new tack, he asks, "Maybe taxi?" and then grimaces as he sees a baggage handler approaching with our bicycles.

Bangkok appears to be hell on earth--a surreal vision of a post-apocalypse Los Angeles, a city of millions sprawling endlessly across a polluted landscape. Huge factories dominate the skyline, and beneath them lie tin shanties, as impoverished as anything we have seen elsewhere, broken and sweltering in the wet, tropical air. An endless stream of cars, buses, taxis, and motorcycles race through flooded boulevards, no one paying any attention to lane markings or signs. Intersections are crammed with motorcyclists, who jam into every available space between cars, and rev their engines as if it is the start of the Indy 500.

The heavy air smells of sweat and diesel, pressing down like a wet blanket. The sky does not exist; in its place is a pale monochrome of smog particles, lit by the floodlights that illuminate the never-ending array of factories, office towers, shopping plazas, and other high rises. We take more than three hours to make our way to Khao San Road, where the backpackers' hotels are located, and by the time we get there, we are drunk on our own perspiration and completely sapped of all strength.

Rooms in the Apple Guesthouse are small and dingy, lit with bare twenty-watt bulbs. The mattresses are stained with ash and semen, and there are no amenities save a small fan, which whirls noisily but doesn't produce much wind. Signs on the door remind us to "please keep cleaning," and "please take off all shore."

Happy to escape the chaos of the boulevards, we take cold showers and then go in search of food. Vendors everywhere sell fresh papaya, pineapple, and coconut; there are steaming *pad thai* noodles and all sorts of curries, fish dishes, and totally unfamiliar sweets. We opt for a sit-down restaurant, which has the most extensive menu we have seen in ages—especially after a month on trails eating *dal bhaat*. The English menu here is most entertaining, offering such entrees as fried much room with mixed stomach, fry carrot with oil snail, and beef barbecue with good teat! There is fried beef shake Thailand, as well as fried beef shake English, along with Seafood Drunkard. We opt for Four Comrades in Fire Sauce, which is excellent, even though we cannot identify half the ingredients. We wash it down with fresh papaya and melon shakes.

The restaurant is a welcome respite from the streets. Large ceiling fans create a soft breeze while animated Thai families socialize, feasting from ornate silver pots that continue to arrive at their tables. Unlike Nepal, where one almost never sees locals eating out, Bangkok's restaurants are packed, giving at least an outward impression that Thais here are doing well economically.

Even after several days of rest, Bangkok doesn't become any easier to navigate. The heat, noise, and pollution make a major ordeal out of trips anywhere other than to the fruit seller on the corner. Giant pillars throughout the city support an elevated motorway which is supposed to alleviate traffic woes, but the project, modeled after the L.A freeway system by architects from California, sits mired in failure. This is partly because corrupt officials have siphoned off much of the funding, but also due to the fact an annual deluge erodes the foundations of the pillars. Bangkok sits under water for several months a year, a flat grid submerged on a flood plain, and the California architects who designed the project failed to take this into account.

Traffic remains grounded throughout the city, and because there is no longer any room for vehicles on the packed road, even the sidewalks have become fair game. Motorcycles make prime use of them, sparing little thought for the few pedestrians who attempt to walk. It takes hours to go anywhere on the public buses, portable saunas that swelter for what seems like days at the endless array of traffic lights. Making travel reservations, getting visas, or obtaining bicycle parts can take all day. Hitomi and I divide all of our chores, and thus cut the misery of movement around town in half.

On a tip, I end up at a bicycle shop which carries imported parts, and I stock up on sorely needed brake pads, gear cables, and tubes. We have travelled just under 4000 kilometers without any maintenance on our bikes beyond inflating tires and oiling chains.

Near the bike shop, I stumble upon Lumbini Park, an oasis of grass and trees where elderly Chinese practice Tai Chi and young children lick ice cream cones. I sit on a bench to give my sticky clothes a chance to dry, and to avoid returning to the congestion only blocks away. A young woman in a miniskirt sidles up and greets me, hands folded together in prayer. In Nepal, the greeting was "*Namaste*," and here it is "*Sawasdee ka*" (*Sawasdee krup* if the speaker is male). I like the gesture, as it seems to embody respect, compassion, honor, and nonviolence.

Without asking, she sits close to me, removes a few loose strands of silky black hair from her face, and studies me intently.

"Hello, you holiday in Thailand?" she asks in broken English.

"Yeah, I guess I am on holiday in Thailand," I reply.

"You how old?" she continues.

"Thirty-four."

"Ooh. Same same my sister," she giggles. "You no look haa-pee," she adds, dividing the last word into equally stressed singsong syllables.

"It's a bit too hot and smoggy for me to have a smile," I answer. "What's your name?"

"Ratree," she grins. "You like Santa Claus." She reaches out and gives my beard a tug. "You han-sum man," she continues in her singsong Thai. "Hello, you me boom boom okay."

She raises her pencil-thin eyebrows up and down and winks suggestively.

I laugh. "I've never heard it put that way before, but no thanks for the boom boom. Actually, I am here with my wife."

She frowns for a moment, then resumes cheerfully, "But you holiday in amazing Thailand, right? Holiday boom boom wife no problem."

I sigh, and we continue to chat for the next half hour. Ratree is from a village in Issan, an area in the northeast of Thailand. There is no work there, and her family cannot make ends meet, so she has come to Bangkok. She works part time in a bar and tries to find foreign men to sleep with for money. When I ask her if she feels comfortable doing what she does, she shrugs and tells me that it isn't all that bad. She meets a lot of different people, has learned to speak more English than she would in school, and saves money to send to her family. But as she tells me this, a vacant and distant look comes to her eyes.

I ask her what she would like most to do with her life. She stares hard at me, then says, "I want do like you do today. Come sit in park and enjoy, no need work, have holiday."

I wish Ratree luck and take my leave. As I go, she calls after me:

"You come back see me! You good man, we boom boom good! This amazing Thailand, right?"

Hitomi and I come to the conclusion that cycling out of Bangkok will be little more than an exercise in masochism. We decide to take a train to the north of the country, cycle for a month and a half, then swing south and follow the coast to Malaysia.

We buy plane tickets from one of the numerous bucket shops that line Khao San Road, and are scheduled to fly from Kuala Lumpur to Auckland, New Zealand, in three months. Our seats are not confirmed, but the travel agent tells us that this is normal. We catch the night train to Chiang Mai, capital of the north.

Northern Thailand is made of steep, impenetrable jungle and mountainous terrain. It divides the numerous ethnic hill tribes from one another and separates Thailand from neighboring Myanmar and Laos. Outside of the cities in the north, there are very few Thais to be found, and every steep ridge hosts a different tribe. Tribes in the north include the Hmong, Lahu, Lisu, Akha, Yao, Shan, Karen, and Khun Satun. The Khun Satun are a nomadic, indigenous group known as Spirit of the Yellow Leaves, named for their practice of leaving their banana-leaf dwellings once the leaves change color.

There are also villages of Kuomintang Chinese. The Kuomintang, or Chinese Nationalists, fled China after Mao came to power; many hid in the jungle here and have never left. We often see large banners with Chinese characters, greeting us outside villages with noodle houses and dumpling shops, where old Chinese men read newspapers from Taiwan. Hitomi and I speak to people in Chinese, dusting off the rusty phrases we collected in the Middle Kingdom.

Many of these villages lie precariously close to the porous border with Myanmar. The Karen and Shan communities, both non-Burmese minorities, have fled here from Myanmar to escape fighting and oppression over the border. The Thais have accepted these groups, although completely on their own terms. The government, in return for these groups' support at army garrisons and border posts—and for a cut of the huge opium trade—provides schools and medical clinics. Access to these resources is free to all in the village in exchange for their acquiescence to being proud members under the Thai flag. Children learn Thai in the schools, and the focus in education is on integration into Thai society. I wonder to myself what will happen to the language and customs of these tribes.

The Akha are an example of one potential outcome. Probably the most visible of all the hill tribes, the Akha have rejected Thai overtures to modernize. Many consider them the poorest and most backward of all the hill tribes, yet they are also the most colorful and exotic. They wander the paths of northern Thailand wearing ornate, colorful headdresses covered in beads, feathers, and flattened coins. They engage in pig farming and opium cultivation, and live in dwellings built on stilts, in villages filled with totems.

The Akha originate from Yunnan, in southwestern China, and have for the most part kept to themselves since migrating here. They are ani-

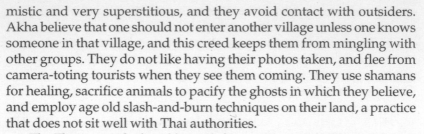

mistic and very superstitious, and they avoid contact with outsiders. Akha believe that one should not enter another village unless one knows someone in that village, and this creed keeps them from mingling with other groups. They do not like having their photos taken, and flee from camera-toting tourists when they see them coming. They use shamans for healing, sacrifice animals to pacify the ghosts in which they believe, and employ age old slash-and-burn techniques on their land, a practice that does not sit well with Thai authorities.

The Thais provide the Akha with few services, and a Thai teacher or health worker will be made to feel extremely unwelcome if he or she stays in a village. Thus, Akha villages tend to be locked in poverty and disrepair. Passing through several, we feel very uncomfortable and most unwelcome.

Just over the hill from an Akha camp is a Lisu village, a total study in contrast. The Lisu hamlet is spotlessly clean, with piped water, an active school, and a health post. Women sit in thatched bamboo huts, chatting away as they stitch clothing on shiny sewing machines to the accompaniment of the Thai pop songs blaring from radios. The Lisu in this village are lychee farmers, making a fortune with orchards full of the sweet, coveted treats. They have been traders and experts in commerce for ages.

Lisu language is close enough to Chinese that many Lisu have gone to Taiwan to work, and have prospered. They have also sought contact with outsiders, rather than avoid it. We stay in the home of a man named Asa, who used to be a trekking guide in Chiang Mai, but now runs a simple and quiet guesthouse, where his entire family lives under one roof. Asa, a model of success, can speak Lisu, Lahu, Karen, Thai, Chinese, English, and enough Akha and German to make conversation. His children will all have an education, and the family has enough money to buy what they need at the market in Tha Ton, a small town just down the road.

I notice that most of the Lisu, especially the men, no longer wear traditional clothing. Many of the children now spend their days in the Thai school, where they speak Thai, have buzz haircuts, and look like any of the kids to be found in any town in the country.

Asa worries that his village is becoming cash dependent, whereas only ten years before, the community existed mostly on barter, growing their own food and using a shaman for healing. Now, if someone is sick, they purchase medicine from the clinic. Much of the food comes from the markets in Tha Ton, and most of the young men in the village have motorbikes, which they use to go to town at least once a day. Asa shudders to think of what might happen if a year of abnormal weather were to come through and kill off the lychee crop.

Putting Asa's skills to work, we hire him as an interpreter for several days. As we wander through the jungle, passing through different tribal territory, Asa explains the beliefs and lifestyles of the tribes. In an Akha village, we are at least tolerated, as they all know Asa. He gives them pocket money and tobacco, something the Thai guides from Chiang Mai and Chiang Rai never do. Unlike in Nepal, most money spent by foreign trekkers in Thailand goes to Thais, and does not trickle down to the villages and tribes they pay to see.

We also pass through Karen villages in the area. They are divided into sub-groups such as Red Karen, Black Karen, and White Karen, distinguishable by the different colors they wear. The Karen are quite different from the other hill tribes; they are a matrilineal society, do not grow opium for money, practice crop rotation as opposed to slash-and-burn agriculture, and are Christian as well as animistic in their beliefs.

A local group of great notoriety is the Padaung Karenni, better known as the "longneck" Padaung and famed for its women, who wear heavy brass rings around their necks. Supposedly, they do this to prevent tigers from carrying them off into the jungle, thinking that by wearing collars that they can't be mauled. The women begin to place these brass rings around their necks from the time they are seven or eight years old. By their teen years, they wear five to ten rings, which weigh over a kilo each; as a result, their collarbones are crushed, giving them the appearance of having long necks.

Every culture has its peculiarities of habit and custom, and I try not to judge any of these differences, but in this case, I cannot stop myself. The longneck women do not look happy; they walk around stooped over, and their range of motion is severely limited by the weight they carry. The rings cannot be comfortable to wear, and though they might protect the wearer from a tiger's bite, they don't appear to serve any purpose other than confining the women—and keeping the brass marketers in a lucrative business.

The Padaung are a sad lot, as they are an extremely small community without any rights. They have not yet been granted Thai refugee status, so they cannot work or own land. Thus, their women are put on display like animals in a zoo for tourists to photograph. The display could be more tasteful, presenting insights into the Padaung's plight, their history, and their traditions, but instead it is a freak show. Tourists

spend twenty minutes snapping off a roll of film, then leave. On the
other hand, perhaps international exposure has brought some support
to their cause. And I suppose that compared to their existence back in
dictatorial Myanmar, life in Thailand might have some benefits.

As we pedal northwards, the hills become relentless, made even
more challenging by the tropical heat. After cycling across the Himalayas,
I thought we could tackle any grade in the world without effort, but
Thailand has been a rude awakening. I understand why we have not
seen a single bicycle on the road.

Our only solace is in food. Thai food, if one likes spice, is hands-
down the best food on the planet. I could live the rest of my days in
Thailand, and maybe even in Bangkok, for this alone. Even in the smallest village, every meal is the best I have ever eaten, and Hitomi and I
approach each challenging hill fueled by the mouthwatering thought of
the meal to be had in the next town.

There are green curries, red curries, and yellow curries, each bal-
anced with a generous amount of coconut milk, lemongrass, kaffir lime
leaves, and fish sauce to mellow the fiery chilies and the appropriately
named "mouse shit" peppers (so called due to their miniscule size).

In most lunch spots, one can find a variety of hot and sour soups,
rice noodles drenched in sweet curry sauce, and exquisite salads. Our
favorite is *som tam*, a pungent creation of shredded unripe papaya, peanuts, dried shrimp, lemon juice, tomatoes, palm sugar, fish sauce, and
plenty of hot chilies, all pounded together in a ceramic mortar and pestle.

We stay in the town of Doi Mae Salong for several days, enjoying
pleasant weather and good food. Mae Salong, it turns out, is a real hot-
bed of illegal activity. It was settled by 2000 Kuomintang soldiers, who
escaped from China under the leadership of General Duan Xi Wen, now
entombed in a mausoleum on the outskirts of town. The new settlers
became involved in the opium trade, which flourished through the 1980's;
in its remote, mountaintop position, Mae Salong is the perfect spot for
such an enterprise.

The Burmese opium warlord Khun Sa made his home in a hideout
near Mae Salong until he was ousted by the Thai military and the CIA.
Some law and order have been restored to the area, but things have not
changed much. The fancy restaurants and hotels are empty, and serve
as fronts for the drug trade, which still functions in high gear, if a bit
more covertly. There is a Thai school in town, and tea and corn crops

now cover the slopes of the surrounding mountains. The official name of Mae Salong has been changed to Santikhiri, which means "hill of peace," in an effort to disassociate the town from its past; however, the poppy fields run rampant just across the border in Myanmar, as well as in Laos, and illicit money remains as plentiful as always.

Leaving Mae Salong, we descend back to the steamy plains at record speed, interrupted only by a couple of flat tires. By late afternoon we have reached Mae Sai, a bustling frontier town straddling the Mae Sai Bridge into neighboring Myanmar.

After a particularly delicious dinner in a local restaurant, we beckon the manager over to compliment him on the meal, and I ask him why the food in Thailand is so continually delicious. He responds, "Because this amazing Thailand."

This reply is the standard answer to any question in Thailand.

Several years ago, the Tourism Authority of Thailand ran the Amazing Thailand campaign, which featured glossy pamphlets with pictures of sandy beaches, an inviting turquoise sea, and dark-skinned nymphs with glowing smiles. There were pictures of elephants in the jungle, teak houses with shady verandas, and endless temples silhouetted against tropical sunsets. "All these seductions are yours, in amazing Thailand," the brochures promised, and tourism revenues increased by large numbers.

The locals seem to have bought the hype that went along with the campaign, so now, in almost any situation, there is one simple reason to come to Thailand. Why are the beaches so nice? Why is the food so tasty? Why are the people so beautiful, and their smiles so broad? Why are the roads so steep? Why are the hill tribes treated so poorly? Why is there such corruption in the political system?

Because it's amazing Thailand, no?

We phone the travel agent in Bangkok to find out if our seats to New Zealand have been confirmed, and are told that they haven't, but that we shouldn't worry, as it's par for the course. We don't bother to ask why, assuming we will be told that it's because this is amazing Thailand. (So amazing that every flight out of the country is booked solid for months!)

We make our way south along the Mekong, through Chiang Saen and Chiang Khong, sleepy towns with old teak houses where Thais lounge in the shade, out of the afternoon heat. The Southeast Asian

Games have begun, and this year, Thailand is playing host to the event. (Of course, the reason the Games are here this year, as an old woman cackles to us, is "because amazing Thailand.") In every town and village, television sets have been dragged onto porches and set up in corner cafés so that the entire population can get into the proceedings.

Because we are on bicycles and half of our team is Asian, people presume that we are involved somehow with the event; everywhere we ride, they applaud and urge us on, screaming, "go, go, champions!" as we cycle through town. In Chiang Khong, a huge crowd is waiting to encourage us, everyone waving and smiling. They are led by a young boy in an oversized pair of diapers, who chases us repeating something over and over, which I later translate as "look at the athletes!"

We bask in the limelight, pretending that we have just entered Olympic Stadium, until Hitomi nearly crashes when a chicken dashes under her wheels while she waves to some children.

Our moment of glory comes to an abrupt end, when I discover that a piece of my rear rim has peeled off and is flapping against the brake pads, threatening to come off entirely. This is the first serious incident of equipment failure to occur since we left Japan, and because bicycles are almost nonexistent in Thailand, I wonder what to do. The rim can only get worse, and at some point, the entire wheel can be expected to collapse.

Fortunately, I have a tip from a man named Alon, who I met in Mae Salong. He mentioned an old man in Chiang Mai who is a bicycle lover and runs a small shop. We have little time to spare, as it is still a long way to Kuala Lumpur, so I leave Hitomi relaxing in a garden hotel, and my rear wheel and I take the afternoon train to Chiang Mai.

Finding Mr. Prem Thawat is no easy task. The address I have is scrawled in English on a tiny piece of paper, so the various shopkeepers and pedestrians I stop to ask have trouble deciphering it. Eventually, I am directed down a tiny lane, where I come upon a small shop with a few old bike tires lying in the dirt out front.

I look around the shop, and am not impressed by what I see. There are a few bike wheels of very dubious quality, scrapped parts, rusted chains, and a seat cover or two.

A frail, bespectacled man appears, introducing himself as Prem Thawat. I show him my peeled rim, and he informs me that I have come to the right place. This is the headquarters of the Chiang Mai Bicycling Club, where all the bicyclists that I have never seen anywhere in Thailand congregate and share their love of the *rot jakrayan*, Thai for bicycle.

Prem disappears into the back of the shop and reappears, smiling and clutching a mountain bike rim. "You are in luck," he informs me, and proudly displays the one piece of foreign equipment he has left in stock, a Campagnolo rim from Italy! I am flabbergasted, as I never expected such a quality component, and I hesitate before asking how much this pretty item is going to set me back. Prem scratches his head and mulls over how long it will take him to disassemble my wheel, relace the new wheel with my old spokes and hub, and then true it up.

"Oh, how about 200 *baht*?" he decides, watching my mouth fall open. This is around eight dollars. Back home, one couldn't even fix a flat tire for this price; here I am, getting a top-notch rim and all the labor on it for eight dollars!

Over tea and dried fish, we talk about cycling—or the lack of it—in Thailand. Other than a few group road rides, the members of the Chiang Mai Bike Club don't do too much cycling. They don't commute, preferring their motorcycles for doing battle on the congested ring roads that encircle Chiang Mai, which looks like a miniscule edition of Bangkok.

When Prem has my new wheel all set to go, he basks in pride while I complement him on his workmanship and thank him profusely.

"Send me a postcard, and let me know if you make it," he suggests, and I promise to do so. I rush back to the train station in time to grab the last train of the day back to the Mekong.

As we cycle south, the hills and wicked grades of the north disappear, but are replaced with heavy traffic and narrow road shoulders. Diesel fumes choke the air, and the heat on the tarmac soars to levels that by late afternoon are quite unbearable. We put our heads down and grind out the mileage, finding diversion in the pineapple stalls that dot the roadside.

We pass through Damnoen Saduak, where people live in houses built on stilts, as the area is underwater during the rainy season. Longtail boats ply the canals through here, heaped with fruit, vegetables, and household goods. They also carry souvenirs, as the colorful "floating markets," as they are known, have become a big tourist draw.

Further south, we pass through Petchaburi, Prachuap Khiri Khan, and Hua Hin. In each town, our hotel for the evening is filled with smiling prostitutes, who whisper, "hello, you two la-dee okay?" to me as we check in for the night. They are outnumbered only by the cockroaches. In Hua Hin, the beach is packed with sunburnt old men, cavorting in the waves with their nubile, dark girlfriends, rented by the hour, day, or week.

Despite the tourism, crowded roads, and bar girl scene, the beaches are indeed lovely. Crescent bays are tucked into each bend of coastline, hidden by curving strands of coconut palms swaying in the wind. Each bay is filled with aquamarine blue water, which softly caresses the sparkling white sand. In even the remotest spot, there is usually a cheerful young girl traversing the beach, hawking fresh papaya, succulent pineapple, or sweet pods from a jackfruit.

Limestone cliffs rise dramatically from the sea, karst formations that look like inverted mushrooms. The water is so shallow that one can often walk to the base of the cliffs, finding some shadow out of the eye of the broiling sun. The water itself doesn't offer much relief, being the temperature of a tepid bath.

Three weeks remain before our flight out of Malaysia leaves for New Zealand. "It still is not confirmed no worries," reports our travel agent in Bangkok. We decide to use this time to do a meditation retreat, something we have thought of doing while travelling in the Buddhist world.

Tucked into the forest near the city of Chumphon lies Wat Suan Mokkhaphalaram, a monastery which offers ten day silent *vipassana* meditation sessions. Suan Mok, as it is called for short, means "Garden of Liberation." The temple complex was founded by Ajaan Buddhadasa, a renowned Thai monk who was labeled a traitor and communist during the 1970's for his criticisms of the military and capitalism. Buddhadasa accepted Islam, Christianity, Judaism, and other religions in addition to Buddhism, and he followed closely Martin Luther King's principles of nonviolence and Gandhi's urgings for simplicity. The monastery reflects these values, as the buildings are simple, unadorned, functional structures, very unlike the opulent, gold-covered pyramids one finds at most *wats*.

Buddhadasa was encouraged by the westerners he met who had interest in Buddhism, so he set up a meditation course for them, staffed by monks who could speak a little bit of English. Under the principle that the benefits of meditation should be available to all, Wat Suan Mok courses do not cost any money, though a donation of several dollars a day is used for food and operating costs.

Hitomi and I check in, pay our donation, and are given a thin blanket, small pillow, and a mosquito net. These are to be our only provisions for the ten day retreat. Each participant is given a small concrete cubicle, with a hard platform to sleep on, over which the mosquito nets are hung. The cubicles are arranged around a large rectangular courtyard, which contains two large rainwater tanks from which one can draw water to bathe. Men and women are housed separately, and contact between the two sexes is not allowed during the course, so Hitomi and I have our last conversation, wish each other luck, and head off to our respective dwellings.

There is no electricity in the compound, but it really isn't necessary, as we will be asleep early in the evening. Besides, activities like reading and journal writing are discouraged, as they take away from the focus of the meditations, which aim to rid the self of all distractions.

Visitors must take a ten day vow of silence before starting the course, and many of the participants worry greatly over whether or not they can manage this. Hitomi and I, comfortable with spending quiet time in nature, have no fear of the vow, and we look forward to the silent inner time.

What we are deathly afraid of is the food situation. We eat over 5000 calories a day just to maintain our weight and stamina. It is mortifying to think of plunging into a routine of total physical inactivity, eating only two meals a day, which we assume will be very basic plates of rice. These fears turn out to be needless, as we find out on the first day that the two meals are all-you-can-eat offerings of vegetarian curries, prepared by a team of enthusiastic assistants, and is some of the best food we have had in Thailand.

The schedule at Suan Mok is rigorous. We rise every morning at four-thirty and go to the main temple hall for a *dharma* lecture, followed by the day's first sitting meditation for one hour. Breakfast follows, and then everyone has an hour and a half of free time to bathe in the local hot springs and take care of any personal needs.

The rest of the morning is spent alternating between sitting and standing meditation. We do an hour of one, then switch, with no breaks until the midday meal. A bell sounds at the end of each session and is our only contact with time during the morning.

The meditation sessions are extremely difficult, even though I have engaged in various forms of meditation in past years. The monks try to have us focus on *anapanasati*, mindfulness through breathing, something that sounds a lot easier in theory than in practice. It is not easy to spend over twelve hours a day doing nothing but concentrating on one's breath.

Amid a jumble of mental activity, I try to follow my breath. I pursue each inhalation, and am aware of the breath at each moment as it enters my nasal passages, as it reaches the back of my sinuses, and as it exits back out of my mouth or nose. This is easy for about five to ten breaths, or even twenty, but just when I think I have mastered this awareness, I realize that I am no longer paying attention. Rather, I am off somewhere else in my mind, thinking about friends and family, problems, issues, the state of the world, a place I would rather be, or perhaps focusing on the heat in the room, or on a fly which has landed on my foot.

The Buddhists call this "monkey mind," a mind which wanders aimlessly through a landscape of a million miles of infinite thoughts. Only by following the breath can one gradually begin to control this monkey, and start to become aware of existing solely in the moment, within the breath.

After an hour of sitting, we alternate with standing meditation, during which time we pick a small area of ground and walk about twenty paces back and forth, again focusing only on the breath. During this exercise, I am able to observe my mind wandering, and I am amazed at the leaps it makes. One minute I am watching my breath; the next minute I am following the journey of a small spider, which sidles along the path next to me. I think about seeing tigers and rhinos in India, then I fantasize about the woman walking nearby me, salivating over her tan, slender legs and well-defined calves. I wake with a start, frustrated, and return to my breathing, counting each breath to help myself pay attention.

There are people from all over the world at Suan Mok. It is most strange to see each other daily, to smile and make eye contact without ever speaking to one another. I am reminded how many labels we create without words, and I wonder if at the end of the ten days, my impressions and expectations about these people will turn out to be correct.

After lunch, there is an hour and a half for resting on one's own, and then we resume alternating between sitting and standing meditations. Later in the day, there is a chanting session. Chanting was never a part of meditating that I enjoyed before, but now I revel in it; led by an elderly monk with a booming deep voice, it is actually far more akin to singing.

There is a tea and fruit snack around sunset, and then a lecture during which people are allowed to ask questions of the monks regarding their practices. I am surprised at the number of people who seem to expect a flash of light to go off in their heads, or to have some "enlightenment" experience after they meditate enough.

A young monk assures everyone that this is not what meditating is about. He states that the whole purpose of meditation and the monastic life is to make people pay attention. Buddhist belief holds that life is suffering. Our attachments and desires create much of this suffering, and if we can separate ourselves from these attachments and desires, we can reduce the suffering. By learning to focus on the breath, we learn to focus on whatever engages us in our lives.

The young monk tells us, "When you are reading a newspaper, read the newspaper. When you are driving a car, drive the car. And when you are talking to your friend, talk to your friend. Do not try to read, drive, and talk at the same time, for this will surely lead to an accident."

"Perhaps," he continues, " if we all concentrated on each action, there would be fewer accidents, and the world might be just a little easier to live in. This is all we are trying to teach."

Even in our small space and daily routine, there are a million funny stories and situations. In the cubicle next to mine, a man arrives a day after the retreat has started. After several days, I realize that he never comes to any of the meditations. I hear him through the walls, listening to his Walkman and talking with the neighbor on the other side of his cubicle. Often the talk is about the physical attributes of women in the course, or of how much good hashish they have smoked in Thailand. During the day, my neighbor sleeps and sunbathes, and then stays up late moaning to himself, presumably masturbating into the wee hours of the night.

During my free time after breakfast, I have taken to doing some maintenance work on our bicycles, and have been working hard at truing Hitomi's wheel, which has gone out of whack. After several days, I realize that I have really messed up the wheel, loosening the spokes on one side far too much without creating a balance on the other side.

Right about this time I am ready to make a complaint about my neighbor, who is using this retreat as his personal holiday and interfering with my experience, especially when I try to sleep. I am sitting in my room with the door open, sweating in the hot air and staring in disbelief at my failed repair job on the wheel, when my neighbor sticks his head in the door and greets me. I am cold and silent toward him, putting my finger to my lips and hissing at him to shut up, but he continues, oblivious to my protests. He begins to ask about the bike, and I have no choice but to give him some curt and whispered answers. He perks up and tells me that he used to be a bike mechanic, then proceeds to take my wheel and put it right, giving me pointers as he goes.

That afternoon, I spin the perfectly trued wheel and reflect that angels are sent in many different guises.

On the eighth day of the retreat, I find myself growing antsy. I am addicted to constant change, especially in terms of scenery, and find myself longing for the changing terrain of the road. So despite the ban on leaving the compound, I sneak out just beyond the walls for an afternoon walk.

To my amusement, I discover that I am not alone. I come across several people smoking (cigarettes are banned from the course), a couple kissing in the bushes, and one woman attempting some rock climbing. Two guys return from the shop up the road with Snicker bars and cans of soda. I figure we would all make pretty pathetic monks.

On the last evening of our retreat, I feel relaxed, peaceful, and extremely well rested. There is a full moon out, and one of the senior monks leads us on a meditative walk through the swamp grass and large strands of causarina trees. I walk slowly, following each footstep as I breathe in and out, and become aware of the senior monk's large, flat feet, planting firmly and gracefully into the grass. It occurs to me that this man's lineage is incredibly ancient, and that he is far more rooted in past and present than I am. If we were to be transported any number of years into the past, my clothing, my gait, and everything about me would quickly brand me as an outsider, from another time and place. This monk, with his long orange robe, shaved head, and flat bare feet, would fit right in, his costume, manner, and purpose unchanging as the years move past.

On the last morning at Suan Mok, we speak at last. Hitomi and I sit, sharing the battles we've gone through and lessons we have learned, and we introduce ourselves to many of the people at whom we have been smiling silently for ten days. This has been a great opportunity to remove ourselves from the whirlwind pace of everyday life, and to examine our every breath and step down to the last details.

Thanking the monks, we load our bikes and wheel out of the front gates of Wat Suan Mok. The flowers by the roadside sparkle with an intensity the likes of which I have never seen, and the lush jungle around us appears illuminated in its fresh greenery. Spinning my legs, I am mesmerized by the kinesthetic movement of my body, and by the sheer beauty of motion. For a moment I feel enlightened, and then it occurs to me that this freshness and revitalization must be exactly what a prisoner feels upon being released from jail.

A large signpost at the Malaysian border announces, "Bringing illegal drugs into Malaysia is punishable by death." A skull and crossbones has been penned in above it.

The official in a khaki suit who sits at a table near this sign says to us, "Hello, marijuana?" He laughs when I flex my calves and pantomime coughing and trying to cycle, then stamps our passports without further ado and waves us through.

The terrain doesn't change on the other side of the fence, but there are more cars, higher speeds, and a lot of shopping malls. Hordes of young Malaysians chatter away on cellular phones while they shop in air-conditioned arcades. People no longer wave or smile at us; as is the case in most developed countries, they are too caught up in their own dramas to even realize that we are there.

Being near the equator, the humidity becomes a heavy, sticky goop, which works its way under the skin and clings tenaciously throughout the day and night. We make our way along the flat highway past tin mines, rubber plantations, and the fragrant roadside *durian* stalls that appear every ten kilometers or so.

The *durian* is considered the king of all fruits in this part of the world. It is a large, heavy fruit with scaly skin, which hangs from its tree like the testicles of a large bull. It is incredibly succulent and exquisitely textured, yet for all its delights, has one major flaw: it smells exactly like a fresh bowel movement. Its stench is overpowering. Throughout Malaysia and Singapore, big signs in buses, trains, and hotels announce, "NO DURIANS ALLOWED HERE." I consider it a marvel of nature that something so foul-smelling can taste so delicious.

Many travellers do not like Malaysia, finding it too modern, too fast-paced, too much like home. Yet Hitomi and I enjoy passing through, despite the sultry weather. Sitting in a restaurant, I watch a young Malay girl in a black veil and headdress saunter past a nearby mosque, which issues forth a call to prayer. A young Chinese lady in a miniskirt, riding her rusty bike down the street passes her, while a Sikh clad in a turban and *lungi* furiously pumps past her on his way to work. In today's multi-ethnic global environment, one might see this scene in Toronto, New York, or San Francisco, but this scenario is commonplace to Malaysia.

Relations between the Malays, Chinese, and Indians are not always harmonious. The Chinese are the minority, yet they own most of the country's commerce and wealth, and riots flare up on occasion. Yet for the most part, Malaysia is a peaceful and prosperous country, and these scenes of ethnic and cultural diversity are heartwarming, especially after we have spent months in countries with very dominant ethnic majorities.

Sometimes the Malays seem lost amongst the noisy Chinese and Indians. In Ipoh City, we come across the Hindu festival of Thiposan, where sari-clad women and dancing *sadhus* throng the city's temples. The sadhus stick pins and needles into their faces and dance as if in a trance, pleading with the gods for good fortune. Around the corner, we check into a hotel run by Mr. Toh, a spry man who looks like Jack LaLane and is seventy-two years old. He is an island of calm in a sea of noise, as the upstairs of the hotel is full of Chinese prostitutes, putting on their makeup and screaming at each other. There is noise from the street, noise from the hall, noise from the televisions blaring in every room, noise from the hookers, even noise from the fans.

We join Mr. Toh for a meal and listen to his stories of growing up in Malaysia. He talks about life under the Japanese during the war, about Malay-Chinese relations, and about the economic boom of Southeast Asia. He apologizes for the ladies upstairs, but informs us that Ipoh is known as the Sin City of Malaysia. We tell him that if hotels are any indication, every city between here and Bangkok is Sin City.

Down the block from the hotel is a Malaysia Airlines office, and for the first time, we have a chance to check on our tickets in person. The woman at the front desk is courteous and apologetic, but tells us straight out that whoever sold us our tickets without confirming them has been stringing us along. The New Zealand flight, which only goes once a week, is booked solid, and there are no available flights for another two months, the onset of winter in New Zealand. The clerk tells us she will put us on high-priority waiting, but estimates our chances of getting a flight at around five percent.

Grimly, we continue south, with five days remaining before our scheduled flight. We pass through Taiping, a city of gardens, and Tanjung Malim, where we catch the latest James Bond film in Chinese. The humidity is suffocating, and both of us have sore throats and head colds, caused by sleeping with too little clothing under the whirring ceiling fans in our hotel rooms, which seems preferable to shutting them off and sleeping in the equivalent of a sauna.

We pass through Slim River, which has a lovely British rest house. The armchairs, large fans, and long verandas are tempting, but after calling Malaysia Airlines and being told that our chances are still very slim, we decide that one slim is enough, and keep pedalling.

The next morning, the day of the flight, we are over 100 kilometers from Kuala Lumpur, and have decided that we will go to Sumatra for two months while waiting for an available flight to come through. Regretfully, we will have to scrap our plan to cycle New Zealand, but such is fate.

Before giving up completely, I call the airlines while we stop for a bowl of noodles, and am told to call back later. Thirty kilometers down the road, I try one last time and am put on hold. A cheerful clerk comes on, acting surprised that I am calling, and rather nonchalantly informs me that we are confirmed for our flight scheduled to leave in five hours!

We have forty kilometers to go, and there is not a lot of time left, so our jubilation over having a flight is overshadowed by the necessity of making tracks. I see a motorway that goes directly to the airport, bypassing central Kuala Lumpur, but motorways here do not allow bicyclists. We race into a nearby police station to explain our plight, and the officers clap us on the back and boisterously urge us to take the motorway. Tentatively, we cycle to the motorway entrance, where a big sign says, "Bicycles and pedestrians not allowed." We ride to the tollbooth and wave to the guards. They wave back, and we hightail it to the airport.

At the Malaysia Airlines check-in counter, big signs (everywhere in Malaysia there are signs, informing one what one can and cannot do) inform us that excess baggage charges are twenty dollars per kilo. After our Nepal experience, we are well prepared. We check in the bikes and just enough luggage to meet the weight limit, then carry the rest with us onto the plane. We are not an exception to the rule, as we see Indian families carting suitcases filled with televisions, cameras, and boxes of chocolates from the duty free shops.

Hitomi and I sit for a moment in the airport lounge, which houses a Kentucky Fried Chicken outlet. Old women in saris inspect the edibles, and nearby, elderly Chinese men look fearful about taking their first escalator ride. We marvel at the clash of the developed and undeveloped worlds, the past and present. We recall days in China when entire villages would stare at us, and we would dream of being in a clean, quiet park in New Zealand with a picnic lunch, a bottle of wine, and a few good books to read. Today we dream of afternoon tea, cool weather, and an end to the chaos that is Southeast Asia. I close my eyes and know that when I wake, the dream will have come true.

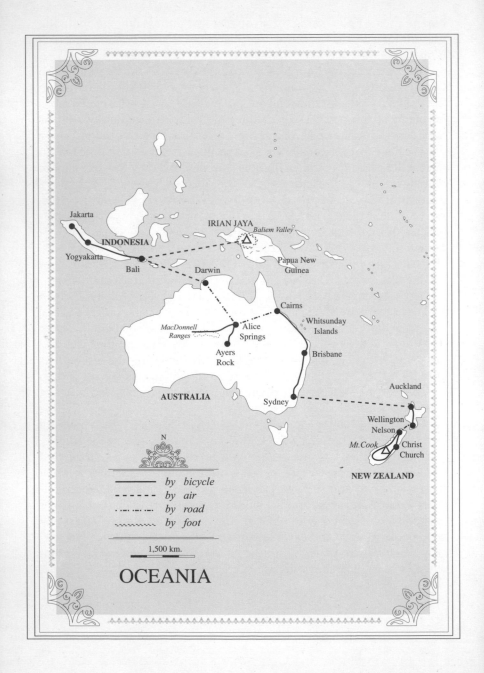

OCEANIA

Part Two

Far Under:
To Oceania and Back

Every man carries within himself a world made up of all that he has seen and loved; and it is to this world that he returns incessantly, though he may pass through, and seem to inhabit a world quite foreign to it.

Chateaubriand

A man who leaves home to mend himself and others is a philosopher; but he who goes from country to country, guided by the blind impulse of curiosity, is a vagabond.

Oliver Goldsmith,
The Citizen of the World

Chapter Seven
New Zealand

> *In Middle English, the word "progress"*
> *meant a journey, especially a seasonal journey or*
> *"circuit." A "progress" was the journey of a king*
> *round the castles, nomad round his pastures, a*
> *pilgrim round shrines. Moral or "material" forms*
> *of progress were unknown until the seventeenth*
> *century.*
>
> Bruce Chatwin

Expectations exist only to be dashed into tiny fragments—and to signpost the way to the folly of one's desires. Auckland turns out to be anything but quaint, cold, and British. The afternoon we arrive, it is extremely hot and sticky out, as if the airline has played a trick on us, and we are back in Kuala Lumpur.

We almost do not make it out of the airport. New Zealand Immigration has extremely strict policies about what may enter the country, as the indigenous plant, tree, and animal populations here are all at risk from non-indigenous bugs and bacteria. An incredulous inspector listens with eyes ablaze as we list all the countries our filthy bicycles, tent, and sleeping bags have passed through. Several fumigators are called in and our gear is sprayed down meticulously before we are allowed to proceed.

The city of Auckland sprawls endlessly, and I am reminded of Los Angeles. First Bangkok, now Auckland; perhaps the entire world is destined to resemble the City of Angels. Traffic is heavy on the wide boulevards, which are certainly not as bicycle friendly as I had imagined they would be. Progress everywhere, we are learning, comes at a tremendous cost.

One pleasant surprise is that Auckland is the largest Polynesian city in the world. The streets are filled with Tongans, Samoans, Fijians, and other South Pacific Islanders, most of them quite large in girth and chatting animatedly. We also see hordes of Japanese exchange students, lots of Chinese businesspeople, and large numbers of Maori natives, so Auckland has an unexpectedly cosmopolitan feel to it. At times, it feels as if we are still in Asia.

In this global village, it can be hard to know where one border, language, or culture ends, and where another begins.

New Zealand does live up to one of its stereotypes, though: our arrival is greeted with fifteen hours of torrential tropical rain. Both of us are deathly ill, and the rain does not improve matters. I have been coughing so much that I have lost my voice and can only manage a few words in a deep rotten bass. Hitomi has sprouted boils all over her legs, and is also having problems with her teeth.

Looking back now through our travel journals, I am amused and shocked by how many entries revolve around exhaustion and illness. In postcards and storytelling, there is fantasy, the lure of the exotic, the drama of adventure; in our journals, there are headaches, backaches, diarrhea, constipation, sore throats, muscle pain, joint pain, fatigue, and fever. Fortunately, the big nasties like malaria, hepatitis, typhoid, and Japanese encephalitis haven't yet found their way into our panniers.

We contact the friends of a friend and are invited to stay with the Morgan family, which gives us a chance to rest up, visit a doctor, and become reacquainted with the western world. For a few days, it is satisfying to be pampered, sleep long hours in a soft bed, and receive invitations to barbecues every evening. I even rediscover the almost-forgotten luxury of perusing the newspaper while sitting on the toilet. But all this grows old fast.

People around us talk about the stock market, the local football teams, and the latest songs on the radio. They inquire about each other's lives, but the questions seem shallow and meaningless. It is as if we are watching a play.

People want to see our slides, and ask us if we have been to the Potala, the Taj Mahal, or the Royal Palace in Bangkok. They say we are very brave, and they wonder aloud if it isn't too dangerous and dirty to travel in Asia. They talk about going to some of these places if they ever have the time and money. No one seems to understand that our days in the developing world consisted of sweat and dirt, or that we spent much of our time washing our few articles of sweat-stained clothing by hand, over and over again.

The Morgans and their peers appear to be doing very well, but seem stressed out that they aren't doing better. I wander through the local mall amid the frenzied consumers, contemplating all the televisions, microwaves, cellular phones, and beds. Life here, with all the trappings, seems like a life that is way out of balance. Then again, who am I to criticize?

Within a week, Hitomi and I are sufficiently recovered to get back in the saddle (or perhaps it is as soon as we are back in the saddle that we recover). The minute we get onto our bikes, the rains stop, and we leave Auckland on a sunny morning with puffy cumulus clouds drifting lazily overhead, blown along by the unceasing New Zealand wind. Outside the city limits, we are thrust immediately into the New Zealand of postcards. We ride past rolling green hills, small dairy farms, sheep, and cattle, enjoying the sparse traffic on the narrow backroads.

We decide to take another break from cycling and make a canoe trip down the nearby Wanganui River. As soon as we dismount, rain pours from the sky without stopping. But the weather is warm, and getting soaked in a canoe will be much more pleasant than getting soaked on the road. We rent a canoe and begin a smooth run through hundreds of small rapids, cruising along at a lovely pace of about ten kilometers an hour.

The Wanganui River is the second longest river in New Zealand, and due to its ease of navigability has always served as a trail from the Tasman Sea to the interior. For years, the Maori had large settlements on its banks, where they caught fish and birds, and used the native plants and berries which were abundant along the riverbanks. Missionaries arrived in the 1840's, and by 1860 a dozen paddleboat steamers were carrying passengers up the Wanganui to grand hotels on the river's upper reaches.

Maori legend has it that the Wanganui was formed during a fight between two nearby mountains, Tongariro and Taranaki. They were fighting over lovely Pihanga Mountain, and when Taranaki lost, he stormed north, leaving a gaping chasm in the ground behind him. A spring issued forth from Tongariro, filling the chasm and creating the river.

As Hitomi and I float downstream, we are impressed and bewildered by the indigenous flora and fauna. There are *ngaio* and *nikau* ferns, *miro* and *rimu* trees, and countless others impossible to identify without a book or guide. We hear the cries of *kaka* parrots and *tiu*, whose sing-song call sounds like a ringing bell.

The Department of Conservation has set up huts at intervals of about a day's paddle along the river, and they are pleasant and well run. The clean, simple shelters are equipped with bunkbeds, small kitchens, woodstoves, and emergency radios. They are staffed by volunteer wardens who show the same generosity we have encountered everywhere in New Zealand, coming out to greet us with steaming mugs of coffee as we emerge soaking from our canoe. The sole exception to this delightful trend is the hut in Wakahoro, an ancient one-room schoolhouse where a grim-faced couple silently hand over cups of tea, then sit and stare at us while they gulp down their mammoth steak and potato dinner.

The rain lightens, but the winds change direction, and we struggle to make any progress at all, even though we are going downstream with the current. Watching another canoe founder in the winds and swirling water, I realize how pathetic we ourselves must look. Fortunately, Tieke Marae is not much further down the river.

In 1840, when New Zealand became a British colony, the signing of the Treaty of Waitangi made land available for British settlers. New Zealand's land grab, unlike those in the U.S. and Australia, was made with the provision that Maori land could not be taken without their agreement and some sort of payment. However, land wars erupted after the signing of the treaty, due to tensions between the settlers, who demanded land, and the Maori, who were reluctant to sell it. A bone of contention remains over the Treaty of Waitangi and its failures, and over how to redress claims of lost or stolen land—even if that land was supposedly sold freely. Still, race relations in New Zealand are probably much better than in most parts of the world, and Maori culture and language are as much a part of education and society today as any other subject.

In some instances, the Maori have chosen to reclaim the land, and the bend in the river where we now sit is one of these spots. The Department of Conservation has recognized the right of the Maori to reclaim their *marae*, or meeting house, but as it is on National Park land, they would like to run it in a partnership with them. The Maori want total administrative rights on the land before this can happen, so they sit at a stalemate.

As a result, there is a private campground on one side of the river, where we notice most of the Kiwi groups go, and a *marae* on the other side. Visitors are welcome to stay at Tieke Marae in exchange for observing Maori protocol and donating any leftover food (on what is one's last night on the river) as a way of contributing.

A teenage boy comes out to meet us as we berth our canoe and leads us up into the *marae*, explaining protocol. We are greeted by elders, who sing their welcome greeting, and then we are escorted to the front of the *marae*. Hitomi follows behind me (customs dictate man before woman here) and sits on the women's bench. I take my place on the men's bench, introduce Hitomi and myself, and then sing a song about my sacred mountain and homeland (fortunately, as a mountain lover I have a few in my repertoire). Following this, we all *hongi* (rub noses and press foreheads together) and then enter the *marae* for tea and homemade buns. Some things British transcend all cultures and squabbles.

Larry, the elder here, is a burly and muscular man with a chiseled face perpetually wrinkled in thought. His partner, who is introduced to us as Ma, cooks up a huge feast of taro root, beets, pumpkin stew, and burgers, served with fresh pan bread cooked over an outdoor fire, while Larry talks about the politics of Tieke Marae. He says that the land here was taken away with the Railroad Act of the 1890s, and the issue never redressed, as tourism followed on the heels of the Act, and then National Park designation. The elders reclaimed the land several years ago and are now engaged in a standoff with the National Park, although neither side has landed any forcible blows.

The most promising result of this strife is that Larry has brought several teenagers—mostly young men from the cities who have tribal roots here—to reconnect with their culture and ways. One young man is a carver, one is a farmer, and another is becoming a canoe maker, proudly displaying to us the second sleek wooden canoe he has built in the past six months. Many of the kids have had trouble with their parents, troubles in school, and problems with drugs and alcohol, so this has been a revitalizing opportunity for them to grow and reconnect with their heritage.

Most *maraes* in New Zealand are set up as tourist attractions, well intentioned, but basically there for cultural entertainment, full of song, dance, and costumes. Here at Tikae Marae, the experience is simple, with no pretense, and all the more enjoyable because the only way to get here is by boat. We sit around the fire discussing local politics and chatting about the boys' various projects, and as I breathe in the smells of fresh bread and taro boiling away on the fire, I marvel at all the stories we hear every day and at the rich lives we encounter.

After stuffing ourselves and talking half the night away with Larry and Ma, we take our leave in the morning and wish them well.

New Zealand's campsites are to be highly commended, and perhaps given some sort of medal for their combination of comfort, service, and scenery. Most sites are located in parks, or on the outskirts of towns, within bicycling distance of a grocery store. The campgrounds are equipped with piping hot showers, clean toilets, full kitchens, laundries, television and reading rooms, and even small bunkhouses available at a low cost if the weather should turn foul.

The caretakers are usually as pleasant as the sites, and Les and Annette Walker, our campground hosts in the town of Taumaranui, are no exception. We arrive just as the first drops of a storm hit, and Les comes striding out to help us pitch our tent ahead of the rain, then carries our bikes into his garage. A tall, gaunt man with a bowl haircut, he chatters the whole time about the dairy farming industry, which he reckons to be a far more stressful occupation than being a campground host.

In the kitchen later, Les has everyone in stitches with his jokes and infectious belly laugh. His amiability and generosity seem all the more amazing when we learn that he has hepatitis, diabetes, hemophilia, and spinal cancer! He disregards these as if they were just a bad joke, then tells us that he has five broken vertebras because he was run over by a truck a year ago!

Later, he offers chocolate bars to whoever can find all the glow-in-the-dark monsters he has hidden all over the kitchen. Together with several Swiss cyclists who have arrived, we spend the next hour crawling around like little kids, searching for dinosaurs, goblins, and other delights.

As we crawl into our sleeping bags for the night, I reflect on human kindness. Despite all the world's horrors, injustices, and cruelties, there are a million kindnesses for each one—and an endless number of people to supply each of those kindnesses. Hitomi and I are often praised for being brave and strong in taking on our cycling challenges, but these pale next to journeys like the one Les is on.

The North Island, though pleasant to meander through, is not what I have come to New Zealand for. The green rolling hills and farms remind me of the American Midwest, and Hitomi and I make tracks to get to the snowy peaks and glaciers of the South Island as quickly as possible.

Locals invite us to an eel fry at a campsite outside of Raetihi with stupendous views of giant Mount Ruapehu. While we eat, we suffer our first theft of the journey; Hitomi's daypack is pilfered from our tent. It contains only postcards, a pen, a Swiss army knife, and a book by the Dalai Lama, but after so many moons of never thinking about safety or security, it is a pity to have this reminder. I am also surprised that it has occurred in small-town New Zealand, which has an impeccable reputation for security. Stereotypes never do quite live up to their billing.

The road flattens out all the way to Wellington, the windy hub at the end of the North Island. Built on steep hills surrounded by bays, the city is more scenic than Auckland. It is home to a liberal university, a community of artists, a bustling financial district, and the seat of the New Zealand Parliament. Refined Victorian and Elizabethan homes grace the city, and cafés line several pedestrian-only thoroughfares in the center of town. Wellington would be an attractive place to live if the wicked weather stirred up by the Cook Straits did not bombard the city with mist, rain, and gale force winds for most of the year.

As usual, when we dismount to wander around town for several days, it pisses with rain the entire time. I begin to wonder if we will sneak all the way around New Zealand without it ever actually raining while we are on our bikes. The last time we donned rain jackets was in Tibet, six months ago, and we are seriously thinking about hiring ourselves out as good weather beacons.

We ferry to the South Island, and the change in terrain is dramatic. Billowing clouds drift over brown heather and trees that are already displaying their fall colors. The temperature drops, and the humidity of the subtropical north is conspicuously absent. There is a very desolate and lonely feel to the land, and even on the main road down the east coast from the ferry terminal, there is almost no vehicle traffic. The wind here whistles, howls, and occasionally screams, and is our constant companion. We are closer to Antarctica here, and the winter storms that rush up from that frozen continent appear to be starting as we arrive. Daytime temperatures are pleasant enough for riding, but it is no longer warm enough to sit outside after dinner, and if we can't find a motorcamp with a sitting room, we snuggle into our sleeping bags early.

We meander down the Kaikoura coast. The road, which hugs the turquoise water, is sandwiched between the Pacific Ocean and the rugged, dry Kaikoura Range. Smells of the sea fill our nostrils, and we breathe

salt, wind, and ocean spray. Seagulls wheel overhead and colonies of
seals snuggle against the rocky coves, drying themselves in the arctic
sun. A penguin with yellow tufts behind his ears wanders across the
road, looking like a lost old man, terrified as our bicycles approach.

The wind roars like an inferno and turns for and against us without
warning. At the point of utter exhaustion, we always seem to run into
other cyclists with whom we can parcel out the misery and trade travel
tales. On one particularly bad afternoon, just when we can go no further,
a rickety bicycle made out of wire appears at the side of the road like a
mirage. Attached to it is a sign: Pedaller's Rest, Working Sheep Ranch
Accommodation.

The ranch, just off the main road, has a bunkhouse, a kitchen, a cute
pet pig, and other amenities for the weary cyclist. The owners, Jim and
Denise, are sheep ranchers who often see forlorn and sickly bicycle riders battling the winds near their ranch; after inviting many thankful
cyclists home for the night, they have decided to make a business venture of it. I tell Denise that places like this are what cyclists dream about.

We leave the coast and head through the Hunderlees and
Hawkswood, rollercoaster hills brown and dry under the azure fall sky.
Mileages are short, locals are friendly, and the ice cream is good. An
elderly Kiwi bicyclist named Paul tells us that days like this are the
"champagne of touring." Other bicycle tourists we meet complain of the
steep New Zealand hills, and we sit back and feel like confident old
pros.

In Kaiapoi, we camp next to the annual Deer Cullers Association
retreat, and despite their friendly overtures, hastily move camp away
from their barbecued stag preparations, which don't complement our
morning oatmeal and coffee. New Zealand is a meat-eating country, and
whenever we are invited for a meal—which is frequently—it is a challenge on the digestive system after so many moons in the world of rice
and vegetables.

We roll into the Cantebury Plain, and Christchurch, the South
Island's only metropolis, a flat, sleepy "British" city with beautiful parks
and attractive houses. My old friend Mark has settled here with his Kiwi
partner, Kim, and we stop to rest and visit for a week. As always, it is
both strange and delightful to be plucked off the road and into the settled
lives of friends. Hitomi and I look on with some envy at their ease and
comfort, and we plunge greedily into the world of books, music, walks in
the park, and dinners with friendly neighbors.

However, when Mark asks us if we ever get tired of travelling, of the constant motion, strange faces and places, and experiences which come so rapidly that there is barely time to process them, we immediately respond with a resounding "No!" He doesn't quite understand until I ask him, "Don't you ever get tired of going to work every day?" (Mark happens to have an occupation that he enjoys immensely). Travel is a job Hitomi and I enjoy a lot. The hours can be long, but the benefits are pretty good: sunsets, mountains, oceans, and all the calories one cares to consume without ever gaining a single pound.

After again abandoning our bikes and hiking for several weeks through the Rees and Dart valleys, along the Routeburn Track and over the Divide, we emerge at the west coast. The place has one of the highest rainfalls anywhere in the world, averaging around seven meters annually. Water pours from every slab and stone, gushing from peak to sea at maximum velocity. Massive granite spires and walls tower over everything, spewing water in the form of glaciers, rivers, and waterfalls into the valley below. It is as if the water is being sent in a thunderbolt from the sky.

After a night of rain, morning peels away the clouds to reveal a glistening sunny day. We wear smug smiles as we get our bikes out of the shed at the Wanaka motorcamp. However, the west coast will have none of our pride, and a few hours after we climb back in the saddle, large drops begin to slip from the blackening sky. The sun breaks out in the distance, though, over Lake Hawea and Lake Wanaka, and we are treated to the spectacle of ten rainbows in the course of an afternoon. We also meet two Swiss cyclists named Reto and Michael, who joke that cycling New Zealand is almost like cycling at home, as every cycle tourist seems to be Swiss.

Descending through the Gates of Haast, a steep and narrow canyon that cuts through the coastal mountains, we slide down to the coast pursued by rain and sandflies. In Haast township, we are told we cannot camp due to flooding, and take a room in a local inn. The local weather forecast calls for five days of uninterrupted precipitation. I guess we are due.

As we resume spinning our wheels up the coast, glaciers, snowy peaks, lush forests of rimu trees, and cascading waterfalls flowing into the Tasman Sea surround us. Unfortunately, we see none of this beauty. Everything is gray, and visibility is about three meters. I can just make out Hitomi's helmet in front of me.

In Lake Paringa ("a charming, serene lakeside spot," according to the Department of Conservation) our tent almost floats away in the night, and its waterproof abilities fail miserably. By two a.m., our sleeping bags are like ponds. Michael and Reto, the Swiss cyclists, opt to camp in front of the bathroom door, as there is a slight overhang. They do stay dry, but the stench from the composting toilet keeps them awake, and the entire sandfly population of New Zealand descends upon them.

At Fox Glacier, we see the tour buses but not the sights.

At Franz Josef Glacier, it is still raining, and the weather forecast calls for northerly winds, plus another seven nights of rain. The only creatures on the road—besides drenched cyclists—are the sandflies, which continue to pour in through all the "breathable" seams in our raingear.

After seven days of continuous moisture, I find I am enjoying the rain. It forces us to slow down, and I am becoming acutely aware of the soaked ferns lining the sides of the road, of the different colors of the cliffs, and of the various speeds and sounds of each new storm. Once we receive the first soaking of the day, it isn't so bad to be wet. Our raingear keeps us fairly warm except during long breaks, which are pretty much impossible to take anyway, due to the sandflies.

In Greymouth, which is indeed gray, we leave the wet coast and climb toward the Lewis Saddle, in the interior. We stop in a place called Maruia Springs, a hot springs hideaway run by Japanese caretakers; it brings back memories of days in Japan. Mark comes from Christchurch to join us for a day, and as we talk of our plans, it hits me that we will be leaving New Zealand in a week.

As we luxuriate in the warmth of the springs, rain pattering gently on the steaming pools, Mark again presses me on our ability to travel so long without becoming tired or jaded. I tell him that although it is physically tiring to be moving all the time, neither one of us can imagine our journey ending.

"I've come to a point," I say, "where I don't see life in terms of fixed friendships or long projects, or even as a continuum that stretches from childhood through adulthood. I see everything now in terms of moments and seconds. Even when I'm with old friends, a moment now is exactly that, nothing more or less, not an extension of the past. Things are here and now, and I focus entirely on what exists in front of me. Past and future don't really exist, because they are only memories and possibilities. With a view like this, it's pretty easy to go on—and on."

When we began, Hitomi often told me that she thought she was moving away from something. I felt like I was moving toward something. Now I don't think either of us feels like we are moving away from, or toward, anything at all. We are absorbed completely in motion for its own sake, and of course for all the magic it brings into our lives every-day.

We bid Mark a hearty goodbye and cycle over the Hope Saddle, our last pass in New Zealand. As we make our way down into the Motupiko Valley, I mull over the journey of Thomas Stevens, whose story I have been reading at night. In 1884 Stevens set out around the world atop his penny-farthing, armed with an overcoat, a pistol, and little else. His tale is nothing short of astounding. He had no maps or guidebooks, and nobody had travelled the route before him on two wheels. Stevens often rode on railroad beds or on tracks that we would today call hiking paths; he often fell, which couldn't have been pleasant, as the seat on a penny-farthing was high above the ground. Compared to his adventures, our journey is a picnic, and I chuckle at how many people think we are either brave or foolhardy.

Along the Motueka River, the change in scenery is astounding. Not only is the sun out for the first time in a week, but we are surrounded by non-native plants. Maple, pine, and eucalyptus trees dot the hillsides, and soon we are winding through fruit orchards. This is the fruit basket of New Zealand, and we cycle next to acres of corn, hops, raspberries, plus orchards of pears, Fuji apples, and kiwi fruit. The air is crisp, the light is golden, and the colors are of fall.

We catch up with Michael and rent kayaks to paddle out to Abel Tasman National Park, at the northern tip of the South Island. The Tasman Bay, which flows around the park, resembles something out of the south of Thailand. We paddle past white sand beaches lapped by turquoise water, and only the sandflies prevent things from being perfect. As we glide through the inlets and small islands of the Tonga Island Marine Reserve, fur seals flip off their sunny rock perches to play with us, biting our paddles, somersaulting over our kayaks, and putting on a natural circus performance. We spend several hours in small lagoons, taking photos and exploring like five-year-olds on a first beach trip. New Zealand is putting on a splendid final show, and we lap it up greedily.

We say goodbye to Michael in the appropriately named Mosquito Bay. He has a few more days of leisurely paddling planned, while we have been invited to speak at a school in Nelson the following morning. Sometimes all the goodbyes are difficult, but as I was once reminded, "goodbyes only mean you get to say hello again."

Nelson is sunny, with abundant produce and a laid-back lifestyle that recalls California. Hitomi and I go to the prestigious Nelson College for Boys, where we are to speak in our friend Tim Robson's Geography class. The school is straight out of an English schoolboy novel, complete with uniforms, a strict headmaster, and ivy-covered stone buildings. The boys are well behaved, attentive, and knowledgeable about world geography, and they are happily surprised when we wheel our loaded bicycles into their classroom. We dispel a few stereotypes and myths about places we've been and people we've met, talk about trip planning and survival, and ask the boys about their own dreams.

They have plenty of these, from film star to banker to Antarctic navigator, but when I ask them how they intend to turn their dreams into reality, they become speechless. When one of the boys asks Hitomi if this is our dream come true, she smiles and says, "Well, yes." Looking out the window at the rain that has begun to fall again, she continues, "But most of the time it's a lot of hard work."

It rains most of the way back to Picton, the end of our circle around the South Island. While Hitomi stops to use a restroom, an older woman approaches and greets me.

"A gooday to ya. Whereabouts are you from?"

I tell her, and she continues, "So what do you think of our fine little country?"

"Not too shabby," I reply. "It's not only beautiful, but so livable. Seems like most folks here can afford a house, some land, and the time to appreciate it all."

She smiles and reflects on this.

"It's changing, like everywhere," she laments, "but we've still got some of the cleanest air and water on this planet, and I wouldn't trade it for anything. You enjoy the rest of your stay here, and you're welcome back anytime."

The ferry arrives to whisk us back across the Cook Straits, where an overnight train to Auckland is waiting for us. Everything is so orderly and smooth. We munch our picnic dinner, only to find that our tickets entitle us to another one, compliments of the train. I figure we can make room for it somehow.

Chapter Eight
Australia: *The Merry Old Land of Oz*

> *Increasingly, our world consists of destinations and goals, with the times and spaces in between them eliminated by jet propulsion. Consequently, there is little satisfaction in reaching the goal, since a life full of endpoints is like trying to abate one's hunger by eating merely the two precise ends of a banana.*
>
> Alan Watts

Hitomi and I walk down the street in a suburb of Sydney, wondering aloud whatever became of Spencer, the flamboyant didjeridoo player we travelled with to Mount Kailash. Minutes later, we wander into a neighborhood park, where a flea market is being held. Under an awning, surrounded by saris and amulets, sits Spencer himself!

Moments like these are true evidence that all things are indeed connected. We babble on about all the moons we have spent since leaving Mount Kailash, and Spencer fills us in on the latest thrill in his life: becoming the father of an energetic baby girl. No trips to India are on his agenda, but he makes do with Sydney's multicultural riches.

Sydney has been yet another pleasant surprise. The streets teem with restaurants representing every culture on the planet. We see *dim sum* next to Ethiopian *injera* bread; Vietnamese *pho* shares space with *doner kebab*; and fish and chips are available twenty seconds away from *masala dosa*.

There is a burgeoning nightlife, a very open gay scene, and the Kings

Cross district, full of strip joints, hookers, and needle users sitting on the streets. It's not exactly soothing to the eye, but it is very alive. We have been so long in sleepy New Zealand, with its peaceful, orderly homogeneity, that the gritty urban realities of Sydney are, at least for a time, invigorating. The people here are free of the sameness that was becoming tiring in New Zealand. Indeed, in a week of being passed from friends to strangers, we stay with a single father and his teenage son; an older woman living with her two friends and flatmates; and a radical lesbian feminist. Munching hummus and pita bread at a corner Lebanese restaurant, we agree that the variety is most refreshing.

Sydney reminds me of San Francisco, the vibrant and multicultural city of my youth. Hitomi says that she could live here, and we talk about lingering. But Sydney is not Australia, and the Land of Oz—as the locals call it affectionately—is huge. With only a few months to see it, we pack up our panniers and take to the road.

The first step for any visitor to Australia is to spend a few days getting familiar with the language. Hitomi comes to me swearing that someone told her to "bring your cozzie to the barby;" it turns out that "cozzie" means bathing suit, and "barby" stands for barbecue or picnic. At the barby, a fellow sits and listens to our travel stories, muttering over and over, "fair dinkum to ya" (honestly). When the tales get a bit too tall for him, he states, "don't come the raw prawn now" (don't try to deceive me).

The ubiquitous "g'day mate" is easy enough to pick up, but we are bewildered by directions to "put the esky in the comby" (put the cooler in the campervan) and "beware of the hoons and larrikins" (delinquents and ruffians) up in Queensland. We look for a restroom and are told that "the dunny's just off the bitumen" (there's a bathroom just off the paved road).

When our host informs us, "There'll be good tucker at the sparrow's fart" (food will be ready at dawn), it occurs to us to pedal out of town as frantically as we can.

On a gray and drizzly morning, we take the narrow bitumen out of the Wiseman's Ferry crossing along the Hawkesbury River, sheltered by the canopy of eucalyptus forest that engulfs the road. I had imagined Australia as sunny and flat, but on this morning, it is neither. Short, steep hills mark the route as we roll towards Wollombi, a historic town on the old Great North Road, an area of coalmines originally worked by British convicts.

In the early 1800's, the American War of Independence left the British without a place to dispose of convicted criminals. Several penal colonies were created in the newly claimed land of Australia, bringing scores of prisoners to a desolate, empty land on the other side of the world. I try to imagine what it must have been like for convicts arriving at this wild, remote outpost. It must have been sheer hell for some, a true place of penance; others may have found the vastness and new horizons enticing.

Hitomi and I whiz past several mangrove swamps and a few banana plantations, and pumping up the steep hills, we are reminded of Thailand. However, by now we feel resilient and mighty astride our bikes, and neither of us considers walking up even the most precipitous climbs.

It is now more than a year since we left Japan, and we break 10,000 kilometers as we rejoin the Pacific coast in Coffs Harbor. Towns here have a laid-back, friendly feel, reminding me of the surfing communities of southern California. People go out of their way to wish us "G'day," and ask where we are going. We camp in a reserve in a gum forest, where we see our first koala bear and are visited by flying foxes at dusk. Our "tucker" for the evening is a smooth Thai curry, Greek salad, loaf of French bread, and bottle of wine, topped off with an entire chocolate cheesecake for dessert. It is almost frightening to think that we each need over 5000 calories a day just to maintain our normal weight and energy level, even on days when we don't ride.

Last night's meal was Indian, the night before Chinese, and before that, Japanese. Sydneyites had warned us that once we got in the bush (or "back o' Bourke," as they call it) we would be subsisting on crocodile steaks, wichity grubs, and kangaroo flank. However, Oz is turning out to be a gourmet paradise.

Towns here are modeled after the American mall and suburb look, for better or worse. The quaint one-room village with a corner market, as found in so much of New Zealand, is gone, replaced by the shopping complex on the highway. Franklins, a mega-supermarket chain, carries a wide array of goodies at unbeatable prices. In the New Zealand markets, food was expensive and the most exotic item on the international food shelf was pasta; here, the aisles are crammed with satay sauces, curry powder, sushi fixings, and more. Twenty dollars buys so much food we can barely carry it.

Climbing over the Sterling Range and Naughton's Gap, we continue along the coast of New South Wales on empty roads. Cycling here is almost dreamlike, and we pedal along in the warm sun with a slight breeze blowing at our backs, daydreaming of adventures yet to come while our legs spin beneath us. The region we are passing through is known as North Coast Hinterland, and is infamous for the "back to the land" movement that started here in the 70's. A hippie guerilla movement against logging the rainforest was successful, and the Aquarius Festival, which celebrates alternative culture, was also launched in these parts. Communes dot the landscape, and many people occupy their time with organic farming, home schooling, marijuana growing, and subsistence living.

The rural communities appear peaceful and well functioning, but the regional center of Nimbin is not in such an idyllic state. Being in the "marijuana belt," Nimbin has attracted young people from the city, who come to experience the freedoms of this hippie haven. With them have come unemployment, harder drugs, and an aura of hipness characterized by designer tie-dyed t-shirts. The town is full of rainbow murals, head shops, artsy stores with psychedelic designs painted on the walls, funky cafes, an Herb Museum, and there is even a Hemp Embassy! Smells of incense and patchouli fill the air, and tattooed young men with Rastafarian dreadlocks sit on the street corners and bang out drum beats and folk tunes, staring with glazed eyes at the world around them.

We make home at the town's youth hostel, which is a farm located on a lovely creek. After a meal of homemade organic tofu, we ward off the persistent herb sellers who hound us as we walk through town. Having grown up in Berkeley, California, Nimbin is nothing new to me, although for Hitomi, it is like stepping into an issue of Rolling Stone. This sort of behavior in Japan just doesn't pass muster. We are relieved to be missing the annual Hemp Mardi Gras and Drug Law Reform Festival, which I am sure, is a real high.

In Binna Burra, bush turkeys steal the pears and giant blueberry muffins we have carried all the way from the coast. These deranged birds will steal anything not anchored to one's tent or bike—and even then they might consider it. They hide under the pungas pines or Antarctic beech trees, then disappear into the forest canopy once they have completed their raids.

We're spending a few days in the Lamington Tops National Park on the advice of a friend in Brisbane, and are happy to have arrived in the rainforests of tropical Queensland. Lounging next to our tents, we watch several pandolins, which resemble small wallabies, waddle by. As in

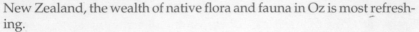

New Zealand, the wealth of native flora and fauna in Oz is most refreshing.

We had asked our friend to show us a place with nice views and an active rainforest. Additionally, he gave us the number of Alex Edwards, "a fellow whom I think you'll find quite interesting," so we place a call. Alex lives deep in the forest, and he gives us a set of very complex directions over the phone, describing various mud tracks and dirt paths. He claims we shouldn't have any problems, as we are on bicycles, then chuckles and says he looks forward to meeting us.

A day later we disappear deep into the state forest, cursing as we hack our way through brambles and circumvent mud holes. However, Alex's directions are impeccable, and after an endless series of rights and lefts into narrow sandy passageways, we emerge in a clearing where there stands a traditional Japanese house!

Alex, it turns out, has lived in Japan, among many other places. A short man with sandy hair, glasses, and a peaceful smile, he welcomes us to his humble abode as if we were old friends and begins to answer our questions about his wonderful home.

He is originally from Canada, and left at a young age to travel the world and escape the monotony of life at home. Later, he fell in love with languages, and spent the next fifteen years roaming from country to country, settling for several years in Japan, Egypt, and various places in Europe, becoming fluent in a plethora of tongues as he went. When he reached Australia during the height of the "back to the land" movement, Alex became enamored with the rainforest. He put together 8000 dollars, bought land and building materials, and built a home perfectly executed after the old tiled-roof farmhouses he had seen in Japan.

In the yard, there are banana, mango, and black sapode trees, several rainwater tanks, and even a Zen rock garden. The rock garden is made of immaculately raked small pebbles, designed to evoke mountains or a great sea.

The only items of any great expense in Alex's home are the *tatami* mats, which he imported from Japan at a cost equal to what he spent on everything else. There is no electricity, the toilet is a composting model, and the bath is a simple rock garden solarium, complete with bucket and scoop. Alex does have a phone, and he retains a car as his only connections to the outside world. Other than this, life on his veranda is pretty simple and serene. He says he wanted it this way to keep his life "deliberate."

"Think about it," he muses. "Your friends call you up and ask you to go out. You say, 'Okay, I'll just have a quick bite and take a shower and I'll be right over.' Out here, I can't do that. I have to light the wood stove, heat water for a wash, and take time to prepare a meal."

"Life is fast enough as it is, so what I have to live with here purposely slows me down, and makes me more aware of time, my environment, who I spend time with, who I am."

Hitomi tells Alex of our travel plans, and he smiles and shakes his head.

"Five years ago," he says, "I might have been envious of you, but not now. I spent so many years doing. Nothing but going and doing. Well, you never know what the future will bring, but for now I am done doing. I'm concentrating on just being. Watching my banana trees bear fruit, and the wet seasons come and go."

I must admit, it all seems very appealing, and we linger late into the evening on the veranda, watching the fireflies flicker on and off in the sultry air. Yet we have an awful lot of doing ahead, and after a night of deep slumber, we oil our creaky chains and ride into the bush.

The savanna of Queensland is a long, flat stretch of coastal plain dominated by stunted acacia trees. We have big tailwinds through here, and cycling is more like sailing; we breeze along effortlessly at high speeds. Traffic is sparse on the Bruce Highway, and on some mornings we spot more kangaroos than cars. Small groups of kangaroos spring along at high speed, making hopping seem like an efficient way to travel.

The townships through here are mainly outposts. Gin Gin, Miriamvale, and Mount Larcom are dots on the map that represent water, food, and perhaps a campsite at the end of the day. Some spots consist of only a handful of homes and a roadhouse, the Aussie all-in-one convenience store/restaurant/pub/gas station. These may be of great relief to the "roadtrains," the giant convoys of eighteen-wheeled transport trucks that rumble through the night across the outback, flattening kangaroos as they go, but after several encounters we have learned to expect nothing from them. The one in Mount Larcom is extremely dismal, boasting a few rotten bananas, a lot of junk food, and a wall of porn magazines.

Hospitality out here is plentiful. Locals like John and Mick, who beckon us to "come sit around the billy with a couple a blokes," often invite us in. They are train drivers who do contract work for Queensland Rail, earning good pay, but working their butts off and rarely making it home. They are big, strapping fellows who enjoy their beer after work—

John drinks two six-packs a day!—then get up in the wee hours and do it again.

Over stories of fistfights, bars, and rugby, John cooks up several very tough steaks with boiled vegetables, then crowds our placemats with beer bottles and proceeds to give us long lectures on tattoos and martial arts. Most of the lectures are directed at me, as Hitomi cannot understand a word of this giant's strong accent.

Sugar cane fields envelop us as we move north, away from the Tropic of Capricorn. Clairview, Sarina, Calen, and MacKay are towns with sugar mills, ethanol distilleries, and little else. With the strong winds still at our backs, cycling through Sugar Cane Alley is effortless, and we can almost close our eyes and just drift over the flat and silent road, listening to the windy sighing of the tall cane plants next to us. The savanna offers open, endless views, and our thoughts follow the pattern set by the landscape. Thoughts in the mountains are narrow and crowded; here they have ample space, and it is easier to follow ideas to their conclusion before they can be interrupted.

The only low note is the abundance of roadkill plastered to the road everywhere. Many animals fall prey to the speeding roadtrains. In the course of a single morning, we see a freshly killed copper snake, a cow skeleton, several cats, and the "roos." Dozens of dead kangaroos are ground into the asphalt, their sad faces etched in agony.

Hitomi has even developed a great sense of sympathy for snakes, creatures she had always feared and hated before. She shudders as she imagines them slithering out of the grass, their bellies contacting the strange asphalt, then freezing up as the glaring headlights bear down.

And of course there are the cane toads. Cane toads were imported from South America to control the population of sugarcane beetles, which were destroying the sugar crops. As is often the case, the solution to this problem brought its own set of consequences. The cane toads ate native bugs and insects in addition to the beetles, and covered the countryside with little toadies, as the female cane toads lay about 30,000 eggs per spawn. The toads took over the forests, their poisonous glands killing any birds, snakes, or other creatures that tried to eat them.

Thus every Australian considers it a civic duty to crush as many toads as possible each time he or she drives. Hitomi and I often see vehicles driving slowly down country roads, swerving back and forth to wipe out as many cane toads as possible.

In 1770, Captain James Cook steered his vessel *The Endeavor* through a passage of about seventy coral islands on the fringe of the Great Barrier Reef. Cook named the islands the Whitsunday's, actually forgetting that it was Monday, as he had crossed the International Date Line. Halfway to Cairns, and a bit fatigued by long days, Hitomi and I decide it's time for a respite on one of the islands.

We stock up with a week's worth of food and enormous drums of drinking water, then find a skipper willing to sail us out to North Molle Island, an uninhabited, reefed island in the Great Barrier Reef Marine Park. Park rangers have informed us that we are the only ones with permits for the island for the next seven days. After hauling all the gear off the boat and setting up camp, we settle in to fulfill a Robinson Crusoe fantasy.

North Molle is a woodsy island with one sparkling white sand beach. There is little to do besides walking the island and snorkeling around the coral lagoon. We peruse every inch of the newspaper we brought with us, and spend hours feeling the sand, looking at the water, chatting, and walking along the coral beach. I feel cleansed, as I did during our stay at Wat Suan Mok in Thailand, with the chaos of perpetual motion brought to a complete standstill. Our greatest challenge is designing a bird-proof box after Dave and Mabel, the two resident crows, throw us a welcome party by shitting all over our tent and attacking our supplies. They manage to open our pineapple juice and steal a slice of pumpkin from our vegetable cache.

Hitomi comments that this place is as about as close as anywhere gets to paradise. We have sun, sand, water, total peace, and no schedule. I am amazed that so few people come here, opting instead for the islands with resorts, bars, and video parlors. Bob, the skipper of our boat, mentioned that those who do come tend to stay only one night, as they get bored otherwise. I guess I used to feel the same way, though now I feel so relaxed, calm, and content that I wish we had brought another week's worth of water.

I wonder how Captain Cook felt here. Did he long for human habitation after so many months at sea, or did he enjoy the silence and solitude of these tropical gems, as we do now?

We rise with the sun and enjoy the coral reef, which is at its best with the morning tide out. The lagoon is filled with a rainbow of colorful coral, which changes shades and hues as the morning progresses. Large, flat batfish, curious and friendly, meander through the reefs. Skipper Bob had told us that they would eat right out of our mouths, and sure

enough, when Hitomi holds a piece of bread between her lips, the batfish glide right up and give her a big kiss!

Each day passes at a languorous and deliberate tempo. We snorkel,
sun ourselves, practice yoga and tai chi, write, cook big meals, and just
be together, watching sunrises glide into sunsets. Dave and Mabel don't
show up, and I guess we have fooled them with our makeshift "esky."

On our last night on the isle, a northerly Santa Ana wind blows
through. It is hot and humid, bringing hordes of mosquitoes and breeding restlessness in our tent. We lay prisoner in our sweat-drenched tent,
listening to the shrill drones of the mosquitoes clamoring for our blood.
Our patience with confinement is amply rewarded when we arise in the
morning and swim.

As we crawl ever further north from the Tropic of Capricorn, the heat
really picks up. It is the middle of winter and 96 degrees. When the
winds are behind us, riding is easy, but there is no breeze whatsoever for
our parched faces; a headwind keeps us cooler, but makes the going
slow and laborious.

South of Bowen, the land grows very dry, and for a stretch is even
devoid of cane fields. Gnarled trees on the horizon are the only signs of
life. Pit stops out here are as harsh as the land; grizzled petrol station
proprietors glare at us when we buy Gatorades, then refuse to fill our
water bottles, offering to sell us a liter for five dollars.

In Bowen and Ayr, the terrain is once again wet, lush, and fertile.
This area of Queensland is the beginning of the Australian breadbasket,
where tomatoes, peppers, melons, and mangoes proliferate. Campsites
here are international workcamps, packed with Sikhs, Pacific Islanders,
Africans, and Chinese laborers picking fruit for ten dollars an hour.

It is sad to read of Oz's high unemployment rate, and of so many
people preferring to live "on the dole" (collecting unemployment money),
as it seems that there are endless vacancies. The work is hard and hot,
but at ten dollars an hour, with twelve-hour workdays and a seven-
dollar camp spot available, it is a real opportunity to save some cash.

I realize that I am starting to see things with the eyes of a foreigner.
The immigrant laborers in the camp next to us tell us that this place is
like paradise. Elsewhere in the world, this type of work earns inhuman
wages in often-horrid labor conditions. Yet many young Australians see
this work as demeaning and ill-paid. I am reminded of Japan, where I
saw the service and labor jobs filled by workers from China, Thailand,
and Iran. The Japanese no longer wanted those jobs that were *kikken*,

kitanai, and *kitsui* (dangerous, dirty, and hard).

In Townsville, a pleasant town on the sea, we visit Greg Jetnikoff, a fellow who pulled over at the side of the road back in Gin Gin and offered us a place to stay when we got up north. Greg lives with his partner Cassandra in the old firehouse, which he has converted into a spacious and charming living space. His backyard is full of fruit trees, most notably the black sapode, also known as the chocolate fruit for its custard-like taste and texture.

It turns out that Greg is a former car, motorcycle, and bike mechanic, a real grease wizard who enjoys maintaining his bicycles for the triathlons and mountain bike races he takes part in. The former engine house has become Greg's workspace, full of bicycles and spare parts. He spends the greater part of the afternoon and evening giving our bikes a thorough going-over, cleaning them and replacing pulleys and cables.

He is flabbergasted by our blackened chains and freewheels, which have gone over 10,000 kilometers without any maintenance other than the occasional dab of oil. According to manufacturers' estimates, the average chain should be replaced every 3000 kilometers.

"Bloody 'ell, mate, I've never seen chains like this in me life," Greg tells me. "I can't figure how in the bejesus you guys are still riding on these things."

Hitomi and I sheepishly look down at our toes without comment. Greg shakes his head again and again, informing us that we are riding moving time bombs, and that we had better take care of things in Cairns. I'm convinced we could probably hold out longer, as I subscribe to the philosophy of "if it ain't broke, don't fix it." However, the next real bike shops will be in Penang, Malaysia, several months and thousands of kilometers away. I grudgingly promise Greg that our steeds will get some prompt attention.

On the last leg of the journey to Cairns, we detour up and around the Atherton Tablelands, an area of rainforest, waterfalls, parks, and small towns. In Milla Milla Falls, we spot a kangaroo rat, the smallest member of the kangaroo family, a shy, silly, tiny creature hopping along like mad. Shortly after this, a platypus catches our eye, skimming along the surface of a still lily pond.

On days like these, we seem to move in slow motion, assuming the pace of the things we see: a bee alighting on a sunflower, a caterpillar curling on a leaf in the sun, a dog lying in the shade of an overhanging eave, too lethargic to even consider disturbing us as we pedal by. I marvel at how this deliberate and circumspect shuffle contrasts with the greater picture of our everyday reality, one of perpetual motion and a mind-boggling assortment of ever-changing stimuli that rip past faster than the images in a music video.

It is up on the Tablelands that we have one of our worst arguments ever. It happens on a rainy morning, cold, damp, and very foggy. Hitomi is ready to leave camp, and I am dawdling, in no mood for my first soaking of the day, and lingering over a second or third cup of coffee as long as I can.

Our arguments usually start from the smallest of things, masking other issues. Travelling on bicycles leaves little room for error, as there is mileage to cover, camp to set up, food to be cooked, and chores to be done, no matter how exhausted we are. Lately, we seem to have very different energies in our approach to these things.

As I am a foot taller than Hitomi, it takes her two pedal strokes to accomplish what I can do in one, so although she is a strong rider, it takes her much more effort to put in the distance for the day. On 100 kilometer days, she needs to get out of camp at an early hour to ensure herself that she will enjoy the day and finish before dark. I, on the other hand, am content to leave late, preferring to enjoy the slow pace of the morning and then push myself once I get on the road. We have tried leaving at separate times, but this doesn't always work in terms of camp breakdown, plus we end up worrying about each other when we are too far apart. Ever since our separation in Osaka at the start of the journey, I have been terrified of one of us disappearing into the bowels of a strange land.

Lately, on the mornings when I have been ready to leave early, Hitomi isn't. The next day, she is up and full of adrenaline, while I laze about camp, still groggy from the beers we drank before bed. One afternoon, she arrives in camp too hot and tired to do much except swim or get horizontal, while I am ready to run a marathon. And the next day, our positions reverse.

At any rate, on this particular morning, this behavior is not okay. Hitomi berates me for not waiting for her, while I complain of her lack of speed. We end up having a screaming match, standing in the pouring rain, unable or unwilling to take back the words that drive us apart. This is one of those fights where, back home, one person or the other would go stay with a friend or sibling for the night, let the tension subside, then come home, apologize, and go back to normal. But out here, that isn't an option. Our house is a tent about three feet wide, and there are no other rooms where we can sit by ourselves.

By the end of the day, in our soggy campsite in Lake Tinaroo, we are too damp and drained to make any effort to discuss the wedge we are driving between each other, and we curl up in our sleeping bags, pressed as far against the opposing tent walls as we can get from each other, and tearfully drift into our separate nightmares.

Morning brings sunshine, drier spirits, and congenial attitudes. Yet strangely, neither one of us apologizes for the previous day, or attempts to discuss it. It is as if the long distances and wide empty spaces of Australia have brought some sort of demons out of our psyches, and all we can do is stop and stare at them.

Several days later, the sun is beating down, the wind is at our backs, and we are sailing down big hills back to the ocean. Hitomi is laughing at the kangaroos hopping along near us, and it is as if our disagreement never happened. Yet years later, when we look back on our journey together, both of us remember this day with precise clarity as one when something changed inside and between us, something that would begin to pull us irrevocably apart.

Reaching Cairns was a major goal when we arrived in Australia. It was a large dot on the wide-open map of Oz, a long way from Sydney. Just like that, here we are. And as with so many goals, we find ourselves completely disillusioned upon attaining it. The means really are almost always better than the ends.

Cairns is a tropical tourist trap, a city of souvenir stalls and dive shops surrounded by the lush and sticky tropics. There are crocodile farms, water parks, and various tropical Disneylands, mostly attended by Japanese tourists. Japanese entrepreneurs are buying up Cairns, creating a climate of mixed feelings; the community welcomes the business, but resents being owned by outsiders.

In a dramatic departure from our daily routine, we try living a soap-opera life at the condominium of Miki and Koichi, our friends from Matsumoto. Paradise Palms is a tacky golf resort cum estate located near the northern beaches of Cairns, among row upon row of lifeless condominiums and manicured lawns. The security gates appear to even keep out the mosquitoes.

It is the beginning of July, and our goal is to be back in Kuala Lumpur by late September, then reach Nepal in time for the onset of the trekking season. Indonesia only allows two-month visas, but we figure that we would rather spend our time there than here—not to mention that we will need all of that time to make our way across Bali, Java, and Sumatra. We are left with about three weeks in Oz, obviously not enough time to bike the thousands of kilometers from here to northern Darwin, from where we will fly to Bali. So we opt to bus to the Outback and do two weeks of cycling around the famous Ayers Rock and the MacDonnell Range.

In Cairns, we play tourist, and are as bad as the rest of the lot, dropping almost 1000 dollars on various transportation tickets, as well as several hundred dollars on complete overhauls of our worn-out bikes. Included in our purchases are roundtrip air tickets from Bali to Irian Jaya, where we have dreamt of trekking among the Dani in the highlands of the Baliem Valley.

We also try taking a bus tour of the area, the first such tour of my life. I have often wondered why people go on such tours, as every time I have bicycled next to a tour bus, it looks like most people on the bus are asleep. Now I understand. Try as I might to make the most out of this luxury outing, I find my eyelids heavy, and soon am deep in dreamland. I awaken to find Hitomi snoring deeply next to me, as if she hasn't slept in years.

It is two days on the bus to Alice Springs, in the center of Australia. After all the long afternoons controlling our own pace and space, it is more akin to a two-year prison sentence. The bus is relatively comfortable, yet we are still cramped, sore from being unable to stretch out. We sit captive, staring out the window as the scenery changes with lightning speed.

The sun sets, fiery and bright over the burning cane fields, which are now being harvested. We cross the Dividing Range and drive through miles and miles of emptiness, across a red and brown land devoid of mountains and flat as a pancake. The landscape is a 360 degree panorama of nothingness. There are no trees, no mountains, and no settlements, just dry scrub and continuous horizon. Roadhouses are 200-300 kilometers apart, and are packed with grumbling bus passengers, hungry roadtrain drivers, and weary cross-country travellers. Cycling across this stretch would have been a challenge.

Uluru, known more popularly as Ayers Rock, was so named by William Gosse, the first white explorer to see The Rock. It is another one of the natural world's power spots, and it is fitting that we spend a full moon at its base. This moon is one in a series that has included Mount Everest, Mount Kailash, and the Yangtze River.

Uluru and its nearby neighbor, Kata Tjuta (or The Olgas, according to the white man, who has an annoying habit of renaming everything he sees), are about 850 meters high, and over 350 million years old, and they used to be higher than the Himalayas. This area was completely glaciated, but it broke down over time, leaving only the core of the sandstone domes. The earth here is ochre red and covered with shrubs. White-barked ghost gums grow, as well as mulga trees, members of the acacia family. The species of vegetation here are 55 million years old, and it is no wonder that Uluru is sacred to the Aborigines, as everything about this region exudes an aura of timelessness.

Up close, Uluru is magnificent. It is not one big rock, but a series of billowing folds, complete with gorges and valleys, around ten kilometers in circumference. Aborigine legends, like the fight of the Snake Woman against the Liru People, explain the formations that appear between the cliffs and rock faces. Whether one believes in the legends or not, they are certainly a convenient way of explaining what is there.

The rocks of Kata Tjuta are just as astounding: thirty-six domes of varying shapes and sizes, which look like white hats or elephant backs (Kata Tjuta means "many heads"). The shapes remind me of drawings in the Curious George books of my youth.

We spot a thorny devil, a medium-sized lizard with soft earth colors on his leathery armor. He looks ferocious, but actually exists solely on a diet of ants. He scrambles off into the shade of some desert oaks, which are actually a type of causarina tree. In order to survive here, the oaks dig their roots down fifty meters below the surface, where they can find water. Only then do they begin to grow on top, their downward-sloping, top-heavy branches aiding in shade and water retention.

Travelling in places like the Himalayas, I have always felt an external delight. The scenery is stupendous, the mountains thrusting out of the earth, the land always feeling so full of excitement. But the Himalayas are a young range. Out here, there is more of a sense of mystery, of maturity. Wisdom, rather than excitement, emanates from this ancient terra firma. Here, the enjoyment of the place springs from something internal, something far older and deeper than I have ever dared to ponder.

"Have bike, will travel." This is etched into a beam in the shelter overhang at the Ellery Creek Bighole campsite. Ellery Creek is a deep and frigid swimming hole, a welcome oasis in the blinding ochre desert of the West MacDonnell Range. A series of watering holes runs through the range, part of cavernous gorges carved by ageless underground rivers that snake through the mountains on their way to the Simpson Desert.

The water holes have long been a lifeline for travellers here, and with the benefit of paved roads, maps, guides, and vehicles, there are certainly more explorers wandering about than in past years. Some may not see them as explorers, but the spirit of adventure is alive as ever. Camped next to us are a German couple who have been sailing around the world for seven years, now taking a break from life on the water. Next to them are an Aussie pair with two young children, who have just driven a four-wheel-drive vehicle 1700 kilometers across an old stock route through the desert, resupplying on fuel via a fairly risky drop of several barrels by bush plane. Everyone does indeed have his or her own dream.

Another seventy kilometers up the road is Glen Helen Gorge, where ghost gums line the sandy bottoms of dry gorges hemmed in by crumbling red rock walls. The Finke River, an Aboriginal trade route, has flowed here for 300 million years, and today services the tourist trade.

Despite the distances and the remoteness of the place, the outback remains well connected. Most outposts retain at least one high-frequency radio, set up for long-distance communication up to 3000 kilometers. The HF radios have been used for school correspondence courses, and are perhaps most noted for their role in the RFDS, Royal Flying Doctor Service. The service started in 1928, and now provides medical treatment and evacuation to communities that are two to three weeks' land travel from any medical facilities.

A spinifex pigeon alights on my bike, looking just like its city kin except for a mohawk atop its head. The diversity out here is awesome—even among the pigeons, this ancient land creates variety. I look back one last time at Mount Sonder, Sleeping Woman Mountain, and say a silent goodbye to this natural wonder that sprawls across the desert behind us, bathed in a myriad of early morning colors. It is 130 kilometers back to Alice Springs, and the last kilometers we will pedal in the Land of Oz.

Australia has a population of about eighteen million people, almost all of whom live in five or six cities along the coast. Unless one travels an incredible distance, opportunities for contact with communities of Aboriginal people are limited. I harbor no expectations of seeing a traditional native community, and I assume that most traditional communities lie far out in the Outback, in private areas that are restricted to non-Aboriginals, as perhaps they should be. I would, however, like to see a community set near a town, going about their daily business.

As luck would have it, in Alice Springs we are introduced to someone who has contact with the Amunanga community, on the outskirts of Alice, and we are able to schedule a visit there the following morning.

The first thing we see in Amunanga is a pack of young kids racing away from the community school. Their teacher, a bedraggled white man, comes out after them, and upon seeing us, straightens up and invites us in for tea. I expect to hear about educational funding woes, or about what he has learned by working in this community, but instead we are subjected to a vicious diatribe describing how horrible the children and their parents are.

Three quarters of the class do not show up at all, and of the handful of kids who do, it is not until an hour after the lunch bell rings. The teacher gives them an art project to complete, consisting of some watercolors and a large piece of paper on which the outline of a giant snake has been drawn. The children have obviously seen this one a thousand times, and after about fifteen minutes, they run away and do not return.

The teacher complains about the conditions here, and engages in a gossiping session with the woman from town who has brought us over. I am reminded of my own days as a teacher; the negative chatter and complaints in the teachers' lounge usually came from those who made little effort with the children, and whose charges rebelled because they could not respect the people who were supposed to be educating them.

Away from the school, the situation doesn't get much better. We are taken to a house in a total state of disrepair. The walls are blackened, possessions are scattered at random across the floors, and nothing has been cleaned in ages. A group of elderly women sit outside, boiling water for tea in a burnt coffee can and staring vacantly into space, while several babies crawl about in the garbage and dust which surrounds the house.

Several of the women beckon to us to sit and have tea, and we strike up a conversation. They ask us if we have any food, and we offer them the packets of instant noodles that we happen to have in our packs. They devour them greedily. One woman implores Hitomi to find her some medication for her eye, which is red and swollen, filled with tears.

Again, I expect a heart-wrenching story from the woman who has brought us here. She is a social worker in Alice, and has worked with the

Aboriginal population for some time. She informs us that the government is trying to help the Aborigines, but they remain "stuck" in their native ways.

"They don't use the houses we give them," she claims. "They prefer to sleep outside. And when we bring them food, they refuse. They'd rather eat things they gather and hunt from the desert. When they get sick, they won't take our medicine, and prefer to stick with their age-old cures."

Yet I am seeing a very different picture than the one she paints. Most of the community appears to be out of work, and there isn't much food. I don't see anyone heading off to hunt, much less engaging in shamanistic rites. The women who have pleaded with us for food and medicine don't look thrilled to be huddling around the fire, and appear to need some basic necessities. Conditions here are absolutely appalling, actually far worse than anything we have seen in China, Tibet, Nepal, or elsewhere. If there were a few hundred more people here, it would be a refugee camp.

In the end, I don't buy claims that the Aboriginal culture is just too much at odds with white culture to fit in. In a community like this one, I don't see people stuck in their old ways, or unable to embrace different ones; all I see is a lack of human kindness and compassion for people in a very sad situation.

Compared to the state of Maori-Pakeha (white) relations in New Zealand, Australia appears to be in the Dark Ages. No words can describe my feelings as we are driven back to Alice.

In the recent past, Aborigines were not allowed to enter cities, a step beyond even the horrible Jim Crow laws of the American South. Given the violent repression of the past, the vast size of the land, and the apparent lack of energy or care on both sides, a happy future is a long way off, up a very steep road.

Our spirits are buoyed when we do run into a more positive face of Aussie diversity back in town. We meet Satoshi, a half-Japanese, half-Native American kickboxing champion who looks like James Dean. Satoshi tells us that he spent a year in a coma after the car his father was driving crashed head-on, killing his entire family.

Adrift, he has reached Oz with his pregnant Japanese girlfriend in tow. He has been working on cattle ranches to make a living while he tries to get his boxing career back in full gear, and is preparing to be a dad. His stories are painful, and his string of bad luck a long one, but he is a survivor, and his adventures are a tribute to the human spirit.

We invite him and his girlfriend to dinner, and listen to Satoshi's tales of cattle drives, dude ranches, and the Australian Wild West. As the sun goes down, bathing all of Alice in a purple glow, it occurs to me that although we have travelled miles and miles to have these adventures, one really doesn't have to go very far. Adventuring is a state of mind, an outlook, a way of being, and every human has a tale to tell, a story to share. Whether we are willing to spend our time and energy listening to them—that's another story.

Chapter Nine
Irian Jaya: *Of Cannibals, Missionaries, and Noble Savages*

In the Descent of Man, Darwin notes that in certain birds the migratory impulse is stronger than the maternal. A mother will abandon her fledglings in the nest rather than miss her appointment for the long journey south.

Life is like riding a bicycle. To keep your balance, you must keep riding.

Albert Einstein

The moist and heavy air of Asia slaps us in greeting when we touch down in Bali at two a.m. Even at this late hour, taxi drivers are hanging out in front of the airport, chain-smoking, chattering, and all vying for our business. Back here in the developing world, life never sleeps.

It is only a few kilometers into town, so we reassemble our bicycles and begin the jaunt to Kuta Beach, past rickshaw drivers sprawled out over their bike seats. Fruit stalls give off wafts of tropical fragrances, guava and mango. Gutters are full of dirty plastic bags and other trash, swept tidily into piles by bamboo brooms, which leave telltale tracks across the dusty streets.

A skinny boy dashes into the street in front of us and asks if we need a room. A year ago, we would have regarded him with suspicion and caution, a con artist out to rip off the foreigners. But now we see him for what he is, a boy with an opportunity to add a few rupiah to his family's meager savings, trying to be of assistance to some visitors.

In the developing world, no matter where we are, or what time of day or night it may be, someone will always materialize out of nowhere, hoping to be of service or just wanting to see what's going on. People here have a curiosity born out of a life lived completely in public, without privacy, where entertainment is not paid for in cinemas or cocktail lounges, but is something seen at eye level from one's own bedroom.

By day, Kuta comes alive. The streets are a frenzy of activity, mostly geared at making a living off the thousands of foreigners who come to enchanted Bali seeking a bit of paradise. If one were to find true paradise, it wouldn't be long until the rest of the world was replicated into exactly what one had found, rendering the exotic mundane.

Kuta Beach looks like dozens of other enclaves we have seen in Asia; I am reminded of Thamel in Kathmandu, Khao San Road in Bangkok, and Penang in Malaysia. Hitomi and I pass endless stalls filled with secondhand books, tie-dyed clothing, and pirated cassette tapes. The merchandise all looks very familiar. The colorful travel bag sold in Kuta is actually the same one hawked on Khao San Road; the "Balinese" mask was also for sale in a Thamel shop; and the selection of native jewelry is less extensive than one might find at a Berkeley flea market. Perhaps in the next decade, all these items will be available in the 7-11 convenience stores that are as common in Kuta as in Bangkok, Penang, or Amarillo, Texas.

Local restaurants follow this trend toward sameness, eschewing their own paradise (which has already been lost) in favor of one far away, which retains its exotic wonders. In Kuta, there is the Mount Everest Restaurant, the Singapore Bar, the San Francisco Pension, and the Himalayan Disco. I think back to Kathmandu, which has the Bali High, the Mango Guesthouse, the Siam café, and a Texas Steakhouse. Khao San Road is home to the Kilimanjaro Guesthouse and the Big Apple, and I even found a menu there offering sweet coffee "Bali style."

Fortunately, Kuta is just a gateway, our pit stop on the road into the unknown, and after storing our bicycles with the proprietor of our guesthouse, we return to the airport for the flight to Irian Jaya.

If Irian Jaya's status as an exotic destination off the beaten track is to be measured by the flight there, we are looking at dropping off of the globe. In Bali, our flight is delayed five hours; completely unprepared for this, we sit in the sweltering terminal, and after five hours have run out of reading material, food, and conversation. When we finally board the dingy and decrepit Air Merapati plane—named after an active volcano and angry god—we are treated to the sight of several gangly workers dangling from the wings of the plane, attempting to tighten some parts with their wrenches.

Eventually, the plane roars off the tarmac, wobbles slightly, and becomes airborne. We reach for our sick bags and hang on to the armrests of our chairs, which have lost most of their padding via large holes in their sides.

As if to make up for the long morning, lunch is served three times in the following several hours. All three lunches are the same: a small cardboard box with miniscule mayonnaise sandwiches on white bread, a very thin slice of cheese that resembles candle wax, a mini bag of about thirteen potato chips, and a plastic glass full of a purple beverage sweeter and stickier than anything I have ever tasted.

There is no movie screen, no leg room, no magazines, and not much of anything else either, although there is a safety manual that instructs us, "Number One of important, if plane should crash, do not panic."

Following lunch number four, we descend into Ujung Pandang, capital of Sulawesi. Here, we are told that our flight will no longer be going to Jayapura, the main city on the coast of Irian Jaya, where we are to connect with a once-a-week flight into the Baliem Valley early the following morning. Smiling officials tell us not to worry, that everything will work out fine, and to "be happy today." They then bundle us back onto the plane, which is now heading to Biak, an island used as a refueling stop halfway between Jakarta and Los Angeles.

Airborne again, we are served our fifth lunch of the day. It has improved; there are now stale biscuits to go with our mayonnaise sandwiches and chips. Almost as soon as we reach cruising speed, we descend again, this time to Ambon, one of the Spice Islands. The island looks very mysterious and inviting, full of jungles and mountainous terrain. Just off the runway is the wreckage of a plane, casually removed from the tarmac but not cleared away. As Hitomi looks at me in disbelief, I close my eyes and suck on my syrupy drink.

Exactly twelve hours and ten mayonnaise sandwiches after leaving Bali, we reach Biak, a tiny coral-ringed island. Smothered in thick jungle, it looks like something out of an Indiana Jones film. We are exhausted from the day's ordeal, though quite full from our lunches, and we prepare to do battle with the airline officials in order to make our early flight connection tomorrow. Surprisingly, this battle never materializes, as the Merapati staff in the tiny one-room air terminal are incredibly helpful. They inform us that there will be an early flight to Jayapura, arriving with an hour to spare before the bush plane to Wamena leaves. Merapati will have a taxi ready, plus a wakeup call in the morning. Furthermore, we are to be housed in the Hotel Irian tonight, with room and board on the house!

Thanking the staff, we are escorted to the Irian, one of the nicest places we have ever spent a night in. The old colonial-style building is constructed almost completely of teakwood. A huge dining room is furnished with vintage pre-World War Two furniture, and large chandeliers hang from the ceilings. Our room has a veranda opening toward the sea, slow ceiling fans, and most importantly, insect netting without tears in it. The area is rampant with malarial mosquitoes.

Dinner is an all-you-can-eat feast of curries served elegantly in engraved silver bowls, and despite our bloated stomachs, we take the opportunity to gorge. We dine with Phillipe and Cecille, a couple from Belgium who slowly smoke elongated cigarettes and tell us of their many previous journeys to this region. Their stories are shrouded in mystery, and they give no details about why they are here. The wait staff surrounding us are very dark-skinned, and look more African than Indonesian. The air is also much heavier than it was in Bali, thick and choking, and even under the revolving blades of the fans, our bodies soak in a constant lather of sweat. As we retire for the evening, both of us comment that this place is like a chapter out of a Conrad novel.

Come morning, we continue to make progress in the same manner as yesterday, via the eternal forty-five minute flight. Today, the small Merapati Fokker flies to Timika, in southern Jaya, before heading on to Jayapura. We are becoming aficionados of mayonnaise sandwiches and sticky purple liquid.

In Jayapura, we have to secure a *surat jalan*, a police travel permit that will let us wander the Baliem Valley. Fortunately we bump into Silas Yikwa, a Dani man from the Baliem whose brother operates a guide service there. Silas takes Hitomi and our Belgian friend Phillipe to the police station, while Cecille and I take care of baggage and tickets in the airport.

By quarter to ten, Hitomi, Phillipe, and our permits are nowhere in sight. Everyone else has boarded our tiny plane, which juices its engine on the runway in preparation for a ten o'clock departure.

By five to ten Cecille and I are frantic, but the Merapati staff, in their usual nonchalant way, tell us, "No worry, okay sir, all happy."

At ten-fifteen, the plane is still on the runway, but attendants are working to remove the entry platforms and secure the doors. Hitomi and

Phillipe rush into the airport, breathless, drenched in sweat and waving our *surat jalans*. The Merapati staff and Silas Yikwa scream, "Go! Go! Run hard and fast, plane now leave!" We lurch across the runway and onto the stairs, seconds before they are disconnected from the plane.

Tibet may be the roof of the world, but Irian Jaya is most certainly its heart and center. Some ninety million acres of impenetrable jungle and forest cover the land, and in spite of recent logging and mining, the interior of Irian Jaya remains more untouched and untravelled than even the jungles of the Amazon. From my window of the plane, I see nothing but vast and endless jungle.

Out of Timika, we skirt the flanks of Puncak Jaya and other towering, dark peaks, which loom silently in the mist. We are near the Equator, yet Puncak Jaya, at about 5000 meters, is covered in glacial ice. It and its nearby neighbor Gunung Nnga Pilimsit are the highest mountains between the Himalayas and the Andes.

The Baliem River comes into view below us, snaking its way through the lush jungle canopy. I still cannot see a single sign of human habitation, even though we are flying quite low. I know that somewhere down there are tigers, large lizards, tree-climbing water rats, crocodiles, snakes, and extremely rare butterflies. The jungle is also home to over 700 species of birds, including dozens of strains of the bird of paradise, which wears feathers of flaming gold, emerald green, and crimson. The Irianese and Papuans call it the "bird of the gods."

Irian Jaya is officially Indonesian, but physically and culturally it is part of Papua New Guinea, which controls the east side of the gigantic island. The coastal Irianese are Melanesian, while the highland tribes are all black skinned, with features like those of the Australian Aborigines or Africans. Inland, often divided by just one small hill or ridge, there are hundreds of tribes, each with their own language.

Like the Chinese in Tibet, the Indonesian government has tried to control Irian Jaya by introducing a transmigration policy. Most coastal towns are now inhabited by more than fifty percent Asian Indonesians; as in Tibet, positions of power, education, and finance have been put in the hands of outsiders. Additionally, Irian Jaya is home to one of the world's largest copper mines, and the foreign-owned Freeport mine is a hotly contested source of revenue. Profits go almost entirely into foreign pockets and the hands of a wealthy few in Jakarta, thousands of kilometers away.

We are heading into the Grand Valley of the Baliem, a lush, fertile, and wide expanse cut by the Baliem River through the Central Highlands of Jaya. In some areas, the place supposedly has remained in the Stone Age. The Dani, Lani, and Yali tribes are the primary inhabitants of the Baliem, though hundreds more tribes are scattered throughout the surrounding forests. The Dani are farmers, growing neatly ordered fields of sweet potatoes and creating elaborate irrigation systems. They get along with their neighbors these days, but as recently as 1960, cannibalism was practiced here. As we begin our descent into the valley, I can swear that I see a naked man brandishing a large spear and racing through the fields below. I get an inkling that we are in for an adventure.

We bump down onto the Wamena airstrip, more like a football pitch than a runway, and as we disembark from the plane into the refreshing mountain air, we are met by hundreds of villagers who have come to watch the spectacle of the landing. Everyone is smiling, either happy to see us or joyous at witnessing the landing of something so extraordinary as this metal bird which has fallen from the sky.

Most of the onlookers are men, many of whom are completely naked except for thin and hollow gourds that cover their penises, held in place by a string around their waists. Women are mostly topless, and wear only skirts woven of grass. Some of the men and women are clad in the most ill-matched clothing: wildly colored polyester trousers, white hats out of Al Capone's Chicago, and extra-small t-shirts with inscriptions like "U.S. Justice Department," "Metallica: Kill 'Em All Tour," and "Born to Raise Hell."

Wamena is a sprawling grid of dirt and gravel lanes, dead flat in contrast to the peaks lining the valley. Schools, missions, *warungs*, and dozens of government buildings are scattered haphazardly throughout the town center. The large outdoor Pasar Nayak market is a cultural treasure, if somewhat dirty and smelly. Wet floors are lined with rotting vegetables and remnants of pig carcasses, but the mélange of faces, customs, and souvenirs make it a delight to get lost here. Dani men wander the aisles, their bodies smeared in pigfat and soot to insulate them from the crisp morning air. Most wear only *horim*, the tubular penis sheaths made from dried gourds, and perhaps an elongated necklace of cowry shells.

The Dani sell fine stone axes called *kapaks*, along with bows made of laurel and rattan, and spears of myrtle, all items that they still use. There are grass skirts, bark string bags, rattan bracelets, Asmat carvings, bone headdresses, shells, bird of paradise feathers, and of course plenty of penis gourds. The Dani are aware that these items have tremendous National Geographic appeal, so prices are high, not to mention that the locals now ask for a rupiah note or a cigarette in exchange for a photo pose. However, there remains a refreshing innocence to it all.

The men are like little children trying their hand at a business transaction. They try to sell items at ridiculously over-inflated prices, then realizing they have been caught doing so, smile sheepishly and look at the ground, their lips forming into an embarrassed pout.

Others wander up, grinning ear to ear, and take us by the hand to show us their friends' wares. One man named Yogorok Willy, with a flattened mop-top hairstyle and painted face, grips our hands like a scared five-year-old and guides us to his acquaintance, who squeezes out a few tunes on his bamboo mouth harp.

Dani women sell most of the produce, the bulk of which is made up of sweet potatoes, carrots, and turnips. Several of them wear ornately crafted orchid fiber necklaces, which dangle above their sagging breasts. I notice that many women are missing the upper joints of up to five or six fingers; when I ask about this, I learn that when a family member dies, custom dictates an axe blow to the hand, ensuring an everlasting memory of the pain and grief of death.

It is amazing that Dani traditions have remained so intact. Although they live far from the rest of the world, there have been attempts to "civilize" them. During the 1970's, the Indonesian government launched the appropriately named Operation Penis Gourd, in which the Dani and other tribal groups were made to put on clothing and vacate their grass huts and tree house shelters. Needless to say, this endeavor failed miserably, as the Dani were stricken with all sorts of skin diseases, and thus left to return to their original ways.

The missionaries have also tried to tame the Dani, arriving in the Baliem in the late 1940's and encouraging the heathens to abandon their nakedness and come into the house of the Lord. The missionaries, to their credit, have done an excellent job of bringing agricultural innovations, first aid posts, and schools into the area, and their air transport service is now the only way to get into the interior without travelling weeks or months on foot. However, they have also brought disease and outside ideas that have caused internal strife. Looking at the culture and technology of the Dani, I don't see that the missions have added any great miracles to a society that in some ways is its own Eden.

Upon arrival, we make the acquaintance of Uraipen, an outgoing and handsome young chap in a Berkeley Music Festival t-shirt. He speaks very passable English, in addition to Indonesian, Dani, and Lani, and we agree to hire him as a guide. We lay out a route, discuss provisions, and agree on hiring one porter to carry food.

The next morning, Uraipen introduces us to Pennius, our porter to be. After the sophistication of the Nepali trekking scene, it is amusing and somewhat disconcerting to see the state of affairs here in Irian Jaya. Pennius, a gangly fellow with a natty and bushy Afro, has no backpack, nor any kind of device for hauling supplies. Instead, he has a burlap sack full of holes, into which is stuffed a disturbingly small amount of food, given the fact that four of us will be walking for almost two weeks. There isn't even a rope tied around the sack, and when I ask Uraipen how Pennius plans to carry everything across rivers and over mountains, Uraipen looks at me with a "how can you be so stupid" grin, and says in a matter-of-fact way, "In his hands, of course."

Pennius's footwear is another concern; extra-large hiking boots without laces flop around on his sockless feet. When we express concern that he will develop blisters, Uraipen translates something to Pennius, who grins like a moron, then giggles like a mischievous child every time we look at him. Hitomi instructs me to pack extra moleskin in our first aid kit.

Eventually we get our ragtag group together and march out of Wamena, past the orderly fields and thatched roundhouses of Dani villages. Bananas and sweet potatoes appear to be the staples here, though we also come across peanuts, pineapple, sugar cane, and a large, fleshy, and very tasty gourd, the name of which Uraipen translates as *buu asli*, Indonesian for "original fruit."

This is the first place we have seen in our travels where men share the burden of life's daily tasks. Dani men stop to greet us as they return from the fields, strapping muscular warriors with children's smiles and the gentlest handshakes I have ever experienced. Each man makes a point of shaking Hitomi's hand, then my own, until I fear that if this continues, we will wear out our arms and make little progress.

The men greet us with resonant cries of "*wa*," a word that means hello, goodbye, thank you, how's the weather, and a dozen other things, making communication here easy and fun. The men often ply us with piping hot sweet potatoes, roasted on beds of hot wood embers, and we gobble these down as we "*wa*" our way down the trail. By late afternoon we reach Abimbak, a tiny village perched on a hilltop, overlooking a steep ravine. The once-warring tribes in this area strategically located most of their villages on high ground, positioned as defensive fortresses.

The local school headman comes out to greet us, and guides us to his home, where we are to stay the night. Uraipen and Pennius begin making supper, a delicious affair of noodles and fried vegetables cooked in shrimp paste and coconut milk. (Uraipen says he learned the recipe from a tourist.) The headman brings out a guestbook full of comments and anecdotes from foreigners who have come before us. The book has a signature section for all visitors, and we are numbers 159 and 160, a figure gathered over four years of tourism in the village. That is only forty visitors per year, in a village quite near a road. In a shrinking world, full of vagabonds bent on exploration, I take comfort in these figures.

One of the primary luxuries of leisurely and aimless travel is having time to be timeless. In Abimbak, we pass the remaining hours of light sitting with Onees, the headman. Villagers come to shake our hands, then join us to sit and take in the mountain air, while we all idly watch the local children play a game of soccer.

Everyone has a contented look and a peaceful demeanor, and there is no sense of hurry or urgency anywhere. I think of my life back home, and how often friends—and I—commented on how the years passed at what seemed like the speed of light. Here, the afternoon could be an eternity.

After eating, we resume our sitting outside, and the children are replaced by a gathering of locals who play various homemade instruments, one of which looks like a large bass cello. The Dani are talented and exuberant musicians, and melodic singers as well, and this evening's gathering to sing, strum, and be together is repeated in every village we visit, night after night. Sadly, one never experiences this in Wamena, where electricity and television have arrived.

The following morning, we realize why Pennius is carrying such a light bag of food. Evidently, we have been unwittingly enrolled in the Irian Jaya Trekker's Weight Loss Program. The program is as follows: eat a few crackers for breakfast, then sweat buckets climbing 800 meters through jungle and mountain in the hot sun.

Hunger aside, we are feeling strong, and I worry that we will wear out Uraipen and Pennius, who have grown soft living in town. Pennius, as expected, has developed blisters, so we make several stops to treat them and give him moleskin, and are rewarded for our efforts with a handful of extra crackers.

Trails here are steep and slippery, with long traverses around valley folds to reach safe river crossings. Out of the forest cover, the going is tedious in the hot sun, and it takes all day to reach villages just a stone's throw across the ridge.

In the hamlet of Bolobur, we come across dozens of men and women sitting on the trail wailing and screaming. Many people are crying so hysterically that they seem to be going into a trance. Uraipen informs us that we have walked into a funeral.

I feel uncomfortable, and am ready to move on and leave the people to their grieving, but the village headman invites us to sit and join them. He points out a woman whose body is caked in chalky white clay, making her look like a ghost. Her husband is the one who has died, and surrounding her are the closest relatives.

Uraipen translates for us, and says that the villagers have been sitting like this for two days. This outpouring of grief will continue for one more day, after which a pig will be slaughtered and a giant feast held to celebrate the departing of the dead man. The headman grins in anticipation when he talks about the feast, and invites us to stay a few days and join them.

Hitomi is stunned by this whole scene, as am I. In our cultures, death is private and hidden, usually filled with nothing but sadness. Here, the entire community has turned out for a therapeutic crying session, followed by a fiesta to celebrate it all. Nobody has even batted an eye at the four complete strangers who have waltzed right into the midst of this.

Many people back home would label this place "primitive." The farming implements and hunting weapons are made of stone or wood, the houses are constructed of straw thatch or grass, and no one is wearing a stitch of clothing other than the woven grass skirts and penis gourds. There is no electricity or piped water, and in this village, no mission, school, or other sign of "civilized" encroachment. Yet as I look at the mourners around us, I think that my modern and "developed" society could learn a lot of very simple and essential truths and skills from this culture. Perhaps, in losing traditions and lifestyles like these in the face of the onslaught of "progress," we are actually making giant leaps backwards.

We alternate between extremely taxing eight-hour days (sometimes gaining and losing 2000 meters of elevation) and gentle three-hour saunters. Yet when we ask Uraipen how the next day's march will compare to the present one, he always answers with a cheerful "same same." We are still surviving on our cracker diet, though only with the help of the sweet potato gifts we continue to receive everywhere. Pennius's blisters have hardened, but he insists on being given new moleskin each morning, taking great satisfaction in watching Hitomi show him how to put in on for the umpteenth time.

Following the Toli River, we stroll into the village of Mamet, a bustling place perched on a hillside shelf. There are several compounds of thatched roundhouses, a gravel airstrip, and a dozen missionary houses, the kind one sees in the "Let's rejoice in the beauty of His world" posters that can be found in cheap restaurants or guesthouses all over the world.

There is also a large church, where Mamet's entire male population sing gospel at the top of their lungs. Shortly after our arrival the men flood out of the pews, holding bibles and wearing more clothing than we have seen in the past week. They are attired in ill-fitting slacks and suit jackets, with top hats mashed down over their thick hair. The scene is like something out of Peter Matthiessen's *At Play in the Fields of the Lord* or Paul Theroux's *Mosquito Coast*.

Hundreds of naked kids escort us across the airstrip and into the village, all vying for the honor of holding our hands, and they lead us to a mission house where we can stay the night. The house is in complete disrepair, barren inside except for a rickety wooden table and bench. The other houses are in the same state, and we are told that the missionaries have long left Mamet, though an Indonesian pastor still flies in now and then to check on his fold.

What amuses me to no end is that half an hour after the Dani men come out of church, I meet them again by the river, this time in their penis gourds, smoking and splashing water on each other. They seem deeply absorbed in the moment, and just roll with whatever life brings, whether singing along in church or hanging out naked at the water's edge.

We descend the steep path out of town to the river, and the entire village follows us down to watch us bathe. This has happened in places like Tibet or China, where people gawked at us, stared obscenely, and would not give us any privacy. Yet here, it is very comfortable. After all, the Dani find clothing repugnant, so there are no hang-ups about nudity, and it is a real event for them to have a bath with the foreigners. We do attempt to gain some semblance of privacy with a few half-hearted urgings of *"pergolah!"* ("scram!"), but we soon give in to the wide smiles around us and enjoy our bath. Half the village joins in, splashing, soaping up, laughing, and making merry.

Our food supply has dwindled to almost nothing, so it is with great relief that we reach the town of Karubaga, which has a guesthouse, several food kiosks and *warungs*, a hydro station, and even a weekly Merapati flight to Wamena.

Sitting down to make some notes in my journal, I am taken aback when Uraipen comes over and asks me to give him money to buy food.

"Uraipen, we gave you money back in Wamena," I tell him. "Our payment for the trek included all food, which we agreed that you would buy, remember?"

Uraipen fidgets nervously and mumbles that he doesn't remember.

Hitomi looks across the room at me and rolls her eyes; she told me earlier that she had an inkling something like this was coming. I tell Uraipen that we will buy the food here, but that the money spent will be deducted from his salary, a plan which he refuses. There is a stony silence for the next half hour, as we aren't willing to play this game, and Hitomi and I finally decide that we are better off making this last segment of our trek ourselves. We can buy food here, the trails have been easy to follow, our Indonesian is adequate enough for dealing with the villagers, and the Dani everywhere have been pleasant and accommodating. Thus we inform Uraipen that we are terminating his services.

Realizing how much he will lose in salary if he leaves now, Uraipen agrees to use the money from his pay for food. The gesture saves face, but at this point, we feel it is better to part, and we tell him so. Fortunately, the Dani do not seem to harbor grudges, and Uraipen is as relaxed about the whole thing as he is towards anything else. Soon he and Pennius are cooking us a last supper and giving us advice on which trails to take in the days ahead.

Pennius, upon being informed that he is fired too, roars with laughter at Uraipen's inability to take us for a ride, then spends the next half hour trying to wheedle all the remaining moleskin from our first aid kit. After he gives me one of the most tender and healing leg massages I have ever had, I concede willingly.

A week later, we are back in Wamena, in time to witness a fighting festival. The Dani and other tribes in the area have long engaged in ritual warfare, mock battles that serve to preserve tradition, sharpen strength and skills, and release tension. Rival clans used to adorn themselves with bones, feathers and paint, then gather on opposite sides of a valley, brandishing spears and bows, taunting each other with derisive hoots, whistles, and yells. Eventually, a frontal assault would take place, and then everyone would retreat for a pig feast. People were rarely killed, and the battles served to strengthen the clans.

The Indonesian government decided that any type of warfare was bad (excluding their own military abuses in East Timor and elsewhere) and outlawed the clan battles. It claims total success in its efforts to pacify the Dani, although there have been reports of clan warfare taking place deep in the jungles of Irian Jaya. However, seeing the potential of such spectacles to bring tourist dollars, the government has authorized annual fighting festivals in the Wamena area.

Tribes and clans gather on a vast expanse of cleared field on the outskirts of town. Each group is elaborately decorated in different colors, painting their bodies and wearing long bones through their noses, ears, and cheeks, with regal headdresses of cassowary, egret, and bird of paradise feathers perched on their heads. Many of the warriors sport armbands made from pig testicles and necklaces of pig intestines, which ward off evil spirits and ensure good luck.

The warriors spend hours primping and preening, flexing their weapons, and making yodels and catcalls, before charging the other side for all of two minutes. The scene resembles a rousing game of Capture the Flag more than it does a battle, and the spirits of the audience and participants are exceedingly high.

The entire town of Wamena has turned out for the event, and we run into Yogorok Willy, who won't let go of Hitomi, clinging to her hand and gently calling her "Mama." We also spot Uraipen, who is very happy to see us, asking if we know of any other tourists who might be interested in trekking here. Pennius is missing, and when we ask where he is, Uraipen replies that he is walking all the way back from the last village to save money by not taking a *bemo* (share taxi). Hitomi asks Uraipen why he is wearing the wool socks that she gave to Pennius as a present, and he turns a bit pale and sheepishly replies that he purchased them from him. We grin, looking forward to Pennius's version of the story.

While the battles are raging, several pigs are prepared for the feast to follow. The pigs are held in the air by several men, who grip their ears and hooves. One man then shoots an arrow into the midsection from several feet away, and the pig is then dropped, squealing and spurting blood, onto the ground, where it soon dies. This method of slaughter ensures that a large wound is inflicted causing rapid bleeding.

The pig is placed on a roaring fire and singed, the skin bubbling and turning black. It is then placed into an earthen oven made of heated stones, and smothered with rattan leaves and smoked until it is ready for eating. Pigs here are very valuable commodities, usually reserved only for funerals and weddings, or used as settlements for wrongdoings. The Dani also perform traditional slaughters for tourists—for a fee of several hundred dollars—but today, the entire event is on the Baliem, and everyone is enjoying themselves.

Long out of film, I glance over at Hitomi, who is as sun drenched, incredulous, and wild eyed as I am. She remarks that if this event were taking place in Bali, Nepal, or even Tibet, there would probably be at least 5000 foreigners in attendance, including a National Geographic photographer or two. Yet here in the Baliem, there are about thirty foreigners on hand to witness this spectacular event, some of them missionaries or expatriates living somewhere in Indonesia. As the sun begins to cast its long afternoon shadows over the valley, I ponder retiring to this simple neck of the woods, trading in my bicycle and panniers for a penis gourd.

Chapter Ten
Bali and Java:
Dancing With the Gods

> *Every trip we take deposits us at the same
> forking of the paths; it can be a shortcut to
> alienation — removed from our home and distanced
> from our immediate surroundings, we can afford to
> be contemptuous of both; or it can be a voyage into
> renewal, as, leaving our selves and posts at home,
> and travelling light, we recover our innocence
> abroad.*

Pico Iyer

When we flew in from Australia, Kuta Beach marked our return to the developing world. Today, returning to Kuta Beach from Irian Jaya is more akin to landing in Manhattan. At eleven p.m. the town is wide awake. Discos blare, vendors ply their wares to gangs of inebriated foreigners, and impoverished women implore visitors to take their daughters for the evening.

Barely clad bodies throng the narrow streets, passing along in a steamy blur, attacked on all sides by a mass of humanity trying to make a living. My ears are filled with cries of "Transport boss," "Hello ring boss," and "Give you morning price, how much you last price." Hitomi is beseeched in Japanese with *"Konnichi wa, ogenki desu ka, yasui omiyage arimasu yo,"* and *"sayonara"* ("Good afternoon, how are you, I have cheap souvenirs, goodbye") as we make our way through the crowded, rubbish-covered streets.

Momentarily separated from Hitomi by the crowd, I run into the arms of a muscular woman saturated in perfume and makeup, who quickly works her hands to my crotch and then my pockets, looking for a wallet. As I tear away from her grasp, I look into her face to discover that "she" is a man, one of the female impersonators known as *orang bencong* who try to separate drunken foreign men from their wallets.

Reuniting with our bikes (which, surprisingly, have not been sold, stripped, or ridden halfway around the island) we make a beeline out of Kuta, and soon find ourselves surrounded by lush scenery. Lime green rice paddies are delicately sculpted into near vertical hillside terraces, next to which lies dense jungle full of creepers and vines. The quiet on the roads is disturbed only by the occasional drone of a motorcycle whizzing past.

The terrain is extremely hilly, but no match for our steel quadriceps, and by midday we ascend into Ubud, Bali's cultural capital. Tucked into the rainforest, Ubud has long been an artists' colony, and most of Bali's eminent dancers, painters, carvers, and musicians hail from this region. Unfortunately, Ubud is undergoing the same fate as Kuta, rushing into the hedonistic dream of free market capitalism.

Every shop in Ubud fronts a sign heralding "artist's home," "master carver within," "painter's gallery," or "learn *gamelan* and shadow puppet from professional here." Ubud is the birthplace of the Balinese school of painting, which favors scenes of local village life over the more traditionally popular scenes from the epic Hindu legend, the Mahabaratra. The shops now offer cheap prints depicting peasant farmers and Indian Ocean sunsets, and these hang on the shelves next to "I Love Bali" t-shirts and batik clothing.

Yet Ubud is not all bad. It is nowhere near as crass as Kuta, and there are places like Pondok Posok, a quiet retreat co-operated by Balinese and foreigners, where cozy rows of futons and cushions are set up under the shade of a banana tree. Here, one can while away the afternoon reading from the extensive multilingual library, or listening to the melodic and peaceful sounds of the *gamelan* floating along in the breeze.

Pondok Posok offers language courses, cooking lessons, dance, massage, shadow puppetry, and art instruction, and a mix of foreigners and Balinese take part in the activities. As Hitomi and I sit and sip tea, a wizened Balinese man with a wispy white beard patiently teaches a German lad how to strike a *saron* and *ketuk*, instruments used in the *gamelan* orchestra. Across the courtyard, an American woman slowly enunciates sentences before a group of young Balinese girls, who take in every word she pronounces.

Perhaps the nicest thing about Ubud is the ease with which one can escape the tourists and craft shops. On an afternoon walk, I spend less than fifteen minutes following a path in the jungle before I am transported to a Bali of myth. The place is a virescent painting, composed of paddies of rice saplings, grassy fields, and swarms of butterflies, with dense forest canopy as a backdrop. Everything sparkles in the afternoon sunlight. The hues and tones of the vivid greenery range from ivy to chartreuse. Traditional homes, picturesque bungalows with storybook fruit gardens, nestle against the deep forest. The silence is so strong that a rice stalk ruffled by the wind creates a symphony of sound.

There are few people about, although a group of women in brightly colored sarongs pass by, gracefully balancing ceramic water jugs on their heads. They walk with hips swaying, humming to themselves as they move through the fields. I chance upon a group of young maidens, bathing bare-breasted in a knee-deep pool of cool, clear water. They seem neither embarrassed nor bothered by my intrusion, and merely smile in greeting before continuing with their ablutions.

Farther down the path, I come across a gathering of men, huddled in a circle and chanting excitedly. They are watching a cockfight, and those who have gambled on the red-plumed rooster—who has torn his opponent into a bloody mess of feathers and slashed skin—are fervently anticipating their winnings. I am given a few suspicious looks, as if I am not supposed to witness this side of Bali.

I marvel that time travel is actually possible here. I have been transported from the fleeting sensations of the chaotic present into a past where time seems to stand still. Back in town, packs of tourists are rushing about, snapping shots of every temple and shrine, never seeing the life that is going on just under their noses.

Inspired by my surroundings, I pause to sit beside a cascading fall and make a sketch of a Dani warrior. It turns out well, and I wonder if I can sell it back on the streets of Ubud for a "morning price."

The arts are an integral part of people's lives in both Bali and neighboring Java. In almost every village we pass through, we come across *gamelan* sessions, ensembles of men and women playing a variety of bamboo instruments that emit resonating and melodious scales. The *gamelan* orchestras often accompany any type of dance or drama in Indonesia, but in the small villages, people gather and play simply to pass a hot afternoon together.

Wayang is another vibrant art form. *Wayang* means "ghost" or "shadow," and is a form of theater practiced since around the eighth century B.C. The shadows of puppets or actors are projected onto a screen lit from behind, while a narrator tells a story. In Bali, *wayang kulit* (shadow puppets) are a big favorite, but *wayang* is also performed by masked dancers, or by actors imitating shadow puppets.

The shadow figures originally represented deceased ancestors, returning to the world of the living to check on their descendents. The puppeteer acted as a bridge between the spirit world and the world of the living, and *wayang* was used as a prayer to appease the gods and ensure abundant harvests, fertile women, and a healthy village. This living religion continues today, and *wayang* address topics including menstruation, politics, and the building of new hotels. Performances serve to educate the rural population, many of whom have little schooling. The shows also preserve tradition and custom, and serve as harbingers of good fortune. Thus the Balinese and Javanese remain well connected to their pantheon of gods, and the countryside is alive with drama, dance, and music.

We cycle on through this celestial land, our eyes dazzled by the verdant feast, ears soothed by the constant musical accompaniment, and even our taste buds are stimulated and sated, as the fruits of Bali are truly the nectar of gods.

Mangoes in Bali are sweeter than any others in the world. Paring the dark green skin of the heavy fruit reveals pulpy orange flesh the color of a perfectly ripe pumpkin. Hitomi and I consume at least a kilo each day at the fruit stalls that line the streets of each village, along with other exotic treats like papaya, guava, and pineapple. There are *rambutan*, litchi-sized balls with a hairy and prickly red skin, inside of which lies a transparent egg, much like a grape but far sweeter. We also sample *mangosteens*, *salak*, stinky *durian*, thirty or forty varieties of bananas, and the giant jackfruit, a ten-kilo spiked football which opens to reveal small, sweet pods.

In spite of the often unsanitary conditions, people here look extremely healthy, with shiny skin and robust features. I credit this to the natural treats that the gardens of Bali provide.

We finish cycling around the island, moving over the steep foothills of Gunung Agung and Gunung Batur, two enormous volcanoes that we stop to climb. The north side of Bali is hotter and less verdant than the south, covered in lava rock and the debris of volcanic eruptions. In Air Sanih, schools of dolphins flip and glide through the calm waters along the coast, while on land, schools of children playfully chase us, cooing, "I love you, I love you." What a way to travel.

Crossing to Java, we see a few visible signs of change. There are more people on the road, villages are a tad larger, and there are not as many tourists. In fact, there aren't any. Locals seem kinder and friendlier.

Another difference is the number of mosques scattered throughout each town. While most Balinese practice a form of animistic Hinduism, the Javanese are predominantly Moslem. Hitomi has worried about travelling in a Moslem country as a female cyclist, but her fears quickly dissipate as we are shown nothing but generosity and kindness everywhere.

Mosques sit next to the road at the entrance to most towns and villages. Usually, someone sits in front of the mosque with a loudspeaker, preaching passages from the Koran and encouraging donations from passers-by. Yet when they see us cycling through, they begin to scream every English word they know, broadcasting throughout the entire village their cries of "Hello! Goodbye! My name is Afi! It is a book, and you are a pen!"

There is chaos on the road. Buses and trucks compete fiercely, swerving to pass the scores of bicycles and horse carts that take up most of the road. People on bicycles carry amazing loads: enormous bags of rice piled high and wide, cords of wood, bananas stacked far above riders' heads, and baskets of almost every object imaginable. There are village-to-village brush salesmen, ice cream and *es campur* vendors, and we even come upon one fellow with a sofa strapped across his back rack, with an old man reclining on the sofa, smoking a cigarette!

Climbing gently around volcanic slopes, we wheel into the small town of Kalibaru and stop at a small inn. The rooms have views of coffee and tobacco plantations, but this is about it for amenities. Our room is full of mosquitoes, and the mattress crawls with bedbugs. Visiting the toilet in the night, I discover that the ladies sitting around the courtyard winking at me are part of a brisk love trade. I chuckle to myself, thinking that despite Allah's missives, the world really is the same everywhere.

The following morning, on the road to Jember and Lumajang, we climb a long and winding pass. Women and children stand in the hairpin road bends and direct traffic, letting approaching drivers know if there are oncoming cars. It all seems pointless, as there is almost no traffic on the road through the forest, yet at every turn there are pointers and wavers. I later learn that drivers are supposed to toss coins to these people, but not one of the few vehicles we see slows down or opens a window. Perhaps the government is now footing the bill. Whatever the case, the array of jobs and services offered in the developing world is beyond description.

There may be no traffic going over the pass, but on either side is an unending parade of bikes, cars, horses, and even water buffaloes. Cycling is pleasant enough, though hot and dusty, and there is a constant supply of food and drink throughout the day. Our lunch is a regal affair of jackfruit curry, potato pancakes, and *gado-gado*, an assortment of vegetables in spicy peanut sauce.

As we pedal through the countryside, I notice dozens of people hanging from small ladders, their legs submerged in the canals that snake throughout the fields. The people look very relaxed and calm, staring out at us as we pass, and I comment to Hitomi, "What a pleasant way to spend an afternoon beating the heat!"

She laughs and tells me to look more closely at the bathers. I do, and am horrified to discover that no one is sitting in the water to cool down—they are relieving themselves!

These canals flow into each town, where scores of people are washing their clothes and dishes in the water. My jackfruit curry begins to gurgle noisily in my stomach.

Our senses continue to be assaulted with a barrage of odors, sights, and sounds. Bells clang, dust flies, the smell of sewage wafts through the air, rice paddies glisten, faces and bodies drip with sweat. Everything is raw, entertaining, alive, and at times, exhausting. For every stalk of sugar cane on the roads north of Brisbane, here there is a human being, and all around us are the sinewy arms and legs of lifetimes of manual labor.

Hitomi and I have been trying to put our finger on why we feel so strong cycling here, doing long hours and long mileage without feeling the slightest bit tired. I think it is because there is so much life surrounding us. It is impossible to become bored here, as a thousand things happen every second of the day. It is sheer exhilaration to cycle among—and be part of—this frantic mass of humanity.

Malang is an attractive enough city, despite its size, and we spend several days there. It is graced with large, shady parks and excellent restaurants, and is an extremely affluent place compared to the stretch of East Java we have just traversed. There are neon-lit shopping plazas, run primarily by the Chinese, whose grip on commerce thrives this far south down the Southeast Asian trail. Well-dressed children with cotton candy stuck to their faces follow their dapper parents on evening strolls. Teenagers ride pirated copies of Specialized and Giant mountain bikes, careening with abandon through the wide boulevards past flower sellers, beggars, and open squares where masked dancers perform late into the sultry night.

On our last morning in Malang, we meet Marijke Van Hoorsten, a Dutch woman doing a Ph.D. on Hindu statues in Indonesia. She tells us that the influence of animism here greatly changed the nature of Hinduism as it spread to Bali. The Pantaran temples are an example of this, not too far off our route, and Marijke urges us to pay a visit, so after breakfast we cycle the flat earthen track leading to the site.

Pantaran is a set of temples dating from the twelfth century, with bas-relief carvings that are still intact. At the main temple, scenes from the Hindu Ramayana epic are carved in stone, with the legendary hero Hanuman confronting winged monsters, demons, and other forces of evil. I usually dislike visiting temples, shrines, and architectural wonders, because it is generally the case that thousands of slaves were forced to toil on the buildings, often losing their lives in the process. Today, however, I take a less critical view. I imagine living before the age of science and reason, unable to explain nature's marvels like thunder, lightning, earthquakes, and volcanic eruptions. Especially in Java, where active volcanoes dominate the landscape, people must have felt a strong need to build these edifices and appease the angry gods responsible for the destructive power of the elements.

We cycle four hours to the town of Trenggalek, where all three hotels are full. Some towns have a bad feel from the minute we arrive, and Trenggalek is such a place. Nobody is able or willing to understand our passable Indonesian, nor can anyone speak English or other languages. As night falls, we cycle to the police station to ask for help and are given the name of one of the full hotels we have visited. The police tell us that we must demand a room more forcefully. We return to the hotel, and I do my best Indonesian version of "give us a room or else," while Hitomi glares at the staff. We get a room.

As we drop onto our springy and bumpy mattress, ready for a long sleep, a festival springs to life outside our window. It is accompanied by the most horrendous blaring music, a wailing din that sounds like someone who has just been poked in the eye or kicked in the testicles. As the madness rages on outside, we give up on sleep, play dominoes, and thank our stars that towns like Trenggalek are few and far between.

The Trenggalekis have informed us that Pacitan is 200 kilometers away and all downhill. We curse them all as we gasp up the steep hills that greet us about thirty kilometers out of town. Most of Indonesia has been moderately hilly, the roads forever skirting volcanic slopes, but the road we are riding now is brutally vertical, and a few hours in the direct sun and soupy air leave both of us debilitated.

I have a very bad heat rash, and Hitomi looks ready to pass out, when we come across the village of Trelambo. It is a handful of shacks, a much smaller village than the significant dot on the map indicates. Nevertheless, it is far more endearing than Trenggalek. A boy, not more than twelve or thirteen years old, rushes out of a house and stands very stiffly in front of me. He raises his hand in salute and screams, "Hello missus!"

He then turns to Hitomi and greets her with "Good morning George!"

This turns out to be the extent of his English. His name is Bagong, and putting our Indonesian skills to work, we learn that he lives with his large and loving family of twelve, in a house that serves as the village *warung*. He takes us there, and over boiled vegetables and tofu with soy sauce, we learn that Bagong is in fact thirteen, that he dislikes girls, except for his mother and sisters, and that he is the proud owner of a Chinese mountain bike, which cost 150 dollars, a small fortune in these parts. We are also assured, by the entire family, that it is truly downhill from here and that therefore we should relax and stay for another glass of iced tea. We end up having three glasses, and enjoying the company of the very animated Bagong, who translates our broken Indonesian into something his family can understand.

We finally take our leave, with all twelve members of the family lined up together waving in unison and chanting, "I love you." At moments like this, I know that all the steep hills, potholed roads, grubby toilets, and parasites have been worth it.

And yes, it is all downhill all the way to Pacitan.

Pacitan Bay is a gem, a long curving beach where crashing surf pummels and polishes the shiny black rocks on the shore. Because it is set in a recreation area, a steep entrance fee prohibits locals from using the area. This is unfortunate, but does leave us with the entire beach to ourselves.

I would love to rest a few weeks here, lingering over sunsets and learning the stories of those who live here, but as usual, Hitomi and I continue on. Our bodies have become so accustomed to perpetual motion that I wonder if we will ever be able to stop.

I have been reading about the ten steps of Shugendo, the religion of Japan's mountain priests. As we climb out of Pacitan, it strikes me that our journey has followed these ten steps pretty closely:

1) *Jigoku*—the body experiences hell (especially in the tropical sun at noon).

2) *Gaki*—survival, hunger, and thirst (perpetual and unrelenting).

3) *Chikusho*—bearing the hardship of animal-like existence (most often felt in the various toilets we have frequented).

4) *Shura*—dispelling feelings from competition and antagonism (too exhausted to argue).

5) *Ningen*—understanding the transient nature of man (joy, anger, sorrow, etc. are all short-lived and unreal. Trying to remember this in places like Trenggalek).

6) *Tenkai*—realizing the vulnerability to downfalls (arriving at the summit, one sees one must go back down…and, of course, back up again).

7) *Homon*—listening to mountain manifestations of divine consciousness, the sound of wind, birds, and trees (and perhaps the belches of diesel exhaust).

8) *Engaku*—grasping the truths and causes of illusions. Forms of nature are undisturbed by wind and rain. Things appear to die in winter, only to be reborn in spring (we often feel like we are about to die at the end of the day, but we get up the following morning and begin the process all over again).

9) *Bosatsu*—spiritual enlightenment, salvation of others through compassion (still looking for this one, although we thought we found some semblance of it on the high passes in the Himalayas).

10) *Hotake*—supreme enlightenment (Buddhahood). No comment, except that it is still another 30,000 kilometers back to the shores of the Pacific.

Travelling this way, we are often told by other travellers how brave, courageous, great, and amazing we are. The locals usually inform us that we are stupid idiots. Hopefully, there is some a balance to be found between the two viewpoints.

A day later, we roll into Yogyakarta, the cultural capital of Java. Yogya, as it is affectionately known, is another sprawling Asian monster city of noise, pollution, and chaos. However, it is less a city than a series of unending villages, and is thus a tableau of scenes of rural life. Farmers chase water buffaloes in rice paddies, and women bear water jugs on their heads and hips as they walk the dusty paths into town.

Yogya is also home to an inordinate number of *becak* (bicycle rickshaw) drivers, to the point where it appears that half the population of the city is employed in the *becak* trade. The minute we separate ourselves from our bicycles, we are constantly badgered by *becak* drivers who demand that we hire them for a day, hour, or week. The drivers who are not currently soliciting our attention can be found lounging in their contraptions by the side of the road, playing cards, chatting, and sleeping in the shade.

I learn from several of the drivers that the average fares number around five per day, each fare being worth somewhere between 500 and 1500 rupiah (twenty to sixty cents). This works out between one and three dollars a day, and I wonder how these people survive. Then again, the per capita income in Indonesia is about 600 dollars a year, so it appears possible to squeeze by, although there isn't much room for error. Between fifteen and twenty percent of people here live in poverty, which is a better figure than other countries in Asia with similar economic climates. Although Hitomi and I have seen a lack of sanitation, education, and medical services in many areas, we have not seen masses of starving or destitute people. Most people have extended families, some sort of dwelling, and enough food to eat for basic health.

Going to do some souvenir shopping, I end up taking a ride with a young man who greets me with, "Stop pollution, take a *becak*!" I ask if I can take a shot at pedalling, and the driver looks at me as if I am insane, but concedes the saddle to me and climbs in the back. We go careening down the street, much to the amusement of other drivers and passers-by. The rig is virtually impossible to steer, and is at least three times as heavy as my own overloaded steed. It is with great humility and respect that I over-tip my smiling driver. I figure that in a past or future life, I have had, or will have, a stint as a rickshaw driver.

Besides its *becaks* and cultural treasures, the highlight of Yogya is its chicken. There is fried chicken, coconut chicken, and chicken with jackfruit curry, which sounds much more exotic than it tastes. Every evening on Jalan Maliboro, the main street, hundreds of vendors set up barbecue stalls and the masses gather for enormous chicken feasts. Because we are some of the only foreigners in the crowd, we are beseeched by amiable Yogyakartans who want to practice their English, find out our story, or just be friendly. It would take an awful lot of doing to become lonely in Indonesia.

Out of Yogya, we pedal up the steep slopes around Mount Merapi, which appropriately means "Fire Mountain." Merapi has erupted countless times throughout history, and as recently as two years ago, when over a hundred people were buried in molten lava spewing out of its bubbling cone. The steep gradient is steamy, but cycling here beats sitting motionless and sweating buckets of perspiration on the plains.

A fellow by the name of Christian invites us to his intimate guesthouse up in Kaliurang. It is a cool resort nestled into a pine forest at the edge of the mountain, and we gladly escape the suffocating heat and settle in for the night. Merapi begins to rumble and thunder, and Christian awakens us at two a.m. so that we can climb to an observation post on the mountain's flanks in relative safety. As dawn breaks, we are treated to the spectacle of Merapi crackling and sparking, and we watch spellbound as fiery red lava rushes down the mountainside under a wide black sky full of stars.

While we sit engaged in this spectacle, Hitomi reminds me that the end of September is approaching, and that we have planned to be back in Nepal. Lately, we have been feeling the need to get off the road for a while, and have decided that Nepal will be the place to do it. We have job connections, friends, and very happy memories there—not to mention that we hope to spend another trekking season in the Himalayas.

Travelling as we do, Hitomi and I try to be good ambassadors for our cultures and countries. Dispelling stereotypes and trying to paint a realistic picture of our homes—something to counter the images that people everywhere receive from television, advertising, and the consumer culture—motivates us to keep moving. I once arrived at a hotel in Malaysia, where a local approached me and asked where I was from. Upon hearing that I was American, he looked me up and down incredulously and asked, "But then why are you so poor?" It was inconceivable to him that an American would choose to travel on a bicycle and not stay in a fancy hotel. Such cultural exchanges certainly give us a reason for being out on the road.

But as constant visitors, we are always taking. We are always the guests, always the ones invited for food, sleep, tea, and friendship. Of course we give of ourselves, and we support local economies with our cash, but we often feel that we are getting far more out of our interactions than those with whom we interact, and many times, we have wanted to give back and go a little deeper. A certain weariness develops when one puts one's head on a different pillow almost every night of the year. It will soon be time for us to settle somewhere for a while, to give something back and take a rest.

Yet with the dawn of every new day, another natural wonder like Mount Merapi beckons, and we rush to our bicycles like little children, eager for the next adventure. I am again reminded of Odysseus, who tried so desperately to return home, but found that he could not leave his ship. He was a captain, able to steer clear of danger and surmount challenges under the blessing of the gods. His men needed him, and he needed his adventures. It is no wonder that whenever he charted a course toward home, another monster or adventure would clutch him in an unrelenting grasp. Perhaps it was a grasp from which he didn't want to be freed.

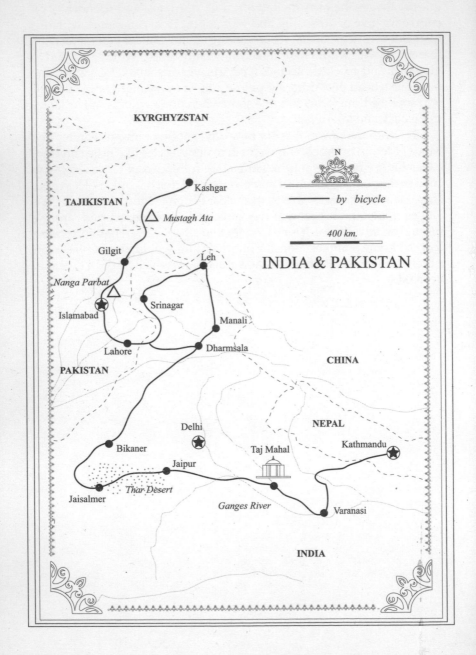

KYRGHYZSTAN

TAJIKISTAN

Kashgar

△ *Mustagh Ata*

Gilgit

Leh

Nanga Parbat

△

Srinagar

Islamabad ★

Manali

Lahore

Dharmsala

PAKISTAN

CHINA

NEPAL

Delhi

Taj Mahal

Kathmandu ★

Bikaner

★

Jaipur

Jaisalmer

Thar Desert

Ganges River

Varanasi

INDIA

N

—— *by bicycle*

400 km.

INDIA & PAKISTAN

Rajasthani beauty, Jaisalmer, India

Monk flashing forbidden Dalai Lama photo, Tibet

Dani men dressed for an afternoon out, Baliem Valley, Irian Jaya

Hitomi battling sheep, Tibet-Nepal border

Ama Dablam, the Goddess's amulet, Nepal

Hitomi with Chinese Moslems, Gansu, China

Thar Desert sunset, Rajasthan, India

Hawa Mahal, Palace of the Winds, Jaipur, India

Hitomi on the open roads of western China, Qinghai Province

"Telepek" hat, the latest in Silk Road fashion, Turkmenistan

Akha woman enjoying betel nut, Thailand

Zaina Beshekeyova under Siberian pines, Kyrghyzstan

Mr. Haidar, host extraordinaire, Karakoram Highway, Pakistan

The "Friendship Highway," Tibet–Nepal border

Field of dreams, Georgian–Turkish border

Desert princess, Rajasthan, India

Warrior dressed for battle,
Irian Jaya, Indonesia

Watchman, Jaipur, India

Pilgrim, Mani Rindu Festival, Nepal

Aghia Sophia, Istanbul, Turkey

Mt. Everest and Nuptse, Khumbu, Nepal

The Eyes of Nepal, Swayambunath Stupa, Kathmandu

In the Ilhara Valley, Cappadocia, Turkey

magical sunsets, the luxury of timeless travel

Part Three

Seeking Shiva, Chasing Alexander: Travels on the Subcontinent and Across the Silk Road

The land of dreams and romance; of fabulous wealth and fabulous poverty; of splendor and rags; of palaces and hovels; of famine and pestilence; of genies and giants, and Aladdin's lamps; of tigers and elephants, the cobra and the jungle. The country of one hundred nations and a hundred tongues, of a thousand religions and two million gods. Cradle of the human race, birthplace of human speech, mother of history, grandmother of legend, great grandmother of tradition, whose yesterdays bear date with the mouldering antiquities of the rest of nations.

The sole country under the sun that is endowed with imperishable interest for alien prince and alien peasant, for lettered and ignorant, wise and fool, rich and poor, bond and free. The one land all men desire to see, and having seen once, by even a glimpse, would not give that glimpse for the shows of all the rest of the globe combined.

Mark Twain, *On India*

Chapter Eleven
Beginnings (II)

This existence of ours is as transient as
autumn clouds. To watch the birth and death of beings
is like looking at the movements of a dance. A lifetime
is like a flash of lightning in the sky, rushing by, like
a torrent down a steep mountain.

Buddha

Motion creates impression. The dynamic fosters ideas, often coming rapid fire and without time for processing. The static, on the other hand, allows for perspective, for examination without external stimuli.

After several months, Kathmandu, the tiny, charming capital of the Himalayan kingdom, is no longer so charming. Its streets are filled with open sewage, and the wealth concentrated in the tourist districts is horribly disproportionate to the hard reality of everyday lives here.

Perhaps worst of all is the pollution. Forty years ago there were no cars in the entire Kathmandu Valley. Today, I can barely make out the shadows of the Himalayas due to the haze, and the city is perpetually blanketed in black smoke. Commuting to work every morning, Hitomi and I join the ever-increasing number of cyclists and motorcyclists who wear face masks to mitigate the effects of the smog.

Not all is bad. I teach Geography at an English school, and every morning, my smiling minions arise as I enter the classroom, shouting in unison, "Good morning Sir! Nice to see you Sir!" Of course, they do this for all the teachers, but I am almost moved to tears each time by their polite and eager faces.

My extensive travels help me turn my classes into a more lively experience for the kids. We put away the dry, factual textbooks they have been using, and instead I bring slides, tell stories, and ask the kids to share their own stories. It is a joy to watch their horizons expand.

I tell the children that I started this journey because I wanted to see the world with my own eyes, hear it with my own ears, and smell it with my own nose. I wanted to form my own impressions, separate from those of my parents, my friends, and the daily newscasters.

I urge them to exercise the same scrutiny out in the daily world; being diligent students, they question me about Australia the following afternoon, and dismiss everything I report as a crock of beans.

Hitomi is across town working for an environmental education project. She tries to make visitors aware of the fragile Himalayan environment, and works to bring Nepalis closer to foreigners by offering free English courses and workshops to porters and lodge owners.

I cycle over to meet her for lunch most days, and we share our joys and frustrations about living in Nepal. Both of us have observed that life in Nepal appears to consist of one long tea party. In my school, teachers often bask in the noon sun, long after the class bell has rung, sipping tea and telling jokes while children patiently wait in the classrooms. Meanwhile, in Hitomi's office there is a perpetual exodus of staff from desk to rooftop, to engage in the same activities.

On one hand, we both find this behavior extremely annoying. I become angry with the teachers for depriving children of educational time, while Hitomi complains that it takes weeks to complete projects that might be done in an hour, if only people would make a concentrated effort.

Yet on the other hand, it is a joy to be in a society that values friendship, conversation, and the joys of the moment far higher than it values work. In Japan or the U.S., one would be fired for drinking tea on the roof merely because the weather was fine.

We foreigners are not the only ones aware of these goings-on. Hitomi's boss, Mr. Sherpa, is a jovial fellow with much money and political clout. He often invites me in to chat during my visits there, and we go to the roof of his building, sip tea, and discuss his upcoming projects and plans. One morning, he points across to the nearby rooftops of various government buildings, where men in long *kurta* shirts and *topi* hats lounge in the sun and speak animatedly. Some are flying handmade paper kites, competing to see whose will soar the highest.

"Dave," Mr. Sherpa says, "do you see my country? Do you see what we are doing? Government workers, supported by our taxes, spending their work hours playing like children."

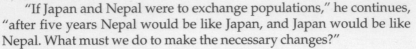

"If Japan and Nepal were to exchange populations," he continues, "after five years Nepal would be like Japan, and Japan would be like Nepal. What must we do to make the necessary changes?"

I don't voice my opinion that it might not be such a good thing if Nepal turned into Japan, or vice versa. I reply to Mr. Sherpa, "What are *w e* doing? Granted, we have discussed a few work-related projects, but mostly we are enjoying the sun, our tea, and each other's company, no?"

Mr. Sherpa looks at me, grins, and proceeds to page a boy on the deck below us to refill our cups.

It has been nice to leave the road for a while, to settle in one place with a routine, and to see the same friends day after day. Getting involved in individual projects has also calmed the tension between Hitomi and me, and given us some breathing room.

Yet just as we are becoming comfortable in our corner of Kathmandu, and thinking of spending the rest of the year under the shadow of the Himalayas, some life-changing news comes from home.

Odysseus was forever being ripped from his moorings, cast out into the open sea in spite of his efforts to sink his anchor. Perhaps this is the fate that awaits us wandering types. This time, however, it is not the road that calls and dislodges us from our nest.

I arrive home one day to find the guesthouse staff all very agitated. They tell me that the American Embassy has been trying to track me down, and that I have to call them immediately. I have not violated any laws or failed to remit taxes, and I still have a valid passport, so my first thought is that there must be an emergency back home.

My suspicions are confirmed shortly after I pick up the phone. My uncle has been trying desperately to find me, and he tells me that my mother has had a recurrence of her non-Hodgkin's lymphoma, a cancer that she has fought off successfully twice in the past. He does not have to say much, other than that my mother's kidneys are failing, and that she is going to die.

This news, so far away, in another world, seems almost as unreal as the call itself. My uncle and I are 10,000 miles apart, talking on a telephone, while in the garden across the street, a farmer stacks cow dung cakes to use as fuel for his cooking and heating fires.

I tell my uncle that I will be there as fast as I can, realizing as I say this that I no longer know how to do things "as fast as I can." I rush to see my friend Rajiv, a mountain-bike-lover-cum-travel agent who has assisted Hitomi and I in our flight plans in and out of Nepal. It is high tourist season in Nepal, and there are no direct flights from Kathmandu to the United States. I must get to either Bangkok or Singapore first, and of course all of these flights have been booked solid for months.

Rajiv calls several friends in the business, and has his assistants do some groundwork, all to no avail. The soonest flight is more than a week away.

"Rajiv," I plead, "I may have a lot of hours to drink tea with you, but I don't have a week, man, I do not have a week."

He looks into my eyes and understands. He has recently lost a family member, and it happened while he was overseas. He has his assistant call back to Singapore Airlines, where another round of "I can't help you" ensues. Rajiv asks for the phone and listens grimly to the person on the other end, and finally says straight up, "You owe me one." He repeats this, enunciating every syllable.

When he puts the phone down, he smiles warmly and says, "Singapore Airlines, tomorrow at ten a.m. Life is about connections, no?"

I hug him, look deep into his eyes, and say, "I owe you one. A very big one."

Suddenly, I switch back into Western mode, mind churning away furiously as I scribble lists of things to pack, notify people here of my departure, and try to prepare myself for what lies ahead. Back at the guesthouse, the staff have told Hitomi about my mom, so she is prepared for the flurry of activity. She will stay for the next few days and take care of our affairs here, before coming to join me. As with the rest of our journey so far, we have very little idea what all this means. We don't talk about it, but there is an underlying feeling that perhaps our journey is over.

My mother died a week after I arrived home, with my uncle and me at her bedside. In the short time we had together, we were able to share loving memories, her thoughts and worries about my future, and also to patch up rifts and unspoken differences that had plagued us in years past. I felt like I was in a strange time warp; jet-lagged and culture-shocked, I now faced seeing how the cancer and subsequent drugs had ravaged my mother. She had been so incredibly strong and independent, and was now wasting away in body and then in mind, in spite of any efforts she made against her condition.

My mother jokingly prided herself on being a model patient, knowing full well how stubborn she could choose to be, and the doctors and nurses in the hospital praised her promptness, cooperation, and stoicism, not to mention the fact that she had never missed a single appointment throughout the ups and downs of her illness.

So it was with great alarm that my uncle tried to pry her from her bed on one of her final mornings, when she told us that she no longer wanted to go to the doctors, and chastised us for waking her in the first place.

Having been so many moons in the East, in cultures where the approach to death and dying is very different, I noticed that my response was not what I expected. In years past, I might have been as adamant as my uncle about the need to preserve my mother's life, wanting to gain for myself another day, hour, or minute with her, to say all the things I had never been able to say, to gaze at her face, and to understand more clearly why I might be who I am.

Yet for the first time I understood that my mom had at last made peace with her cancer, her life, and most importantly, her impending death. As she told me—with my uncle also there beside her—she was ready to rest. Sometimes it is important to struggle, as it gives one great strength and the ability to overcome obstacles. But at other times, struggle is hindrance, and acceptance is what brings peace.

In this case, I could only weep. I wept tears of sadness, and of the pain of loss. But I also wept tears of relief, for my mother's transcendence of her bodily illness, and for the rest that would come for her spirit.

Hitomi arrives a few days later, having put our life in Nepal on hold indefinitely, and at least initially, I relish her love and support. Many family friends also go far out of their way to share grief, relive memories, and try to make my transition to living back home as smooth as possible, given the circumstances.

Yet despite the outpouring of support and love, I feel as if I have lost spiritual stability. I cannot explain this feeling to Hitomi, who treats me with compassion but has never herself lost a parent or sibling. I wrap myself in my grief and try to avoid dealing with the strange society I see on the street everyday, which I can no longer comprehend.

Death is a taboo in America, at least compared to Nepal or Tibet, where it is common to talk about terminal illness, to see dead bodies, and watch public cremations and the scattering of ashes into rivers leading to the Ganges. Death is an inevitable part of life, and it seems that even young children in Nepal have a healthy understanding of what happens to the human body as it ages and expires.

I wander through streets full of riches, where water comes out of the tap, and the electricity works all the time. Yet there is also abject poverty, and I see faces filled with spiritual desperation everywhere I turn. I grow annoyed with people whom I see as spoiled and pampered, and become viciously critical of everything I see, replacing my grief with anger. Hitomi gets tired of my brooding and returns home to Japan for a few months to visit her parents, while I fill my days dealing with lawyers, paperwork, and the bureaucracy of death, tying together and tidying my mother's possessions and the memories of my youth.

I know that I must return to the journey, yet my heart is neither here nor there. I feel as if I am suspended in a limbo. But when I think about what my mother would have wanted, the answer is clear. She would want me to climb high, go far, and make all the journeys she never could.

I also consider the words of a good friend, who correctly accuses me of being a starter but not a finisher. She talks about all the ideas and plans I have had in my life, and how I have gone ahead with so many of them, only to pick up something new when the going got tough, or when a new idea caught my fancy.

These thoughts weigh heavily on me, yet produce no action, and I remain sullen and sluggish, unable to do even the most basic of chores. When Hitomi calls to ask if and when we will return to Nepal, I cannot answer.

This goes on for a few months, with no end in sight. I wake up, drink tea, answer the mail, putter around in the garden, and stare at the walls, wondering what happened to all of my energy and wonder. These things seem as dreamlike as do the stupas and rickshaws of Kathmandu, thousands of miles—if not lifetimes—away.

In the end, it is a simple radio ad that produces action. I am listening to the news one morning when an advertisement comes on for something called a Body Toner. The ad promises that one will become hard bodied and lose ones love handles without doing sit-ups, or any exercise for that matter. Just slip into this new invention while watching TV or lying on the couch, and presto! Fitness arrives.

I have heard this type of claim countless times during my stay here. "Be comfortable! It's easy! Enjoy the good life here in the richest country in the world!" It is a claim that is so pretentious, so full of itself, and most of all, so opposite to every conviction that has driven me on my journey since the beginning.

Within two weeks, I have reserved space on a flight back to Nepal.

Chapter Twelve
Mother India

> *I should be sorely tempted, if I were ten*
> *years younger, to make a journey to India. Not for*
> *the purpose of discovering something new, but in*
> *order to view in my way what has been discovered.*

Goethe

> *A good holiday is one spent among people*
> *whose notions of time are vaguer than yours.*

J.B. Priestly

I always find the journey back to the developing world easier than the other way round. It is simpler to go from fast to slow, and from order to chaos—at least for me. Perhaps I am more used to it, after so many years of travel. Maybe it is because everyone is so damn personable in the Third World, and because there are no strangers there.

Nibbling *dal* and rice, in a small café back in Kathmandu, I watch a man arrive and sit next to a woman at the opposite table. They engage in friendly banter, and I assume that they are husband and wife. Yet when another man enters the café, joins them, and then beckons me over, I learn that the couple is actually not a couple, and that this is the first time they have met!

I return to our guesthouse where Hitomi has been napping. I explain my surprise at what I have seen to my friend Ningma, who laughs and tells me how boring it would be to eat lunch or dinner by oneself—or to do anything else solo, for that matter. Of course, he says, one should join another in a public place and not be bashful about it.

Ningma informs me that he has heard we don't do this in America, and that over there, "if no friend, no talk." He finds this idea completely incomprehensible.

Hitomi has been back from Japan several weeks now, and appears as eager as I am to get back to the journey. She has enjoyed spending some time with her parents, but misses the thrills of the road, and the physical addictions to cycling each day. She's happy to see me in higher spirits, and we quickly map out a route from Nepal to India via the old and little used Rajput road.

It takes us only a few days to climb out of the Kathmandu Valley and over the foothills of the Himalayas, after which we drop into the Terai, the vast plains that constitute the Nepalese-Indian frontier. Countless acquaintances have warned us of what to expect in India. Robbery, sickness, tigers, con artists, and a host of other misfortunes await us; after several travellers tell us that India is worse than China, we wonder if we should reconsider our plan to spend nine months in the country.

Stopping in Lumbini, we go to visit the famous Bodhi tree, where the Buddha allegedly received enlightenment. The site is a serene spot, surrounded by temples, fields of rice, and the chirping of cicadas. We pass a reflective moment under the tree, meditating on the events of the past month and the journey to come. Our silence is broken up by a small boy with large ears who gives the all too familiar "hello, one pen" salute.

We cross the border at Sunauli, a chaotic armpit of a town filled with travel agents, moneychangers, and rickshaw drivers. Women are conspicuously absent. Customs officials thumb through our passports and chastise me for not writing more legibly on my declaration form. One fellow with a bushy handlebar mustache eyes our bicycles and asks where we are going. When we inform him that we are headed to Varanasi, he looks at us as if we are mad, and yells, "Surely you are not travelling with such contraptions as these!"

Gesturing at our overloaded steeds, he continues, "I am thinking you are taking leave of your senses, and recommend that you are finding a proper transportation immediately!" We pull away, wondering what will be next.

Some borders are merely arbitrary lines drawn in the sand, and other than the flags flying on either side, there are no real differences to be found crossing from one side to the other. The India-Nepal frontier is not one of these. Although the terrain doesn't change—the endless miles of rice fields and pipal trees continue, desolate in the cold morning mist— we are immediately aware that we have entered another country. People are everywhere, even throughout the rural countryside. Men wrapped in shawls appear out of the mist, standing silently by the side of the road, or flying down the road on their one-speed bicycles, hell-bent on riding next to us and staring.

We see almost no women in shops, restaurants, hotels, or anywhere else, unlike in Nepal, where most business proprietors tended to be women. Hitomi finds this unsettling at first, but as the men appear harmless, and stare at me as much as they do at her, she soon begins to enjoy their attention.

Most amusingly, there are turds in the road every ten meters, so evenly spaced that it seems like someone has measured where they should be placed. In China they were everywhere, but here there is definitely an order. We joke that we won't need kilometer markers or our cyclometers—distance here is measurable by counting crap!

The state of Uttar Pradesh, home of the Ganges Plain, is one of India's most populated areas. Wherever we go, there is nothing but people. Stop to admire the countryside—people. Stop to eat lunch—people. Stop to look at the map—people.

In every town, orange juice vendors set up their bicycle carts at the side of the road. We stop in each place for a glass, and at ten cents a shot, they can't be beat. Of course, as soon as we stop: people. Hundreds of skinny men surround us as we drink, silently staring, marveling at each sip we take. I whip out my camera for a few shots, but it is impossible to take individual pictures, and each look through the viewfinder reveals a sea of brown faces.

Between towns, bands of scantily clad children chase us, screaming, "*Angreji! Angreji!*" ("English!"), as they run down the road after us. Women slap dung cakes together for fuel; men fill earthen jugs from handheld water pumps, people make cloth on spinning wheels; and hordes of figures in turbans and blankets wander throughout the foggy land, apparently without purpose. Mahatma Gandhi's rural India has not changed one iota in the last fifty years.

In Nautanwa, the first town where we attempt to find lodging, nobody can speak English. When we try to get directions in our stuttering Nepali-cum-Hindi, we are told to go left, right, straight, back the way we came, another few miles, and that there is no hotel in town. Eventually, we manage to uncover a decrepit lodge, where the manager disappears with my hundred-rupee note without making change.

There is nothing resembling a restaurant, though we do find a filthy stall which serves up something that is supposed to be *dal* but looks more like a basin full of morning sickness. As starving cyclists, we dutifully lap it up, a spoon in one hand and the other on our stomachs. We stagger out, still functioning, but still hungry. Fortunately, there are orange, pomegranate, and banana stalls along the street, where we are able to sate ourselves.

For a large town, the pickings are slim. In China, there were always restaurants, cinemas, and shops, but here, they are hard to find. There are parts shops everywhere, with parts for autos, parts for bicycles, parts for hand tools, parts for parts. Most shops seem to be little more than a collection of nuts, bolts, and bric-a-brac. There is no toilet paper, which concerns us after the meal we have just downed. As always with first impressions, I wonder if this town and its trappings are typical of all of India.

Judging by what we have witnessed today, we are a long way from home. The advances of the Internet are still a thousand years from the hovels we have bicycled by, and existence is basic out on the plains of the Terai. People's only possessions seem to be bicycles and dung. Nobody has any money, not to mention electricity, warm water, or even running water. Yet everyone seems to have unlimited time, and nobody appears to be starving.

Drifting on toward Gorakhpur, we shiver in a damp cold that we did not expect to find here. Bedraggled figures in bedsheets squat by the roadside, clutching wooden staffs. The mist creates a deep chill, and I wonder when we will next take a bath, as we have seen no signs of hot water anywhere thus far. I also begin to doubt that the socks and underwear I washed three days ago will ever dry in the coming months. Suddenly, reaching the monstrous Indian cities becomes most desirable.

Our Western road atlas, "the most up to date and fully researched set of maps on India available, with all roads personally driven by the researchers," is completely useless. Half the roads are wrongly numbered or do not exist, and the unmarked junctions and towns make it a sure bet that the authors have never visited this part of the world. Still, the roads are in good shape, traffic is almost nonexistent, and if it weren't for the cold and lack of amenities, the going would be quite pleasant.

Outside Gorakhpur, we come across a large political rally. It is election year in India, and one local candidate's zealots parade up and down the highway, blocking the road. As we enter the throng, the crowd

of mostly young men begins to cheer us on at the top of their lungs, as if
we have entered Olympic Stadium on a victory lap. We smile and wave,
but suddenly, several of the fans decide to chase us, and a mob scene
ensues, with hundreds of bodies storming at us and pressing against
our wobbling bikes. Most fortunately, the crowd is benign, and our pur-
suers merely shriek "Thank you, thank you," at us, eventually allowing
us to escape.

I have heard stories of crazed and hysterical riots between the Sikhs
or Moslems and the Hindus, and I shudder to think of what could happen if these people had different reasons for being out today.

Wheeling into Gorakhpur, we see how everything in India exists at
an extreme. Well-lit streets boast shops packed with appliances, food,
and all other manner of consumer goods, and the gaunt stick figures of
the countryside have been replaced by corpulent men and women, who
waddle from shop to shop. Traffic has gone from the rattle and squeak of
bike chains to a complete ocean of bedlam, with cars, trucks, buses, rickshaws, and thousands of cyclists and pedestrians competing for every
inch of space. Policemen blow whistles, wave batons, and conduct traffic with authoritative voices, but although they control the traffic well,
they are completely inept at giving directions, and send us in circles as
we search for a hotel.

Eventually we find the Marine Hotel, posh, sparkling clean, and
with staff lined up at the door to greet our arrival. The hot bath is itself
worth the rather inflated price of the room.

We opt for the fanciest looking restaurant in town and feast on *palak
paneer*, a homemade cheese and spinach concoction, with *gobi*, a spicy
dish of peas and potatoes, and *naan*, a fresh unleavened bread baked in
a clay tandoori oven.

Families large in both numbers and size surround us. Women in
saris feast as if there were no tomorrow, along with barrel-chested Sikh
men, identifiable by their turbans, long beards, and arm bracelets. Couples
chat in Oxford English, and obese children stuff themselves and laugh
merrily.

Overwhelmed by all that we have taken in during one day's travel,
we retreat to our room and watch the World Table Tennis Finals on
television. The match, between China and Japan, seems a million miles
away from the world outside our door.

It is several hundred kilometers to Varanasi, the holy city on the

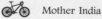

Ganges, and the cold grows worse as we move south. We now cycle in tights and gloves through a flat, gray, and gloomy land where the sun no longer exists. Our days have a sameness to them: by day, we ride through fields lined with excrement, the monotony of the terrain broken by the occasional juice stand, and each night, we arrive in a chaotic town where we recharge our batteries to do it again the next day.

The odd character adds spice to this routine, such as the waiter in Azamgarh who informs us that he used to be a tour guide, and that he can speak five languages.

"English, Hindi, Bengali, and Punjabi I am having complete capabilities in," he proudly informs us.

When I tell him that this is only four languages, he nods his head and replies, "Yes, I am speaking five languages," and proceeds to name the four again.

Indians and Nepalese have this habit of wagging their head from side to side and rolling their eyes when they are answering questions, and the wag is so vague that I can never understand whether it means yes or no. When we ask if we are on the right road, or if a certain meal is available, or if there is a bucket of hot water, we always receive a silent smile and a bob of the head that in no way resembles an answer.

In one *dal* stall, I ask the server to bring us two plates of *dal*. He wags and grins. After twenty minutes without service, I ask if our order has been forgotten. Again, he wags and grins. After another ten minutes, both of us are irate and very hungry, and this time Hitomi beckons the man over and asks where our order is. He wags and grins some more, as if nothing has happened. When we point to the other patrons' plates and then to our own mouths, he says, "Oh, you want to eat," then wags his head, grins, and finally brings us some food.

Five kilometers from Varanasi, a city of some several million, we plunge from the world of hovels and dung onto the Grand Trunk Road. It is India's most major thoroughfare, running from Calcutta, on the Bay of Bengal, all the way to Lahore, in Pakistan, and our arrival at the Grand Trunk Road also marks our entry into holy Varanasi.

As the last meters of dung peter out, we descend into a traffic jam resembling Woodstock. Hundreds of thousands of bodies mount every form of transport imaginable, and in some cases, transport mounts bodies. A cacophony of horns, engines, and black soot envelops us, and we proceed into the throng, grinding to a dead halt. The only street leading off the main highway into town is so packed that even cyclists and pedestrians cannot move. We stand still among rickshaws, cattle, and people hauling carts of bananas, iron beams, steel rods, cement slabs, dripping blocks of ice, and everything else imaginable.

Initially, it is rather terrifying, as the competition for space is intense, and bodies and machines hurtle recklessly toward any vacant spot. However, once we get the hang of things, we start having fun. None of us can move more than a few inches, and from the man next to me—who is propelling at least a hundred pounds of silk on his rickety handheld cart—to the stalled rickshaw drivers on the other side, we are all together, all vividly alive in this throbbing mass of humanity.

After an hour, we near the Ganges and the road disperses into a series of small alleys and lanes, some so narrow that we can barely fit our bicycles between their stone walls. Riding becomes close to impossible, so we dismount and are almost immediately surrounded by a group of very young boys. They clamor for our attention, asking in English and Japanese which guesthouse we want to visit; at eight years old, they speak more Japanese than I can, though they have never been out of the alleyways of Varanasi. We settle for a small, clean place near Dasaswamedhh Ghat, which is a bathing platform on the Ganges named after ten horses supposedly sacrificed here by the Hindu deity Brahma.

The Ganges is referred to as the River of Eternal Life, but it may also be a river of sure death. In Varanasi, it flows languidly with the sludge of human output. It is used by thousands as a toilet, bathhouse, laundromat, garbage dump, and cremation depository. Yet these excesses are what makes the Ganges so appealing.

The river is flanked by *ghats*, platforms which descend into the river and provide access for Varanasi's millions. The ghats teem with life, and my senses are assaulted by a barrage of sights, sounds, and odors. Men in loincloths lather themselves with soapsuds, laughing with abandon as they immerse themselves in the murky brown water. At the next ghat, women submerge themselves fully clothed in saris, and young maidens slip gracefully into dry saris under large towels, held up by grandmothers with watchful eyes.

Dobi-wallahs, the laundrymen of India, beat hundreds of sheets, saris, and pajamas with large wooden paddles. As they finish, hordes of boys swoop down with straw baskets, carry the stiff clothing to waiting rickshaws, and return with yet more garments in need of laundering.

The ghats are active from the first pink rays of dawn, as are the labyrinths of passages surrounding them. Perfume and spice merchants set up their wares, sadhus chant incantations, yogis engage in bodily contortions, and cows trample through the charcoal fires that warm the cold street dwellers. Boats ply the waters of the Ganges, shrouded in early morning mist, and we haggle a passage onto one and float aimlessly along the riverbank. Grizzled barbers are already out shaving the heads of eldest sons who have lost family members, as tradition dictates. The shorn locks, like everything else, are tossed into the river of no return.

Near the barbers are the cremation ghats, where logs are piled in giant funeral pyres. Bodies lie on wooden planks, wrapped like mummies in white cloth, awaiting the fires. After they are burned, the ashes are put into small clay pots and handed over to the bald sons. The men scatter the ashes into the Ganges and perform purifying pujas, completing their living attachments to the deceased.

These rituals stir deep emotions as piercing as the pungent air, redolent of burning bodies, cow dung, and a potpourri of spices. Our spirits are assaulted here by death, by life, by all the things that at home we relegate to the unopened closets of our minds.

I reflect on my own mother's death. She chose to be cremated, and my uncle and I followed her wishes, enacting our own ritual in returning her ashes to the sea in one of her favorite spots. Yet the entire process was far removed from our own emotions and struggles at the time. The cremation happened in an incinerator; the ashes were discreetly locked into a sealed case; and my locks were certainly not shorn in memory and sorrow.

Our sorrow and grief remained private for the most part, and perhaps this is the great luxury of a culture of material wealth and open space. Here in India, death—our greatest fear—is completely public, and all its emotions, demons, sorrows, and trials are thrust in our face everyday. Perhaps in facing death openly, we begin to understand what it means to embrace life.

I sit on the banks of the Ganges and meditate, following my breath in and out. Around me, astrologers offer consultations, women hawk buckets of fresh curd, and beggars ask for alms. The nearby streets are pictures of bedlam: bells clang, seekers chant, rickshaw wallas pursue customers. Yet there is harmony in all the chaos. Amid this assault to my eyes, nose, and ears, I am completely at peace. I feel as if I could stay in this one spot, even die here, without ever needing to move again.

We stay for almost three weeks in Varanasi, studying Hindi, sitting by the Ganges, and immersing ourselves in the ongoing spectacle of life that pulses throughout the ancient city.

Although we are well known to the touts, rickshaw wallas, hotel boys, and others on the streets, we are still treated as if it is our first day in India. Silk salesmen offer us their "best" rates, ten times higher than the normal prices. Boatmen promise "special tours," the only special thing being the hourly wage they will receive. The rickshaw driver who took us across town the past two days for ten rupees, tells us that today he will give us a real bargain of a ride for only twenty!

Rickshaw drivers wait outside five-star hotels, refusing all offers for passengers for weeks at a time, waiting for the one wealthy tourist who will give them a monthly salary in one fell swoop. Never mind that they could have earned the equivalent by taking other customers—or that they might not end up with any rider at all. They are far more content to laze in the sun, waiting for their pot of gold.

I start to get the sense that in India, everything that runs according to my western logic may be turned on its head. The school where I study Hindi has been founded by a renowned "Specialist of Languages," who has received several awards for his "non-grammatical" method of instruction. However, we spend a lot of class time learning pronouns, gender, and sentence structure.

When I point out to the teacher that this is the study of grammar, I am given a long diatribe about why the school's method is world famous, why I am learning Hindi so quickly, and a list of points needed to master the language. It is as if my question has not been heard.

Going to and from class everyday more than makes up for the struggles with the teacher. I am constantly late because I get caught up in mammoth crowds, consisting of Jain festival processions, bodies being carted through the streets to the burning ghats, elephants trampling down narrow roads, or Sikh men following a procession of musicians, dancing wildly as if in a trance. I reach the classroom out of breath, and hurriedly scribble notes into my journal while reciting my grammar points with the other students.

As if the daily intensity was not enough with a clear mind, there are the *bhang* shops. *Bhang* is the leafy part of the marijuana plant, and although it is against the law in India to use marijuana, there are govern-

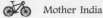

ment *bhang* shops where it is completely legal to obtain the drug. Hitomi and I wander past one during an afternoon stroll, and the menu board offers cakes, biscuits, and chocolates containing marijuana, hash, and opium. I opt for a marijuana chocolate, which tastes like cow shit dipped in nuts and honey, and it sends me on a four-hour high during which I dance wildly with the Sikhs in the street, and begin to wonder if all of India is not on *bhang* all of the time.

Hitomi, who wisely has chosen not to partake, leads me back to the hotel, where we go to the rooftop to escape the madness. Yet in India, even the rooftops pulsate with action. Thousands of boys fly handmade paper kites, battling for position and open space, scrambling up and down flimsy pipes and sometimes jumping across to adjacent roofs.

We engage in sunset bouts of tai chi, which brings some of the kite-flying frenzy to a halt and draws a crowd of curious young smiles. A bold young boy steps up to me and asks, "Uncle-ji, is it kung fu that you are doing?"

In class one morning, my teacher Sonu tells me about the riots here between the Hindus and the Moslems and Sikhs. Varanasi is about thirty percent Moslem, a figure that seems high, but Sonu says they come here to weave cloth for Hindu silk merchants. Moslem-Hindu riots have occurred often, and are usually set off by a new law or local dispute. The Hindu-Sikh riots of 1984 began after the assassination of Prime Minister Gandhi by her Sikh bodyguards.

Riots here are usually short-lived and terribly brutal. People are beaten and set on fire by enraged mobs, with the victims' community retaliating against the attackers in the same way a short time later. The violence is so horrible that people will desperately try to erase their identity. Sikhs have removed their turbans and cut their long locks, and Moslems have removed their *shalwar kameez* outfits. Sometimes, disguise is impossible, as when Moslem attackers ripped the pants off disguised Hindu victims to discover whether or not they were circumcised.

Knowing how crowded and chaotic the streets are normally, I try not to imagine what things must be like during these times of madness. It is easy to see why these riots happen, though, as the intolerance and prejudice here run very deep. My teacher is a well-educated man from the highest caste (Brahmin, the priest caste), yet he seems as ignorant as someone without any education or experience. He tells me that all the riots have been started by Moslems, that Hindus never start fights, and that Brahmins are pure and above the law. According to him, Brahmins only teach, govern, and bring goodness to all of India.

I am reminded of other places in the East, where the hand of fate is far stronger than in the West. While in my culture people often try to change situations that aren't to their liking, in India, things are accepted as inevitable. To tamper with them is to tamper with the work of the gods, something beyond the role of mortals.

A month later, we begin to curve away from the Ganges, leaving some of the masses behind and heading into forests and jungles that slowly begin to give way to the deserts of Rajasthan. On the main road to Bharatpur, I make out what I swear is a bear ahead in the afternoon haze, standing on its hind legs in the middle of the road. When I tell Hitomi, whose eyesight is not as sharp as mine, she looks at me as if I have been eating *bhang* again.

But there is indeed a bear standing in the road. It is on a leash, tethered to a man in a suit jacket who waits at the roadside for the cars to slow down. Once they do, he ambles onto the highway and demands baksheesh from them in order to remove the bear. Once he receives his money, he retreats to his post and the bear takes its position as a traffic barricade once more.

It turns out that the man and bear belong to the Kanjar, a nomadic subset of the Sudra, or "untouchable" caste. The Kanjar have been breeding bears in captivity for hundreds of years and bringing them to the roadsides to earn a living. During the reign of Rajiv Gandhi, Gandhi's brother Sanjay's wife led a campaign against the Kanjar, saying that their practices were a form of animal cruelty. The Kanjar went to the magistrate, claiming that this was their only source of income—as well as their destiny—and won the case. They are now back on the roads with their bears.

In China, the authorities would have built a shoe factory and put everyone to work, but here in India, the world's largest free-market democracy, one can sit by the roadside with a bear on a leash! Anything to earn a living.

Hitomi argues with the bear's owner, informing him that because we are bicyclists, we should not be subject to the car toll. We are also irate over the position of the poor bear, which looks miserable standing out on the tarmac. But it is to no avail. We pay our baksheesh, have a hearty laugh, and cycle on.

We cross the Aravali Range, arid hills that separate the desert from the forests. The India of millions at last seems far away, though we return to it every evening, coming into chaotic towns and villages.

Near the Sariska Tiger Reserve and the Kholadeo Bird Sanctuary, we see Siberian Cranes with startling yellow eyes and red bills, sitting in fields of mustard. Moorhens, mallards, point herons, darters, and egrets inhabit the waterways, and we even chance upon greater spotted eagles, perched in nests overhead. Nilgai (a horse-like deer) and sambar (a moose look-alike) trot out of the brush and across the road, as do wild pigs, which dash crazily to escape our onrushing wheels. I even spot a giant python, curled around a large rock and looking extremely menacing.

The bushes and brush fall away, specks of sand begin to appear along the roadside, and within minutes, it is as if a giant hand has lifted one backdrop and installed another. Camels emerge slowly out of nowhere, pulling carts driven by men with sun-blackened skin. Women in saris glide barefoot through the sands, balancing huge ceramic jugs on their heads and pausing to stop and stare as we pass, aliens on strange flying birds.

Only the yellow swatches of mustard flowers remain to reassure us that we are still in the same country. We have entered Rajasthan, the land of kings.

Rajasthan was ruled for years by the Rajputs, warrior clans renowned for their fighting prowess. The Rajputs were bound by codes of chivalry and honor, leading a romantic lifestyle much like that of the knights of medieval Europe, and were praised as being fair rulers who provided their subjects with land and employment. They outlasted the Moghuls, and even forged alliances with the British—although the Maharajas of more recent times squandered their fortunes on opulent lifestyles—and eventually they fell from grace during the rise of independent India. Although the Maharajas are long gone, their palaces and fortresses still remain, and Rajasthan is straight from a chapter of the Arabian Nights, with its colors, ancient history, and desertscape.

Hitomi and I pedal into Jaipur, a sprawling city of millions and the modern showpiece and capital of Rajasthan. Every other shop takes Visa and MasterCard, ATM's stand on most street corners, and the major boulevards are one endless stream of rumbling Tata trucks. Yet as in most of India, the ancient and the new are never far from one another. The scores of old palaces and forts scattered throughout the city are composed of red sandstone, which glows pink to ochre in the late afternoon sun, and Jaipur is appropriately known as the Pink City. As part of their code of honor, the Rajputs originally painted buildings pink, the color representing hospitality.

The Moghul Empire and the dynasties of Maharajas have left their imprint on Jaipur, and the architecture and design are spectacular. The intricate latticework and the ornate gates, doors, and windows all bear the mark of a labor of love. Wall murals are of the Rajput Moghul school, miniature designs that under a magnifying glass reveal the most carefully detailed scenes. Having grown up in another culture which so often focuses on its own history, I am astonished to see what vibrant works have been taking place in this faraway land.

As in Varanasi, we move between extremes, from ancient history to the present, from the lap of luxury to the wretches of poverty. Unlike in America, where we can drive through the inner city hidden behind the tinted glass of our automobiles, here we are thrust back and forth between the different worlds hundreds of times each day.

We rise in the mornings and wander through the bazaars on the large rectangular boulevards of Jaipur, for once not getting lost. Jai Singh, the Rajput founder of the city, based his plans for the city on an ancient Hindu treatise, the *Shilpa Shastra*. The entire city is laid out on a perfect grid, and the perfectly proportioned shops, mosques, and temples conform to a symmetry found nowhere else in India.

At the cycle bazaar, rusty chains and bald tires surround mechanics who sit on tiny stools in the dust doing repairs. The fruit bazaar is teeming with housewives, pinching and squeezing the offerings and bartering with the eager merchants. We see a gem bazaar, textile bazaar, silver and gold bazaar, silk bazaar, and utensil bazaar, to name but a few. Office workers in neat slacks purchase goods with credit cards, while in a neighboring stall a family loads their purchases onto a camel-drawn cart. At the nearby *lassi-walla,* members of every caste line up for cool and creamy *lassis*, a thick yogurt drink served in throwaway ceramic mugs. The mugs are tossed into the street, where they are trampled by shoppers and wandering cows throughout the night; come morning, they have become dust, ready to be molded into mugs again. In India, nothing goes to waste. Those who cannot afford the seven cent cup of refreshment linger next to other drinkers, hoping to scrounge up a half-finished glass before it is thrown away.

Yet in the air-conditioned Surya Mahal restaurant around the corner, we are insulated from the beggars and hungry children who prowl the streets outside. Not a single table is empty, and we could be in Paris,

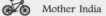

London, or Toronto. Middle-class families, well groomed in their Kashmiri sweaters, pick from tables piled high with *masala dosas* and *chole bhature*.

In Nepal, Indonesia, and other spots we have travelled, Hitomi and I have often felt uncomfortable visiting middle-class establishments. They were the clubs of the wealthy, invariably filled with tourists, and almost no locals could afford to eat in them. Nor did locals in those countries partake in trekking, museum hopping, or visiting sites of world renown, as they were too busy working. In India, however, about twenty percent of a population of one billion are identified as middle class, which makes for some huge numbers. Seeing and interacting with this middle class makes it all the more enjoyable to dine in family joints and visit tourist attractions.

Yet then, only seven blocks from where we sit, entire streets are congested with figures who seem barely alive, lying on the pavement, many without limbs. There are lepers with open wounds and unwashed skin, their eyes reflecting complete despair. Some groom each other, plucking lice from scalps, but most lie on their backs. Blankets and cups, their only possessions, hang on the walls behind them.

Jodhpur is known as the Blue City, as its extensive Brahmin population paint their homes powder blue, a symbol of purity. The Jodhpur Government Tourist Office tells us that the guesthouse we have chosen is full and too expensive anyway, so we should choose one of theirs. Of course, when we ring the guesthouse, it is neither full nor expensive.

We try the Tourist Office the next day, and opt for their city sightseeing tour, which promises "a detailed information filled plan of looking all sights of important Jodhpur history." The tour bus is decrepit, with a chain-smoking and betel-nut-chewing driver who spits red juice at our feet and drops us off at a handful of sites. There is no guide, information, or anything else, and we could have taken a public bus for a fraction of the price.

We drop exhausted into bed every night, overwhelmed by the barrage of experiences. Yet every morning, we awaken like drug addicts, wearily staggering out into the madness for yet another fix.

Trying to leave Jodhpur, we run into some sort of religious festival. Soldiers are stationed at each intersection in a series of roadblocks, and unable to find a route out of the mess, we try to cut through a barricade. We are immediately surrounded by angry soldiers. A man who seems to be in charge stomps up to us and barks, "And exactly what business are you doing?"

"We are going to Jaisalmer."

"By road," he states rather incredulously.

"No, by plane," I answer, no longer in the mood to sit here stalled.

He eyes us up and down, and then, pointing at Hitomi, looks at me and screams, "And what is that?"

Thoroughly disgusted, I scream back, "That is a human being, and she happens to be my wife!"

Hitomi, smart enough to bow out of games that cannot be won, has already started cycling in the opposite direction, knowing full well that this is one barrier we will never cross.

We finally make our way out of the mess in Jodhpur and head west through a landscape of sand and dry grass, the beginnings of the Thar Desert. This is not a tourist route, yet every man, woman, and child we pass on the road cries out, "Hello one pen!"

If we ever find life on Mars, the first thing the Martians will say is, "Give me a pen!"

At dusk, we reach a hamlet of mud-baked, thatch-roofed huts near the village of Shatawa. Nobody here has a phone, television, or even a bicycle. Yet the handful of herders here do have all their necessities. There are camels, water (from a pipeline provided freely by the government), and lots of open space. Locals live on milk from camels and goats, *dal*, wheat chapatis, and *sangri*, a delicious and versatile vegetable. The people are healthy and peaceful, and do not ask for anything in return for their hospitality.

As we approach the western reaches of the Thar Desert, rolling sand dunes dominate the landscape. Winds rage in our face most of the day, and several army trucks stop to offer us lifts, but we refuse, opting for pain and suffering. These feelings are an integral part of life, to be borne as much as happiness and joy, and I wouldn't trade this experience for anything in the world. Besides, after our day in the Quaidam Basin back in China, could anything be worse?

India's way with natural recycling continues to impress. A fresh steaming pile of cow dung sits in the middle of the road, a large truck bearing down upon it, when out of the desert, a young woman in a pink sari and veil rushes into the road. She scoops the precious poop into her

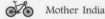

ceramic pot just before it is splattered; out here, it is valuable fuel.

In the town of Pokaran, members of the ear- and nose-cleaning caste approach us and ask to be of service. These men have long and rusty needles with which they probe, twirl, and remove wax and snot from the ears and noses of their customers. They often greet us with, "Hello cleaning sir," proudly displaying little vials filled with previous pickings. In this land of no waste, I wonder where the contents of the vials end up. In candles, perhaps?

Villages here have more mosques than we have seen elsewhere, and the men dress in light blue *shalwar kameez,* pajama-like outfits with long shirts that hang down to the knees. The men tend to have long beards, and the women are often veiled, a sign that we are close to the border of neighboring Pakistan. Another sign is the camouflaged bunkers, tanks, and bases of the Indian army taking up much of the desert sands. Around the army bases, villagers tend to be sullen and inhospitable. Kids taunt us and make lewd comments to Hitomi. One day, she is riding about a kilometer ahead of me when a group of boys races after me on their bikes, blocking the road and screaming at me in a mix of incomprehensible Hindi and English. One of them snatches a newspaper strapped on to my rear rack, and I warn them not to touch my bike while I am riding. They continue to taunt me, several of them even hurling small stones at my head.

Finally, one gangly kid cycles up next to me, reaches over, and grabs my handlebars. I glare and tell him that if he does this again I will beat the crap out of him. He grins and does it again, and without thinking I turn my front wheel into his bike, forcing him to stop, and fling him and his bike to the ground. I jump off and begin to pummel him as he screams for mercy and cowers on the ground. His friends flee into the desert.

After uttering a litany of curses, I release him and he rides off, looking surprised that I have spared him from a more gruesome fate. As he pedals away, I sit there amazed. I am a pacifist, and am quite shocked at my actions—and at how wonderful it felt to take out my anger on the kid. I wonder if this rage has been in me all the time, and if it has taken the rawness of life here to bring it to the surface.

I catch up with Hitomi, who sits shaking her head at my story, not so much at my reaction, but at India, a land that seems to know no bounds when it comes to surprises.

At dusk we pedal into Jaisalmer, another city out of a page in *The*

Arabian Nights. While Jaipur is the pink city, Jaisalmer is a city of gold. Buildings of golden and yellow sandstone sparkle in the rays of the setting desert sun, reflecting a magical light and blending into the surrounding sands.

The Jaisalmer Fort towers over the city, guarded by a hundred bastions and a set of imposing gates. It has not been turned into a tourist attraction, and a fourth of the city's population still lives inside of its walls. The fort was built in the twelfth century, and little has changed in its cobbled lanes. No vehicles are allowed, and the turbaned men and veiled women scurrying through the tiny passageways are dressed as if they have travelled forward through time.

Jaisalmer hosts a yearly Desert Festival, which coincides with our arrival. The festival is a colorful pageant of camel polo, turban-tying contests, and mustache competitions. The former Mr. Mustache, a man with a six-foot-long handlebar on each side of his face, was beheaded in a blood feud ten years ago!

We stay two weeks in Jaisalmer, the longest we have stayed anywhere since Varanasi, then once again return to a life lived out of packed bags, confronting great unknowns and moving perpetually. Yet it is with great sadness that we say goodbye to the many locals who have befriended us during our stay here, and we often stop to gaze back at the fort dominating the skyline as we spin out into the sands once more.

Time always speeds up on our rest days. While cycling, we get into a groove and never really think about just how hard we are pushing ourselves day in and day out. However, once we stop, it sinks in just how intense a pace we are maintaining. On days where we lounge around and do nothing but eat and drink, evening comes with blinding speed—along with the reality that we must head out into the heat and dust again in a few short hours.

On our way out of Bikaner, the "something always happens in India" journal entry for the day is our discovery of the Karna Mati Temple, in the village of Deshnok. Legend has it that a contingent of dead storytellers were turned into rats to spare them from the wrath of angry gods; these rats, present incarnations of the narrators of tales, are now enshrined in this safe haven.

The interior of the temple is a pit of rats, who fill every crack and crevice and have full run of the shrine. The holy rats are extremely large, fed on milk and balls of candy brought by the temple priests and thousands of devotees. The scene is like something out of a horror film or nightmare. Shoes are not allowed inside the temple, and the rats swarm over everyone's feet; the pilgrims react to this much more ecstatically than we do. Wire mesh is strung around the entire compound so that birds of prey cannot enter and harm the holy rodents.

To ensure good fortune, the priests urge devotees to eat bits of *prasad* that sit mixed and trampled with the rat turds on the ground! We figure we are blessed enough to give this a miss, and rather shocked, we make our way out. I am convinced that someday we will read about the entire city of Bikaner being decimated by the plague, but then again, where else on the planet do rats get such devotion and respect?

While Rajasthan is a land of palaces and fortresses, it is also an impoverished state that suffers countless droughts, famines, and other calamities. Few people have even a grade school education or any knowledge about the outside world.

So it is a shock to cross the border and enter Haryana and the Punjab, two of India's most affluent states, which produce over sixty percent of India's rice and wheat, as well as much of her industry. We ride into the city of Hisar, pursued by a skeletal Rajasthani man who races alongside us on his squeaky one-speed bike, asking me repeatedly what I have in my bags.

Hisar looks like a prosperous place, with a bustling downtown full of hotels, restaurants, appliance shops, and wide boulevards with trees and flowers. We make a beeline for a fancy ice cream parlor, and almost immediately, three gorgeous young women in stylish pants suits come over to our table and socialize. They are veterinarians who graduated recently from the university here, and they inform us that it is their duty to help us during our stay in Hisar.

It has been three months since I had an intelligent conversation with a woman not covered with a veil, other than Hitomi, and it is a nice change to share ice cream and stories without being stared at. Our bicycling friend sits mutely at the neighboring table, gawking at us. In his village, ten kilometers back in Rajasthan, he is undoubtedly head of a family and clan, but here in Hisar he is invisible. He sits in embarrassed silence, watching all of us gab away in English, and during a lull in the conversation even leans over and whispers, "Sahib, these ladies here, where are they from in America?"

Our trio wants to take us home to meet their families, but we are exhausted and politely decline. The ladies direct us to a hotel, wish us well, and tell us not to hesitate to call them if we need anything.

Before parting, one of them leans over and asks Hitomi, "So really, how is India?"

Hitomi looks at her, smiles, wags her head and rolls her eyes in jest, and replies, "India is…unique!"

The ladies nod in complete understanding and agreement.

The Hotel Palkin has carpeted and air-conditioned rooms, color television, hot water, a banquet hall, and no manager telling us what to do. In fact, the concierge is a prepubescent teen who almost falls off his chair when we enter the lobby, and only overcomes his shyness when he learns that we do not bite and can actually converse with him in Hindi.

In our giant suite, we tune into the BBC, which informs us that the United States is about to bomb Iraq. The Winter Olympics are being broadcast live on ESPN from Nagano, Japan, where our journey began. We leap briefly into the modern world of CNN, mega-events, and hurried lives, leaving for a moment this other world of tea stalls; this world of villagers who have never heard of CNN, the Olympics, or even the village twenty kilometers down the road; this world of lives that move at a pace in rhythm with the wind whistling between our wheels.

Life on the road in the Punjab is sheer joy. There is no excrement, no kids hollering for pens (I do believe that they are actually in school here), and no crowds surging around our bikes. We are greeted everywhere by turbaned Sikhs, who gather a polite distance from our bikes to discuss the gears and drive trains. Most are only curious and friendly, coming over to find out where we are from and where we are going, or to wish us good luck.

On par with the camaraderie and clean surroundings is the Punjabi food. Roadside *dhabas* serve thick and creamy *dal* with lots of chilies, cilantro, and yogurt, and freshly baked naan bread.

Leaving the desert, we ride through corridors of eucalyptus trees surrounded by wheat fields and agricultural heartland. The weather begins to cool, and by the time we arrive in Sirsa, it has begun to rain.

It rains all night, a deluge that keeps us awake half the night. In the morning, the street looks like a beachfront, with waves washing against the buildings, but we set out into the downpour and ride to Mansa under a dripping canopy of eucalyptus.

In the sprawling town of Mansa, every street is either underwater or swimming in mud. We reach the town center, every inch of our bodies streaked and spotted with mud, and a smiling restaurateur beckons us in for giant plates of steaming *dal, chapattis,* and vegetables. The patrons get a kick out of us, treating us like warriors emerging victorious from a fierce battle. We don't bother to wash anything off, as there are still thirty kilometers to go before Barnala, which we hope to reach by nightfall.

A howling gale springs up behind us, but our grimy bikes and bodies make it to Barnala just after dark. We are worried that hotels may turn us away, but tonight our karma is good. Hotel manager Zakir Hussain, a West Bengali, rolls out the red carpet for us. He carries in our filthy, wet bags, brings us steaming mugs of chai, fills several buckets with steaming hot water for bathing, and serves us a six-course feast for two dollars!

Zakir also sets up a separate room with the fans on full blast to dry things overnight. In the meantime, Hitomi and I wheel our bikes into the giant bathroom and hose down everything we own, at least making our wheels look somewhat respectable again. It is a tidy ending to the day, though more than just the day almost ends for Hitomi when she emerges from the bathroom and goes to ring the room service buzzer with a hand that is still wet. As she reaches for the buzzer, connected to a tangle of wires for the lights and television, she receives a tremendous shock, which throws her to the floor halfway across the room.

I race over in a panic, ready to begin CPR, but she is surprisingly intact, with no ill effects other than a sore hand and a huge fright. Zakir, who has arrived by this point, offers endless apologies for the wiring system, asks us what time we want breakfast delivered, and stays to tell us about his family in Calcutta. Work brings him here for nine months a year, and he misses the food in West Bengal, the spontaneity of the Bengalis (he finds the Punjabis rather stodgy), and the more relaxed pace. However, like most people we have met here, he accepts his lot with a smile.

As Hitomi and I snuggle in for the evening, listening to the rain outside, I think of how often people at home ask me, "Are people over there really happy?" I know that if I were to ask an earwax picker, bear breeder, hotel manager, or rickshaw walla if he were happy, he would shrug, smile, and answer, "It is my life, sir."

It is three days from Ludhiana back into the Himalayas, and we decide to break for a few months in Dharmsala, home of the Tibetan government in exile. Leaving Ludhiana, we pass through clouds of pollution and shantytowns that go on forever, where the corrugated shacks of migrant city workers sit amid mounds of garbage and sewage. We put our heads down and pedal hard, reflecting on the consequences of industrial progress.

Eventually we escape the city and get onto the excellent Grand Trunk Highway, with its wide shoulders, rest areas, and abundance of fancy restaurants. Marijuana plants grow along the roadside, and even on the center divider, but none of the plants are touched, the Sikhs likely being too industrious to indulge.

Within a day, we begin climbing into green foothills. Large snow-covered peaks are visible in the distant haze, and we begin to pass through mountain villages, where light-skinned, barefoot peasants work rice terraces. Food is sparser in this region, and we spend some evenings putting together meals of bananas, tomatoes, and potato *pakoras*, along with dozens of cups of sweet tea from roadside stalls.

We struggle up the steep Beas River Valley, our effort made bearable by the fresh air, hawks and eagles flying overhead, and howler monkeys, which sit at the roadside and stare comically as we ride past.

We find a guesthouse in Rani Tal, a village on the shore of a lake, where a signboard proclaims, "Fit for nature lovers and intellectuals." A full moon rises over the distant Daludhar Range, the twenty-sixth moon of the journey since we left Japan. Over the next rise, in Dharmsala, *Losar* (the Tibetan New Year) has just gotten underway.

I recall the first moon of our journey, an orange harvest moon above the Yangtze River in China, more than two years ago now. It is strange to think that after all our adventures, we are in a way returning to the early stages of our journey—to the Tibetans. No matter how much we look for difference, we repeat ourselves again and again.

Chapter Thirteen

Borders: *Between Countries and Souls*

Hate is not the real opposite of love. The real opposite of love is individuality.

D. H. Lawrence

Traveller, there is no path. You make the path as you walk.

Antonio Machado

P laces of meditation and healing can often turn out to be quite the opposite. Space, time, and opportunity for reflection can bring deep-seated fears and issues to painful light. This is always for the better in the long run, but the immediate pain can be quite severe.

Our stay in Dharmsala lasts just short of three months. Dharmsala is the home in exile of the government of Tibet and the Dalai Lama, who fled here from Tibet during the 1959 uprising. It is a thriving community, thronged with monks, Tibetan refugees, Buddhist scholars, pilgrims, and tourists. Nestled on a ledge under the magnificent Daludhar Range, it is—at first glance—a sanctuary of peace, and a ray of hope in the all too often bleak Tibetan political and cultural struggle. Foreigners come to study Sanskrit, teach English to Tibetan refugees and monks, or work on various aid projects. Others throng to receive the teachings of His Holiness, the Dalai Lama, who gives public teachings and greets visitors throughout the year. Still others come just to breathe the clean mountain air and take in the brilliant surroundings.

Dharmsala, like other hill stations, is supposed to be an oasis away from the chaos, crowds, heat, dust, and intensity of Indian life, but of course every supposed nirvana has its own pitfalls. The tiny town has perhaps overgrown its boundaries, and all the visitors have a terrible impact on McLeod Ganj, as the upper portion of Dharmsala is known. The garbage situation is one of the worst we have seen in India. Plastic water bottles, soft drink cans, and beer bottles are strewn over hillsides deeply eroded by the never-ending construction of guesthouses, bakeries, restaurants, and shops.

The town is now on the "full moon party circuit," a series of wild orgies that take place every full moon in travel spots like Goa, Ko Phangan in Thailand, Kathmandu, and now Dharmsala. Thousands of travellers descend on these small places in search of Ecstasy, trance dancing, and rabid escape from who they are. Hundreds of young Sikhs from the Punjab arrive, minus their turbans, inspired by dreams—and Bollywood films—to search for loose women and a wild time.

And while His Holiness gives teachings on compassion, nonviolence, simplicity, and freedom from desire, up the road from his temple, young monks pack tiny rooms to watch pirated videos featuring gratuitous violence, cafés serve as bicultural meat markets for lonely souls, and local youths struggle with their anger and disenfranchisement.

Within a short time, Hitomi and I begin to miss the chaos and color of the plains below.

But perhaps our dissatisfaction is internal. Pausing from the thrills and demands of everyday bicycling has again revealed the growing distance between Hitomi and me, space that we no longer know how to fill. Perhaps we are no longer even interested in filling it.

We have repetitive disagreements over our future, having children, work, and where we want to live, but these all seem so far away, and at least for me, unfathomable at present. On a more immediate level, Hitomi doesn't feel she is as mentally strong as I am; she has feared since Australia that I could leave her at any time, and that she would be unable to carry on by herself.

I tend to agree with some of this, and I should let her know that I will not leave her, and make her aware that she is actually far stronger and more independent than she believes. Instead, however, I lose my respect for her and belittle her efforts at improvement, all the while shoving my own cockiness and self-confidence down her throat.

I can see what is coming, and so can she, but we rather naively put faith in our journey, which has served to hold us together in the worst of times. She gets involved in the Tibetan community, goes to Dalai Lama teachings, studies tai chi, and hangs out with new Japanese friends, while I study Hindi, climb mountains, and go off to festivals to take photographs.

When we are apart, sometimes I think I have an answer or solution, but when I return, the look on her face tells me she doesn't want to hear it. Unable to speak, we retreat into our private worlds. Yet we go on, and on the first of May, leave Dharmsala to return to the plains and head for Pakistan.

The plains are now in the throes of the pre-monsoon buildup, and the heat is becoming unbearable. After our settled mountain life in Dharmsala, we are sluggish and lethargic, and we have to stop often on inclines. The heat on the road becomes a hazy inferno, far worse than anything we have experienced in the tropics. I drink five liters of water in a few hours and still feel dehydrated, and Hitomi is completely spent by early afternoon.

Fortunately, scattered along the road are *gurdwalas*, religious hospitality centers run by the Sikhs, with food, water, and cool dark halls in which to rest. We douse ourselves from head to toe in water, which seems to help, though the searing heat dries us again within five minutes.

At around five we roll into Amritsar, a large border city that houses the Golden Temple, the most revered site of the Sikhs. We find a hotel, watch the sunset at the Golden Temple (a gilded dome said to resemble an inverted lotus flower) and then head out to celebrate our last night in India, taking stock of the half year we have spent in this vital and amazing land.

Hitomi snaps at me during our rickshaw ride to the restaurant, and again in the restaurant, over tiny things, and far more viciously than she is apt to. I become angry, and we again hit that wall where it seems more sensible to retreat into silence than to provoke and come to blows. Yet tonight, the silence is horribly oppressive, and it feels as if we have reached some point of no return. Stupidly, I blame it on the terrible heat, and presume that with a good sleep, we can start fresh in the morning.

Morning comes all too soon, as neither of us has slept well. Even at six a.m., the heat is ghastly, assaulting my brain like a jackhammer, pounding away relentlessly. Heat usually slows me to a tortoise's pace, but this morning, for whatever reason, I am up and antsy to be on the road. Breakfast is done, my bags are packed, and I am outside stretching, waiting for Hitomi. Returning to the room to see what is taking her so long, I discover that she is nowhere near to being ready, and as I chide her and mention the growing heat, she slows down her packing efforts even more.

We are soon shouting at one another. She yells that she always waits for me, and that I must do the same for her, while I scream my own version of the story. Our ranting escalates, until, unable to deal with any more, I inform Hitomi that I am leaving for the border, and ask her whether or not she will be joining me. Very calmly, she looks me in the eye, and answers, "No."

At this point, we are beyond acting or speaking rationally, and we begin yelling and crying, accusing and blaming each other for all the things that we haven't solved or dealt with. In the end, we are both spent, but are unwilling to back down from the separate roads we have chosen. I take the tent and cooking pots, shakily cramming them into my already bulging panniers, while Hitomi goes to a corner of the room, unable to look at me anymore.

I look at her and try to speak, but the words will not come. I do the only thing that I know I am capable of: I wheel my bike out onto the road.

I pedal furiously into the heat, on a road packed with Sikhs on their bicycles. Many ride next to me, asking where I am from, what my name is, and if I am married. I don't quite know how to answer them.

When I stop for tea, a man saunters over and asks me where I started this journey. It has been exactly three years since we left Japan, so many moons ago. The man probes further into my personal life, asking questions which lead to dead ends.

"You are being married, good sir?"

"Well, um, yes I am, or was as of about an hour ago."

"And where is your kind missus being now?"

"Um, she's back in Amritsar, but maybe she isn't there anymore."

"And when will you be again joining with your loved one?"

"Um, I don't think we'll be joining again for a very long while."

Eventually, he wanders off shaking his head, while I think that I might be the first person trying to bicycle around the world who has gotten married, lost his mother, and then his wife, all on the same journey.

After ten kilometers, the road completely and rather eerily empties of all bicycles. I travel the last seven kilometers in India totally alone, at last reaching the only open crossing on the heavily fortified border that divides Pakistan and India.

On the Indian side, the passport official greets me with a cheery, "Hello *baksheesh*, hello money," to which I scowl and laugh. My bike and gear are randomly scrutinized by a guard, who points to various items and asks me what they are, but doesn't understand a word I say. Thus we have a rather useless encounter, in which he points, I say "tent," or "sleeping bag," and he smiles and points to something else.

The official asks if I am travelling alone, and I look back down the empty road, expecting to see Hitomi come riding along. After all, how many times have we put differences and arguments behind us and gone on? But today it is not to be, and after forlornly glancing back down the road into India, I tell the guards I am on my own. Several officers in paramilitary garb open a locked gate, and with one last wistful and rather desperate glance back to the east, I cross into Pakistan.

The Pakistan-India border is a result of the carving job created by India's independence from the British after World War Two. Here in the Punjab, thousands of Sikhs crossed over to live on the Indian side, while the same numbers of Moslems went to the Pakistani Punjab.

In the first settlement I reach on the Pakistani side, the streets are thronged with beak-nosed men, most of whom are taller than their Indian counterparts. Everyone is dressed in *shalwar kameez*, the pajama-like national dress of Pakistan. When I say "everyone," I mean men. While at least a few women were visible in the fields and eateries of India, they are nowhere in sight here, other than young girls out playing near the roadside.

People pause as I cycle by, then raise an arm and shout *"Salaam aleikum."* ("May God be with you.") I am to hear this everywhere for the next several months, often followed by an invitation for tea. Some traditions have no borders.

It takes roughly an hour to get to Lahore, the capital of the Pakistani Punjab and the third-largest city in the country. Under the British, Lahore was a highbrow city of grand architecture and prestigious universities, but today it looks like most other cities on the subcontinent: polluted, crowded, and chaotic. However, it seems to be missing the intensity and *joie de vivre* that characterize most Indian towns. People here appear to be more serious—or less foolish.

I find a hotel downtown with a windowless room that is a cross between a prison cell and an oven, where I take a nap and then head out in search of food. It is Friday evening, and men are heading into mosques for afternoon prayers. It is also a holiday of some sort, and many of the restaurants are closed. The ones that I do find open are a drastic departure from the wonderful kitchens of India that have sated me for the past half-year. Almost all the dishes are full of meat, and after six months without it, my stomach is not ready to handle it. I ask in one place if they can do any type of vegetarian cooking, and the waiter looks at me sadly and says in a singsong voice, "Sorry sir, begetable unabailable."

I find another place with *subji* (vegetables) on the menu, and order it with a bowl of *dal*, only to be brought a plate of mutton with a couple of tiny peas and carrots beside the meat. The *dal* here is much drier than in India, without much sauce, and is served with large dry *roti*. As I nibble glumly through my meal, I start to wonder how the food will be in the countryside, if this is what one gets in a major city.

I sit alone in the empty restaurant, feeling sorry for myself. The events of the day seem unreal, and I still expect Hitomi to come wandering down the road at any moment. This is just temporary, right?

I feel elated to be free, on my own, no longer engaged in mental and emotional battles. But it has been a long time since I ate in a restaurant by myself. It will take some getting used to.

I wander over to the Shalimar Gardens, another masterpiece by Shah Jahan, builder of the Taj Mahal and scores of other exquisite palaces and buildings. The gardens are done in Mogul style; pools and fountains surround the marble causeways, and multi-tiered arches frame spacious lawns and fruit trees. The gardens are a pleasant reprieve from the heat, pollution, and dirt of Lahore, and this is the first place in Pakistan where I see couples, as well as several unveiled women, relaxing on the grounds.

As I sit, a businessman named Sachafid Khan joins me. He welcomes me to Pakistan, and we exchange pleasantries for ten minutes before our conversation rapidly degenerates. Mr. Khan leans over and declares that sex must be easy in America, then asks how quickly I can get a woman into bed back home. I inform him that most women will not just jump into bed with you, and that this is generally the case around the world, but Mr. Khan will have none of it. In a sly voice, he informs me that "Pakistani men are very very warming," which I discover means horny. Premarital sex is a no-no here, and the expectations of the sex that will come with marriage seem completely inflated and unrealistic. It must be something of a letdown.

Mr. Khan, who is married, tells me that he plans to go to Europe to find a woman, because European women are always in heat! He tells me that European nipples are of the highest class, though when I ask him what the difference is between a Pakistani nipple and, say, a French or British one, he is at a loss for words.

We sit in silence for a time, watching children chase each other around the fountains, and then a pair of western females appear, toting cameras and guidebooks, and Mr. Khan hastily bids me adieu and heads off in hot pursuit.

Back on the streets, I can't help but think that Pakistan is like some sort of bizarre science fiction tale called *Planet of the Men*. Men are everywhere, holding hands, chatting animatedly, and strolling arm in arm. Boys play cricket and fly kites. There are no women. All these men and boys must have mothers and grandmothers, sisters and wives, yet the women remain completely invisible. Perhaps it is for the best that I have crossed the border alone.

I awaken the next morning feeling exactly the same as on the previous one: flat, low, miserable, overheated, and ill. Deciding that action is the only cure for this lethargic state, I pop downstairs to order tea.

For the third day in a row, I am asked, "Mixed or separate?" and I assume that this refers to how the milk and sugar is served. On the first day, I ordered "separate" and received a carafe of milk and sugar on the side, but yesterday the tea arrived creamy and highly oversweetened with the same order. I ask for black tea, and am told by the staff that this is impossible.

"But isn't that what separate is?" I ask.

"Sorry sir, not possible," my waiter answers. "But you can be having green tea."

"Aah, green tea." I reply. "That would be lovely," I reply. Ten minutes later, I am served a cup of light black tea.

At seven a.m. the temperature is already 110 degrees, and I take to the road in a very foul mood. Conditions are far better than in India, but I have decided that I do not like Pakistan. The food is crap; there is no cold beer to be had after a long hot day (this being a strict Islamic country, alcohol is not sold openly); and there are no women to look at or speak with. Great place to start off my single career, I think to myself.

Even worse, there are no mangoes! Just thirty kilometers away, on the Indian side of the Punjab, the streets are packed with mango sellers. Yet for whatever reason, on this side there are none.

I am in some sort of a bad dream, descending into the Pakistani version of Dante's Inferno. Every meal is a venture into the unknown. Tonight's menu reveals a "mixed vegetables platter" hidden in the mutton section of the menu, and I end up with some very overspiced peas and carrots, with tasteless rice that is full of bits of worms. I am also asked if I would like a glass of "barf tea," which after careful thought I conclude must mean iced tea, as *barf* is Hindi or Urdu for snow or ice, but just the thought of barf tea with my worm-filled rice makes dinner all the more unpalatable.

In the morning, I have diarrhea again, which isn't much of a surprise. The thermometer on my pannier is registering 115 degrees. I groan and pack my bags.

The road drifts on under the wrath of a merciless sun, melting in the heat. Villages and towns through here all look exactly alike: ugly, filthy, and dusty. I dream of an American supermarket with fruit, cheese, bagels, a carton of orange juice, and a freezer section.

People stare at me as I pedal along, a few riding alongside me on their own bicycles to ask the usual questions. Urdu, though supposedly the same language as Hindi, is turning out to be rather indecipherable. I cannot understand what most people say. On most days, I make a sincere effort with language, but today is not one of them. It is easier to play stupid, and to keep my eyes on the road and my mouth on the water bottle.

I end up in the town of Gujarat at ten, and decide that I will go insane if I continue to cycle in this heat. Within half an hour, I am naked under a ceiling fan in the rather dreary Melody Hotel.

I begin to imagine a lifetime like this, dwelling like some small insect in tiny cubicles with slow fans, the whole of existence hinging upon the revolving whoosh of the blades, which bring slight relief from the scorching air outside.

The proprietor of the hotel, a jovial old man, has seen with one glance that I am not doing well. He continually pads down the hall to my door, bringing me buttered toast and tea, and recommends that I should not ride a bicycle during this time of year.

As I try to sleep, a pounding on the door awakens me. Four young men barge into my room, all brandishing pens and clamoring for my autograph. It turns out that they are members of a local cycle racing team, and word has spread that I have arrived; the grapevine on the subcontinent moving at a speed that puts even the fastest Internet connection to shame.

The guys are quite sweet, though like all the Pakistanis I have met, they talk hopelessly about their country, wanting desperately to go to the U.S. or Europe. They are quite the opposite of their Indian brethren, who would spend the same energy talking about all the merits of India.

They ask me for all my particulars, and as I am tired of having to explain my recent parting with Hitomi, I tell them I am separated from my wife, to which one replies, "Oh, you and your wife live separately from your parents? You are lucky indeed!"

The boys have me autograph their aftershave lotion boxes with personal messages, then warn me to take care the day after tomorrow. It will be the holiday of Ashura, during which a sect of Shiite Moslems beat themselves silly with chains and spiked clubs. As I prepare for bed, it occurs to me that if I lived in this heat, surrounded by thousands of horny men, I might take up such methods of celebrating.

Fortunately, the absolute worst of the past week appears to be behind me. The following morning, I begin to climb away from the searing plains under an overcast sky. An old man cycles beside me for most of the morning, never saying a word except when I pass him, to which he responds, "Allah be praised," and gives a burst of power to get back ahead of me.

He leaves me when I stop for my first tea break, in a small café where several men immediately come up and ask me to take them with me to America. When I ask them why they want to go there, they respond in unison, "In America, sex is free and good." I don't dare to dash their hopes.

One asks me for my sunglasses, to which I point up to the sky, trying to explain that I still need them. Perhaps because it is cloudy, the fellow misinterprets me, and asks me if Allah needs my sunglasses. I think to myself that if Allah needs a two-dollar pair of sunglasses, well...

I travel on, crying for joy when I see some green hills. In the town of Dina, I find a fancy-looking hotel where I break for lunch, but beat a hasty exit when the first thing I read on the menu is "soft pricks and hot pricks." I opt for an outdoor fruit stall on the other side of town, where I stand eyeing mushy musk melons and withered bananas when an old man with a skullcap comes up and asks me "English or Yunnan?" I know that the Urdu word for Greece is Yunnan, so I give him this answer, to which he replies exuberantly in Greek, *"Kalimera filaki mou, ti kanete?"* ("Good morning my friend, how are you?")

His name is Ahmed, and he invites me to his house, plies me with tea and biscuits, and tells me a bit about his life. He lived for several years in Greece, doing construction work, and his broken Greek is certainly better than mine. He tells me about his struggles living in a foreign country, adapting to the strange food and customs, and missing his wife and family. I also learn from him that men from each village in Pakistan go to work in some foreign country, be it Greece, France, or Libya.

For perhaps the first time in Pakistan, I am reminded that we all are the same deep down. We all seek a way to make a living, a way to find love, a way to make our place in this huge yet tiny world. I feel connected and whole again, ready to lay the past to rest and move on.

I bid adieu to my Greek speaking friend, despite his urges to stay forever with his family, and set my sights on Islamabad.

Chapter Fourteen
The Karakoram Highway

> *The important thing about travel in*
> *foreign lands is that it breaks the speech habits and*
> *makes you blab less, and breaks the habitual space-*
> *feeling because of different village plans and*
> *different landscapes. It is less important that there*
> *are different mores, for you counteract these with*
> *your own reaction-formations.*
>
> Paul Goodman,
> *Five Years in Europe*

> *Travelling is a fool's paradise. Our first*
> *journeys discover to us the indifference of places.*
>
> Ralph Waldo Emerson,
> *"Self-Reliance"*

From what I have heard and read, Islamabad does not sound promising. The Pakistani capital is reported to be a sterile and soul-less city, little more than a diplomatic enclave for the well off. However, these reviews have obviously not been submitted by anyone arriving off the searing plains by bicycle.

Approaching Islamabad from the southeast, I am greeted by green hills, and for the first time in weeks I see mountains in the distance: the Margalla Hills, foothills of the western Himalayas. The road becomes a beltway with a ten-foot shoulder, surrounded by plants and trees. Under cool gray skies, I could be on the freeway rolling into Seattle or Portland.

A Greek architect designed Islamabad in 1958, creating a grid system that divides the city into eight zones by embassies, industry, education, and so on. The boulevards linking the zones are spacious, lined with jacaranda and hibiscus trees, and are flanked by large parks full of roses and bougainvillea.

Traffic is thin, and is controlled by the first roundabouts and traffic lights I have seen in more than a year. Helpful and attentive policemen guard every intersection, and everything looks sleek and efficient. I gaze up at the fancy office towers under construction everywhere, and decide to nominate Islamabad as my favorite city in Asia. Beauty truly does lie in the eye of the beholder, and it really is totally a matter of perspective.

There is even a campground right in the heart of the city, a peaceful haven surrounded by trees and a rather murky river. It costs ten rupees (twenty-five cents) a night, and there are hot showers, a kitchen, and several bunkhouses. Exhausted, yet ecstatic to have made it this far, I pitch my tent in the woods to settle in for a week.

A fellow bicyclist wanders over before I can even begin unpacking, sporting a colorful skullcap and a wide grin. He embraces me in a warm bearhug without saying a word, and I know that it is going to be a long night in the teahouse.

Paco is his name. He is a Spaniard, and has cycled over 75,000 kilometers in the last eight years. I have been strutting it pretty high as a long-distance cyclist ever since I learned that my name meant God in Nepali, but Paco's journey reduces me to very mere mortal status. He left Spain and travelled through the U.S. and South America for several years before moving on to Africa and Asia. He reached the Taklamakan Desert in the dead of winter, crossed China, and finally arrived in the Philippines, where he fell in love. He returned to Spain to find work, but had no luck, and is now on his way back to the Philippines.

Paco has just come from Afghanistan, which is supposedly off-limits to foreigners, torn by civil war and under strict control by the ruling Taliban, who have turned the country into a fundamentalist Islamic republic. When I ask Paco how he obtained a visa to travel there, he tells me with a laugh that he didn't.

He tells me in his thick accent, "I go to the border, no. I sitting long time with my *bicicleta*, nobody talking to me. After three hours, some Taliban guards, they invite me for tea. We drink tea one hour, two hours; finally I ask them if it possible I visit Afghanistan. We sit two more hours, drinking tea, watching the sun. At last one big boss comes. He ask me how I come so far on this bicycle. I tell him 'Allah helped me.'"

"He smile very very big! After this, they give me address of Taliban generals in every city, and also give me big bag of money because they say I no find bank! Then they open gate and I go in."

It sounds like an incredible adventure, though his description of the state of Afghani roads is enough to scare me off, not to mention that no books other than the Koran are now allowed in the country; with such a policy, I have no desire to set foot (or wheel) in the place.

Yves Perault, the other cyclist in camp, soon joins us at the tea table. Yves has been on the road six years, leaving Paris for Africa and eventually settling for a time in the Reunion Islands. He has just cycled the length of India, and is now crossing Central Asia on the old Silk Road, a route that I also intend to follow.

It is most refreshing to meet kindred spirits, and we talk giddily until we are barely able to stay awake. I am delighted to listen to the colorful journeys of others for a change, as so often I am the one asked to tell the tales. As we stroll back to our campsites, I think how fortunate we are to have chosen the open road, and the adventures that it brings day in and day out.

In an Islamabad restaurant, I watch a woman enter, following in her husbands footsteps. She is covered from head to toe in black, her eyes peering through a slit in her veil. The waiter brings her husband a menu; he orders, and they eat, the woman discreetly slipping morsels of food under her veil and into a hidden mouth. Her husband rises to leave, stalking off as if she does not exist, and she follows silently. I wonder how kosher it would be for me to ask her the time.

A debate takes place in camp on the subject of women in Pakistan, with all the male residents giving their expert opinions. One fellow tells me that he finds it sexy that women are covered up, leaving everything completely up to a viewer's imagination. I tell him that while I find a woman in a bikini or a mini-skirt more titillating than one not wearing a stitch, I certainly don't find someone dressed as a piece of furniture or a mummy to have any charms, sexual or otherwise.

I leave Islamabad on a misty morning amid an endless stream of transport trucks. Pakistani trucks are a sight to behold, absolute works of art which belong in a room in the Louvre, rather than out on the dusty roads. They are covered in finely detailed Moghul-style paintings, with religious motifs and blessings offered to Allah. Themes of the drivers' fantasies are sketched around the sides and back; on one truck, a city boy yearns for the pastoral peace of the countryside, and on another, a yokel dreams of the bright lights. Doors look like they have been pilfered from an antique shop, many made of wood carved into exquisitely detailed patterns.

Drivers take great care of their masterpieces, driving slowly over bumps and weaving cautiously around potholes. They give me a wide berth, and are actually the most courteous truckers I have come across anywhere in the world.

The same cannot be said of the bus drivers. The buses are also ornately painted, but the drivers are absolute lunatics, racing side by side at insane speeds. Buses here are all privately owned, and all leave towns at the exact same time. Since the first one to the next town gets all the passengers, drivers drag race on narrow two-lane roads and do not back down for oncoming vehicles or anything else.

It is hard to believe that between 300 B.C. and 400 A.D. the area I am riding through was considered the world center of Buddhist art, history, and philosophy. Alexander the Great rested at nearby Taxila on his way to India in 326, and Emperor Ashoka built a Buddhist University 100 years later. Buddhism spread to China from here, and Indian and Greek art were fused on this spot. Today, it is an average, ugly, congested series of dusty bazaar towns. I wonder if this is progress.

Near Mansehra, I pick up the Karakoram Highway, the famed high road to China. Built in the 1960's, the KKH took over twenty years to construct, and more than 900 Chinese and Pakistani workers lost their lives laying down the 1200 kilometers from Islamabad to Kashgar.

Kara koram means "crumbling rock" in Turkish, and the KKH winds through behemoth glacial valleys where the Asian and Subcontinental geographic plates collide. It traverses some of the world's most inhospitable and physically violent terrain.

Passing Mansehra, I climb into high valleys full of wheat fields and pine trees. Snowy mountains stand guard in the distance, draped in tufts of cumulus cloud, and I take solace in returning to an environment where man is clearly humbled by nature.

The mighty Indus River, which I last saw as a glacial trickle at the foot of Mount Kailash, surges between the jagged mountains to the east and the more rounded domes to the west. During the war with the former Soviet Union, the Indus valley served as a funnel for weapons from the CIA to the *mujehadeen*, the Afghan resistance. Small towns here are full of Pathans and Afghanis armed to the teeth with Uzis and rifles, which are sold in dozens of gun shops along the main streets. The combination of age-old hostility and modern arms is a recipe for disaster, and as I ride, I wonder if I am heading into a passage of no return.

This section of the KKH is known as Indus Kohistan, a series of remote valleys isolated from the outside world. When Pakistani and Indian Kashmir were one, most travellers avoided this route, which was subject to banditry and violence; even today, buses and trucks travel in convoys and seldom stop.

Part of the reason people fear the area is that it is not subject to Pakistani law. The highway is under government jurisdiction, but the law ends the minute one steps off the KKH, and anything off the road is tribal. I have been warned to alert the village chiefs to my presence upon arrival, as the only way to remain safe is to be accepted under their protection.

The first hamlets I pass through in Kohistan are ratty jumbles of stone and dirt, where bratty boys yell at me and throw stones. The places reek of poverty and ignorance, and feel extremely inhospitable. Fortunately, the towns are few, and for the most part, I have the road to myself.

I relish the chance to cycle in the middle of an empty road, and my eyes wander off to the high peaks, the green valleys, and the chocolate Indus.

I reach the town of Besham by early afternoon, a bit anxious about spending my first night in Kohistan. But my fears are assuaged when I meet Mazhat Ali Khan, a young Pathan from Swat, who brings me to meet the village headman and then shows me to a room in a guesthouse. Mazhat hopes to become a doctor, is a devout Moslem, and is horrified by my stories of stone-throwing children and inhospitable adults. He says that if only everyone would pick up the Koran, these problems would not exist.

Mazhat takes me to meet several of his friends, and then we go to sit by the banks of the Indus, watching an old man perched on a boulder reciting verses from the Koran. During a lengthy discussion about religion, Mazhat tells me that there is no law but Islam, and that the biggest problem in Pakistan is that the Shiites don't understand Islam the way the Sunnis do.

I take issue with this. Everyone I have met here takes such pride in Islam, but not everyone follows it. The Koran says nothing positive about throwing stones, or about keeping women in a state of ignorance and imprisonment, yet these go on without change. The will of Islam cannot be questioned.

Perhaps this is why India seemed more relaxed and friendly, in spite of all the chaos and poverty. People laughed at themselves, their lives, and their gods.

Back at the guesthouse, the owner asks all the usual questions and is shocked to learn that I am separated from my wife. He looks at me in utter despair and tells me that separating here is close to impossible. Yet when I ask him if this makes for stronger couples, he falls silent and then looks around to make sure no one is listening.

"No," he says, "many, many struggles at the home."

Life everywhere is the same; only our approaches are different.

Journal entry: The Chinese Buddhist pilgrim Fa Hsien crossed this area on foot in 403 AD, describing the road as difficult and broken, the mountainside as a 10,000 foot stone wall, and the way as exceedingly treacherous. His description is accurate. The KKH delivers eight hours of punishment, and without my past experiences in bearing suffering, I don't think I would have made it today.

By late afternoon, the heat is over 105 degrees, and the climb along the Indus is savage and relentless, with never a flat stretch to rest. I dream of finding a swimming pool, a masseuse, and a very large bottle of beer.

The scenery and grandeur are beyond superlatives. Hamlets cling to crumbling canyon walls, and torrents of water pour across the road from towers of rock, plunging over steep cliffs into the frothing and churning Indus below.

In Pattan village, children throw stones at me, and the adults make no effort to stop them. Trucks pass, carrying men wrapped in Pakistani flags, screaming slogans that I cannot understand. For the first time in six years, I fall off my bike, to which several locals respond by laughing hysterically while I brush myself off and apply bandages to my cuts.

I press on, bruised, bloodied, and parched as hell. Pursued by a very angry sheepdog, I ride gingerly into Dassu, where hundreds of men with rifles flung over their shoulders throng an open-air bazaar. Their prominent beards and noses are right out of an Arabian tale, and riding in the dust and dirt, I feel as if I have gone back into feudal times.

I pass a cricket pitch, where scores of men are watching a match. Two cute young girls, the first I have seen in ages, step out into the road in front of me. I smile, and one responds by bending down, picking up a very large stone, and chucking it right at my face, missing narrowly. I look at the cricket fans, who are now watching me, and implore them with my hands to reign in their children. They all scream at me, and I know I have to keep moving. As I cycle away, dozens of stones zing off of my bike and helmet, and my only recourse is to pedal, despite my exhaustion and anger.

Fortunately, on the other side of town, I find the Khyber Afridi Hotel, which is a total contrast to the scene I have just left behind. Its plush carpeted rooms overlook the Indus, with views of mighty peaks off the balcony. The staff are as gentle and welcoming as they come, and I find slippers waiting by the door.

Despite the daily battles I wage in Pakistan, I am coming to the conclusion that Pakistani hotel managers are the most gracious souls in the world. There is never a hassle, a rip-off, or an argument, and this seems well in accord with Moslem hospitality, which dictates that even an enemy be wined, dined, and given safe haven while a guest—though he can be shot the minute he walks out the door.

In the dining room, I am invited to sit with three men. Safid, Rachman, and Farik are Christians from the Punjab, here teaching "moral development" for the Christian Brothership of Pakistan. I inform them that they have a brutal task ahead, and within minutes I am pouring out all my exhausted and pent-up feelings.

Farik tells me not to feel bad. Stoning and alienation are common greetings for all outsiders. This area is made up of hundreds of tribes, their connection to the outside world as tenuous as the road I have been riding, weaving through the boulder-strewn debris of colliding mountains.

Rachman informs me that the trucks filled with angry young men are protesting a nuclear test by India in the desert of Rajasthan, where Hitomi and I were cycling only a short time ago! As I look on in shock, Safid urges me to keep my spirits up, and says that I should be able to get through the rest of Kohistan unscathed, as long as I control my temper and get off the road before dark.

I leave Dassu early the next morning, anxious to be moving before the stone throwers have finished their breakfasts. As I ride out of town, I see two signs painted in English on houses up on the hillside. One says, "Fuck the USA;" the other, "Support Islamic Fundamentalism."

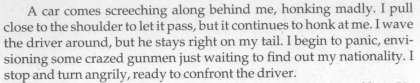

A car comes screeching along behind me, honking madly. I pull close to the shoulder to let it pass, but it continues to honk at me. I wave the driver around, but he stays right on my tail. I begin to panic, envisioning some crazed gunmen just waiting to find out my nationality. I stop and turn angrily, ready to confront the driver.

It turns out to be the hotel manager. I have forgotten a bag of fruit. He waves and drives off, accepting my profuse thanks without any fanfare. I glance back at the signs on the hill, shudder, and cycle on.

At a bend in the road, which is carved into the mountainside and covered with debris, four young men run out and grab my bike, forcing me to stop. They tell me that they own the road, and that I must pay them to pass.

Enraged, I ask them if they would do this to fellow Pakistanis. The oldest boy, perhaps seventeen, says to me, "All Moslems are brothers, but you are a Christian," and then threatens to throw me over the cliff.

I am furious, and am ready to fight to the death, but there are four of them, and I am on a deserted road in the middle of some of the most savage terrain on earth. So I ignore their threats and walk with them up to a small crest where the road swings downhill. Here, I tell the leader that I am not a Christian; that he is not a Moslem; that nobody with any real religious belief would act the way he has; and that he does not know Allah, or any other decent being for that matter. I push off and zip downhill, away from their clutches, although a hailstorm of stones follows my tracks.

An hour later I am in Shatial, a collection of shacks trying to pass as a town. The children here look unkempt and diseased, wide-eyed with fear and hopelessness, and everyone stares at me in disbelief, running away when I attempt to speak with them. Most fortunately, I have a note from Safid, Farik, and Rachman, and another from the Chief of the Department of Forestry, who has made provisions for me to stay at the Forestry Resthouse here in town. Eventually, I find a man who can read, and he takes me down to a rundown bungalow by the Indus.

The *chowkidar* (caretaker) brings me two buckets of filthy water for washing, and a carafe of drinking water with fish and worms in it. My water filter breaks, but I guzzle the cold murky water anyway.

On the main street, I find a filthy hovel that serves something resembling *dal*, and I buy several pieces of watermelon at a stand covered in flies. Nobody attempts to speak with me, other than one man who asks if

I am Indian. When I tell him that I am not, he tells me about the recent Indian nuclear explosion, and adds, "*Inshallah* (God willing), we shall run our own test as soon as possible."

I retreat to my bungalow, where I spend fifteen minutes in the dark trying to insert the right key into the lock; I have a set of twenty that look and feel exactly the same. I then spend an hour trying unsuccessfully to fix my broken water filter. Exhausted, I lay back and stew in my sweat, wondering what possesses a man to go through such daily trials.

Fortunately, Indus Kohistan is not large, and leaving Shatial, I realize I am in its last reaches. The Indus here becomes a blackish brown, running through a barren moonscape reminiscent of Nevada or Death Valley, only with 7000 meter peaks rising behind the barren hills.

Around Chilas, a tractor passes, and a young man flings a piece of sugar cane at me. It strikes me in the chest, and like that, Kohistan comes to an end. Around the next bend in the road, I come across wheat fields and fertile gardens. The countryside here is inhabited mainly by the Shinaki people, who smile, don't stare as intensely as the Kohistanis, and don't throw stones. I still see no women, and all the men have long, bushy beards, reminding me of the Amish of Pennsylvania.

The valley opens up, and I am treated to my first views of Nanga Parbat, the eighth-highest peak in the world at 8100 meters. Farther north, I can make out Rakaposhi, Dubani, and Haramosh. I am close to the heart of the Karakorams, and I feel that the struggles of the past days have indeed been for a reason.

In Talechi, a tiny oasis of trees and garden plots in the desert, I find a peaceful government resthouse with a verandah, ceiling fans, and functioning electricity. The *chowkidar* serves me a spinach curry, fresh from the garden, and I swear that it is the best meal I have ever eaten. I fall asleep to the sound of the evening prayer call from the local mosque. The call is not prerecorded, as is often the case, but is made by an actual villager, who climbs up to the minaret and sings in a deep resonant voice, beckoning all to give thanks.

The following afternoon, I roll into Gilgit, the largest town on the KKH. The town itself is rather drab and dusty, but is surrounded by towering cliffs and peaks, and high desert terrain.

The denizens of Gilgit are friendly and used to tourists. I even see women walking on the streets and shopping. All the men here wear hats, which identify where along the Indus they come from; the flat brown wool beanies of the Hunzakots are the most prevalent. I find it a marvelous way of identifying oneself, and I even spot a few members of my own clan, the ones with the colored bicycle helmets, wandering through the bazaar.

I check into a place called Tourist Cottage, an absolute haven after the rigors of the past weeks. Dinners are served on the veranda, and are lively affairs with ravenous travellers and a handful of locals drinking tea, smoking pipes, and sharing tales. I meet Coleman, a British gardener who barters his skills in exchange for room and board. Each fall, he works the grape harvest in France and Switzerland, making enough cash to finance his yearly overseas journey, which has brought him to the Karakorams this year.

I also take a shine to Audrey and Craig, a couple of doctors from Boston. They are making their way home after a year of interning in South Africa. Audrey is well travelled, has lived in China, and has a heart full of adventure; Craig has played outdoors his whole life, as a beach bum in Santa Cruz, a yurt dweller in Colorado, and a solo winter traveller in the wilds of Alaska. We seem to share the same energy and sense of wonder, so we make plans to meet for a trek farther north of Gilgit.

After Kohistan, every minute north of Gilgit is a day in paradise. The weather is sunny and cool, the road is empty, and the asphalt is in good condition, in spite of the landslides that seem to occur every few minutes. Checkerboard mesas are carved above the river, well-irrigated gardens full of trees and flowers, in total contrast to the barren rock and furnace-like desert where I have spent the past weeks. High peaks are now my daily companions, towering over the road with blocks of ice spilling from their overhanging glaciers.

People here are friendly and inviting. Inns have decent, garden-fresh food, and children here chase after me with big smiles on their faces, waving and panting as they run beside my bike. Stopping for tea in a roadside garden café, I meet Robert, a Dutch cyclist on a three-week holiday, and we spend the next several days cycling together.

Robert and I enter the Hunza valley, thought by some to be the setting of the mythical Shangri-La, where people live to be 100, fruit drops from the sky, and the air and water are fresh and abundant. Hunza is home to the Hunzakots, Ismaili Moslems with a view of Islam as wide as the Kohistani view is narrow. The Ismailis follow their spiritual leader, the Aga Khan, an extremely wealthy and generous benefactor who lives in Switzerland, and the area is awash in schools, medical clinics, and development projects.

In the Ismaili world, women are on equal footing with men, and in Hunza, it is as if we have arrived in a new country. Women in colorful pillbox hats greet us with boisterous *"Salaam aleikums"* and invite us in for *burus* and *phitti*, a buttermilk cheese served with whole-wheat bread.

The literacy rate here is high, and girls get the same education as boys. Most locals are fluent in Urdu, Burushaski, and several other local languages. Of course, English is now studied with a passion.

Even the mosques are silent, in a land where prayer calls often awaken travellers from the deepest of slumbers at ungodly hours. According to the Ismailis, if you want to go to the mosque, you go. You certainly should not need to be reminded to go—or what the hour is.

The town of Karimabad is the center of Hunza, snuggled under the foreboding Ultar Peak and glacier. As Robert and I ride in, we find the road blocked by a huge procession of schoolchildren carrying large signs that say, "Keep Hunza Green," "Plastic Causes Cancer: Keep Hunza Polystyrene Free," and "Plant Trees, Stop Deforestation."

We are stunned to find this on the roof of Asia, seemingly so far from the "developed" world. Our jaws drop even further upon arrival in the center of Karimabad, where trashcans are lined up everywhere! In one kilometer, I see more trashcans than I have seen in three years in Asia. When I go into a shop to ask about the garbage, I am told that it is taken weekly to an uninhabited valley, where it is burned and buried. Perhaps we are in Shangri-La after all.

On the town's main street, we come across Coleman, Audrey, and Craig, happily ensconced on a guesthouse veranda, drinking tea and staring dreamily out at the mountains. We join them for a feast of *dauda*, a thick vegetable stew, with spinach curry, chicken in mint sauce, and kidney beans, all served by the amiable proprietor, Mr. Hussain.

We sit back and admire the mountain setting, colored by birch and poplar trees. As we play cribbage and chat non-stop about how much magic there is in the world, we realize that among the five of us, we have covered almost every spot on the planet. As darkness descends, Coleman trips over the manager of the lodge next door, Mr. Haidar, who is out praying on his mat; this sends the entire lodge into endless peals of laughter. Clouds roll in and spit rain, and from our veranda, the world is a very okay place.

Morning brings a chance to more fully appreciate the wonders of Hunza. Since ancient times, the entire valley has been laboriously sculpted into a series of irrigation channels, tiered over 1000 meters up the steep slopes of the Ultar Nala. The channels have irrigated a previously barren swath of mountainside, and have turned Hunza into a mecca for apricot, almond, and apple trees. Every shop in town has an abundance of dried fruit and nuts for sale, as well as homemade cheese and bread. It is no wonder that the Hunzakots of yore lived such healthy lives to ripe old ages.

Strolling through town, I meet two Dutch cyclists on ancient bikes that don't look as if they will make it down the KKH. The riders tell me that they have run into Yves, the Frenchman, about a week ahead of me; they have also met Paco, who has come down with malaria and is resting in Gilgit. There are days where the world seems to shrink to about the size of a teacup.

The barrage of wild scenery continues relentlessly as I move north. Triangular rockets of granite rise from the valley floor in glorious amphitheatres. Glaciers and scree rush to the edge of the road, undoubtedly to cover the asphalt in years to come.

Just out of the village of Gulmit, my rear tire explodes, after 7000 kilometers of good use. My spare is not much better, but it is all I have. The locals get a kick out of watching my roadside repairs, and I carry on, only to find myself nursing a flat within twenty minutes. This time, my pump breaks while I try to inflate the spare tire; tragically, I have left my spare pump back in Gilgit, along with a few other "nonessentials." My water filter broke two weeks ago; my camera went on the blink in Karimabad; now my pump has stopped working. I wonder if someone is sending me a message.

I drag my bike up three very steep kilometers to the top of a pass, where I find the village of Passu and its famous Cathedrals, an exploding series of rock spires and serrated peaks that burst straight up from the valley below. The scale of sky, space, and land is of epic proportions, and I feel as if I am at the end of the earth, living amidst an age of upheaval.

I descend from the pass standing up, trying to take some weight off my rear rim, which bounces and clangs noisily against the pavement. Rain begins to fall, and I am drenched and grow hypothermic, but I don't care. I wobble down the mountain totally immersed in a natural living wonderland, feeling like I too may crumble and disintegrate at any moment, to return and be remolded into another form in the evolution of centuries.

Passu is full of boys with red hair and freckles, blue- and green-eyed girls with white skin, and other European-looking people; they are the Tajiks, Kyrghyz, and other groups of the high Pamir. Yet the *shalwar kameez* remind me that I am still in Pakistan—as does the sobering news I pick up from the BBC on my short-wave radio, which announces that Pakistan has conducted two nuclear tests in response to the blasts by India.

The locals gather in concerned silence, and I learn that they are a politically astute bunch. Several tell me that they support a strong Communist China and its suppression of their Uighur Moslem "brothers" across the border; China serves as a buffer zone to protect them from the fanaticism of the Afghan Taliban to the west, and the same narrow mindedness that is creeping up from the south.

I go outside to do yoga in the rain, staring at the soaring Cathedrals and realizing that the mountains have no care about nuclear weapons. A blast here would only hasten what they do each day anyhow: move, crumble, and change.

I find Audrey and Craig again, and once more we talk into the wee hours, joined by Ghulan Mohammed, our latest in an unending line of gracious and caring innkeepers. We feel like old friends now, and in this remote and strange outpost, perhaps we become aware of the meaning of giving time and listening in a way that is no longer possible in the busy spaces of our lives back home. Yet Mr. Mohammed reminds us that life here is just a slower version of what we have all left in our backyards. He tells us that fifteen years earlier, the people here all farmed, herded, and wore animal skins. The road brought trade, clothing, and a cash economy; today, tourism is nearly the sole source of employment. It has certainly brought a more convenient and easier life to the inhabitants of Passu, yet at the same time, Ghulan Mohammed feels that life here is now expensive and complex.

The answers? "There are none," says Mr. Mohammed, "and those that there are, are in the hands of Allah."

As a tureen of heavenly spinach soup arrives from the kitchen, we all heartily agree.

Audrey, Craig, and I decide to spend a week trekking along the Batura

Glacier, so we stock up on provisions and hire two local lads to serve as porters. Trekking etiquette here in Passu is impressive, and porters are rotated so as to ensure fair employment for all. The village seems free of the competition and pressure I felt in Nepal, India, Irian Jaya, and elsewhere. We are introduced to Sultan-Din and Karim-Jan, two sturdy and amiable sixteen-year-old boys on school vacation, eager to pick up some pocket money by carrying our food and equipment. Our party saunters out of Passu under gray skies and the watchful eye of the soaring, snowy Cathedrals.

We set up camp next to a shepherd's hut in a pasture. Rain falls for the next several hours, but there is a potbelly stove in the hut. We sit and listen to the radio, and the BBC informs us that Pakistan has closed its banks in anticipation of a capital drain. The U.S. and Japan are going to apply economic sanctions in response to the nuclear blast. We are so near, and yet so wonderfully far from all of this mess.

After arising to apricot and rice porridge prepared by Karim-Jan, we spend several hours picking our way across the moraine-covered Batura Glacier amid towering stones, boulders, blocks of ice, and deep crevasses. Higher up, we head through ablation valleys filled with juniper, birch, and willow, rapidly approaching the snow line. Wild rhubarb and small shoots poke out of the ground, and summer still seems a far off promise.

In the late afternoon, we stumble into Yashpurt, which means "horse's flat ground." It is a busy summer village, old stone houses set on a grassy knoll under the mighty wall of the Batura Ice Flow. A congregation of women runs out to greet us, and they shake our hands, chat amiably, and even encourage us to take their photos. With their long pleated braids, sunburned and wrinkled faces, and embroidered pill box hats, the women resemble Tibetans, although the Wajid language they speak sounds far closer to Russian. They spend summers tending the goats, driving them higher into the mountains as the summer comes in order to find suitable pastures for grazing.

I ask where their husbands are, and learn that the men spend summers working in Karachi, Bahrain, and New York! The women seem to relish this time together, away from their men, and we certainly enjoy their warm company. They ply us with fresh goat yogurt and yak cheese as we listen to the nearby sounds of rockfall and avalanche.

We help several villagers corner their goats, play hackey-sack with the children, and settle down under kerosene lamps for a sumptuous stew and our daily round of cribbage. Another splendid day—although we cannot find the large bars of chocolate we thought we had packed.

Above Yashpurt, the valley narrows and the scenery goes beyond sublime. Fluted frozen walls of ice and cornices rise directly above us, the noise from their unceasing activity often deafening and frightening. The power of the land is stunning, beyond words. This is a savage, pristine place of accelerated and perpetual change, uncontrollable by man and his technologies.

We spend several days in this natural wonderland. The weather is often stormy, but serves to heighten the drama of the scenery and sounds around us; thunder echoes off the glacial seas above us, while lightning crashes against hanging rock towers. Life, in all its chaos, is close to perfect—except that we cannot find the cans of sardines and the large block of cheese that we swear were in the food bag.

In the morning, Craig and Audrey take me aside, and half jokingly ask me if I am getting enough food. They wonder if with my cycling appetite, I have had need of late night forays into the food bag. I laugh and tell them I have been wondering the same about them. We sit down and come to the sad conclusion that Karim-Jan and Sultan-Din have been pilfering food while we aren't looking. They don't seem to eat enough, although whenever we have asked them to eat more, they refuse, and instead go off to find a bit of "Hunza water," the local moonshine. As we are almost out of food, we decide to return to Passu and deal with the situation there.

Ghulan Mohammed is waiting for us on his veranda, watching the cherries ripen on the trees in his garden. He pours tea and asks about the high pastures and our trek. We try to downplay the missing food, as everything else has been so wonderful, but we do bring it up. We are most surprised when the Village Welfare Committee shows up half an hour later, asking for details of what has gone missing, and how much each item costs.

Several hours later, the Welfare Committee returns, along with a glum Karim-Jan and Sultan-Din. We all sit together and take tea, and the boys confess and apologize. The head of the Welfare Committee decides on a monetary figure to be deducted from the wages we are to pay the boys, and asks if this is okay with us.

Because I have experienced porter problems in Irian Jaya and Nepal—and because I was once a sixteen-year-old myself—I do not hold a grudge, and readily agree, as do Audrey and Craig. What is amazing is how professionally and competently the village has solved the issue, especially as it involves outsiders. The entire community of Passu is to be highly commended.

An hour later, everyone in town knows about our trek, and a lot of good-natured jokes are made about the two boys, who turn out to have committed a slew of rather harmless pranks in the past years. We run into the pair early in the evening, and are happy to find that neither side harbors any resentment. An escapade that could have escalated has been discussed, dealt with, and closed forever.

Audrey and Craig are continuing on to China before returning home, and it is time for our paths to diverge. We say a heartfelt goodbye, and they hop on a van headed to the border, while Mr. Mohammed tracks down an old Chinese pump to reinflate my tire. On a half-inflated tube, I make my way north against headwinds and drizzle, watching the terrain become devoid of human habitation. About twenty kilometers on, my bald spare tire goes flat again, and soon I am stranded by the roadside, wondering how I will weasel my way out of this one.

Most amazingly, I see a bicyclist approaching from the other direction. He is an American named Jeff, who has lived in Japan for seven years, married a Japanese woman, and bicycled across China. We quickly trade tales, and I put Jeff's pump to good use. I make it into Sost, the last town in Pakistan, before dark.

Sost is an ugly frontier town of banks and grubby overpriced hotels, most unlike the other towns of the northern Karakoram. Military officers rub shoulders with Chinese traders, who smoke, spit, and make a lot of noise in the local restaurants and karaoke bars. My attempt to watch the World Cup in a local café is terminated by a broadcast of the Prime Minister's speech on the Pakistani nuclear test.

I have planned to go up to the top of the Khunjerab Pass, the border with China, but my energy level is low. After it rains all night and morning, I find that my tire has gone flat yet again, and I decide to hop on a wagon back to Gilgit and return to India.

It is sad to end my stay in these mighty mountains surrounded by angry men spitting mutton bits on the floor. However, things do have a way of revolving full circle, and I recall that my entry into Pakistan ran somewhat along these lines. I order a Coke and retire to my hotel room, listening to the rain beat down outside my window.

Chapter Fifteen
Travels in Ladakh and Kashmir

*For my part, I travel not to go anywhere,
but to go. I travel for travel's sake. The great affair
is to move.*

Robert Louis Stevenson

Several weeks after leaving Pakistan, I am back in northern India, headed east of Dharmsala into the Khangra Valley. It is refreshingly lush after the barren and parched valleys of the Karakorams. The monsoon rains are threatening imminent arrival, and the skies are swollen and the air thick and wet.

As I cross out of the Khangra and into the Kulu Valley, I meet a fifty-five-year-old British cyclist who calls himself Cube, and we ride together for several days in misty pine forests reminiscent of America's Pacific Northwest. At the top of the Kulu Valley sits Manali, an overcrowded bazaar town packed with Indian tourists and young Israelis. The Israelis smoke ganja by day, and dance to trance music and techno-pop all night long. I presume that things were like this here in the 60's—though I doubt that banana pancakes were available in the local restaurants then.

Despite the party scene, Manali is a decent place to break for a few days. There are hot spring bathhouses across the Beas River, fine for sitting out of the persistent monsoon drizzle and watching the mist creep through the forested slopes surrounding the town. Decent food is also readily available, and Cube and I enjoy the comforts of town life while we complain to one another about the hedonistic behavior of the Israeli contingent that has inhabited most of upper Manali. We agree that many of the younger generation of travellers seem to have no sense of discipline or purpose, and that they appear only to be running away from things in their lives, rather than moving toward something.

Cube sets out for Ladakh, but I decide to rest for a few more days. The high passes still have not been cleared of snow, and the bridges over major rivers are still out. With all my gear, I need to proceed slowly and with more care than Cube, who is riding with minimal weight.

Ladakh means "land of the high mountain passes," and is a place I have dreamed of since reading Andrew Harvey's classic *Journey to Ladakh*. It is a remote, high-altitude desert, nestled amid the Karakorams and Himalayas, and an extremely barren and savage environment. It is a hotly disputed territory; Pakistan and China have both claimed portions of it for themselves, and parts of the road are on the "line of control" that the Indians and Pakistanis argue over. The main road from Srinagar is no longer stable after the troubles in Kashmir, and the high road from Manali is only open two months a year, due to heavy snow.

There are five passes en route from Manali to Leh, the Ladakhi capital. Three are over 5000 meters, and one is the second highest motorable pass in the world. The road is not yet open because of the snow, so once I reach the second pass, I will be totally alone. I find myself missing Hitomi, who will not be here to share the joys and hardships, or lend solace.

I have tried not to think much about our separation, and so far, it has been easy; I have been surrounded by people, and have not spent long periods of time by myself, face to face with my thoughts and fears, without room for diversions. Perhaps I have let Cube go ahead of me because I need to be alone with this time and these challenges. It is time for me to find out if I still have what I thought I had when this journey started— what I somehow feel I have lost.

The Rohtang La, at just under 4000 meters, is the lowest pass on the high route into Ladakh. Rohtang means "piles of dead bodies," a fact that doesn't improve my mood as I wheel out of Manali and begin to crawl up the Beas River.

Initially, the ascent is straight and steep, and I feel sick as I struggle to haul my seventy pounds of gear. After ten kilometers, the road begins to switchback, and I feel like I am making progress. Himalayan lammergiers with wingspans larger than my bicycle appear overhead, swooping down to see if I am fair prey, but my loaded steed and over-powering body odor seem to deter them from coming any closer.

It is only fifty-six kilometers to the pass, but by about thirty-five, I have climbed over 1200 meters, and have run completely out of steam. To my delight, a small cluster of *dhabas* appears over the next rise, a tent village of Tibetans from the Khangra Valley. A friendly woman shows me to a tent with cots, cooks up a hot meal, and informs me that an older foreign cyclist stayed here several nights before. I retire happy in the knowledge that Cube has found the going as taxing as I have.

It rains all night, but morning brings clear skies, with mist floating up from the valley below. I leave early, along a road that becomes a small river of runoff from the melting walls of snow that line my passage. As I near the top of the pass, I pass shacks renting out coats, hats, and gloves to the throngs of Indian tourists who come to the Rohtang, and I even see families with skis arriving to zip down the ten-meter snow slopes!

The other side of the pass is a nightmare, as the road becomes a river of rocks, washouts, and water crossings. I creep downhill, stopping several times to fix tire punctures. A cyclist appears at around two p.m., coming in the opposite direction. He looks wind-whipped and in a state of shock, and doesn't say much to me, other than that the road is not good. His headset has come apart, and is tied to his bike with a piece of string. As I grip my handlebars and try to dodge boulders and read river crossings, I feel like I have entered a land of no return. The road begins a steep climb, and I get soaked with all the water crossings. The cycling—and often walking—consumes me, and I no longer take photos or revel in the scenery. It is just my two-wheeled pal Odysseus and I, taking on Mother Nature. She always wins, but we do make some slow progress.

It is a mere fourteen kilometers up the Barilacha La, but they are undoubtedly the worst fourteen I have encountered anywhere on earth. A rutted and washed out track climbs steep and relentless switchbacks, covered in water, ice, and snow. A bulldozer has cleared a narrow passage between huge walls of snow, which eventually take over the road; I discover the bulldozer lying flipped and broken in a snowdrift. I have to carry my gear over and around this mess, onto a more stable ridge of snow, where at least there are some foot tracks to follow.

I stumble blindly through a bleak world of white and gray, and the footprints disappear under fresh snowfall. I walk and carry my bicycle, and after two hours, I am lost. Nothing remotely resembles a path. I decide to follow the occasional animal tracks I come across, hoping that the animals have taken the path of least resistance. The slope I am on does appear to contour around the mountains the way a road might.

After six hours of wretchedness, I am treated to the most beautiful sight in the world. Ahead of me, through the falling snow, I can make out the multitude of colors of the Tibetan prayer flags that signify the top of the Barilacha La. I begin to weep in exhaustion and relief, falling to my knees and giving dozens of *namaskars* and *la la la tso*'s to the heavens and gods above.

I am filthy, sunburnt, out of breath, and have a bad headache from altitude, but the tribulations of the day are far from over. The descent is horrible. Snow, rocks, and torrents of water take the place of what should be a road, and I have to continue to walk. To think that cyclists informed me that the road to Ladakh was better than the Lhasa–Kathmandu road because it was "paved!"

Just when I feel my spirit is going to break, the water and mud begin to dry up, the skies open, the sun comes out, and the road descends into a lovely valley. I see enormous chocolate mountains, barren desertscape, grassy fields, wild rivers, and not a hint of human habitation. The road is rough, but a superhighway compared to what I have been through, and I fly down the valley at thirty kilometers an hour, body whipped absolutely senseless, screaming at the top of my lungs in sheer ecstasy.

I am either a masochist, a fool, or something like the worker who goes blindly to work every morning even when he knows it is time to find a new job. Perhaps I am all three rolled into one.

I rise at five a.m., my body aching from the previous day, gulp down some oatmeal, dust off Odysseus, and head into a very frozen valley, where the long climb begins to the Lachulung La. It starts out pleasant, ascending twenty-one well-graded switchbacks. Several signs along the way praise the Indian Army Corp of Engineers for this feat of construction. However, the switchbacks end at 4600 meters, and I ascend onto a high ridge where a howling headwind greets me. I walk much of the way, feeling physically defeated for the first time on this journey, and I resolve to get rid of as much of my gear as possible upon arrival in Leh.

I eventually reach the top of the pass, which is not much to celebrate, as Lachelung La is a double pass, and I must descend 200 meters to a river before climbing another five kilometers to the true summit, at over 5000 meters. I walk nearly all the way, stopping constantly to suck air, and wonder why I am engaged in such madness. The sun is out in full fury, and it bakes me to a crisp as I worm my way upward. I no longer sweat, as the air is so dry and windy, but my lips are parched and my throat burns. My body has reached its true limit.

Around yet another bend in the road, I see the prayer flags. Again I weep with exhaustion and gratitude. I try to give a yell of triumph, but not much comes out. I can only cry and clasp my hands in prayer.

The sound of an engine drifts in above the wind. I think I am imagining it, but several minutes later, a jeep appears, carrying army officers to Sarchu and to Pang, the next camp on the road. The officers look at me with pity, stopping to give me two shiny red apples before driving on.

I sit and look at the apples as if they were some strange apparition. Then I greedily devour them, letting the juice run all over my face and beard, and get to my feet to dance a rather wild jig. It dawns on me that I have eaten almost nothing all morning, and that if I keep going at this rate, I will resemble most of the sticklike Biharis I have seen working on the roads up here.

The descent takes me through a narrow canyon lined with flesh-colored walls, along a river of silt. Sand begins to appear on the road, and soon I am engulfed in a sandstorm, with my gears grinding noisily, and grit finding its way into my eyes and mouth. It is phenomenal how much different terrain one can pass through in such a brief physical distance. Snow and ice, water and mud, rocks and sand; all offer their own beauty and harshness.

I set my alarm for four a.m. and sleep through it, dreaming that I am in a hot tub in the mountains of Japan, surrounded by voluptuous women who massage me from head to toe. At five, I wake alone in my sleeping bag in a freezing tent in Pang camp. I will need to get moving if I am to have any chance at getting over the Taglang La today.

At the start of the steep climb out of the beautiful Pang canyon, I feel sick, cold, and unable to breathe. Eventually I warm up, then reach the high plateau known as the More Plains, where fierce winds begin to blow. The last two days have been grueling, but I know that today may be the worst of them all, and I try to stay calm, focused, and composed. I often feel like today will be the day that I won't make it, but I just keep pedalling, trying not to look too far ahead.

By eleven, I am only twenty kilometers below the Taglang La. At 5330 meters, it is the second highest motorable pass in the world, and like all the passes before it, this one takes the rest of the day to achieve. The wind howls in my face and makes riding nearly impossible. Even when I can ride, the altitude makes my legs feel like lead, and I have to pause to rest my heart, which pounds wildly.

I walk at least thirteen kilometers, content to concentrate on a mantra of "one more step," focusing on my breath.

With five kilometers left, I emerge onto a hillside shielded by the wind, and can now pedal slowly. A veil of tension and fatigue lifts from me, and I begin to know that I have pushed my body to its limits and succeeded.

At just after three p.m., the prayer flags are in front of me. In the distance, the mountains of Zanskar appear, with the peaks around Leh also not far in the distance. As I dismount, I do not weep, but this time scream long and loudly at the top of my lungs.

All the land I have traversed in the past week is visible behind me, as are the pain and intensity of the last days. As I snuggle into the crack of a boulder for a well-deserved rest, I truly understand that nothing, absolutely nothing, will prevent me from finishing my journey.

Leh is clean and prosperous, and its setting quite magnificent. The town is nestled into a hillside beneath the looming ruins of a medieval Tibetan palace. To the southwest, the Indus River, my constant travel companion of the past few years, flows languidly underneath the snowy flanks of Stok Kangri, a triangular peak that towers over the Leh Valley.

I find Leh much more modern than its high-altitude sister Lhasa. Perhaps this is because I have arrived from such a taxing journey through sheer wilderness, and the bright lights of the big city have me in awe. Or perhaps it is familiarity that I feel; the Ladakhis in the tourist trade here can speak English, and many of them now go to live in Delhi during the cold winters, so they have exposure to a life away from their home.

During my stay in Ladakh, I speak with many foreigners who share the viewpoint that Ladakhis are losing their culture. Yet I began to question whether this notion of lost culture can be based solely on the fact that people are no longer doing what they did ten or twenty years ago.

On my second night in Leh, I rejoin Cube—who has made it through on his bike far more unscathed than I—in a cozy family lodge. The family is one of the many that have prospered with the arrival of tourism. The kids are well educated, can speak many languages fluently, and certainly live more affluently than their parents did at their age. Cube and I stay up with the family late into the night to watch France upset Brazil in the World Cup. The visiting neighbors ooh and aah over each goal, while our host Nawa and his daughter Kelang ply us with homemade pizzas.

The children do not spend the day spinning prayer wheels and chanting mantras; nor do they wear *chubas* or pointed hats, as do the older Ladakhi women, and they spend far less time doing agricultural work than did the generations before them. They do, however, revere their family and the Dalai Lama, attend *chaams* (dance festivals), and retain strong family and community ties. They can speak their own language, as well as Hindi and several others, and they have great pride in the land they inhabit.

I am not sure that their enjoying the World Cup or eating pizza makes them any less Ladakhi than my eating Thai food or playing in a *gamelan* orchestra makes me any less American. Perhaps we are always gaining our cultures, not losing them.

On the other hand, Ladakhis do face some bona fide issues. Dawa, the eldest son, tells me that many Ladakhis now go to Delhi for the winter, rather than stay and deal with the long, cold winter at home. He feels that they are becoming soft, unable to live in a society that for so long has prided itself on its ability to survive in an extremely harsh physical environment.

Dawa also talks about the family time in winter, when all the tourists and their demands have gone away. It is a time for stories, for working together, and for sharing; Dawa believes that in Delhi, amid the noise, pollution, and distractions of city life, this family time is disappearing.

During my time in Leh, I have begun to meet a lot of women. At first, this is very appealing, and I begin to enjoy the fruits of being single once again.

There is Yvonna, a masseuse from California; Offra, an Israeli with mesmerizing green eyes; and Pina, a bouncy Italian who meditates and does yoga in the guesthouse garden every morning. Pina has just ended a seven year relationship, selling her share of the stone house she and her lover had built together, and is now in Ladakh taking time to see where her life should go.

I share much in common with these women, as we are all seeking new ideas and approaches to living, and we share a love of travel, culture, and the great outdoors. We are all young, open minded, healthy, and very free, and I certainly score a few kudos with the reputation that has preceded me into Leh (my reputation, in fact, has reached the point of ridiculous rumor; people say to me, "Oh, you must be the guy who has ridden for ten years." By the next conversation, the figure has become twelve or thirteen!).

Yet as I flirt with these women and bask in their attention, I often ask myself what I am looking for. In six months or a year, the novelty of a new relationship wears off, and the idea of working out personal issues with someone who is more or less a complete stranger seems very unappealing to me. I daydream about going back to Hitomi, who knows me better than anyone in the world.

However, this is not an option. I receive a letter from Hitomi, saying that she has gone back to Nepal and is seeing a guy there, still unsure about everything, but needing to be there picking up her own pieces. She is as sorry as I am, but still feels a great lack of trust and comfort, and is unable to go into the past with me.

As always, in moments when I grieve and feel incapable of decisions, I return to what comes naturally to me; the hard saddle of Odysseus.

In early August I cycle out of Leh, heading west toward Kashmir. The verdant valleys, rushing rivers, and high mountain peaks are supposed to be the most beautiful in all India, but the road ahead promises nothing but trouble.

India and Pakistan have been arguing over Kashmir for years, but this summer has seen an escalation in the fighting. The line of control, a rather arbitrary and imaginary corridor, has been the scene of fierce clashes. Most of the line is well away from main roads and tourist routes, but one spot just outside of the town of Kargil is in the line of fire.

Kargil was shelled two weeks ago, with twenty people killed. Surrounding villages have been evacuated, and the highway closed for days. In spite of the horror stories, I decide to head west as far as I can go, making my decisions on a daily or even hourly basis. I want to avoid the high route back to Manali, and to see another part of Ladakh—and if at all possible, Kashmir.

Initially, the route to Kashmir is much easier than the high road I took from the south. The road follows the Indus River valley, passing through colorful fields of mustard seed and golden barley.

Small, sleepy hamlets dot the valley, and I pass traditional Tibetan adobe houses with brightly painted window frames, straw roofs, and abundant apricot trees in the backyards. *Gompas* of varying sizes sit on the hillsides, their *chortens* glowing white against the blue sky, and monks skip to and fro, engaged in their daily chores.

Conditions are good, and I ride along contentedly, though my image of the peaceful and easygoing Ladakhis is shattered when several fellows on a passing bus hurl fistfuls of apricots at me for sport.

I pass many Bihari road workers, who give me smiles and appreciation. Bihar is one of the poorest states in India, and wealthy land barons known as *zamindars* still control most of the land, forcing the poor to work the land for them like slaves. Armed thugs carry out the orders of the *zamindars*, and use violence to control the local politicians. Therefore, many Biharis come to Ladakh to work in the summer, earning a pitiful twenty rupees (fifty cents) per day for high-altitude road building. Even though they are outfitted with coats and gloves, they are still woefully unprepared for the extreme conditions in Ladakh. They often look like savages, standing dazed and wide-eyed next to boiling pots of tar, or moving rocks across the road one at a time.

On one particularly grueling pass outside the village of Lamayuru, I pedal past a large group of Biharis, who drop their tools and stare at me as I pant and pedal uphill. With a sudden cry, one of them runs up behind my bike and begins to push me along. His coworkers join him, and soon there are dozens of hands pushing me effortlessly up the steep pass. The smiling workers erupt into Bihari folk songs as they push me upward, showing mouths full of gleaming white teeth.

Forevermore, on steep passes, I will remember the joy I feel in this moment.

In Mulbekh, the cultural boundary between Ladakh and Kashmir, I sit in a café where a little boy flicks dried peas in my face, while the family guard dog eyes my bike with a very evil eye. Two foreigners tell me that shells rained down on Kargil all night when they were there, and that I am an insane lunatic if I go anywhere near the place. I listen to the detailed reports from the BBC on my short-wave radio, and decide to inch closer and see for myself what is going on.

In a guesthouse the following morning, I awake to the sound of forty French tourists clamoring for soft drinks and potato chips. They are Buddhists, here to see their lama, and I figure that the guesthouse owner could give them instructions on how to behave a little more appropriately.

Almost immediately out of Mulbekh, the *chuba* is replaced by the *shalwar kameez* and veil as the villages change from Ladakhi to Kashmiri. Grubby *dhabas* appear, serving greasy mutton, watery omelets, and oily vegetables, and it feels like I am back amidst the culinary wonders of Pakistan.

Outside Kargil, traffic is backed up for several kilometers, and as I ride to the front of the line, I wonder if the town is again being shelled. It turns out that the Indian Defense Minister has flown in for a look, and that everyone is merely being told to wait for his helicopter to leave. Strangely, when the soldiers see my bicycle, they wave me ahead, and I cycle into town alone.

Kargil is dusty and shabby, full of shops selling things I don't need, like pantyhose and plastic shoes. I see no signs of recent shelling, though several shops are closed, and a lot of armed soldiers wander around. Life appears quite normal here, and without the recent reports, I might not know that I am in a war zone. In light of the recent troubles, all Kargil's hotels sit empty, and I take advantage of this by naming my price for a carpeted room and hot bath.

Over a bowl of mutton curry submerged in oil, I ask a restaurateur named Mohammed about the recent troubles.

"Troubles?" Mohammed asks. "What troubles? Nobody is ever killed here, and Kargil is as safe as all other towns in the world. Actually, the fighting has occurred fifty kilometers from here."

As I return to my room, I figure that this fellow is either in very deep denial, or that the news services have made some seriously erroneous reports.

I go to bed, and Kargil passes the night in peace until one very large explosion wakes me up in the wee hours of the morning.

The road out of town resonates with fear. Nervous soldiers man sandbagged posts every five kilometers or so, stopping me to check my passport. They tell me that it is safe to continue, and I figure that I will have to put my faith in the Indian army for the next ten kilometers. The road is eerily deserted, and the weather gray and windy as I fight my way uphill. Initially, steep mountains flank the narrow valley and I feel quite safe, but suddenly the mountains fall away, and I enter an open meadow stretching for about five kilometers. Large Howitzers line the side of the road, manned by anxious Indian army officers, and aimed at the hills on the opposite side.

I pause briefly and look up at the hilltops, where I can very easily make out the Pakistani artillery. It is pointed directly at where I am standing, on full alert, and with guns just as large as the ones on this side.

I take one look at the size of the shells being fitted into the Howitzers, gulp very deeply, and begin pedalling like a man possessed. Not that it matters; if the gunners on the hill decide to engage in a bit of sport, my odyssey will come to a very rapid and insignificant end.

Fortunately, it must be teatime. I thank the gods above and turn my thoughts to battling the wind, which continues to howl up the valley and into my face. The river rushes next to me, completely unconcerned with the nearby conflict, and the mountains grow near again, standing somber and looking as disinterested as the river.

The Zoji La, the pass which will return me to the green slopes of the Himalayas, lies just ahead. It is a very narrow pass on a dangerous stretch of road, and vehicles are only allowed in one direction at a time. Until midday, traffic goes up from this side, and afterwards, it comes from the Kashmir side. I have read and heard countless stories describing the horrors of the Zoji La, many of them involving accidents with foreign cyclists. When I reach the top and see the other side of the pass, I know why these stories exist. The road descends crazily through a series of narrow switchbacks on a track of slick stone, mud, and water.

As I begin my descent, 500 trucks come roaring down behind me. I am splattered in mud and nearly run off a cliff when I misjudge a huge rock and my bike lurches wildly in the air. The passing drivers all laugh. They take up all the available road space, making passing or stopping pretty near impossible, and it isn't until one fellow's rig stalls that I am able to get around the pack and head for more stable ground.

I hit the valley floor on the other side just in time for the arrival of hundreds of trucks headed the other way. Although the road increases to two lanes, the steady stream of big rigs keeps me pinned to the muddy ditch at the road's edge. Another day, another battle; yet once again I emerge relatively unscathed.

The road winds into Sonamarg, which means "golden meadows," and the place lives up to its name. Pine forests surround green hills full of wildflowers, and majestic granite spires and glaciated peaks ring the valley. The vale of Kashmir, in its alpine splendor, is even more beautiful than I had expected.

Unfortunately, I cannot buy a beer to celebrate my arrival, as liquor shops have been gone from Kashmir since 1989, when Islamic militants began blowing them up. I celebrate with a feast in a *dhaba*, surrounded by a family from Calcutta who gleefully inform me, "Your legs are being that of Superman, is it not?"

Leaving Sonamarg and its pristine alpine scenery, I ride through exquisitely lush countryside, with fields of corn and wheat on one side of the road and dense forest on the other. Army checkpoints appear every ten or twenty kilometers, and soldiers are everywhere. When I stop to pee along a deserted stretch of road, a voice from the underbrush whispers, "Hello," and I make out the smile of a camouflaged soldier, clutching a Kalashnikov.

A day later I roll into Srinagar, the capital of Kashmir, and a city in a time warp. The British made Srinagar a summer capital during their tenure here, charmed by its lovely lakes and mountains, and little has changed since then. There are scores of crumbling and beautiful old homes set along quiet canals, buried under a tangle of vines and creepers. London buses still ply the main streets, and there are bobbies on every corner.

Yet modern Srinagar is a city under siege. Bunkers sit on every block; buses have screens over the windows so people cannot throw bombs through them; and many of the city's former hotels have been turned into Indian commando headquarters. All of the shops and offices are closed upon my arrival in a solidarity strike for a *mujehadeen* leader who was killed recently.

Yet the locals are as welcoming as ever. A man by the name of Amrit invites me into his home for *sochiwol*, sesame seed bagels, and he is most surprised when I tell him that I eat these for breakfast every day back home. When I thank him and leave, I am mobbed by Kashmiris, who cannot believe I have ridden a bicycle here from Ladakh. I am even questioned by dozens of women in full *burqua* (veils with screens over the eyes, covering the full face); they gossip loudly and occasionally pinch my skinny frame, presumably discussing my suitability for marriage.

After the commotion dies down, Amrit takes me down the street, past women wrapped in *burqua*, nearly naked *sadhus*, and camouflaged soldiers. We arrive at the shore of Dal Lake, in the center of Srinagar, where he recommends that I stay on a houseboat. He beckons a *shikara* (a rowboat which serves as a water taxi) and sends me on my way.

Houseboats were an integral part of British life in Kashmir, and the old boats that plied the lakes and waterways of Srinagar were equipped with armchairs, canopy beds, claw tubs, and dining terraces complete with chandeliers. When the British quit India, they left all this behind, and the boats still serve as a most welcome respite for weary travellers.

Most of the time, the magic of exotic travel is more a fantasy than a reality. The road is dusty and rugged, the transport overcrowded and slow, the bathrooms filthy, and the food rarely as good as a home-cooked meal. But on Dal Lake, reality far exceeds my expectations, and I spend most of the following days laughing in both glee and disbelief.

The Sumbol houseboat occupies a sleepy corner of the lake, next to other boats with names like New Mexico, Sheherezade, Acropolis, Holiday Inn, Plato, and the curiously named Aristotile. The Sumbol is actually a set of two medium-sized boats, complete with Mogul-style sculpted wooden verandas. Bedrooms come complete with Kashmiri rugs and hand-carved chests of drawers, while the living room is furnished with divans, armchairs, china cabinets, and even a stereo. In the bathroom sits a porcelain bathtub.

My host on the Sumbol is Sultan, a thin man with a permanent smile and a look of grace. He lives on one of the boats with his wife, mother, father, daughter, and his elegantly bearded brother-in-law, who is the local crier for the mosque's call to prayer, and climbs a nearby minaret several times each day to sing beautiful Islamic hymns in his tender voice.

Sultan tells me that what is his is mine. He sets me up in the finest bedroom and leaves me to a much-needed nap, before gently awakening me for an elegant dinner of sautéed eggplant, thick *dal*, and fresh vegetables. We share a pipeload of hash after dinner, and I fall asleep on the veranda to the sound of the water gently lapping against the side of the boat.

I spend a week aboard the Sumbol, pampered and doted over by Sultan and his clan. Sultan often comes to sit in the armchair in the dining room, and tells me of how wonderful times were in Kashmir. Hippies flocked here in the 70's and early 80's, and Sultan spent much of that time partying and dancing with them aboard his boat, amazed by all the strange and colorful creatures who came from the other side of the world. As Kashmiris love to sing and dance, he had no problem with the hippies' love of celebrating; as for the hash, marijuana grows like a weed all over Kashmir.

Even ten years ago, 600,000 Indian tourists were coming to Kashmir every year, in addition to 60,000 foreigners. Two years ago, the total number of tourists dropped to 5000, and only in the last year have Indian tourists started to trickle back as word gets out that Kashmir is fairly safe again.

Tourism has been the lifeblood for many of the people here, but Sultan doesn't make too much of a fuss over the lack of visitors. "We take what Allah gives," he says with a smile.

I tell him that I find it absolutely charming, and that I feel like an explorer in the days of old. There are none of the tourist hordes I saw in Leh, and in the following week I glimpse only a few foreign faces, gliding by on *shikaras* in search of a place to stay. I spend my days reading on the veranda, snacking on *sochiwol*, drinking tea, and talking with the family. There is no need to go anywhere, as *shikaras* ply the lake loaded with fruit, apple juice, toilet paper, drinking water, and all other essentials. There are even boatmen offering massage, haircuts, tailoring, and "water trekking."

Sultan is on very good terms with all the boatmen, and he has no interest in commissions at the expense of his guests' relaxation. He asks me to let him know if I feel pestered by any of the salesmen, and even gives me my own small boat to explore the canals and waterways of the ancient city.

During one outing, I find the papier-mâché painting shop of Yusuf Abdul Rahman, who comes from a 200 year legacy of the craft. Yusuf shows me his workshop, and I get a glimpse into just how labor-intensive the painting of the papier-mâché is. Yusuf etches detailed scenes from life on Dal Lake onto the sculptures, brushing in the tree-lined and algae-filled canals down to the minutest detail.

Yusuf's trade may well end with him, as his children are the first literate and educated ones in his family. Both Yusuf and his father are urging them to become doctors or lawyers, without too much regret over the possible death of their trade.

Although Yusuf is neither literate nor formally educated, he has picked up decent English over his years in tourism, and his business skills are impeccable. He tells me about how bad things were in Srinagar just two years before, when there were nightly shootings, bombings, and even raids on the houseboats by militants and soldiers. He talks silently about the atrocities committed by the corrupt Indian army, and about the two factions of militants, those who want Kashmir to be a part of Pakistan, and those who want an independent Srinagar.

I ask Yusuf what he would like for Kashmir, and he looks at me with kind eyes and says, "A peaceful place for my children; a chance to sell my paintings; to watch the night stars as I did as a child, without a sign of tracer bullets in the sky; and to paddle along the silent canals with my friends, Hindu and Moslem alike."

As I paddle back to the Sumbol, I notice that the leaves on the trees have begun to change color, and realize that autumn is near. Winter will come swiftly to Central Asia, and I dread being stuck halfway across. With sadness, I realize that it is time to leave the magical diversity of scenery and people I have found on the subcontinent, and all of the hospitality and adventures that have come with it in the past year.

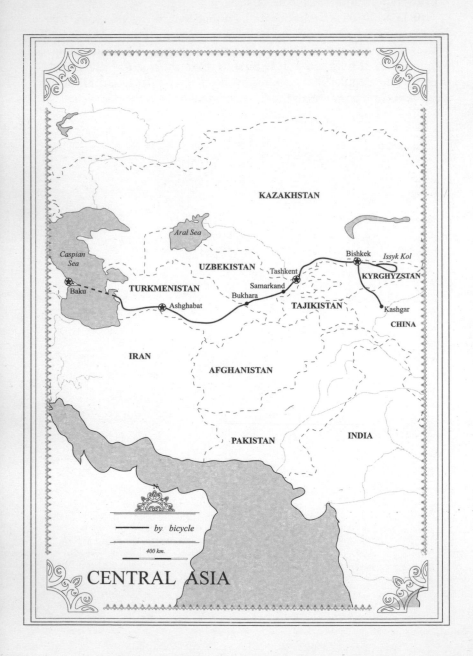

CENTRAL ASIA

by bicycle

400 km.

Chapter Sixteen
A Journey Through the 'Stans

And the road becomes my bride. I,
stripped of all but pride,
So in her I do confide, and she keeps me satisfied,
gives me all I need.
And with dusty throat I crave, only knowledge
will I save
To the game you stay a slave...
Rover, wanderer, nomad, vagabond, call me what
you will.
But I'll take my time anywhere, free to speak my
mind anywhere.
And I'll redefine anywhere.
Anywhere I roam, where I lay my head is home.

Metallica,
Wherever I May Roam

The only information I have been able to glean on the mountain kingdom of Kyrghyzstan comes from my Kyrghyz Cartographical and Geodesical Services map, which guarantees "a high quality and short terms of performance." The map also promises "distortion of earth's surface, stereo topography of glaciers, and geodesical ensuring of towns," yet the junction where I arrive on the eighteenth of September is not on it.

All I know of Kyrghyzstan, other than what my map promises, is that the country is small and extremely mountainous. Upon reaching Naryn, the first town of any size, I am surprised to find Russians still living here, and as I wander through streets full of tall, blue-eyed blondes, I get my first inkling that Europe may not be too far away.

Kiosks in Naryn are stocked with sardines, Snickers, orange juice,

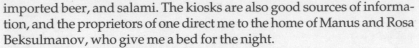

imported beer, and salami. The kiosks are also good sources of information, and the proprietors of one direct me to the home of Manus and Rosa Beksulmanov, who give me a bed for the night.

I am the only tourist here. Nobody speaks a word of any language other than Russian or Kyrghyz, there are neither tourist services nor infrastructure, and local banks will exchange no currency besides American dollars or Russian rubles. After months on what was often a well-travelled Asian trail, Kyrghyzstan promises to be interesting.

I set off from Naryn and follow a silent road into the nearby mountains. The land is devoid of human habitation, except for the occasional wheat field and the traditional yurt dwellings used by the Kyrghyz nomads. There are virtually no cars on the road, and the ones that do pass are ancient Russian Ladas. Almost all of them have smashed windshields, which leads me to believe that there is either a high rate of robbery in Kyrghyzstan, or else a lot of drunk driving. The second possibility seems the more logical one, as vodka costs less than a dollar a bottle.

Every thirty kilometers or so, I pass abandoned railcars where a few families have set up shop. Tables in front of each car display the same provisions for sale: Snickers bars, vodka, beer, and Pepsi. I figure that the Snickers will sustain me halfway to Europe.

Outside the settlements, the only people I see are Kyrghyz nomads, usually riding horses across the windy mountain slopes. They have ruddy cheeks, Mongoloid features, and could easily be taken for Tibetans, except for their tall and pointy felt hats, engraved with animal designs and other totems. These cowboys usually approach when they see that I have my own form of horse. As I cannot speak Kyrghyz, and as they do not understand my miserable attempts at Russian, I spend most of the day without speaking, merely listening to the wind howl.

There are few towns in Kyrghyzstan, and in the ones that exist, food is a problem. Restaurants all serve the exact same fare of *lagman*, the Kyrgyhz national dish, which is a greasy noodle soup full of giant globules of mutton fat, served with shots of vodka. Pickings are better at the small street markets, where wrinkled old women sell jars of fresh *ayran* (a liquid yogurt), fresh *nan*, and of course the ubiquitous Snickers and vodka.

The language, or lack of it in my case, is very frustrating. In India and Pakistan, I could have intelligent conversations with people everywhere I went; thus far in Kyrghyzstan, I can say "*Amerikanski*" (American), "*velosyped*" (bicycle), "*adyeen*" ("one," in Russian), and "*kayeda*" ("where," in Kyrghyz). These words spoken, I listen mutely as people around me pepper me with unintelligible diatribe.

In Cholpon Ata, I stay a week with Elena Ivanova, the matron of a small pension. Elena comes from a city on the Volga in Russia, and spends six months a year with her son Yuri in this home, which she bought twelve years ago. She used to have a steady stream of guests, but nobody comes anymore, and I am actually the first guest to show up in over a year.

Tanya Bakuryeva, a young language student from Moscow, is staying here for her holidays. She looks rather ill, but her English ability is a godsend, and she helps me converse with the Ivanova family throughout my weeklong stay.

Yuri is an enormous man with an even more enormous belly, who brushes aside all stories about my journey, instead asking me how I like the naked ladies featured on the front pages of his tabloid magazines.

Elena Ivanova treats us to the largest feasts that I have seen since India. Plates of stuffed peppers and tomatoes appear, along with bowls of meat stew and trays of *pilmeni* (dumplings stuffed with corn), and endless mugs of hot tea. Over our meals and several toasts of vodka, Yuri tells me of his heroics as a military man. He has survived the war in Afghanistan, and is now retired. He encourages me to find a Russian wife, believing that they all look as inviting as the girls on the tabloid covers, while Elena concurs that a Russian wife might be just the thing for a nomad like myself.

I stay until I cannot take any more of the Ivanovas' treatment. I am constantly plied with food, heaters are brought next to my bed, and I am sent twice a day to the family bath, which is actually a sauna. The sauna is heated with hot larch branches, and is completely relaxing, though Yuri follows me in for each bath, wanting to beat me with the larch branches as the honored guest.

Elena Ivanova loves playing grandmother, and she means well, but is forever bossing everyone around, screaming at all of us as to how we should eat, drink, bathe, wash, and work. Yuri gets the brunt of all this, but is well used to it, retiring behind his tabloid pictures, while Tanya goes off fishing and swimming, the sun doing wonders for her ghostly complexion.

On the morning I leave, Elena Ivanova fills my already overloaded panniers with fish, fruit and bread, and then proceeds to touch and bless my bicycle and all my bags. She insists that I should find a girl-friend, and that Yuri could introduce me to a few eligible ladies. As I leave, Yuri gives me a "special Russian handshake," swinging his arm back as if to throw a punch, then giving me a low five soul handshake, followed by a massive bear hug. Next comes Elena, weeping loudly, embracing me, and imploring me to stay with them forever. It is all so dramatic that I too am close to tears as I take my bike out.

As I roll out of the driveway, Elena Ivanova's voice carries after me: "You are too skinny. You are too alone. You will surely be killed. I will worry about you all night…"

Back on the road, I meet Klemens and Sylvie, a couple of German cyclists en route from their home to Hong Kong. We trade tales as we cycle beside one another, moving against a strong wind and arriving in a small hamlet just as a howling storm begins to leave fresh snow on the mountains above us. As we ask around for a homestay, we are directed from one house to another, and are finally deposited at a very neat and prosperous-looking farmhouse. A sturdy Kyrghyz woman in workboots and a colorful apron sees us coming and rushes to the kitchen with a huge smile on her face.

I spy her heating up the samovar, and soon we are seated around a warm fire, drinking tea and eating thick homemade rye bread with freshly churned butter and boysenberry jam. The woman's name is Kashia, and we are very welcome here, but that is as far as our language skills go. We want to know how much it will cost to stay, but Kashia says it is up to her husband to decide on the financial matters, and he is not home yet.

Klemens and Sylvie insist on knowing what the charges will be, fearing that we will be overcharged, and that if the cost is indeed too much, we must leave now in order to find a suitable campsite before dark. They ask my opinion, and I answer that we are taking tea, and that once this is done, everything will work itself out.

They continue to fidget and fret, venting their worries and asking what I think we should do, and again, I tell them to relax and enjoy the hospitality. It occurs to me how long I have been in Asia, and how accus-tomed I have become to the way of life here. Tea drinking is an integral part of life. It is a way of slowing down, focusing, being present, and preparing for what lies ahead. In business, it is also a tool for breaking the ice between parties, letting them relax and get acquainted before dealing with financial matters or other serious subjects. Whereas to westerners, this taking of tea might look like a waste of time, a stalling tactic, or a way of hesitating to get to the point, in Asia it is perhaps the most important part of any interaction.

Fortunately, before we make any decisions, Kashia's husband Ermek shows up. A very fair figure is agreed upon for meals and lodging, and for yet another night, I settle into the lap of luxury, thanks to the kindness and generosity of a local family.

Over supper, and well into the night, via a pocket dictionary and a variety of charades, we try to talk about our lives and homes. Ermek, Kashia, and their son Adamek survive on the small farm, growing vegetables and raising several pigs and chickens. Life is hard, and I am surprised to learn that the couple are only forty-two years old, as they both look well into their fifties.

As with so many families in rural communities, their big hopes for the future lie with their children, in this case Adamek, who will shortly be off to Bishkek to attend the university. It will be very expensive to send him there, and his helping hand will be missed on the farm, but Ermek and Kashia know there is no economic future here. They see the drunken young men who sit idly in town watching their lives pass by, and they do not want this for Adamek or their grandchildren.

We leave a day later, cycling along the lake of Issyk Kul on a lovely fall day. The leaves are turning yellow and amber, and the sun shines down upon the water. Children chase after us, yelling, "Sportsman!" as we wheel by, and villagers sit out in the mellowing late September sunshine.

The area is sleepy, peaceful, and charming, yet all the villages are horribly economically depressed. We can see desperation on faces in the bazaars, behind the limited supplies and imported goods that few can buy, and in the eyes of the young men who sit swilling vodka by the abandoned railcar stands, eyeing us with suspicious glances as we pass through.

We reach Kara Kol by nightfall, the only real city in the region, and a place that on first glance looks like Newark, New Jersey thirty years past! Ugly concrete tenements, decaying and rundown, grace every avenue, and Kara Kol sprawls for miles, with the feel of a ghost town. At the Kara Kol Hotel, the lobby is full of old Russian women engaged in a trade far older than they are. We are greeted with suspicious stares and told that there is no room for us.

After a further search, we arrive at a series of collapsing tenements, which look like something out of the Great Depression. Young Russian

girls with out-of-date hairstyles and wailing babies lounge on rickety
stoops, while men in dirty shirtsleeves smoke and guzzle vodka. The
neighborhood looks terribly unsafe, and we are shown to an apartment
where the lock is falling off the door. There is no hot water, kitchen, or
indoor toilet, and the tenants want fifteen dollars from each of us for a
night in this misery. We cycle away from drunken comments and the
screams of the children, wondering what our next accommodations will
look like.

Fortune smiles upon us as we arrive at the home of Valentin and
Bubulina, a pair of hearty Russians who live in a large old Russian
house. We are ushered in with a heartfelt welcome and urged to throw
our sleeping bags anywhere we want. As I carry my panniers upstairs, I
am surprised to hear my name, and I turn to find Boaz and Elizabeth,
Israelis I had met near the Chinese border! My astonishment turns to
disbelief when I learn that we have arrived just in time for a Rosh
Hashanah celebration, and a feast fit for a king has been laid out in the
dining room.

I am soon seated among smiling faces, digging into fresh trout, salad,
and thick Russian rye, all the while treated like a long lost son by Valentin,
who says he has never met a man who has seen as much of the world as
I have. Our merrymaking goes on into the wee hours, and Valentin tells
us of his dream to start an adventure tourism business here in Kara Kol.
Obviously, he has already become well known in the Soviet bloc, as
halfway through the evening, a group of nine whitewater rafters from
Moscow arrive, all set for a nearby expedition.

During my travels in Asia, I have often dreamed of finding a spot in
the world where only true explorers or adventurers might end up, a
place still relatively undisturbed and unchanged by the coming of tourism. I have seen glimpses of such a place in Irian Jaya and other spots,
but these places were terribly remote and wild. Yet Kara Kol, at the edge
of savage mountains and rivers, is still easily accessible by road, but still
so unknown that it might as well be off the map.

I watch Valentin arranging details with the rafters, who are incredibly vibrant and burly men with huge beards and the builds of lumber-
jacks. They are attempting for the fifth time to raft a Class Five and Six
river (six meaning unraftable and suicidal) into China; on each previous
attempt, they have lost one member of their party.

Valentin tells them that I have ridden my bicycle 23,000 kilometers
around the world. The rafters look me over from head to toe and pull out

a bottle of vodka to toast my craziness. I toast back to theirs, and retire to my sleeping bag, drifting off to the sounds of the Russians wrapping their boxes of equipment with swaths of duct tape.

Valentin appears to be in on every operation that comes to town, as several days later, a film company from Bishkek shows up at his place prior to setting out on a job. Yevgeny Barishnikov and Tuligen Sidikov have come to make a documentary for a German television company on the traditional Kyrghyz mountain life; Valentin's friend Zaina Beshekeyova, who comes from a mountain village nearby, shows up to guide them.

Zaina asks if I would like to come along to see the beautiful mountains of Kyrghyzstan for the day, and I accept without hesitation. Soon we are bouncing along a rutted track, climbing above the abandoned sanitarium of Jeti Oguz to enter the Kyrghyz wild west. Red sandstone cliffs and canyons give way to pine forests, and hot springs gush forth from the rocks.

When Zaina tells me that a house and land next to one of these hot pools costs about 4000 dollars, I seriously consider moving in.

Though she lives in a tiny mountain settlement with her mother and two brothers, rosy-cheeked Zaina is a bit more cosmopolitan than meets the eye. She spent several years as a member of the Communist Party in Moscow, has a large collection of Russian literature on her shelves, and engages me in some longwinded discussions about the fall of communism and the future of the ex-Soviet republics.

After lunch, we take horses up a meandering valley past a magnificent ranch that Zaina points out as the property of famed Soviet cosmonaut Yuri Gagarin. Soon the valley narrows, and we enter one of the most gorgeous forests I have ever seen, full of Siberian pine, which unlike its relatives, changes color in the fall, and has turned to a surreal mixture of amber and burnt yellows. I romp through the valley like a child, taking photos until my film is gone.

Yevgeny and Tuligen spend the afternoon filming, and we watch a group of cowboys arrive and begin the laborious process of pitching their *yurta*. The *yurta* is a geodesic structure, the outer shell made of wooden poles lashed together with rope. The frame is then covered with the hides of yaks, sheep, or even horses, and the hides are tightened down to create a very warm and weatherproof shelter. Carpets are laid on the floor of the *yurta*, and samovars and vodka bottles are brought out for the feasts that follow the raising of the shelter.

The nomads know Zaina, and we are given a warm welcome. They invite us to join in the camp chores, and to partake of the sheep that has been slaughtered to inaugurate this temporary hunting and grazing camp. As the foreign dignitary, I am the guest of honor, and thus I am served the most valued piece of the sheep—its eyeball. I cannot refuse, as scores of eyes scrutinize my every move, so I close my eyes, look heavenwards, and begin crunching away, visualizing chocolate ice cream all the while.

We feast and guzzle vodka all afternoon, and I am the subject of endless toasts. After enough alcohol, I discover that my Russian has improved dramatically, and I spend a blissful afternoon wondering if I will suddenly wake up from this magical dream.

I want to linger in Kara Kol forever. Zaina is ready to adopt me, Valentin wants me to stay and help him run a trekking agency, and most of my free time is spent in hidden valleys, hot springs, and enchanted canyons, where autumn colors rage under the amphitheaters of glaciated peaks. However, Europe is 7000 kilometers away, and under the pale October sun, I know that the weather will only grow colder in the coming weeks and months. I say yet another sad goodbye, and hit the road once more.

It takes only a few days to zip down from the highlands into Bishkek, the capital of Kyrghyzstan. Bishkek is an odd place, small yet sprawling. It lies snuggled against glaciated mountains, but without feeling like an outdoor paradise, and is seemingly caught somewhere between the Roaring Twenties and the Great Depression. Fashion-conscious shoppers and dapper Soviet-Kyrghyz couples walk arm in arm along sweeping boulevards, stopping for lamb burgers and ice cream, while all around them, drab Socialist architecture decays, scores of homeless squat in doorsteps, and vacant-eyed youths toss syringes into the gutters.

It snows heavily in Bishkek, and I delay my departure for several days. I pass the time at the bazaar, gorging myself on burgers, chocolate, and ice cream, and I go to see the circus, which is a Russian institution. This one has a particularly Central Asian flavor, with Kyrghyz trapeze artists, Kazakh horse riders, Uzbek strongmen, and clowns and Playboy bunny wannabes in leggy stockings from all over.

There is no border post between Kyrghyzstan and Kazakhstan, although a policeman flags me down shortly after my entry and asks sheepishly if he can have my autograph. This happens again after ten kilometers, when a man in a big fur hat driving a belching Lada screams at me to stop. He disembarks waving a pen and paper, yelling, "Sportsman, *atkudah*?" (from where?) over and over.

Temperatures remain bitterly cold for the next several days, though no more snow falls. I am forced into my tent by the early afternoon, usually camping in an empty apple orchard, where I melt snow on my stove, heat some soup, and nibble chocolate bars before snuggling into my sleeping bag.

My water bottles freeze at night, but my spirits remain warm, as people continue to treat me with unabashed kindness. On my first night in an orchard, the owner of the land arrives on his horse just after I have brewed my tea. Startled to find an American on a bicycle camped out in the snow, he invites me for food, telling me that I am very brave to travel the *Jibek Jalu* (Kazakh for Silk Road).

At Kazakh truck stops, gorgeous young women come chasing out after all the drivers who pull in, inviting them in for a meal. When I see this, I assume that the women are prostitutes, as the minute I stop, they are stroking my beard, cooing softly, and trying to lead me into their railcars, which serve as makeshift diners.

Unable to resist the charms of one young lady, whose miniskirt reveals the best legs in the universe, I let her lead me to a railcar, telling myself to have an open mind. Her name is Aika, and while she purses her lips and sticks out her ample chest close to my face, she looks through my dictionary and finds the words "handsome, married, available," and other suggestive vocabulary. She takes my frozen hands and begins rubbing them, and I close my eyes, imagining that I am Alexander the Great, surrounded by a harem on the Silk Road.

But my fantasies are only a pipe dream. My bowl of stew arrives, and Aika runs outside to bring in more customers. I realize that all the girls here are just perky and flirtatious twenty-year-olds, out to bring in diners for their family restaurants, and having fun while doing it. Ever the sucker, I stop in teashops and diners every fifteen kilometers or so to have my ego stroked. My mileage dwindles to almost nothing, yet I have no regrets whatsoever.

The weather warms up, the snow melts, and I am soon back into shorts, forgetting that winter had even made an appearance. My route through Kazakhstan takes me along the edge of the Steppe, the world's largest prairie, which runs from Hungary all the way to Mongolia. It stretches flat and endless to my right, while snowbound behemoths rise 3000 meters up from the plains on my left. The road is flat, and a brisk tailwind pushes me along.

The small towns are as picturesque as the scenery, and everywhere I go, the hospitality is better than the last place. Military patrols stop me to shake my hand and wish me luck. Several women pull over, ask if I am married, and then jokingly demand that I take them with me to America on the back of the bike. A young man stops in the middle of the road and has me autograph his passport photos! I am convinced that the modern Silk Road is every cyclist's dream.

Emerson wrote that "travel is a fool's paradise," and sure enough, just when I think that it really all is downhill, my ride is rather rudely interrupted. Thirty kilometers outside of Shimkent, five minutes after I have celebrated passing the 24,000 kilometers cycled milestone, my front rim cracks.

A terrible whumping sound comes from my wheel, and I discover that the rim has begun to peel apart. There is little I can do. I release the brake so the wheel can continue to revolve, and I proceed very slowly with my fingers crossed. Shimkent is a large city, and I hope I can find something.

Shimkent is indeed a big place, an ethnic madhouse of Uzbeks, Kazakhs, Tajiks, Turks, and a few Russians. Its bazaar is the mother of all bazaars, a labyrinth of stalls selling clothing, food, and every part, bit, and piece known to man. There is a very extensive bicycle part section, full of saddles, spokes, tires, and frames, but sadly, there is no such thing as a twenty-six inch wheel to be found.

I press on toward Tashkent, and the hilly terrain makes for frightening riding, as I have no front brake, and fear that my rim will implode at any minute. The day seems to take forever, but I reach the Uzbek border unscathed.

Convoys of soldiers patrol the frontier, and suspicious police sit behind glass barricades. A group of Uzbek women, all with mouths full of gold teeth, wander over to sell me Uzbek *som* at the black market rate, and when they find out where I have come from and where I am going, they insist on giving me a pile of money to buy tea and food. I refuse adamantly, but without success, and all they are willing to take in exchange is my autograph.

A Kazakh woman in a car leans out and asks if I have been on television. A minute later, she leans out again and asks if I would be interested in marrying her. She smiles, I smile, the Uzbek women smile, and as I ready my passport for inspection, I vote Kazakhstan as the most pleasant spot on earth.

Tashkent is the hub of Central Asia, a huge and modern city with many vestiges of the Soviet days still visible. I walk along palatial boulevards and through tree-lined parks full of cafés. The government buildings are unsightly, but the underground stations of the sleek metro system are ornately decorated with chandeliers, marble columns, and various communist motifs. Around the crowded Amir Temur Plaza, hawkers sell paintings, books, and souvenirs, next to well-dressed young Uzbeks, who sip cokes at streetside eateries, looking chic in their designer jeans, sunglasses, and slick hairstyles.

Supermarkets are stocked with cereal, cookies, and imported European goods like Greek orange juice, Danish feta, Belgian chocolate, and Norwegian herring. Yet I sense a desperation in Uzbekistan, far different from life in Kyrghyzstan or Kazakhstan. Inflation is rampant, and black market traders are gathered at almost every intersection. People wander the streets clutching dollars in their hands; if one has only *som*, one may be penniless by the following morning.

I take a room at the Khadra Hotel, which is inhabited by Pakistanis. The management is friendly, there is an excellent restaurant with *dal* and *subjee* downstairs, and I meet a Japanese traveller named Yuki Endo, who is also on a journey across the old Silk Road, though by public transport. It turns out that Yuki is an avid bike tourist and mountain climber, and we spend hours playing cards, singing, talking about our respective adventures, and becoming steadfast friends.

No rim is available in Tashkent, but I call my friends John and Sonja back home, and they agree to air courier me a new rim. It ends up being very expensive, and not exactly convenient, as courier runs come into Tashkent via Frankfurt once a week, and it is more than two weeks before I receive my rim. However, I appreciate the chance to rest and explore Tashkent.

After several weeks, my new wheel arrives and I am mobile again. As I set out for Samarkand on the first of November, the Indian summer continues to hold, with warm days and cold nights the norm. The frozen mornings make rising difficult, and with dusk coming earlier each night, my cycling hours become limited.

The Silk Road through here is modern and ugly. The outskirts of Tashkent are industrial wastelands, and the whole countryside looks like an over-cultivated scrub desert. It is hard to believe that this land once grew most of the produce for the entire Soviet Union. Even the famed Uzbek cotton fields are brown and desolate. The road is very poor, made of large blocks rather than continuous pavement; this means that I go over a giant bump every ten meters, and after a few hours, I feel like the inside of a dropped thermos. Little boys perch on the concrete dividers between the lanes, jeering at me.

It is a far cry from the scene envisioned by James Elroy Flecker, who penned the following words in 1913:

> *We travel not for trafficking alone*
> *By hotter winds our fiery hearts are fanned*
> *For lust of knowing what should not be known*
> *We take the Golden Road to Samarkand*

Though the road is not so golden, the magic of Samarkand remains. I cross into the city at dusk, surrounded by the giant domes of mosques, medressas, and mausoleums, all glowing with the final colors of the day, and I feel that I have truly reached the heart of Central Asia.

Samarkand sits in the Zarafshan River Valley, a major water source in this dry land. Its prime location and talented Sogdian (Iranian) merchants made the city a major center on the Silk Road. The Silk Road, contrary to popular belief, was actually not one road, but a series of arteries on which Chinese silk caravans travelled from China to Europe. All these caravan routes converged in Samarkand.

Samarkand is also the city of Timur i-Lenk, known also as Timur the Lame, Tamerlaine, or Timur the Great, the despot of Transoxiania who followed in the footsteps of Genghis Khan and his Mongol hordes. Timur was a butcher, but he did gather craftsmen, artists, and engineers from all over Central Asia in his efforts to make Samarkand the capital of the world. The monuments that he built here rival any of the other manmade wonders of the globe.

Navigating with my headlamp through dimly lit streets, I manage to find the colossal Samarkand Hotel, where I reunite with Yuki, who has already been here for several days. He shows me to our spacious and well-furnished rooms, complete with chests of drawers, cabinets, and armchairs that look as if they have been here since Marco Polo travelled through the region.

I ask how Yuki has been spending his time, and he tells me that the friendly ladies on the floor above ours have taken a fancy to him, and have been more than willing to practice Russian. I go up to investigate his claims, and return to inform Yuki that we have taken up residency in the town brothel, which leaves him looking rather embarrassed over his ignorance. Later in the evening, some of the ladies come looking for him, and he asks them how much they charge their local clients. Their answer of a dollar-fifty leaves us dumbfounded, and gives a picture of just how bad things really are in Uzbekistan.

Morning comes, and I rise early, excited to see the city's monuments in the daylight. I come first to the Bibi-Khanym Mosque, a monumental structure now in a state of ruin. The mosque was built by an architect who fell in love with Bibi-Khanym, Timur's wife, and he said he would only finish his work in exchange for a kiss. Timur subsequently beheaded him, and instituted the wearing of veils by women to ensure that such a thing didn't happen again.

The nearby Registan was built by Timur's grandson, Uluzbek, who loved arts and intellect rather than bloodletting. The towering blue domes and medressas of the Registan are decorated with turquoise mosaics, marble, and glazed bricks, and are the showpieces of Samarkand. The Registan rivals the Taj Mahal in grandeur, yet whereas the Taj receives thousands of tourists every day of the year, on this November morning, I am virtually alone standing in front of the leaning pillars and majolica tiles. The local cleaning ladies are my only company.

I sit on a bench beneath a willow tree and watch the various centuries go by. Old men on their way to market wear traditional *doppe* (black skullcaps) and *tapan* (long quilted overcoats), and women wear long gowns called *kurta*, with silk pantaloons of the gaudiest psychedelic colors underneath. The gold and glitter worn by the ladies is not the world's most appealing fashion, but it does match their teeth, which are uniformly all gold! When I meet a young woman selling bread in the bazaar with perfect pearly whites, I almost want to fly her to another country for dental work, as I know what the future here holds for her smile.

I spend the rest of the day taking pictures of characters from seemingly every lost tribe of the Kyzylkum Desert: Tajiks, Turkmen in knee-high leather boots, Afghans in baggy pantaloons, turbaned men right out of the Caliph of Baghdad, and women in shawls, robes, embroidered gowns and scarves. It feels as if I have stumbled into a history textbook or medieval fable.

There are few Russians in Samarkand, though the ones in military garb do continue to hassle me, and I am amused by what a game it has all become. One soldier asks for my passport, peruses my weathered array of visa stamps and wrinkled pages, then clutches the passport and orders me to come with him. I ask why, and he says there is a problem. I tell him that if there is a problem, he should call his administrator, and if there are still any issues, he should give my *pazaleesta* (embassy) a call. With a sheepish grin, he returns my passport and tells me to proceed.

Locals, frightened of police and soldiers, avoid them at all costs. Not having grown up here, and at least theoretically believing that I have rights, I do not fear the authorities, which gives me the freedom to challenge them. It also helps that my passport is the right color.

The sunny and cloudless days come in bunches, and I cannot believe it is November. I roll on across the cotton fields, and I spin the pedals and daydream of autograph-seeking Kazakhs, Kyrghyz mountains, and Russian hospitality.

I arrive in Buchara, a medieval desert city, and another famous trade stop on the Silk Road. Although it has fewer towering mosques and epic architectural wonders than Samarkand, it is a far more beautiful place. Samarkand's old buildings are surrounded by a concrete Soviet-style jungle, while Buchara still seems to be living in the eleventh century. There are domed bazaars, centuries-old religious schools, tiled fountains, and marble bathhouses that have not changed since Alexander the Great rumbled through. Genghis Khan found Buchara so impressive that he spared it the razing that took place in all of the other sites of his conquest.

One morning, while purchasing yogurt at a corner shop, I meet a young lady named Raynov. She and her brother Shavkhat want to guide me around and practice their few words of English; I tell them that I am not interested in hiring a guide, but I encourage them to tag along while I go to the bazaar. The pair show me around the various sections of the bazaar, where Raynov seems to know every other merchant, and we spend a timeless day together. We do it again the following day, and on the third day, I realize that Raynov is flirting with me. At one point, Shavkhat asks me if I like his sister. I tell him that she is certainly an attractive and intelligent young woman, but that she is about fifteen years younger than I am. He shrugs his shoulders, and disappears soon after.

Raynov and I spend the rest of the afternoon walking around together. She is twenty-one, but her street sense and her responsibility as the eldest of six children make her seem far older. I am impressed by her determination to take care of her family, who, by her stories, appear to need all the help they can get.

I am staying near the old Russian bathhouse, which has private cubicles, and when I tell Raynov that I plan to go there in the evening, she asks if I would like her to join me.

I am speechless for a moment, but staring at her dark eyes and full lips, I say yes without further thought. She agrees to meet me at eight, and we part with a longing stare.

Back at my guesthouse, I take a nap and oversleep my alarm. At half past eight, I get dressed and run to the street, but there is no sign of Raynov, and I make my way to the bath alone.

I have a very long and leisurely soak, then wander home along the quiet lanes, past the beehive-shaped terracotta domes of the old bazaars, silhouetted against the night sky. As I pass near Raynov's home, a nearby gate opens and several eyes peer out at me in the night. It occurs to me how close I have come to complete foolhardiness. After a week, virtually everyone in these cramped quarters knows who I am, and though it may be a thrilling adventure to live out a harem fantasy in the land of One Thousand and One Nights, a steamy liaison with a young tart in ancient Buchara would probably have every one of her male cousins on my tail within half an hour.

As I shut my own guesthouse gate, I am torn between my rational prudence and the desires that haunt my dreams.

While preparing a rather discreet departure from Buchara, I discover that my front rack is broken in several places. I use hose clamps and duct tape to hold it together, and head out for my last day in Uzbekistan.

The temperature has dropped by at least twenty degrees, and a rather ominous lenticular cloud is hovering over the border with Turkmenistan, not far ahead of me. The Aral Sea, the only source of water in this area, is drying up, and the land has a dead feel to it, like the eerie Quaidam Basin Hitomi and I crossed many moons ago in China.

The frontier appears by mid-afternoon, and the Uzbek customs officers ask me to fill out a new currency declaration, rather than giving them the one I received upon entering the country. This makes absolutely no sense, but I make no quarrel. At the Turkmen post, the fellow who stamps my passport wants to keep all my books so he can study! He is very skeptical that I should need a Russian-English dictionary, three novels, and a guidebook for travels through Turkmenistan.

The Turkmen side of the border looks no different than the Uzbek side, except that there are giant billboards everywhere, proclaiming, "*Halk Watan Turkmenbashi*," which means "Long Live the Head of All Turkmen." These banners are erected even throughout the barren desert, where there are no road signs or kilometer markers. Saparmurad Niyazov, Turkmenistan's president, has created a personality cult greater than anything Lenin, Mao, or Stalin, could come up with, and most of Turkmenistan's oil-generated revenue has been spent on signs, busts, pedestals, and portraits displaying his magnitude.

Niyazov has gone as far as to rename himself Turkmenbashi (Head of All Turkmen). He has renamed towns with this moniker, put his picture on every banknote, and produced scores of leaflets and newspapers that boast of his exploits and glories. The populace doesn't seem to be benefiting from his endeavors however, as money changing seems to be the sole occupation here.

There are no tourists in Turkmenistan, but I soon learn why the moneychangers are everywhere. The day I cross the border, the *manat* is trading on the black market at 6000 to a dollar; a day later, it is at 8000, and three days later, at 10,000. Conditions in Uzbekistan may have been bad, but in Turkmenistan they are wretched. Hotels and restaurants ask for dollars. Local currency is worth about as much as the sands that blow in from the Kyzyl Kum.

It is gray and cold, and I am in a wind-ravaged desert, feeling like I have truly found the end of the earth. Few cars pass, save a few Iranian and Turkish trucks and a scant collection of Turkmen buses that resemble dilapidated shacks with wheels. Crosswinds thrash me, and I pedal past scrubby thorn bushes and weeds until dark, thinking only of how godforsaken Turkmenistan is.

Except for jotting a few notes in my journal, I do nothing but ride. I don't read; I don't listen to the radio; I don't fix my gear. I only set up my tent, boil water, sleep, and get up to do it again.

There are few cities in Turkmenistan, yet some of the tiny settlements have lodging houses. Nobody in these places has ever seen a foreigner, except perhaps on television, and hordes of children follow me upon my arrival, running beside me and gaping as if I am an alien. Rooms are grubby and malodorous, but they cost only a dollar, and the owners are usually friendly, smiling women with gold teeth, who drool when I tell them that I am *Amerikanyets,* and make pathetic clucks when they learn I am alone.

"*Drook nyet, nyet karasho,*" they croon over and over ("no friend, no good"). They make goo-goo eyes at me, while I stand wearily in front of them.

I ride next to the Kopit Dag, a chain of small mountains separating Iran and Turkmenistan. The bustling Iranian city of Mashad is just over the peaks, but could be on the moon for all I care, as out here, there is nothing but sand. It is thirty-eight degrees, and I spend all day singing every song I can recollect to relieve the monotony of the endless road.

Turkmen are traditionally noted for their clothing: women wear colorful dresses and scarves, and the men dress in wooly *telepeks,* hats that look like giant Afros, to go with their baggy pants and knee-high boots. However, although I see a few small *telepeks,* most people are attired in the same Montana Sport jogging outfits and tennis shoes. The outfits are made in Uzbekistan, and I cannot find a single thing here that appears locally produced. My guidebook notes that Turkmenistan cannot even produce its own matchboxes, and the whole situation of the country seems as bleak as the weather.

Police posts are functioning, but even these are a joke. At one of them, a group of drunken law enforcers chase after me with batons, screaming at me to stop, which I completely disregard. They pile into their car to give chase, but the engine won't start, and they are left cursing behind me, their voices carrying on the wind.

After a week, I reach Ashghabat, the capital, which is a real surprise. The city sprawls across the desert, looking like Albuquerque or Phoenix, and on its northern edge are a series of gaudy five-star resort hotels, built for the Middle Eastern elite who have yet to come and buy up Turkmen oil. There are golf courses, department stores, grand mosques, and fancy high-rises funded by Turkish and Iranian entrepreneurs. Everyone I talk to complains about the poverty and the rampant daily inflation, yet from every street corner, Mr. Niyazov smiles down from a billboard, assuring that all is peachy fine in his democratic paradise of natural gaslands.

The one saving grace of Ashghabat is the Sunday Tolguchka Market, one of the most phenomenal spectacles I have beheld anywhere. *Tolguchka* comes from the Russian "to push," and true to form, the market is a sea of shoving shoppers. This gathering of tribes takes place every week, with a vast array of carpets, livestock, artwork, and souvenirs laid out over a large swath of desert on the outskirts of the city.

Women in patterned headscarves of yellow, orange, green, and blue sit in coordinated groups, showing off their wares. They are members of a series of clans with a long lineage in the Turkmen deserts, and they sell colorful and ornate carpets, mittens, caps, robes, and vests. Buchara rugs—which really come from Turkmenistan—can be had for fifty dollars, an incredible bargain, as the rugs will fetch up to 200 in Buchara, and over 500 in Istanbul. Turkish carpet sellers come here to stock up, and I am tempted to buy one for myself, but since I have no more room aboard my mount, I settle for only memories.

My layover in Ashghabat does me well, but it is still 600 kilometers to the Caspian Sea, and I cannot rest long. The weather continues to be cold and overcast, but I leave the city with a raging tailwind pushing me along at over thirty kilometers an hour.

It takes a short afternoon to cover the largest distance of my entire trip, 185 kilometers. I am tempted to do 200, just for posterity, but I discover that my front rack has broken in four more places, and that one of the hose clamps is eating into my front spokes. I pull off into the sands to do some repairs and set up camp for the night.

If there is anything to recommend about Turkmenistan, it is that the country is truly the world's greatest campsite. Pick a dune, any dune. The only drawback with the fine selection is the endless gritty sand, which finds its way into every bowl of soup, cup of tea, or appropriately named "sandwich" that I make.

On these roads, one can learn just how joyless travel is. On endless lonely stretches, I pass destitute settlements and crumbling hotels, with only my thoughts to break up the monotony of the barren desert. I wonder what would happen if Hitomi were here. Would we relieve one another's misery, or would we be close to cutting each other's throats?

There are however, shards of joy to help make it through the day, such as the Turkmen wedding processions that come through the desert from Ashghabat. The Turkmen celebrate marriages by loading entire wedding parties into their cars and driving drunken, at breakneck speeds, into the nearby sands. The car of the newlyweds is usually decorated with an enormous and hideous plastic swan affixed to the top of the vehicle, and everyone chases them, honking and screaming at the top of their lungs.

And then there are the giant Iranian transport trucks, the only other vehicles on the road. When I get a flat tire and can barely put a patch together, due to the gale that rips everything out of my hands, two truckers stop to create a wind block for me. I think of how far these guys are from their own homes and families, and reflect that in such dire places strangers bond rapidly.

I make another 100 kilometer run with the winds at my back, but don't bask in my accomplishments, as I see the road turn back nearly 180 degrees into *Nebit Dag*, the Oil Mountains. Soon I am riding into a violent sandstorm, and what was once a helpful tailwind becomes a furious crosswind. Huge drifts of sand blow across the road, and the futility of my endeavor hits home when I see a large plow truck trying to remove the dunes that are building up on the asphalt.

Twenty kilometers from Nebit Dag, traffic increases, and it is no longer safe or sane for me to be cycling. I cannot look ahead, as I will be blinded, and even peering to the side away from the wind, I am coated from head to toe in fine sand, spitting out the grit as I go. I stop and try to hitchhike, but no one stops, and I must keep riding or become buried in onrushing sand. As I struggle on, I think to myself that I could be at home with a house, perhaps with a wife, watching a movie, sitting on the couch with snacks in hand. Even going to a mall would be far more enjoyable than this misery. This is not fun. I cry out loud, "Why on earth am I doing this?" but the screeching winds blow away my words.

Halfway to Nebit Dag, it becomes so awful that I begin to laugh at the absurdity of the whole situation. I even get out my camera and try to photograph the sand billowing across the road. Passing drivers stare unabashedly, marveling at the lunatic who stands wrapped like a mummy, huddled over his bicycle.

After several hours, I struggle into Nebit Dag, exhausted but alive. The town is a dot in the desert, with basic amenities available; after my ordeal in the sands, the luxuries of village life are a godsend. At the Nebit Dag Hotel, a trio of charming old women with mustaches ooh and aah over my arrival, make up a room for me, and tell me that my life would be far better if I had a Turkmen woman. I decline invitations to meet their daughters, and go off to take one of the better hot showers of my life, ridding myself of the grains of sand that have made their way into every pore and crevice of my anatomy.

This luxury is short lived, however, as it is 160 kilometers to Krasnovosk and the end of Turkmenistan. I arise at dawn, hoping to get a head start on the winds, and am pleased to find that they are negligible. Yet I am not pleased to discover that my left knee is in severe pain, perhaps as a result of yesterday's winds, or perhaps due to the excessive mileage I have been pedalling for the past several weeks. Years earlier, a touch of bursitis in that knee forced me to abandon a trip, and I can only pray that this will not happen out here.

The area is an eerie moonscape, full of wild Bactrian camels and rocky outcroppings in the desert. The weather holds most of the day, neither too windy nor excessively cold, but I cannot enjoy it because of my throbbing knee.

The Caspian comes into view for the first time, just a shoreline in the haze at first, but soon a shimmering emerald sea. Beaten and weary, I give a half-hearted cry of relief as I descend to her shore, and I soon see the lights of Turkmenbashi up ahead. Grimacing with every pedal stroke, I crawl into the outskirts of the city, where I discover a large and rusted cargo ship berthed in the harbor. I learn that it is the good ship Dagestan, and that it is preparing to leave for Baku, Azerbaijan.

I hastily change my remaining *manat* at a huge loss, and then limp my way aboard the ship, paying an overeager crewmember a small bribe for a cabin berth. I end up sharing this with a chain-smoking Azeri man, who belches unendingly and flicks his fingers against his jugular to indicate that I should join him for a nip of vodka.

I take several anti-inflammatory pills and prop my knee above several pillows. Glancing at my bike, I discover that the front rack has broken in several more places, and I wonder who is worse off, Odysseus or myself.

The travel book I read on the voyage repeats itself often about the folly and sadness of travel, and I wonder if it is trying to send me a message.

Chapter Seventeen
Winter Blues:
The Frozen Caucasus

> *Homesickness is one of the traveller's ailments, and so is loneliness. Fear; of strangers, of being embarrassed, of threats to personal safety, is the traveller's usual, if often unadmitted companion. The sensitive traveller will also feel a degree of guilt at his alienation from ordinary people.*
>
> Paul Fussell,
> *The Norton Book of Travel*

> *When one realizes that his life is worthless he either commits suicide or travels.*
>
> Edward Dahlberg,
> *Reasons of the Heart*

Baku is gray and rainy, exactly the same as the Caspian on the other side. We dock at dawn, but immigration officials tell me my visa is no good, and they want forty dollars to process a new one. Tired and crotchety, I tell them to call my embassy, and after four hours of power games, they reluctantly stamp my passport and tell me to get lost.

Baku is an oil city, swarming with expatriates waiting to cash in on the black gold, and there is only one cheap hotel in town, called the Kompass. It is located on an old ship in the harbor, and the rooms are grubby little berths with tiny damp beds and filthy portholes. As in most hotels in these regions, ladies of the night seem to have the run of the place.

I bargain the desk clerks down from forty dollars to ten, and they ask if I have any souvenirs. I give them some postcards of San Francisco, which they look at rather crestfallen. One asks me to give him my personalized keychain, while another requests to search my panniers for something that he could use.

Baku itself is pleasant enough, full of old architecture ranging from medieval mosques and palaces to Gothic mansions built during the Russian oil boom of the late 1800's. The oil is still flowing today, a recent seven billion petrodollar pipeline deal with America the latest moneymaker. The change from Turkmenistan is profound.

New BMWs tear down the boulevards, driven by men screaming into cell phones; pot-bellied foreigners pass business cards in French and Italian restaurants; vendors hawk English newspapers listing the latest NFL games on satellite television. I notice that the glossy magazines for sale give generous advertising space and accolades to British Petroleum, Arco, Elf, Shell, and Texaco for their various achievements.

Well-heeled Azeri kids in colorful cardigans play on electric cars and other rides in the spacious seaside parks, while their parents sip tea and eat kebabs at adjoining stalls. Nearby, crowds jostle to buy oil revenue checks being hawked by ambitious moneychangers. President Aliev has recently given everyone a once-in-a-lifetime petro-dollar check, something like Alaska's oil profit bonus, and there is a brisk trade in the sale and resale of these checks.

Two dapper Azeri businessmen named Nik and Elmar pick me up. They take me to a jazz café, show me an Internet center for catching up on mail, and cannot understand why I refuse their entreaties to go eat in McDonalds. We take a sightseeing tour in their Mercedes, whizzing past policemen who stand in the middle of traffic waving batons, blowing whistles, and screaming for people to pull over. Elmar tells me nobody pulls over if they can help it, as otherwise they will have to contribute to the officers' vodka fund.

My clothing and demeanor aside, I fit in with the crowds for the first time in ages. Mongoloid faces are completely gone, as are Russian ones. Everyone looks Greek or Turkish. Old men with thick eyebrows sit at cafés and spin their worry beads, drinking thick Turkish coffee, and when I walk past, almost nobody gives me more than a cursory glance.

I wander through the narrow lanes of the old town, a far cry from the bustling boulevards nearby. There are minarets, terracotta beehive domes, and bathhouses throughout the area, and it feels like a slightly less magical version of Buchara. But the weather is cold, my knee is still sore, and I don't feel much like sightseeing, so I spend much of my time resting with my leg propped up back on the ship.

In my small cubicle, I reflect on how much space I needed to occupy before I left home. In America, we pride ourselves on space, and we revere open land, palatial homes, and breathing room. Yet in Asia, people take pride in coexisting in overcrowded spaces, and I marvel at how content I have become with just a small enclosure. Given that privacy is usually nonexistent out on the road, this is an absolute luxury.

I look at my map, and at the quarter moon in the sky, and take satisfaction in knowing that when it turns full again, I will be at the Black Sea, well within the reaches of Europe.

I leave Baku on Thanksgiving morning in a windy, humid drizzle. My mood does not improve when I realize that I have forgotten my water bottles in the hotel for the first time in six years, and I have to ride an extra ten kilometers to retrieve them.

Exiting Baku along the Caspian coast, it doesn't take long before I begin to see the cost of the city's prosperity. Oilrigs, tankers, and drilling platforms dot the land and sea, and the shoreline is a burnt, desolate, oil-belching strip. The beaches are ruined, blackened and strewn with garbage, and I think of the magazines in which the oil companies claim how "eco-friendly" they are. I pity the future generations of Azeris, who will bear the consequences of this mess.

The wind, rain, and cold continue, much like in Turkmenistan. The road is poorly surfaced, and the only markers on the dead landscape are ugly electrical pylons. The few people I see are sullen, either taking no notice of me whatsoever or staring rudely as I pass. After ninety kilometers, my knee stiffens, and I have to take a long break in the small town of Kazi Mohammed. Children on the road sell steamed corn, along with some stray pomegranates and mandarin oranges that have made their way up from Iran.

A few old men wander over to look at my bike, quizzing me in Azeri, of which I cannot understand a word. It is a very guttural language, and sounds a bit like an ostrich speaking Swedish. As I cannot make conversation, I wearily plod on.

Every day becomes worse. I head into screaming winds and soaking storms, my knee throbbing in pain. I fear I won't be able to walk by the end of the day, and if someone offered me a ride, I would be in the car in two seconds. It rains harder, and all I can do is pedal. I suppose the sensible thing to do would be to stop, but I have lost all traces of sense long ago. Fancy Turkish buses roll by with TVs, cafés, toilets, and all else on board, all of which I want and don't have. All I get are waves splashed over me by speeding cars.

By late afternoon, it has once again become so miserable that it is absurd, and I know that I will survive another day. My motto becomes, "If I can make it today, well, maybe I can make it tomorrow."

I slide into the small settlement of Kurdamir shortly before dusk, happy to get off the potholed and flooded road. I ask several people where I can find a hotel, and they tell me there aren't any. People appear suspicious and ask lots of personal questions, oblivious to my exhaustion.

While searching for accommodations, I am stopped by a policeman who wants to know if I have visited Armenia. Although the two countries are no longer at war, an air of tension remains, and outsiders are not a common sight here. In broken Russian, with a few Turkish words thrown in, the policeman informs me that the town's hotel is closed, full of refugees from the war, and that there is nowhere for me to stay. I sympathize, but I cannot go farther, so I plead my case.

Eventually, the lawman stops a group of kids, gives them instructions, and tells me to follow them. The kids lead me through a maze of muddy lanes, and eventually stop at a small hovel surrounded by a quagmire of sewage. A small-boned woman emerges, looking horrified at the sight of this alien on a bicycle standing in her yard, and her wizened mother looks even more overwhelmed, even though I promise to pay a tidy sum.

They reluctantly show me into the house. I learn that the woman's name is Gariba, and that she lives with her son, Tamam, and her aging mother. Gariba's husband died when Tamam was only three, and judging by their living conditions, they are having a very hard go of it. Their two-room home is furnished only with a lumpy bed, a broken television, a radio, and a ceramic heater for cooking. Several black and white pictures of Gariba's grandparents hang on the cracked walls.

There is no bath. An outhouse in the corner of the yard consists of just a few narrow wooden slats with a cutout, and water is pumped from a small spigot at the edge of the muddy bog. I am torn between embarrassment at intruding on these people's lives, and relief at having a roof over my head.

Within half an hour, half the neighborhood has heard of my arrival. Locals pack the small rooms, sitting on the floor and staring as I wrap an Ace bandage around my knee and fumble through my first aid kit for some pain relievers.

A young tough leads the queries about my journey; evidently, he has been appointed as the inquisitor due to his brashness, and his knowledge of a hundred words of English. Immersed in my own pain, I am standoffish at first, but eventually warm to his attempts to communicate.

My hosts begin to lament their misfortunes, and I see that life in Kurdamir is light years away from what I have seen in Baku. The town is packed with refugees from the Armenian conflict, and there are no opportunities for work. Even doctors here earn only ten dollars a month, and they are lucky if they can find a job. Inflation is running rampant, and nobody here has heard a word about President Aliev's oil dollars. The young tough gives me a list of all the ills and failures of Azerbaijan, and then pounds his fist desperately against the wall in anger, telling me that life here is horrible. I look at the floor, unable to think of anything positive to tell him.

I hobble over to my bags and take out a tin of sardines and a package of ramen noodles. When I offer to share it with the group, they of course refuse, and I am relieved, as it is the only source of sustenance I have. We sit in uncomfortable silence, me eating, and everyone else watching.

I can barely walk, my gear is soaked, and my spirits are lower than I can remember them being in years. Yet I say a silent thanks for being here, surrounded by the peering eyes, as unfair or troubling a situation as it may be.

I leave early the following morning, my hosts seeming rather eager to see me go. I give them some extra *manat* for their kindness, and for their willingness to take in a complete stranger. As usual, a freezing rain greets me as I head to the highway, and for the first ten kilometers, my knee is in so much agony that I think I am going to collapse.

As my body warms up, I am somehow able to tolerate the pain, which subsides to a sharp throb every time the pedals revolve. I try to think that someday I will be able to laugh at this and tell stories of how bad it really was. As I grind out every kilometer, I learn to concentrate on small things. Pee breaks. Blowing my nose. Stopping to eat my daily Snickers. Watching ducks waddle across the road. A lovely pine forest that I come across in the afternoon. Anything to distract me from the pain, and from the moist cold that penetrates my bones.

Out of the mist, a place called Yevlax appears, with a large hotel full of refugees, their wet clothes hanging in the rain. I ask if there is a spare room, and am given a damp cot to lay my head on. Again, I am thankful, even though there is no water, heat, or electricity in the hotel.

On the other side of town, I discover a bathhouse with shower stalls full of mildew and slime, but it is the only place in Yevlax with hot water, and I embrace the showerhead like a man who has not seen his lover in years.

Returning to my cold room past the vacant stares of men in the lobby, I wonder if it would be any different to travel through here in spring. Does the bleak cold of winter here make the people so sullen, or is it the aftermath of the war with Armenia? People in India and Nepal were far more poverty-stricken, but they were almost always smiling and welcoming. I wonder if their caste system, or their belief in fate and karma, allowed them to accept their situation more easily.

The hotel caretaker awakens me at seven, demanding that I get out; for some reason, he will not even let me eat breakfast before leaving. I don't protest too loudly, as it is thirty-four degrees in my room, and I am by now immune to the frigid sleet which falls outside.

Two hours into my morning, a group of Scottish oil pipeline workers pull off the road to ask how I am doing. They are just returning from Tbilisi to Baku, and they tell me horror stories about Georgian drivers, corrupt militia, and the snowy and mountainous terrain just ahead. It all sounds revolting, and I again try to block everything from my mind, focusing instead on the steady spinning of my legs.

It is a relatively short stretch into Ganja, the second largest city in Azerbaijan. The city is sprawling, industrial, and ugly, but well stocked with provisions. The staff are welcoming in the palatial Hotel Ganja, where I decide immediately to take a day off. Electricity is intermittent, and the only water in the hotel is a stagnant and murky pool in my bathtub, but there are big blankets to wrap myself in, and my room has large windows through which I can watch the rain and snow continue to fall.

People in Ganja are friendlier than in the towns I have passed through across Azerbaijan, especially my hotel staff, who bring imported Polish gingerbread biscuits to my room and wish me *"yakshi yol"* (good road, or happy trails) whenever I leave the hotel. Yet an aura of suspicion remains throughout the city, and a rather interrogative style of questioning takes place whenever I go into teashops or restaurants. In one teashop, a man asks where I am from, then asks if I have a passport. I say that I do, and he asks if he can see it, to which I reply that he cannot. He stares at me while I drink my tea and study my map, then asks where I got the map.

I tell him I bought it in a shop in Baku. "What shop?" is his immediate retort. "A map shop," I snap back, and so it goes.

In my pitiful condition, rest days pass all too quickly, and again I arise to gray skies and a thermometer reading thirty. Snow falls on the dark streets, and I go back to bed, but muster the courage to get up and leave when I discover that there is still no water in the hotel, and that the toilet is full of unflushed crap.

It is so cold on the bike this morning that I cannot change gears because my fingers are frozen; I have to stop to warm them against my chest before each hill that requires a shift. Visibility remains at about ten meters, and cars come far too close for comfort, appearing out of nowhere. Near the Armenian border, the road climbs through small mountains that divide the two enemy states, and the only sign of civilization is a series of destitute and forlorn roadside furniture shops.

People remain obnoxious and inhospitable. Several police try to make me halt, blowing whistles and shaking batons, but they only want bribes, so I pay no attention. Even if the police have cars, they do not have gas for them.

Fortunately, before it can possibly get any worse, the Georgian frontier arrives. The Azeris stamp me through, scowling all the while, and I fear the worst on the other side, given what I have been told about the Georgians. Approaching, a band of young Georgian soldiers, wearing camouflage and flak jackets and brandishing Uzis, look eagerly through all my passport stamps. To my surprise, they touch my bike in admiration, and are beginning to wave me through when one of them screams for me to wait. He disappears and returns with a giant box of oranges and pomegranates, which he tells me to take. I smile and thank him, but tell him that I cannot possibly fit the box onto Odysseus, to which he raises his Uzi in mock anger and orders that I take the fresh fruit at all costs.

Buoyed to be out of Azerbaijan, I grit through my knee pain and climb into cedar forests. Then the road descends into a broad river valley, marred by the industrial city of Rustavi: rows of concrete apartment blocks, surrounded by garbage, industrial waste, and smokestacks billowing black stench. It looks like something out of a Doomsday Book, and I expect to see feral children emerging from the litter, prowling for scraps.

I follow the Kura River into the heaviest traffic I have seen in months as I approach the outskirts of Tbilisi, the Georgian capital. Policemen are everywhere, stopping motorists by the side of the road to engage in sessions of vodka drinking and toasting. I cannot help but laugh at the local system of law enforcement.

Several hours and traffic jams later, I am at the Vokzal, the main bus terminus in central Tbilisi. Buses arrive and depart from Moscow, Prague, Budapest and Berlin, and suddenly Central Asia begins to recede behind me. I find a desk where homestays are available, and am given the address of a family near the station that will house me. These homestay desks exist in every major city train station across the Soviet world, and are a great boon for the weary traveller.

Shortly thereafter, I am standing in a courtyard filled with several crumbling apartment blocks. There is a frenzy of activity: people washing clothes and pumping water, children playing tag, and men in leather jackets working on old cars. I knock on the door of Venera Tateshvili, a kindly woman who stands wringing her hands in amazement at the sight of my overloaded bicycle before ushering me into her flat.

Venera gives a shout as we enter the apartment, and I am greeted by Viola and Alain, Venera's daughter and son-in-law. Viola speaks several words of English, Alain less, and Venera none, but they are very cheery, and are patient in their attempts to understand my muddled Russian. Their flat is a single large room, partitioned with curtains to create some semblance of privacy. There is one double bed (which somehow mother, daughter, and son-in-law manage to share), a functioning black and white television, a small makeshift kitchen, and a ratty sofa bed for visitors.

Conditions here are just as bad as in Azerbaijan. Viola and Alain are doctors, and both have been out of work for several years. The few dollars that visitors bring in through the rail station accommodation scheme help to pay for food and other necessities, but travellers these days are few.

The Tateshvilis share a grotty pit toilet with a dozen or so other families, and there is nowhere to bathe in the apartment complex. The nearest bathhouse is a twenty-minute walk away, and at almost a dollar for admission to the overcrowded public bath, is an expense most people can only afford once a week at most. Electricity is intermittent, heating is an added expense, and in the cold and dark climate, daily life looks to be quite a struggle. Yet the Tateshvilis welcome me with open arms and make me feel like one of the family. Viola practices English with me, happy to get off of her feet, as she is seven months pregnant. Alain is very curious about other parts of the world, and quizzes me about the costs of living in many of the places I have been. Venera is constantly running around, filling the teakettle, stirring soup, and complaining about the state of affairs in Georgia.

Despite the hardships around me, I am most grateful to have a place to rest. The Georgians seem to live on dairy products, and eateries on every block serve slices of *kachapuri*, filo dough pastries stuffed with several types of salty cheese. Thick fresh yogurt is also a staple, and rows of men and women near the rail station hawk glass jars of their own freshly made wares.

Tbilisi in some ways is actually a lovely city, full of gallery houses, palatial baroque buildings, ancient brick and stone churches, and winding cobbled streets that meander through the old town. However, Tbilisi appears to be on the downswing. Buildings are disintegrating, and schools and hospitals look as if they have seen much better days. Traffic is horrendous, with scores of men in rusted Ladas moonlighting as taxi drivers and evading the vodka-swilling policemen. Young men, out of work and with nothing to do, hang out on cold street corners, and old *babushkas* sit bundled at the roadside selling single cigarettes or packets of nuts to make a few coins.

Things may be far safer than during the massacres by the Soviet army in 1990, and better than the chaos that followed the nation's newfound freedom, when thousands of refugees from the conflict with Abkhazia poured into the capital, but stability is still a long ways off. There have been several assassination attempts on President Eduard Shevardnadze, and rumors have it that a local Mafia is running the country. I certainly see a lot of shifty-looking men with cellular phones driving expensive automobiles around town.

It is sad to see the state of decline in Georgia, as I sense a *joie de vivre* underneath the hard times. In contrast to the heavy and brooding Russians, Georgians have always been known for their love of dancing, singing, and throwing parties, and are far closer in temperament to their Mediterranean cousins in Turkey and Greece. The Georgian *supra* (a celebration, which literally translates as "table") is noted for copious drinking and toasting to women, God, and country, which of course

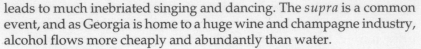

leads to much inebriated singing and dancing. The *supra* is a common event, and as Georgia is home to a huge wine and champagne industry, alcohol flows more cheaply and abundantly than water.

An old Georgian creation legend says that while God was creating the world and allocating land to people, the Georgians were out partying. Angered, God came down and scolded them, wondering how they dared to enjoy themselves so much while he was working. The Georgians laughed and replied that they were merely toasting and celebrating in his honor, then invited him to join their table in merrymaking. God was so impressed that he gave them the most beautiful land in the world, the one he had been saving for himself.

From atop the Metexi Church on the valley wall, I look over the bare trees and the Kura River to the distant snowy peaks of the Caucasus, shimmering in the sunset. All my energies are focused on reaching the Turkish border and Black Sea, but I think about returning to Georgia the following summer, when I am in better condition and everything is warmer and full of life.

My altimeter's barometer drops on my last day in Tbilisi, a harbinger of yet another dose of evil weather. Thus far, Georgia, while bitterly cold, has at least been free of snowstorms or the freezing rain that followed me across Azerbaijan.

I spend the day wandering the central market and eating *lavash*, a flat chewy bread shaped like a manta ray. Young Georgian beauties walk by, most of them dressed in elegant black dresses and coats. Most of the ladies here sport light down on their upper lips, which gives them a rather sultry look, though this soft hair tends to evolve into full-blown mustaches when they are older. Inside the bazaar, some middle-aged women sell little mustache clippers, and spend time between sales yanking hairs.

Back at Venera's place, Alain quizzes me on travels in India, and wanders the flat with a melancholy presence, as if he feels stifled by his position as an expectant father with no work. Still, I am continually impressed by how well the family makes the best of their situation. Mother, daughter, and son-in-law share the same bed, with their daily life nothing more than a set of endless chores. There are no vacations, no shopping trips, and few of the luxuries that people in my country use to break up the monotony of their routines. Yet for the most part, Venera, Viola, and Alain laugh, tell stories, and get on with their daily business without ado.

I think of friends back home who are seeing therapists for problems that are so trivial compared to the dilemmas people here face on a daily basis. Perhaps in gaining wealth and ease, we forget the simple things, all the basic cogs in the wheel of life.

As I begin packing to leave, Venera cries, and tells me that I have been a most welcome guest. The last visitor couldn't speak any Russian, so she couldn't talk much with him. I ask where he was from, and she says that he was a Japanese boy. I ask if he was carrying a guitar, and she replies yes, and how did I know such a thing? Yuki!

I roll out of Tbilisi on a warm and cloudy morning, rested enough to know I am going to make it to the Black Sea. I have an early start, the road is well surfaced, and except for the insane drivers racing past, the world is perfect once again. I follow the Kura River into a mountain valley where churches are perched on the edges of steep cliffs, and I feel stronger and happier than I have in ages.

Just as I begin to relegate the last days in Central Asia to some hidden mausoleum in the recesses of my mind, my ride in Georgia comes to a pathetic end. I come around a bend, and suddenly cannot get any friction when I pedal. My chain seems to not be catching on the freewheel. I stop and examine the drive train, which is deeply worn and saturated in grit, but surely still functional. Digging down to the bottom of my panniers, I find the spare chain I have been carrying for the past six years, but even with the new chain, the pedals just revolve uselessly, unable to find resistance.

It takes a few minutes for me to realize that my entire freewheel has collapsed, and that I will not be able to fix such a thing in Georgia. Waiting two weeks in Tblisi for an overseas shipment is out of the question this late in winter, and the nearest parts and service are in Istanbul. For the first time on the entire journey, I stick out my thumb and begin hitchhiking, and wait about an hour before a van full of drunken men give me a lift, blowing cigarette smoke in my face and sticking vodka bottles under my nose as they interrogate me about how much money I make in America.

The border crossing into Turkey is a cinch. There are neither bribes nor baksheesh to be paid, no grumpy officials, and my passport details are even entered into functioning computers. On the Turkish side of the frontier, gleaming taxis sit in the sun, their drivers chain-smoking and playing backgammon as they wait for fares. There are plenty of decent hotels to choose from, all with hot running water. Banks have ATMs, spiffy Renaults and Mercedes cruise the streets, and well-dressed, over-fed schoolchildren with ruddy cheeks cart their satchels to class.

I climb aboard a plush Mercedes bus bound for Istanbul, complete with soft drinks, tea, garbage pails, and attendants catering to my every need; Odysseus is secured in a hold on the side of the bus. As we begin the long journey along the Black Sea coast, with the attendants doling out cologne and face towels, I realize that this is the bus ride I dreamed of while cycling through the frozen misery of Azerbaijan. I close my eyes and luxuriate in the warm seat.

Part Four

The Bridge from East to West: *Pedalling Through Turkey and Europe*

When I was very young and the urge to be someplace was on me, I was assured by mature people that maturity would cure this itch. When years described me as mature, the remedy prescribed was middle age. In middle age I was assured that greater age would calm my fever, and now that I am fifty-eight perhaps senility will do the job. Nothing has worked......In other words, I don't improve, in further words once a bum always a bum. I fear the disease is incurable.

John Steinbeck, *Travels With Charley*

Farewell Monsieur Traveller: look you lisp and wear strange suits, disable all the benefits of your own country, be out of love with your nativity, and almost chide God for making you that countenance that you are, or I will scarce think you have swam in a gondola.

Shakespeare, *MacBeth*

Oh public road, I say back I am not afraid to leave you, yet I love you. You express me better than I can express myself.

Walt Whitman

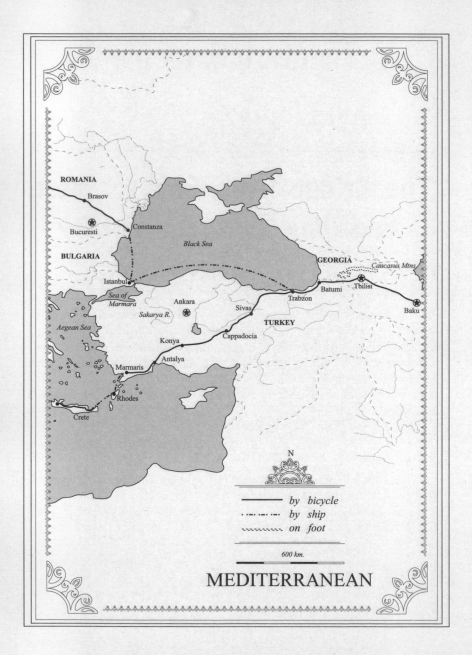

ROMANIA
Brasov
Bucuresti
Constanza
BULGARIA
Black Sea
GEORGIA
Caucasus Mtns.
Istanbul
Batumi
Tbilisi
Sea of
Marmara
Trabzon
Ankara
Baku
Sakarya R.
Sivas
Aegean Sea
TURKEY
Konya
Cappadocia
Marmaris
Antalya
Rhodes
Crete

N

by bicycle
by ship
on foot

600 km.

MEDITERRANEAN

Chapter Eighteen
Greece and Turkey: *Club Med*

Wherever I travel Greece ruins me.

George Seferis

*Travel is the most private of pleasures.
There is no greater bore than the travel bore. We do
not in the least want to hear what he has seen in
Hong Kong.*

Vita Sackville-West,
Passenger to Teheran

The bus crosses the bridge over the Bosphorous, where a large plaque reads, "Welcome to Europe." I hadn't quite intended to see this sight from the window of a bus, but fate has decreed otherwise. The driver threads his way through heavy traffic, and we eventually arrive at the behemoth *Otogar*, Istanbul's main terminus.

I try to come to terms with the currency exchange, as each dollar yields over 300,000 Turkish *lira*. My cab fare into the city runs a whopping five million, and I feel a bit like Howard Hughes as I hand over a wad of notes.

It has been sixteen years since I was last in Istanbul, and with the exception of the giant mosques that stand guard over the city, I cannot recognize a thing. I know that I have reached the district of Sultanhamet when I see the towering Blue Mosque, the mammoth Aghia Sophia Church, and the elongated walls of the Topkapi Palace, but when I try to navigate, I find myself completely disoriented. Sultanhamet used to be a hangout for backpackers and hippies in the sixties and seventies, full of cafés, bunkhouses, and cheap eateries; now it feels like any other western capital, full of people with deadlines, high-stress jobs, and little time for chat. I can only gape at these busy people as they whiz past me.

Wheeling my bike through the narrow streets, I come across the Lale Pudding Shop, which I do remember. It was an institution in its day, full of books, message boards, and longhaired westerners taking leisurely drags on water pipes and sipping small cups of thick Turkish coffee. I am shocked to see not a single backpacker in the Lale, nor any sign of a well-worn divan or a notice board. There are only well heeled tourists inside, eating expensive meals and taking photos of each other.

Dazed and exhausted from my long bus journey, I make my way to a guesthouse, where I am surprised to find Yuki sitting in the lobby. After cries of delight and bear hugs, we catch up on our respective journeys. I ask Yuki how he finds Istanbul, and he looks puzzled as he tries to find the words.

"It is very easy here," he begins. "Lots of travellers to talk with, all conveniences in the shops. But I feel strange. For so long, my goal was to reach Istanbul, and now that I am here, I don't know what comes next, or if I am ready for it."

It doesn't take long for me to feel the same way. I spend days walking around in a daze, doing nothing and feeling lost, both physically and emotionally. I look like half the Turks walking down the street, so nobody gives me the attention I have been so used to receiving. The travellers here are a different breed, and most of them are on short, guidebook-planned holidays, taking a break from studies or jobs back home. They tend to be young and European, and the majority have never been to Asia or anywhere else in the developing world. When I tell them about my travels, they stare at me in incomprehensible horror.

The world of wealth and consumerism begins to take hold of me, and I grow alarmed by my own newfound greed as I walk into all the latest music and clothing shops in Istanbul. I find myself thinking about CD's I haven't heard, books I haven't read, winter clothing I might need, and new bicycling gear. It is frightening to think how far removed I have become from this world, living in one based only on experience and survival, not consumption. In my naiveté, I somehow assumed that while I was gone, the modern world had somehow drifted away, and had been replaced by something far more ideal.

CNN reports that the U.S. has bombed Iraq on the eve of the presidential impeachment vote. I dream of cycling along country roads, far from it all.

I decide to spend the winter in Greece, on the isle of Crete. As I disembark from the ferry in the port of Chania, I wheel into a past life: thirteen years earlier, I spent a season in Chania as a grape and orange picker, having some of my first travel adventures. I am pleased to see that some things have not changed in the slightest. The old Venetian harbor is still sleepy, especially in winter, with couples sitting under trellises in waterside cafés, sipping *ouzo* and eating hors d'oeuvres, while gnarled old men play backgammon and drink their thick Turkish coffee.

A café is still constituted by one rickety table and two chairs, often with several cats curled up on the woven straw seats. Ordering one tiny cup of thick grinds still gives one the right to inhabit the same table and seat for an eternity. Men still stop to play with children and dogs, while keeping short tempers with their wives. Women are still dressed in black, and strangers continue to chat over the newspapers outside the plentiful *periptera* (kiosks).

The Greeks still tend to be noisy, rude, and abrasive, although like cacti, they are soft on the inside. In several shops, I am berated as a tourist, though once I speak in Greek to the proprietors, I am treated like a long lost brother.

I take a small apartment on a lonely beach outside of town, with views of the snow-clad White Mountains. I had presumed that I would be able to rent a villa for a pittance in the dead of winter, but the locals have made a killing off heavy tourism, and it is difficult even to find a place. Trying to bring my rusty language skills back up to par, I enroll in a Greek course, and am soon living a quiet and rather humdrum existence, my days full of studying, walking along the beach, and taking stock of the journey past and of that to come.

A friend of mine, who has just completed a long bicycle trip, writes a discouraging letter about landing back at home. After years of planning, preparing, and working hard to make her journey a reality, she has lived it, and it is now a rapidly fading memory. She and her partner have split up; she is back working in the rat race; and few people take an interest in the places she has been and things she has seen.

It occurs to me that the same thing will happen to me within a year, and though I am still miles from home, I get a taste here of what it may be like. Most of my fellow students are Europeans who have come to settle here, the wives or girlfriends of Greek men. They complain about their husbands and living conditions, and don't have many interests past their backyards. I try to invite them on weekend outings to nearby mountains or villages, but they are too busy cleaning houses or washing clothes.

I feel like I have lost much of my edge, my confidence, and my achievements. When you speak about the Himalayas and nobody around you even blinks, you know you're no longer in your element.

My happiest moments during the wait for spring come during visits from friends back home. Phil Tierney, a longtime outdoor travel companion, comes to see me after a sojourn in Ireland, bringing gray and rainy weather with him.

Refusing to let it dampen our spirits, we head out on bicycles for the weekend, riding under dramatic skies with rainbows and swirling clouds. We ride over the White Mountains to the southern side of Crete, through villages with stone houses and terraced olive groves, where shepherds call out, "*Yasou, filaki mou,*" ("Hello, my friend,") from the hillsides. The bells on their goats tinkle in the wind.

We ride through small hamlets, where locals make us feel welcome. My memories of this land, where I travelled years before, come alive again. We descend out of the mountains through fields of white boulders, past olive groves, and into terrain covered with orange trees, a sign that we have reached the sea. The Libyan Sea comes into view, glowing emerald under the rays of light that shine down from somewhere above the storm clouds. The village of Chora Sfakion appears, a harbor town nestled into a rocky cliffside above the azure water, and Phil and I make it into the only open *taverna* just as a squall begins.

Coming home several days later, I sprint ahead of Phil, racing along in high cadence next to the sparkling Mediterranean coast. For the first time, it occurs to me that I will be reaching the Pacific Ocean in ten months if all goes well, and laying this journey to rest. I will run out of land and stories, and I wonder what it will be like cycling those last ten kilometers to the ocean. Will it be emotional, or just another day? Probably a bit of both.

The PKK (Kurdish Workers' Party) has declared tourist areas of Turkey to be a war zone following the capture, trial, and sentencing of Kurdish leader Abdullah Ocalan. The United States and NATO are bombing Kosovo to shreds, with Greeks demonstrating in scores of towns in solidarity with their Orthodox brethren. And in the Caucasus, the supporters of Chechnyen rebels set off bombs in Vladikavkaz.

I am riding into a maelstrom, yet I feel light as a feather, ready to put my long journey to rest. My dreams of late have been haunted by specters of death, most likely symbols for the deaths I have witnessed in the recent past, of my mother, of my marriage, and of the coming end of this eternal bicycle odyssey.

My classmates in Chania, realizing that I really am remounting my steed and riding off into the sunset, have suddenly opened up to me. We have long conversations about our fears and dreams, and I wonder why they have become so suddenly intimate with me. I suspect that they feel safe telling me their secrets because they know they will never see me again. Perhaps my departure also represents a type of death for them; when we realize that we do not have any more time together, we drop all the labeling, stereotyping, and pretense that cloud the daily routine, and stop taking each other for granted.

Heart beating, nose running, and legs pumping, I celebrate my birthday and the arrival of spring by taking once again to the road. This is truly the last time, or so I think. My bags are full and heavy as usual, but my knees are rested and the new biopace crank I have installed on my steed seems to make riding up hills easier.

Signs of spring are everywhere, most notably in the blossoms that blanket the Cretan coast. The *amigdalo*, the almond blossom, covers the rocky terrain, its light petals of pink and white clinging tenaciously to fragile branches. The beauty of the blossoms is fleeting, as the slightest breeze dislodges them to earth and sky. According to the Cretan author Nikos Kazantzakis, author of the epic *Last Temptation of Christ*, when someone asked Jesus for a miracle, he replied, "You want a true miracle, take a look at an almond tree in full bloom."

I meet a pair of Belgian cyclists in the seaside town of Rethymnon, just starting on a journey that will take them to India and Nepal. They are fresh and full of dreams, a welcome sight for my jaded eyes and world-weary heart. I am grateful for the camaraderie we share, and they listen wide-eyed to my tales of lands they have yet to cross.

Spring here is fickle, and stays on the side of winter more often than not. Cold rains drench me daily, and as I sail from Crete to Rhodes, and then on to Turkey, a sea of mist envelops every island and outcropping that the ferries pass. Greek isles, famed for their whitewashed houses with blue trim silhouetted against the turquoise Mediterranean, lose much of their appeal shrouded in the clouds.

Hail and water pour from the thundering sky as my hydrofoil docks

at the Turkish port of Marmaris. The customs official greets me with a wide grin and says, "Welcome to Turkey." Locals approach quickly, offering to buy me small glasses of sweet fruit-flavored tea and raving about the capture of Mr. Ocalan. They inform me that Turks and Kurds have no quarrels with each other, and they berate the vilification of Turkey by the western press. I avoid expressing political opinions, and just bask in the warmth of being a welcome stranger once again.

The Mediterranean coast south of Marmaris is vastly different than the coast of Greece. Hillsides are covered in pine trees, eucalyptus, and liquid amber (frankincense), and the rains have carpeted the land with a soft green down. The terrain is severely mountainous, with winding roads completely unsuited to bicycling. By midday, my legs are like jelly, and I curse under my breath at the unrelenting grades.

However, in contrast with Istanbul, this part of Turkey has not changed a wink, and the friendly locals more than make up for the punishing climbs. I am invited to stop every few kilometers by fishermen, construction workers, and beekeepers, who greet me with wide-toothed smiles. After plying me with sticky baklava, tea, and fruit, they wish me well, and say, *"Gulay gulay,"* which literally means, "go smiling."

Completely strange men hug and kiss me whenever I stand to depart, while their women force slices of fresh *burek*, a cheese-filled pastry, into my hands. As I pedal away, I conclude that if there is anything I have learned in the last seven years, it is how to take up an invitation for a cup of tea.

This coast is normally swamped with tourists, but due to the Ocalan situation, the coastal resorts are completely empty. In village after village, I find sparkling new pensions, complete with marble tubs, seaside verandas, and catered breakfasts. They are worth twenty or thirty dollars, but are going for about five. Perplexed owners throw their hands to the heavens with a "what can I do?" look, and toss me the room keys.

Rarely does reality live up to expectations, yet the Turkish coast exceeds even my grandest fantasies. The scenery continues to dazzle, with verdant pine-clad slopes rising at near verticals from the soothing azure sea below. Tea invitations abound, food is tasty and reasonably priced, and each night I roll in to clean, comfortable accommodations and warm Islamic hospitality.

Poppies and daisies dot the roadside, the peaks above are still bathed in snow, and the crescent bays to my side offer chilly swimming possibilities. This stretch of the aptly named "turquoise coast" used to be part of the old Lycean Way, and most of my overnight stops are in former seats of Lycean governors. Hidden in the wooded coastal hills lie ancient amphitheaters, oracles to Apollo, and the ruins of Perge, Thermissos, Xanthos, and Olympos.

I spend several days in Patara, where a twenty-kilometer stretch of untrammeled white sand sweeps along the coast, flanked by rolling dunes. Loggerhead turtles come ashore to lay their eggs here, and due to conservation efforts by environmental groups—and the fact that there is a protected Lycean ruin just off the beach—there has been no development in this area, a far cry from the resorts to be found elsewhere in the Mediterranean.

The tourist drought brought on by the Ocalan debacle continues to keep the coast empty, and the German Embassy is now offering full refunds to anyone who purchased a plane ticket to Turkey. The pension owners ask me if I feel safe, and angrily throw up their hands to ask why the west is portraying their beautiful country in such a rotten light. I don't try to give too many answers, and sneak off to the beach, which I have completely to myself.

My journey has become a series of moments, pictures, and interactions with strangers. I still have a goal to reach, but I drift along like a tumbleweed in the wind. Other than an anticipated destination for each evening, I have no plans. I do not sightsee anymore, and without a travel partner, I suppose I am rather lonely and bored. Though in fact, I feel more at peace than I have even been in my life.

My day is made complete by the simplest of events. As I ride away from the coast into the Toros Mountains, I stop for water in a tiny village of brick houses. As I dismount and begin to pump from a local well, a young beauty with hazel eyes rushes out of her home and says hello. She asks, "*Turkje biliyormusan*?" (Do you know Turkish?)

I reply, "*Yok*" (no), and she says, "*Tamam*" (okay). We stare at each other for a few more minutes, and then she smiles deeply and goes off.

I watch her depart, look at the blossoms on a nearby almond tree, and think to myself that life really is perfect, every scene a painting, and the world full of magic.

Turkey is a quilted pattern of rich farmland, blossom-covered valleys, and alpine lakes, stitched next to snowy volcanoes, narrow rocky canyons, and pristine coastal waters. My journey takes me through each segment in a matter of days, and I emerge from the Toros Mountains onto the Anatolian Plateau, a high-altitude steppe with accompanying moon-scape.

I am following the ancient Royal Road, the path the Lycians and later Selcuks travelled from Babylon to Ephesus. Dilapidated and mold-ering caravansaries lay scattered across the steppe, and although they may be gone in form, they remain in substance, as I receive warm wel-comes from their modern-day counterparts wherever I rest my weary legs.

The sprawling city of Konya sits on the Anatolian plateau, smack in the center of Turkey. Konya is rumored to be a conservative and pious city, and is said to be where the old Turkey and real Islam begin.

I have heard that there is no alcohol available in Konya, but this proves to be a myth. Two jovial truckers named Mehmet and Ismail flag me down outside the city, then proceed to pull out endless cans of beer for an impromptu picnic. After we wish each other well, I dizzily spin my way into Konya's labyrinth of circular boulevards and bottleneck lanes. The staff at the Dervish Hotel emerge to congratulate me on arriv-ing by bicycle, help me bargain down my room from six million to two million, and carry all my bags upstairs.

The hotel is near the behemoth bazaar, home to a pungent cheese market; there is also an entire market dedicated solely to stoves, where one can purchase anything from tin pipes and barbecues dating from the Selcuk Empire to the latest heating appliance. In one alley, the shop-keepers call me over to join in a dance, and we twirl slowly to the tune of a traditional musician playing something resembling a banjo.

I am reminded of something I heard in India, that "commerce equals community equals commerce." Indeed, in most of the developing world, people's "business" spills right into the street they live on. Food ven-dors, butchers, salesmen, and knife grinders all set up stools and tables in front of their shops, drinking tea, playing cards, and gabbing with the neighbors. Work and community are the same, and the integration of the two shows on people's faces.

I reflect on America and the rest of the rat-raced world, where we do our business behind closed doors and rush home at the end of the day to get to our communities—which are also usually located behind closed doors. The looks on the faces in these situations are markedly different.

The deep forests and turquoise bays of the coast are far gone in

Anatolia, and I could be back in Tibet for all I know, as there are nothing but grasslands, small farms, and windy moonscape. The only rise on the horizon is the bulk of Hasan Dagi, a snowclad volcano.

As I move east, the land begins to transform into a series of strange shapes, which from a distance look like sculptures molded out of clay. I am nearing Cappadocia, a region of Turkey composed of tuff formations created by the eruption of Hasan Dagi and other volcanoes in the region several million years ago.

I wander through the deep gorges surrounding Ilhara, where Byzantine monks carved cave churches and dwellings deep into the tuff formations. Some of their churches are chiseled deeply into the rocks, often requiring a challenging climb to gain entrance to their sanctuary. Though there is a rushing river and good soil at the bottom of the gorge— a perfect spot to build homes—the monks built their dwellings like fortresses, and I wonder how severely they must have been persecuted by Ottoman invaders to need to do such a thing.

Several churches and caves are connected by elaborate passageways, but rather than seeing this as a testimony to the ingenuity of the inhabitants, I see it more as an indicator of their fear, of their constant concern over security and escape.

The scenery in the heart of Cappadocia is an endless swath of natural wonders in a myriad of colors befitting canyon country: red, ochre, sepia, and every shade between. I am greeted at every bend in the road with troglodyte dwellings, Swiss cheese castles, and fairy chimneys, and I check into a pension in the town of Goreme to enjoy the landscape for a few days.

I go on long walks each day, winding through vermilion cliffs and sliding down tuff chimneys like a child in Disneyland, and encountering nobody but the occasional farmer. When I ask my pension owner why Goreme hasn't changed over the years like so many other places, she laughs and calls it the world's best kept secret. She tells me that local farmers have continued to rely on their traditional lifestyle, rather than jumping on the tourism bandwagon, and she also praises group tourism, remarking that it "keeps all the idiots together in one place, zips them in and out, and keeps the backcountry quiet."

I agree with her, and wander several more days through the Sword Canyon and Valley of the Fairy Chimneys in solitude, clambering over a lunar landscape that is like descending into Alice's rabbit hole, or wandering through the spaces of an intense acid trip.

Back at the pension, a South African tour guide has arrived, taking a short sojourn from his busy guiding schedule. He has resolved to fly back to Istanbul tomorrow, having just spent a harrowing eight-hour bus ride to get here, and he rambles on endlessly at the dinner table about how horrible his journey has been. When I ask why, he tells me that there was no one on the bus to talk to, as they couldn't speak English! I can only chuckle.

East of Cappadocia, the well-trodden tourist trail of Turkey ends. Not that there are tourists this year, but the occasional fighting and instability over the years among the Kurdish population has been enough to deter most sightseers.

The tuff formations disappear, replaced by open farmlands with wheat fields and strands of poplar, all under a blue sky that appears so low overhead as to blur all distinction between ground and air. After several long days of cycling these empty reaches, I arrive in Sivas, a university town of 200,000. The inhabitants seem to have unlimited time on their hands, and spend their time watching the world go by, turning every little event into a spectacle. A bulldozer working a street corner attracts a crowd, while a fender-bender between a donkey cart and a motorcycle fetches 200 people. My arrival doubles this.

My contact out east is solely with men. Women do not make eye contact, and are often sequestered behind their men, heads wrapped in scarves, eyes downcast. All the circles I move in are staffed and frequented by men, and in teashops, hotels, restaurants, and markets, it is as if the women do not exist. By this time, I have learned that they are out working; this rather pathetic situation is one that I have seen repeated all over the globe.

At this stage in my journey, the days often roll on without incident. I ride, arrive in town, rest, fuel up, and do it again the next day. Little fazes me anymore, yet every so often, along comes a day full of surprises that I could never have imagined when I crawled out of bed at sunrise.

Leaving Sivas in the middle of May, I arise to foreboding skies and a dramatic drop in temperature. For the first time since my trials in the Caucasus, I have to stop to change into all my cold-weather gear, and even then I am still chilled to the core. I stop in a small village café for a hot bowl of soup, and the locals inform me that I am headed over a mountain pass where PKK terrorists have been killing people.

Frozen and miserable, I shrug off their concerns and head out into the wind. I pedal on, driven by sheer will and discipline, figuring I have done this enough times before to muddle through. It takes several hours to approach the Camlibel Pass, where snow is falling, and in the whiteout conditions I cannot even see the pass. Eventually, the wind, grade, and pain from my icy fingers make it so I cannot ride, but I walk on, blindly determined.

Rather than sing songs, think of friends, or imagine a warm room, I tell myself over and over, "Here I am on a frozen pass in the middle of Turkey, out in all the elements, walking my overweight bicycle up a hill." There is no focus on joy or sorrow, just on the cold and bitter present. As I reach the crest, I gaze at the trees drenched in white frost, and I imagine that my face must look the same, my beard full of icicles and my nose running like a spigot.

Over the top of the Camlibel, there is a tiny hamlet of the same name, where I fall into a teashop deeply relieved. I guzzle several glasses of tea next to a woodstove, while the owner and his cronies gaze at me wide-eyed, telling me with various hand motions that I still have one more pass to cross, and warning me not to carry on.

Back outside, the winds have become brutal, and I cycle in a daze, feeling like I am going to fall asleep. Cycling becomes nothing but pure instinct and deep resolve. I know that in several weeks I will look back on all this with a laugh or fright, so I try to remember it for all it is: the glaze on the pine trees, the snot running from my nose, the tire tracks Odysseus leaves in the snow.

After nine hours of madness, I reach the Kizilinish Pass and offer profuse thanks to the deities above. Caesar did battle here in 47 BC, ousting King Pharnake II, and remarking, "I came, I saw, I conquered." He certainly didn't do it on a bicycle.

It is thirteen vicious downhill kilometers from the pass, and my digits feel as if they will all fall off, but mercifully, my day is done, and I sail into the town of Tokat just after dark. In a most appropriate end to the day, it turns out that Tokat's claim to fame is that it trains all the best masseurs in Turkey. Within minutes of arrival, I am headed for the Tarihi Ali Pasha Hamam, the cavernous Tokat bathhouse, where I opt for the royal treatment. I reheat myself on hot marble slabs, after which a burly attendant scrubs me with a sponge resembling a Brillo pad, scrubbing off layers of grime and skin. This is followed by a tortuous massage, in which every limb and joint is pulled, twisted, and pressed until I can stand no more.

I emerge from the bath breathing deeply in ecstasy, and am then swathed in towels from head to toe like a mummy. In a private cubicle, I recline on a divan while an attendant named Umit ("not *humid*," he cackles) brings me cups of tea. Umit tells me that the hills ahead are even worse than what I have come over today, but I am too warm, exhausted, and happy to listen to him, and can only marvel at the extremes I have traversed in the last twenty-four hours.

The Black Sea coast, after the hinterlands of the Anatolian Plateau, is modern, prosperous, and hopping. Children zip around on mountain bikes, women without veils walk through the streets, and pedestrians throng the shopping arcades. The downside to all this progress is the atrocious traffic, and I spend much of my morning evading buses and trucks, eventually losing my temper and flipping off obnoxious honking drivers as they nip past.

Halfway through my morning, as I cycle through a small village, I swear that I hear my name called, and look around to see the two Belgian cyclists I met in Crete. Hadewych and Patrick have come a long way since I saw them in Greece. Gone are the looks of fear and wonder, and in their place are the focused stares of road warriors. The couple are ecstatic to see me, as they have had a rough go of it and haven't met any travellers to chat with until now.

They have become accustomed to the rigors of the daily ride, and to living in a foreign culture, and after we ride together for a few days, it becomes apparent that the three of us make excellent riding partners. We are all strong and able to put in the miles, yet at the same time we share a relaxed approach, and we truly appreciate the freedoms of bicycle travel. We end up spending several weeks together, creating the bonds of a friendship that will go far beyond the confines of Turkish roads.

The Turks have told us that the inhabitants of the Black Sea region are the friendliest in Turkey, which I find hard to imagine; the amiability of everyone in the country thus far has achieved five-star levels. Yet they are right, and it seems that we cannot ride more than a few kilometers without being invited in for tea.

In Ordu, a man who has lived in Berkeley, California approaches us, and demands that we stay for *pide* (Turkish pizza) while he recalls his wonderful time there. Down the road in Tirebolu, a family who lived in Holland for fifteen years buy us drinks and practice Dutch with Patrick, who answers in Flemish. Wherever we stop to make purchases or ask directions, chairs are brought out, tea and snacks served, and we are asked to stay and share stories with our gracious hosts. Boys on bikes eagerly escort us to hotels at the end of the day, racing their small two-wheelers next to us, proud to be helping the strangers. Everywhere we go, people approach to greet us, crying, "*Hosh geldeniz!*" ("Welcome, my friends!")

It is a pleasure to cycle in the company of Hadewych, as she is an amateur botanist, and provides a running commentary on the bountiful vegetation that surrounds us. The Black Sea coast is extremely humid, and thus home to all sorts of creepers, vines, and subtropical plants. We travel for days surrounded by abundant hazelnut orchards, and as we move east, these are replaced by terraced plantations of tea bushes, for which the region is famous.

Along with the tea, we begin to encounter the Laz and Hemsin, ethnic minorities in Turkey, far less well known than the often-discussed Kurds. The Laz are supposedly descended from Christians inhabiting the Georgian coast of the Black Sea, perhaps the original guardians of the Golden Fleece sought by Jason and his Argonauts. They tend to be fair-skinned with beak noses, and Laz women are recognizable by the bright red striped scarves that they wear.

The Hemsin are a group with similar origins, and Hemsin women are very identifiable by the black and gold headscarves and mesh headnets they wear, decorated with dangling silver sequins and coins. The Hemsin are famed bakers of bread and pastry, and among the treats on the shelves of local bakeries we find gigantic round loaves of Trabzon bread, which look like large cushions and often weigh up to four kilos! One loaf is enough to feed an army—or at least a trio of ravenous cyclists.

Trabzon, the Black Sea's bustling capital, sits upon a tabletop mountain—its name comes from the Greek *trapeza*, for table—and is surrounded by slopes of densely packed tea bushes. It is an impressive city, replete with charming cafés and crowded bookshops, and like many of Turkey's larger cities, it is caught somewhere between the past and present. Fishermen sell their daily catch in the perpetually misty harbor, next to Laz women who offer baskets of freshly picked strawberries. Young girls in somber headscarves and Metallica t-shirts make their way to school, while Azeri shoeshine boys wax the loafers of suited city slickers. Perhaps most interesting of all are the "Natashas," who have become an integral part of Trabzon's newfound wealth.

When the former Soviet Union collapsed, its sealed borders opened and sent dealers, traders, and prostitutes roaring into Trabzon, following a gold-rush-like frenzy from Moscow and Kiev down through Georgia and into Turkey. The entire northeastern seaboard has become a giant bordello, with Trabzon at the epicenter. Russian hookers with the pathetic nickname of "Natasha" have become local fixtures, decked out in miniskirts, high heels, revealing tops, and loads of makeup. They make a striking contrast to the conservatively dressed Turks.

The towns around Trabzon are small versions of the same thing: they are prosperous, relaxed, and full of rampant development and hideous concrete structures in the middle of an otherwise pristine environment. Heavy mists boil up off the Black Sea, drenching the tea plantations and spraying us relentlessly, but I find that the constant precipitation increases the beauty of the verdant landscape. Rhododendron trees are blossoming en masse; frothy rapids roar down to the sea from the nearby Kackar Mountains; and ancient stone bridges and granite diorite spires peek out through the fog.

In Hopa, on the Georgian border, Patrick tries to find us a hotel room, and the staff in several places tell him that he cannot stay if he is not interested in a "madam." We end up in a room that smells of used contraceptives from which a kissing couple departs exactly as we arrive. Pale, anemic women drift through the hallways, some with needle-scarred veins. Several are lying in adjacent rooms with doors open, their frail skeletons wasting away on beds, looking more like corpses lining coffins.

We joke about our surroundings, but there is a grim undercurrent to our humor. From our bedroom window, we watch the prosperous streets below, filled with boisterous and eager eyed Turkish young men. Truckers come and go from the hotels, and the sun descends and disappears into the cloudy Black Sea.

Our last night in Turkey is spent in Ardahan, a dusty frontier town back on the Anatolian plateau. We are tired and quiet for a change, probably dreading tomorrow, when we will part ways. Conversations between Hadewych and Patrick have been tense lately, and all the signs point to a coming explosion in the long hard days on the road. Their tensions remind me of the troubles between Hitomi and me, and I say nothing, wondering privately if they will make it to India intact.

Yet our partnership has been fantastic. Before they came along, I had been longing to wake up to the same faces every morning, rather than moving on relentlessly. For my part, perhaps I have given them relief from the intensity of one another's company—and a dose of familiarity in a landscape that is still quite alien to them.

The hotel owner heats bath water on a wood stove, and asks if we need anything else. Hadewych jokes that she has been fantasizing about ice cream for days; half an hour later, the proprietor returns with a liter of chocolate and vanilla, which he serves to us as we lie on our beds. We go to sleep saying that we will miss each other and Turkey very much.

On a windy morning, under heavy skies, we dawdle over our goodbyes at a remote junction that feels a million miles away from the other side of Turkey. Patrick tells me that the two of them have learned not to hurry any longer, and I tell him and Hadewych that when they reach the Himalayas, they will look back on what seem like tough times thus far and laugh at it all. It has been a rare pleasure to have such easy company, and we take photos and hug endlessly, but we both have ground left to cover. I swing north for the Caucasus, and they head east for lands I have already traversed. I watch them disappear like particles of dust, swallowed by the high plains.

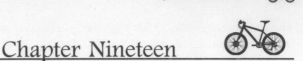

Chapter Nineteen
Georgia: *Under A Bad Sign*

A journey is like a marriage. The certain
way to be wrong is to think you control it.

John Steinbeck,
Travels With Charley

As for man, his days are like grass; as a
flower of the field, so he flourisheth. For the wind
passeth over it, and he is gone.

Psalm 103

The Turkish-Georgian border is a swamp, knee-deep in mud from the past day's rains. Truck drivers wait patiently in an endless lineup of truck convoys, playing backgammon and arguing with fellow drivers to pass the time. I join the queue, standing amid a long line of Natashas who are waiting to enter the Turkish health post.

I reflect on my wait in the train station in Matsumoto, seven years before. Back then, I wondered how many times I would be stuck in similar situations, wet, lonely, and miserable. 30,000 kilometers later, I reckon it really hasn't been too bad.

The Chief of Customs invites me in out of the mud, serves me tea and food, and asks how I like Turkey. Bowled over by the hospitality, I almost weep as I assure him that his country is as big, beautiful, and accommodating as any I have ever travelled in. He sends me out ahead of all the Natashas, toward burly policemen who ask me for three U.S. dollars in exit tax. I do not have any small bills, so they shrug their shoulders and wave me on.

In the past weeks, I have noticed that I am growing jaded. Sunsets are still pretty, but are no longer as gorgeous as ones I have seen in the past. The snowy peak in front of me is not as spectacular as the ones in the Himalayas; the ocean here is not as blue as the one near the Barrier Reef; the meal is not as tasty; and the beautiful woman who beckons me for tea is not as friendly or beautiful as the one I met in *that* place at *that* time.

Obviously, I am burnt out by my perpetual motion, by the flood of experience that bombards my every waking hour. Yet I feel a deeper malaise, an internal dissatisfaction with all things present, and I think that I have truly become like Odysseus, trying so desperately to get back home, but damned to wander forever, drugged with the elixir of the exotic and the sublime. As I cycle along, I fear what may happen when I return home. Will I go out with friends and be bored to tears by the scenery, the conversation, and the company? Is this the price I must pay for truly seeing the world? Or have I forgotten how to pay attention to the present and live in the moment?

The here and now beneath my wheels on Georgian soil is not a pretty one. The road has disintegrated into a track of rocks, holes, and mud, possibly the worst thing I have attempted to ride since China. It is impossible to cycle without pain, and as I weave along, trying not to damage Odysseus or myself, I curse the gods at the top of my lungs.

Yet a resounding answer to all my morning musings lies just ahead, waiting to deliver a major slap to the face of my self-doubts.

Cresting a hill, I begin a descent into a valley. The road does not improve, but I am suddenly surrounded by fields of wildflowers truly unlike anything I have ever seen. Poppies, irises, and daisies rise around me, red, purple, and yellow, packed tightly together and shining against a backdrop of verdantly carpeted hills.

The fields stretch out over acres, so densely packed with color that I could be cycling through a painting by Monet or Van Gogh. I am completely awed, stopping every five meters to take dozens of pictures and savor the miracle that surrounds me. I begin to chuckle, and am soon laughing wildly.

I am both humbled and empowered by this instant answer to my earlier malaise. Never underestimate this earth; there is more beauty here than one can ever imagine.

The landscape is quite a contrast to the carcasses of towns I pass through, ugly old Soviet housing blocks with overgrown yards full of broken glass and rusted metal. The only shops are kiosks selling champagne, vodka, and Snickers.

Akhaltsikhe, the first town of any size, does have a small bazaar with fresh cherries and surprisingly decent *maroozhna*, Russian ice cream. Vendors sell various bric-a-brac: nail clippers, water heaters, deodorant, cigarettes, lighters, razors, and toothpaste, most goods coming from Turkey and Armenia. The heavy overcoats of winter are gone, yet most people are still dressed in black, with men in slacks and button-up shirts, and women wearing see-through black lace dresses and short skirts. It is quite a shock after conservative Turkey.

At night, Akhaltsikhe turns into a ghost town, as nobody appears to have the money to go out anywhere. Even the fanciest restaurant in town, a large place with lacy blue curtains, has only one table occupied by a pair of army officers swigging vodka. Elderly waitresses bark away in Russian, playing cards, gossiping, and watching a fashion show on a black and white television. Everything here is like a relic, as if time has been frozen for forty years.

Roads continue to be bumpy, wet, and full of holes, but I give them little thought, occupied by the continuing scenery and total lack of traffic. The occasional Lada passes, stuffed with more people than I had thought possible, but other than this, the entire country seems asleep. I see a couple walking down to the Kura River with their kids, the father carrying a fishing net and picnic basket. They walk slowly, almost as if in a trance, and they don't bother to look up or react as I pass by. Like the rest of the country, they appear to be in slow motion.

I reach Borzhomi, a sleepy spa town famous for its mineral water, which bubbles up from a spring in the middle of town. The derelict remains of elegant old wooden homes grace the banks of the Borzhomi River, and several sanitariums and an old palace have been turned into apartment buildings. Dirty laundry flutters on their rotting balconies.

There is one giant hotel in Borzhomi, a former five-star Intourist monstrosity, which also looks abandoned. After wandering its cavernous halls for a time, I come across a concierge, who agrees to give me a room. It is surprisingly pleasant, with wooden floors, an armchair, chandeliers, and great forest and river views from the balcony. Of course there is neither power nor water, though the concierge promises they will both come on within several hours. At five dollars a night, I am paying five times what I paid for my previous night's accommodation, but for five stars, Georgian style, I decide that it is well worth it, and decide to take a day's rest.

After seven years on this journey, I have still not had a genuinely horrible experience. Yes, there have been moments of despair and hardship as I faced headwinds, diarrhea, stone-throwing children, snowstorms, broken rims, and boils; many times, I have wished I could be elsewhere. But there hasn't been anything that I would truly call *bad*. A traveller in Turkey mentioned to me just how remarkable this was, to come this long and this far without incident, and claimed that I was sailing under one very bright star. In Borzhomi, this streak comes to a very abrupt end.

I wander up to the water park on the river, where people come to picnic and collect mineral water. Tired, I keep to myself, napping under a tree and writing in my journal. Three teenagers arrive and sit next to me, smoking, spitting, and asking me questions I cannot understand. Upon realizing that I am a foreigner, they continue to prod me, so I move away from them to finish my lunch in peace. I have heard that there are hot pools several kilometers up the river, and I head that way to see if I can find them.

I pass a series of bridges, and see a few families and the occasional couple having lunch in the park, but at the fourth bridge, the picnickers end. I notice the three teenagers walking not too far behind me, and I get the sense they are following me, so I stop to see what they are up to. They pass me, then stop to wait just ahead. Feeling threatened, I turn around and go back to the last bridge, where there are more people, and again they come back past me, stopping several hundred meters below me this time. Bored youths with nothing to do, I think to myself.

I make my way back up the river, stopping often and looking back to see if the boys are still following me. They appear to have given up, and I continue, relieved. I pass an empty swimming pool which probably used to be a mineral spa, but is now derelict and overgrown with weeds like everything else here. As there is still no sign of the boys, I continue onward, soon finding myself on a small path along the rushing Borzhomi River.

The scenery is exquisite, yet I am unable to enjoy it, feeling strangely unnerved. It occurs to me that I should have left my money belt back in the hotel, as a robbery here would certainly leave me in dire straits, with no money, no identification, and minimal language skills in a place with no infrastructure whatsoever.

Not finding any hot springs, and telling myself that this is supposed to be a day off, I turn around to head home. As I round a bend, I see the trio of young men coming towards me. For a second, I consider jumping into the bushes to hide, but I guess that all these years of travel without an incident have left me feeling invincible. The boys come up to meet me, then turn around to walk with me, and I know then and there that I am in a bad situation. Tense, I begin to make small talk. The leader of the trio says his name is Vaxo, and he is here on holiday from Tbilisi. He asks repeatedly if I have any dollars, and I tell him that I carry only *denge checks* (traveller's checks), which I have left in my hotel room.

Vaxo tries to get me between himself and his taller friend, and I duck out of this and walk on the outside of the group. It all feels horribly wrong, but I keep moving and talking, crossing another bridge and knowing that in two more bridges there will be picnickers and safety. The boys speak excitedly with each other in Georgian, and I sense they are discussing what to do with me. One is much taller than I am, and Vaxo is quite muscular—and drunk. I can smell his foul breath as he walks next to me. I consider running away, but I am in my sandals, and I am carrying a stuff sack of camera gear, books, and water.

Suddenly, out of the corner of my eye, I see Vaxo bend down and pick up a large and very jagged rock. I turn to confront him, and he smiles at me with an ugly grimace, as if to assure me that it will all be over quickly. He grabs my shirt, ripping it as I struggle to break free. I have always wondered how I would respond to a situation like this. Would I try to defend myself, showing off some Tai Chi moves as if I knew a martial art? Obviously not. In this case, panic takes over completely, and I break free from Vaxo's grasp and run wildly.

This is a mistake. Within seconds, Vaxo is upon me, and I slip into the mud, a fallen prey. I can sense my mortality with every passing second. I look up at Vaxo, his hand clutching the rock in a death grip, and I try to cover my head with my hands, expecting a blow. My entire journey flashes before my eyes; I feel saddened that my odyssey—and perhaps, my life—will come to an end here on a muddy path in a forest in Georgia. Nobody will ever even know what happened to me. As I await the inevitable strike, I think of Hitomi, her small strong body working to climb a steep hill on her overloaded bike.

Too many seconds go by, and I realize that I am still alive. In a blur, I see the tall boy jump on his friend Vaxo, who is just as surprised as I am, and wrestle the rock away before Vaxo can swing it. Perhaps he has felt a prick of conscience, or has realized that the consequences of what they are doing may be more severe than he had thought.

In the confusion, I scramble to my feet and begin to run, sensing the trio will be back after me within seconds. And they are—but not before I have scrambled up the mountainside, using all my strength to clamber onto a rock ledge and into forest cover where I can hide. I am back in my element, and I traverse the ledge, crawl across a ravine, and have soon buried myself in a hollow under a fallen tree. The boys scream in the distance.

I wait almost an hour before moving. When I inspect myself for damages, I don't find any, though I am covered from head to toe in mud, and feel emotionally raped. The boys are nowhere in sight. Still fearful, and wild with adrenaline, I avoid going back down to the river, and instead spend two hours bushwhacking through the forest.

I return to my hotel completely despondent. Feeling violated, I want nothing more than to wash the mud from my clothes and body, hopefully erasing some of the memories of the afternoon. Of course, the water is not running in the hotel, and it is unbearable to sit in my room, so I go in search of a bathhouse. Several people in town tell me there is no public bathhouse, and one woman suggests that I go to the Water Park. I look at her as if I have seen a ghost. As I trudge back to the hotel, I am stared at by countless eyes, and can only wish that they would all disappear.

Unable to get clean, I figure that food may be the next best thing, so I head to the only bistro in town. It is a cheerless place with no customers, and a staff of six or seven with nothing to do but drink vodka and sing folk songs. I watch them miserably, again reflecting on how the poverty of Georgia has affected these people's lives and my own. No customers; no money; what's left but to be drunk and singing?

While I eat my greasy *katchapuri* cheese pie, one of the waitresses sidles over and asks where I am from, what I am doing here, and why on earth I am so filthy. I answer as best I can, and she shakes her head angrily as I relate my tale of the afternoon's encounter. Several minutes later, the owner of the restaurant comes and stands in front of me, and asks if I like Georgian music. Neither wanting to offend him nor to engage in further conversation, I nod my head wearily. He glares back at me and cries, "Moment!" then disappears into a back room.

He returns with a drum and an accordion, and he and another man lurch into a frenzied chorus of traditional Georgian tunes. The music is almost hypnotic, sounding like the bouzouki or mandolin ballads one hears in Greece or Turkey, and the scene grows surreal as the waitresses begin to dance. I, the lone diner, sit with my plate in the corner.

Moments later, waitresses come to my table and take my hands, dragging me away from my food to dance. I resist at first, in no mood for merriment, but the ladies insist, not letting go of my hands, so I join in, twirling slowly to the intoxicating beat. Soon I am dancing on my own, as the others clap, shout, and stomp their feet, yelling, "Bravo!" and passing shots of vodka around the room. For the first time in hours, a smile breaks across my face, and soon I am laughing uproariously.

In a timeless, magical moment, I catch myself feeling completely healed from my ordeal. Where else on the planet might one be attacked, and a few hours later, be dancing like a wild man in a restaurant with strangers? I order a beer, and shake my head at this very strange country.

Leaving Borzhomi without further ado, I pick up the main road from the Black Sea to Tbilisi. Although the road is in far better condition than what I have been traversing for the past days, there is also much more traffic. Red Cross jeeps whiz by, on their way to and from the crises in Abkhazia and Ossetia. Oil workers en route to Baku pass by in air-conditioned luxury.

Still expecting Vaxo and the boys to be lurking at every bend in the road, I am more attuned to the signs of poverty that are all around. In one town, people have put their beds out in the road for sale. Some of the beds are family heirlooms, and would be worth a fortune elsewhere in the world, but here they are being squandered for the price of a few meals. Farther on, an entire generation stands behind sparse pails of strawberries, hoping motorists will stop and purchase their meager offerings. I cannot carry an entire pail, but stop to give a donation, and do accept a few of the choicest berries from the grateful family.

Policemen are everywhere, trying to pull over cars. Because they are not receiving their salaries from the government, this is the only way they can make an income; despite this abuse of their power, I pity them, especially when I see that few cars stop when requested, instead flooring their accelerators in an effort to escape.

When drivers do stop, the police saunter over to the vehicle, and a short discussion ensues, hands are shaken, a wad of money is discreetly placed into the officer's pocket, and then the entire party shares a bottle of vodka before moving on!

I roll into Gori, another decrepit post-industrial monstrosity of a town. Its main claim to fame is that it is the birthplace of Josef

Vissarionovich Dzugashvili, more familiarly known to the world as Josef Stalin. Stalin spent his first fourteen years in Gori, and in the city's main square sits the only bust left in the former Soviet Union commemorating his reign of terror. There is also a Stalin Museum, with thousands of photos, memorabilia, and other proofs of Josef's greatness.

The museum, like my hotel, has no power and no visitors, and is drab and ghostly. There are Stalin keychains and postcards of the mega-lomaniac for sale in the lobby, but the most striking feature of the whole place for me is the collection of photos of Gori one hundred years ago. Absolutely nothing appears to have changed.

In front of the museum, elderly pensioners sit hawking small bags of sunflower seeds, trying to make some pittance of a living. I return to my hotel, watching drunken men stagger into bars. The desk clerk is nodding off in the foyer, while a black and white TV blares away in the corner. I wake the man to ask for a cup of hot water, and he launches into a tirade about how much better things used to be. The Intourist used to be full every night, with Soviet tourists paying fifty dollars a head, and now look at it, empty and rotting away.

"We need a man like Josef, strong and able, to get back on track again," the clerk tells me, flexing his biceps as he mentions Stalin's name. "Josef *karasho*!" (Josef good!) he exclaims. "Gorbachev and Shevardnadzhe (the president of Georgia) *nyet karasho*!"

Not wanting a debate, I inform him that it would be *karasho* if the water in my room would work, and he promises to see what he can do. An hour later, when I turn the tap on the bathtub, rust-colored water begins to pour from the sink. As I sponge myself off with the dirty water, it occurs to me that the desk clerk bears an uncanny resemblance to Stalin himself. Georgia is beginning to depress me.

On the first of June, I return to Tbilisi. As I cycle past the spot where my freewheel collapsed six months earlier, I raise my fist triumphantly above my head, as I have completed the leg of the Trans-Asian journey.

In the heat of summer, Tbilisi is far more upbeat and welcoming than it was six months earlier. The rest of the country may be a wreck, but an oil pipeline deal with the United States has brought development to the capital, and an agreement with an American power company has ensured that Tbilisi now has electricity for much of the day. There is a new McDonald's, built to resemble a Georgian church, packed with youthful worshippers in designer jeans; I wonder if they serve *katchapuri*. Avenue David Agmashenveli has countless new shops and restaurants, and even a Baskin Robbins ice cream parlor. A Swedish film festival has just swept through town; the new Star Wars is being shown in Russian; and the Metechi Palace's grand hotel lobby is swarming with foreign businessmen and shady local characters.

I am welcomed like a long-lost cousin at Venera Tateshvili's, where things have also changed. Her homestay space has been cut in half by the arrival of Viola's twins. The price of their homestay has doubled, and despite Venera's complaints about how expensive things have become, I notice they are now buying expensive milk protein, rather than breastfeeding, and also using disposable diapers, which cost a pretty penny.

I take a break from cycling, planning to take a bus back to Turkey, and then a ship across the Black Sea to Romania, where I will begin my European leg. Yet I have one final journey to make in Georgia, and that is up into the high Caucasus, a region renowned for its incredible scenery.

I will have company for this jaunt, as my friend Elke will be flying in to meet me. Elke is a seasoned traveller, always in search of a good adventure; on a summer trip tracing her ancestral roots, she has been captivated by stories of the Caucasus. I have told her of the beauty of the land, and of the Georgian love of celebration and hospitality, but have not said much about the general conditions here. Fortunately, she has a good sense of humor and has done some hard travelling, and shortly after her arrival, we have bargained our way into a clapped-out collective van, headed for Upper Swanetia. With ten other locals, we jam into torn seats without seatbelts and begin an arduous journey northward.

Upper Swanetia is a remote region of the Caucasus, an area isolated from the rest of Georgia by mountains, language, and culture. In Tbilisi, people would look horrified at the mention of Swanetia, calling it a land of bears, ice, and savages. Yet although Swanetians are as independence-minded as inhabitants of the other Caucasus regions—the Ossetians, Abkhazians, and nearby Chechnyans and Dagestanis—Swanetia is supposedly still safe, while those areas remain in chaos and conflict. Supposedly.

Well-armed Russian soldiers in military vehicles patrol the Abkhaz side of the Inghuri River, which pounds through the valley far below us. Our van races along at crazy speeds, and Elke moves closer to my side of the vehicle when she sees how close our bald tires are to the cliff's edge.

Soldiers and perilous drops aside, we find the locals extremely welcoming, and their exuberance and extroverted manners are a welcome change from the dour faces we have seen in the cities. When we ask whether there is a hotel in Mestia, the village we are aiming for, we are told that there is not, but the locals exclaim that we needn't worry, as we are in "Svaneti."

After six hours, our bottoms are bruised from the bumpy road, but we forget the pain when we see the dramatic and overwhelming scenery. The enormous icy ridges of the high Caucasus come into view, with the highest mountain peaks I have seen since the Himalayas. Mount Ushba and Mount Shkhelda, two 5000 meter sculptures with immense fluted walls of ice, stand guard like sentries over the entire valley, portals into a hidden land.

Mestia appears shortly afterward, a large village of old houses and garden plots sprawled out across a broad alluvial fan. Stone towers rise all around the village, ancient features of the Swanetian landscape which served as lookouts for the clans that dwelt here long ago. Nestled under the mountain shadows, they give the village a timeless feeling.

Our driver takes us through small lanes to a large house where several people are milling about in a courtyard. The owner, a strapping former mountaineer and guide named Zakro, bids us welcome in Swanetian, which sounds something like a chicken trying to speak Russian. He settles us into a comfortable room upstairs and serves us a meal of thick homemade bread, fresh cheese, and green onions and cilantro from the courtyard garden. Soon we are introduced to the neighbors, one of whom is a young woman who speaks fluent English, and she begins to answer our questions about this strange place.

Eteri Jorgoliani is well educated, giving, and easygoing. She left Mestia to attend university in Tbilisi, something fairly rare for a villager here, and she had ample opportunities to find a job in the medical field. Yet she chose to return to her childhood home—where there is no work— in order to take care of her family.

As elsewhere in Georgia, we see rampant unemployment and alcoholism, but at least in Swanetia, people are used to being self sufficient. Everyone has an old house, a garden plot, and sheep or goats.

Our host Zakro was a full-time guide, and his house a beehive of climbers and trekkers. During the Soviet times, scores of Russians made their way over the Caucasus and down to the Black Sea for holidays. Now he feels like an old man with a head full of memories. Eteri tells us that he is happy to see some new faces—though she adds that despite the hard times, he will ask for an arm and a leg if we opt to do any climbing with him. The few tourists that pass through these days come in prearranged groups, their itineraries arranged by adventure travel agencies, and as I have seen so many times the world over, in barely functional economies these tourists truly look like money trees, their abundant fruits ripe for the picking.

Many people in town are drinking heavily, and a soused Zakro is soon pestering us to employ him as a climbing guide. Elke and I spend hours trying politely to worm our way out of the situation and avoid making agreements. It occurs to me at one point that I am in a situation not unlike the one up the creek in Borzhomi, only here, we are surrounded by a town half filled with the intoxicated descendants of warlike clans.

We escape the inebriated tensions of town by going into the mountains. Eteri arranges a jeep for us, driven by a fellow named Nadari who takes great pride in his task of shuffling the foreigners around safely—and alcohol-free. He is an excellent chauffeur, keeping his eyes glued to the narrow and precipitous mountain road while he gives us a running narrative on the history of the towers, the names of mountain peaks, and the story of his endeavors to keep his family afloat by using his beat-up jeep as a taxi.

At the end of the road lies a small settlement called Ushguli, a smaller and far more charming version of Mestia. The entire area is an endless rolling carpet of green fields, and as Elke and I hike into the surrounding mountains, we find ourselves in the middle of a Technicolor dream. Primrose, anemone, and wild tulips abound, along with pink, white, and burgundy rhododendron bushes. Higher up, bountiful patches of forget-me-nots cling tenaciously to the slopes, in delicate contrast with the savage gullies and ice chutes that tower above them.

The Caucasus ridge stretches for hundreds of kilometers on all sides of us, an alpine fantasy, seeming far from the incessant human conflicts on their lower slopes. We are probably looking into Russia, at far-off Chechnya, and perhaps a few other countries as well, but up here there are no borders. There is only white, green, and the deep blue sky. I pity the locals' loss of income with the collapse of tourism, but I am drunk on the open space and glad to have this grandeur completely to one comrade and myself.

Back down in Ushguli, we find that Nadari has ended his sobriety after being invited by a farmer named Mahmood to sample the local moonshine. Mahmood is a real gem, playing duets with his daughter

Anna on homemade instruments resembling mandolins; both musicians are adorned in wide-brimmed straw hats, and sing at the top of their lungs under the mountain sky.

We know the toasts by heart now. Women, Georgia, and God, always in the same order. For better or worse, chauvinistic or not, I figure these folks at least have their priorities straight. We join in, downing the fiery homebrewed wheat alcohol, and soon we are clapping and singing along ourselves. Mahmood dances wildly, gyrating to Anna's strumming, singing of how life is hard, yet he wouldn't trade his mountains for any of the riches below. The word spreads of our party, and soon half the village has arrived, and everyone is drunk. What else is there to do, hemmed into these isolated, stupendous mountains?

Nadari fortunately has a grip on his alcohol intake, and we all know that it is time to return to Mestia, so we weasel our way out of the party. We give a final toast to Mahmood and Anna, and to their gorgeous piece of the world, and all hug and kiss goodbye.

Unfortunately, a wonderful afternoon is tainted when a few drunken young men from the village surround the jeep and begin eyeing Elke. One of them sticks his face into the car, looks us over, asks us where we are from (Elke is German), then raises his arm in a Nazi salute and says, "Geil Gitler." He repeats this until we realize what he is saying; Russian pronunciation tends to turn the *h* sound into *g*.

I fear the worst, but the man just looks at us all again, grins like a lunatic, and slurs out, "My good, good friends. Geil Gitler." Nadari steps on the gas, and my final impression of Georgia as I look back is of this treasure of a town, surrounded by scenery that jolts my senses, with a crowd of banshees singing, dancing, and howling at the moon, their jugs by their sides. It is a bittersweet country on a permanent holiday; out of work, out of luck, and forever toasting the whole affair.

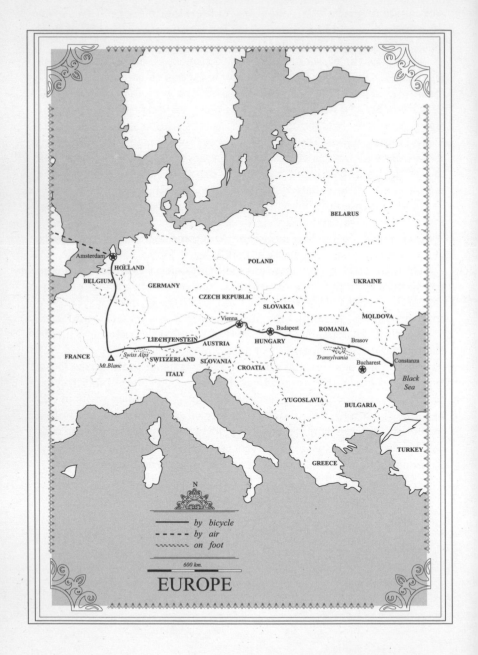

Amsterdam
HOLLAND
BELGIUM
GERMANY
FRANCE
Swiss Alps
Mt.Blanc
SWITZERLAND
ITALY
LIECHTENSTEIN
AUSTRIA
SLOVENIA
CROATIA
POLAND
CZECH REPUBLIC
SLOVAKIA
Vienna
HUNGARY
Budapest
YUGOSLAVIA
GREECE
BELARUS
UKRAINE
MOLDOVA
ROMANIA
Brasov
Transylvania
Bucharest
BULGARIA
TURKEY
Constanza
Black
Sea

N

—————— by bicycle
- - - - - by air
⌇⌇⌇⌇⌇⌇ on foot

600 km.

EUROPE

Chapter Twenty
Eastern Europe:
Into the Old Country

> *Your true traveller finds boredom rather agreeable than painful. It is the symbol of his liberty — his excessive freedom. He accepts his boredom, when it comes, not merely philosophically, but almost with pleasure.*
>
> Aldous Huxley

> *Travelling is like flirting with life. It's like saying, "I would stay and love you, but I have to go; this is my station."*
>
> Lisa St. Aubin de Teran

I have heard nothing but bad stories about Romania from both friends and fellow travellers. "Beware of the pickpockets," they say. "Beware of the Gypsies." "Everyone is a con artist." And so the tales go. So I am a trifle nervous as I disembark at the port of Constanza, stumbling from the boat half-asleep.

Constanza is a beach town, a former Soviet resort on the Black Sea, and in the middle of summer is festive and crowded with sun worshippers. It looks like the entire city has gone to the seaside instead of work; with Romania's troubled economy, this may be the best option. Life here appears to be one big party, though true to Soviet form, the beach resorts are ugly as sin. Concrete high-rise hotels tower over litter-strewn water and tightly packed beaches, where Russian rock and roll blares from loudspeakers, and teens have full run of the sand.

Nicolae Ceausescu, the former Romanian dictator, banned contraceptives and abortion for years, and in 1966 mandated that all women should have at least five children. This resulted in one of the world's largest orphan populations, as well as the highest infant mortality rate in Europe. However, if the beach scene is anything to judge by, there is no dearth of children, and I spend most of my day feeling like I am in a teen party film.

I manage to find a more secluded spot toward the end of the beach, away from the loudspeakers, but my peace is shattered by an enormous woman who comes and bathes topless next to me, belching loudly every thirty seconds. Her pendulous breasts are burned as red as beets, and she spends much of her time doing laundry in a nearby creek, waddling over my towel as she passes back and forth. She suspends her immense underpants from stakes planted in the sand, to dry in the warm breeze.

The Gypsies also frequent this end of the beach, coming down to the sea with their horsecarts to wash both horse and cart in the murky Black Sea. They stand apart from the rest of the Romanians; women in long colorful dresses bundling scrappy kids, and usually one man presiding over the entire clan.

More properly known as *Roma*, the Gypsies are a caste society, coming from India in the fifteenth century. They have been persecuted heavily since then, through the Holocaust, by Ceausescu, and still today, but the warnings I have heard about them don't seem warranted. They certainly are not bothering anyone today, mostly keeping to themselves, and occasionally hawking baskets of peaches or popcorn to beachgoers. The prejudices I encounter never seem to run out of borders.

As I near the Carpathian Alps and Transylvania, the terrain steepens. The wheat fields of the plains are replaced with deep pine forests under jutting limestone crags, and soon I am seeing palatial Gothic mansions and German Renaissance palaces nestled in the trees.

I am entering the domain of Vlad Tepes, better known as Vlad the Impaler, a warlord who impaled hundreds of Turks on a daily basis during his bloodthirsty reign. Vlad was the head of the Draculean Order, and possibly the character upon which Bram Stoker based his *Dracula*. It is not known if the legendary Count really stayed in the castle here that bears his name, but as I crest a hill and see its imposing turrets and walls rising above Bran town, I do manage a shiver.

I find a friendly pension in town and decide to linger several days and explore the mountain scenery. Crucifixes hang in each room of the pension, and my landlady gives me strict instructions to lock my door at night.

Wherever there are mountains, there is legend: Bigfoot, Yeti, and now Count Dracula. Perhaps these tales and creatures help justify our human fright at the grandeur of wilderness, its raw, savage, and unknown terrain. I tend to gravitate toward these places of myth, so it is no surprise that I find myself heading into the Carpathians the following morning.

I leave Bran on foot, following age-old paths in the woods that eventually become climbing routes. Limestone outcroppings loom above me, their steep slopes reminding me of the Japan Alps or Washington's North Cascades. My so-called trail, the Valea Crapatari, is a scree gully running straight up the edge of a towering rock cleft. The slope is extreme, and it takes several hours of brutal slogging to climb out of the forest and onto the Piatra Craiuli ridge. I begin to climb rock faces that have cables attached to aid in ascending, realizing that I will not be able to descend this nasty terrain if I run into difficulty higher up. The views are stupendous, but so is the vertigo, as there is tremendous exposure on either side of my feet. I try to forget about my fear, and focus on where I am placing my hands and feet.

Eventually, I reach a level area and feel the worst is over, though dehydration begins to set in, as I am out of water. Even at 2000 meters, the heat of the sun is relentless, and as I stagger on, I wonder what possesses me to do this stuff. A movie, a swimming pool, and a cold beer would be far preferable, yet day after day I end up chasing rainbows and pushing my body to its limits, whether on my bike or with my feet.

Perhaps, as I have heard mountaineers say, "If you're not living on the edge, you're not really living at all." I think of all the intense experiences and challenges I take on every day, and how they have become my normal world. This world has become intrinsically satisfying, albeit extremely addicting. I can remember being in places where people were asked, "What would you do if you found out that you only had six months left to live?" Most answered that they would go to some exotic place, have a fling, or do something really wild; this suggested to me that they weren't really satisfied with what they were doing every day. I recollect not having much fear of dying, as I felt I had truly lived.

I eventually reach the Cabana Curmatura, a high mountain hut set in a glorious meadow full of wildflowers, overlooking the deep valleys below. Romania has a well-routed trail system through the mountains, with strategically placed huts where one can grab a bunk, food, and plenty of good beer.

Many young students are camped outside the hut, coming in only for warmth and beer. When I ask why they are staying out in the cold, they tell me that the two-dollar overnight charge is too expensive, so they lug everything up the steep trails to avoid the costs. Our conversation soon grows animated with the arrival of a pitcher of *tsuica*, a fiery Transylvanian plum brandy, and after several shots, I am joining the students in renditions of mountain folksongs, finding more Romanian vocabulary than I ever dreamed possible.

A girl named Anka takes out a volume of poetry and translates a passage by Vlahutsa, the "bard of the Carpathians." I close my eyes, hot and dizzy from the alcohol, and listen to her words ring true:

When you are high up here, you are seized by a vague restlessness as if you were ready to fly. There is something so magnificent around you that you suddenly forget you are tired, hungry, or thirsty, and refuse to sit down, gazing in amazement all around; a strange feeling of joy and pride makes you lift your hand and look around as if you too had helped to create all this beauty, and the hosts of mountains were singing a hymn of praise to you!

After a few wonderful days in the mountains, I return to Bran and pick up Odysseus, more rested than I, and resume my journey west. Temperatures are over 100 degrees every day, making cycling a miserable proposition, and I yearn to sit in the shade of a cafe come early evening, opening the first of many Ursus beers. Romanians tend to stick to themselves, and I notice that my journal entries are no longer filled with stories of a multitude of characters, as they were in India and the Far East.

It takes several days to reach Sibiu, a historic town with beautiful old homes with red tiled roofs. The Saxons built Sibiu and the surrounding townships in the twelfth century; the townships were later taken over by the Austro-Hungarian Empire, and the cathedrals and other monuments to these civilizations are still standing. Coats of arms are still plastered on crumbling stone walls, and Austrian churches remain upright despite their failure to convert the Saxons to Catholicism. Today's young people appear to have converted to another faith; they sit in the main *piata* sporting Chicago Bulls, Michael Jackson, and Metallica t-shirts.

In my hotel room, I listen to the BBC on my short-wave radio. Only a few hundred kilometers away down the Danube, the city of Belgrade, Yugoslavia is being bombarded by NATO warplanes. Just a few hundred kilometers in the other direction sits Vienna, with one of the highest standards of living in Europe. It doesn't make sense.

The Apuseni Mountains are the last hills I will see before the Alps, and are another sleepy part of Romania, with beautiful evergreen forests, traditional farming villages, and summer cottages of the wealthy from Bucharest. I take a break in Garda de Sus, a small hamlet on a river, at a cabana run by an old woman with one tooth.

As she serves me a big plate of meat, fries, and Timosoara Bitter beer, I watch a family who are camping next to me, and who look like something out of a sitcom from the 1950s. They have an old car and an older tent, and sit at a bent metal table, having a picnic. The wife's hair is in curlers, and the husband reads a Romanian equivalent of *Field and Stream* magazine. A barely functioning cassette player croaks out "Mabeline, Why Can't You Be True," and other American classics from before I was born. Their sulking teenage son, obviously disgusted with the whole scene, climbs into the car and begins to listen to Black Sabbath on the radio at full blast.

En route to Oradea, the last town in Romania, it rains incessantly, and I am covered in mud as I descend out of the mountains. Traffic picks up, and soon I am battling trucks on the narrow road into the city.

Oradea is a wonderfully preserved city of gothic cathedrals, baroque churches, and Austro-Hungarian palaces. I take a room in the Vultura Neagru (Black Vulture), a charming hotel in an Art Nouveau building from the early 1900s, which overlooks the town square. For five dollars, I receive a carpeted and spacious room with antique furniture, and a balcony with a sweeping of various renaissance, baroque, and rococo architectural wonders.

Oradea's terraced cafés and lovely promenades are filled with some of the most beautiful women and men I have ever seen, and as I sit in the *piata* watching scantily clad young women walk arm in arm with dapper dark men, I am again amazed at how everyone on the street appears to be under twenty-five. The legacy of Ceausescu lives on, and there is something revitalizing about all the youthful and vibrant energy about. As I sip my excellent beer and enjoy the magnificent buildings and gorgeous faces around me, I realize that I like Romania very much.

At the Hungarian border, I leave the Old World behind. Gone are corrupt officials asking for donations. My passport is processed through a computer by expedient guards who don't blink at me or Odysseus. Rough dirt tracks are replaced by smooth tarmac, and everything from the fields to the houses looks tidier.

I have entered the Great Plains, known in Hungarian as the Nyagyalfold, a flat swath of corn and sunflower fields that stretches all the way across Hungary and resembles the corn belt of the United States. It has a mythological stature in Hungarian literature of brave cowboys and sweeping grasslands, but to me, it looks a lot like Kansas or Nebraska.

So far, in each country I have visited, I have either studied the language or been able to relate it to a neighboring one. So it comes as a shock to discover that I have less verbal ability in Hungarian than a two-year-old. Hungarian is of the Finno-Ugric language group, and aside from its extremely tenuous relationship with Finnish, has absolutely nothing in common with any other language.

At first, I don't think it will be a problem, as I hear many people saying "hello," but by day's end I realize that it is the only word I recognize. Arriving in the town of Puspukladny at dusk, I make useless queries about local campsites, and my shouts of "kamping platz" (German) and attempts to mime erecting a tent are met with vacant stares. I feel like an idiot. I do discover an ice cream vendor, though, who has no trouble translating "five scoops" and "chocolate."

I eventually track down a campground near the famous thermal baths, which I have long been looking forward to. Yet with the temperature still over 100, a hot soak is not appealing, and there are at least 500 people crammed in and around the thermal pools. I pitch my tent under a shady tree and collapse in the heat.

Everything functions in Hungary. Hot water comes out of hot water taps, toilets flush, drinking water doesn't need to be purified, and restaurants are air-conditioned. The highways are free of blemishes, and the sleek cars obey posted speed limits.

Yet I am not impressed. The raw and vital edge that I have felt in so many places is missing. Cities begin to look the same as I move westward, full of gas stations, mini-markets, and chain stores selling items that are found the world over. Big Macs and Pokemon toys represent the good life. I begin to dream of the pulsing and colorful markets I have left far behind.

The language barrier remains brutal. Few people speak English or German, and I spend much of my time struggling to do the simplest things. In a bank in Szolnok, after trying to exchange traveller's checks, I am shooed out for no apparent reason. In another bank, my requests are understood, but the computers are down.

In a third bank, I try to ask if there is a commission on checks. "*Commissione*?" I plead. "*Commisye*? *Denge*? *Tarifa*? *Dinero*?" The tellers look at me with vacant stares. One whispers something to her colleague, probably saying, "Look at the foolish foreigner."

Eventually, my checks are cashed, without commission.

The roads of Hungary do provide great moments of interest. Since entering the country, I have seen women tanning themselves on the highway. Often, women in bikinis hang around on the roadside pullouts, and my first thought is that they are out of their minds, standing on the hot black asphalt rather than going to a park or the beach. On the following day, I see more women, not in bikinis, but this time in their underpants! As I watch the ladies solicit several drivers, then climb into the cars and drive off, I rather sheepishly realize that this is just the way the Hungarian love trade works.

In one rest area, I am approached by two bronzed and buxom girls, who wave and give me an exuberant "*Hallo!*" I wave back, and soon one is practically astride my bicycle, sticking her bosom in my face.

"*Hallo, kompleet zex*," she croons. It is the first Hungarian I have understood, and I congratulate myself on this. Trying to be polite, I point to my sweating and filthy torso and then hold my nose. She merely laughs, and points off to the nearby cornfield. I guess being sweaty and having no car make no difference.

I mime exhaustion, and this seems to work, but I ask her out of curiosity how much she charges. She quotes me a price in Austrian shillings worth about a week of groceries. As I pedal away, I wonder to myself if there is a different price for incomplete sex.

A few days later, I arrive in Budapest, the sprawling capital of Hungary, via a speedway for cars and airport buses. The road has no shoulders or exits, and drivers honk and scream at me. I am no longer an object of curiosity, but an annoyance and inconvenience to the rushing populace.

Budapest is steeped in history, and almost every block has a huge stone edifice or domed basilicas. The thick stone buildings engulf the streets in a very different way than do modern skyscrapers, and pockmarks on the bricks show where they have withstood Turkish sabers, German guns, Soviet tanks, and countless other attacks.

I indulge in pleasures that I have long forgotten. I dine at a sushi bar run by a couple from Osaka, enjoy a vegetarian meal in the chic Gandhi Restaurant, buy an Italian *gelati* from a corner stall run by Genoans, browse bookstores stocked with newspapers from around the globe, and take in a Woody Allen film in English. Yet I feel I am merely biding time, letting my body rest a few days before moving on. In India, Uzbekistan, and many other countries, I would have been invited into peoples' homes and treated as a family member. Ahead in Europe, I will stay with friends and feel more like a local. But here, I feel anonymous, with little connection to the place. I am overwhelmed by the large buildings and their history; after so many years in Asia, it is a history I no longer feel part of.

Within days I steam out of Budapest with furnace-like winds howling at me. The mighty Danube river flows languidly here, and I repeatedly get lost trying to follow the supposed bicycle path that should run along it through towns such as Visegrad and Esztergom. These towns still sport thirteenth-century fortresses and cobblestone streets, and indeed, there are still invaders in these places; they are no longer members of the Roman Empire, but balding French, German, American, and Japanese tourists, chattering loudly and toting video cameras.

As the bike path becomes more navigable, I begin to see cycle tourists, their clean panniers, gleaming chains, and bright Lycra clothing a total contrast to my ragged and grubby gear. Elsewhere in the world, the sight of another cyclist with bags is cause to stop and find a café, but here people just pass by, often without even returning a smile.

I feel like an alien, seeing sights that used to be familiar with completely different eyes. I watch the Hungarians wait endlessly for the lights to change at empty street crossings, and follow loudspeaker instructions in the shopping malls. After so much time in places were there are no signals or directions, I find it bizarre. In one small town, I leave a narrow and crowded bike path, only to be pulled over by a policeman who informs me that I am breaking the law by cycling in the street. I tell him that the path is poorly maintained and unsafe, and he answers that he will arrest me if he sees me off the path again.

I am shocked at being told how to ride after cycling 33,000 kilometers among chickens, goats, diesel trucks, and dancing bears. I pedal off in disgust, returning to the road a kilometer later.

My general feeling of weariness is growing, and I realize that I am only putting in the miles now to finish. I criticize what is around me because I am not able to deal with it, yet I am becoming a slave to my dislikes. I am also growing more introspective without the sights, sounds, smells, and people that surrounded me in the East.

I stop in front of a mirror and take a good look at my dusty bike, my weathered gear, and myself. The face in the mirror is haggard, with an intense gaze. The eyes reflect a hint of madness. Is that what others see?

I resolve to cheer up, but arrive in Gyor by night to a campsite perched on a litter-filled bog, right next to the freeway, with an owner who chastises me for interrupting his television program. The mosquitoes are atrocious, and I end up eating my dinner in the tent, my sweat stinking of insect repellent and soaking my loftless sleeping bag. As I lay down to rest, I resolve to skip Hungary next time, and decide to make an immediate beeline for the pastry shops of Vienna in the morning.

Chapter Twenty–One
Western Europe:
To the Alps and Beyond

> *The soul of a journey is liberty, perfect*
> *liberty, to think, feel, do just as one pleases. We go*
> *on a journey chiefly to be free of all impediments*
> *and of all conveniences; to leave ourselves behind,*
> *much more to get rid of others.*

> William Hazlitt,
> *On Going on a Journey*

> *Never a weary traveller complained that*
> *he came too soon to his journey's end.*

> Thomas Fuller

The Austrian roads are so neatly paved they glisten, and for every inch of tarmac for cars, there is another one running alongside for bicyclists. I think of all of the maniacal truck drivers and drunken speed demons who have come close to my wheels, and of the corrugated washboards, dirt, passes full of snow, and rivers I have crossed, and let loose a most hearty laugh.

There are thousands of cyclists out. Grandparents, grandchildren, racers, tourers, families, and couples ride everything from tandems to recumbent bikes. I even spot a unicycle amongst the crowd. It is an average weekend in Vienna.

My return to the western world starts with a bang, as I round a bend of the Danube and almost run over dozens of naked women who are strolling across the bike path! I chuckle to myself that Austrian prostitutes are the most forward I have met yet, but when I see hordes of nude men frolicking nearby, I realize that I have not entered a red light zone, but a nudist park on the outskirts of the city.

I pause to wonder if it is kosher to wear clothing as I ride, as I have indeed learned the "when in Rome" lesson inside out. However, nobody seems to mind. As the humidity increases, I soon stop by a shady stretch of river, and doffing my own bike shorts, slip into the cool and refreshing Danube.

Vienna is a fine city. There are shopping malls and fast food outlets galore, but they are relegated to the outskirts of the city, and the center is a pleasant car-free zone. It is against the law for motorists to come within two meters of a bicycle, so the city is covered with separate bike lanes and arterial bike routes, and is a joy to pedal through.

The architecture, needless to say, is superlative. The St. Stefans Cathedral graces the center of town, its soaring spires laced with meticulous thirteenth-century latticework. Tourists wander in awe beneath it, weighed down with guidebooks, cameras, and ice cream cones dripping in the summer swelter.

The Viennese are some of the most polite city dwellers I have ever encountered, taking time to assist me with directions, and despite living in a world of deadlines and high tech, they seem far less stressed than their counterparts across the Atlantic. Cars stop unfailingly for pedestrians and cyclists, and even the city's bike couriers—who tend to be madmen anywhere on earth—are more subdued here. In my entire week in Vienna, I only encounter one cyclist whom I judge to be zipping along the bike path a bit recklessly.

I have a home in Vienna with my friends Patrick and Sabine, a couple I met in Turkey, and their roommate Klaus. Gazing around their apartment at the shelves of books, the CD collection, the guitar, the skis in the closet, and the spice rack in the kitchen, I am reminded of the life that I left, and I long to be home, sitting around a dining room table with friends.

Yet I am quickly reminded of how illusory these comforts can be. Sabine leaves on a business trip, and Klaus and Patrick take me down to a nearby *heurigen*, a tavern and beergarden serving homemade wine. Over giant plates of barbecued ribs and colossal *kruegels* of beer, I trade travel stories for snippets of the lives Klaus and Patrick lead in Vienna.

Klaus tells me about his work on a Masters degree in Psychology; about the band he and Patrick play in; about his skiing and mountaineering weekends in the nearby Alps; about his close circle of friends here; and about all the conveniences and culture of Vienna. Yet he confides to me that he feels he has "not yet done anything with his life." He feels burdened by his possessions, by his busy schedule, and sometimes by the friends and city around him, and often yearns to trade it all for something unknown and completely different. He asks a lot of questions about my experiences, and after finding out that I am eight years his senior, tells me that perhaps he still has enough time left.

As I pedal homeward, I will hear this theme repeated over and over again. People with lives that seem stable, comfortable, and rich tell me that they are dissatisfied, and that they long for freedom. As a bicycle nomad, I guess I embody some of their dreams, and I take satisfaction in encouraging them to think twice about their aspirations and their every-day routines. I do not tell them that my adventure is as repetitive as theirs. I wake up, ride, eat, drink, and sleep.

I also don't mention that freedom, for me, has also entailed brutal headwinds, strange people throwing stones, and bouts of diarrhea in filthy and alien hotel rooms.

After over a week of leisurely breakfasts with Klaus and Patrick, I force myself to hit the trail once more. Not more than five kilometers from their apartment, I hear a thumping noise coming from my rear wheel, and sure enough, upon inspection I discover that the rim is broken, the third one of the journey. I am tempted to turn around and go back to the apartment, but it is late July, and I have many kilometers left across Europe. I cycled on a broken rim in Uzbekistan; doing it in Austria will be a piece of cake. I disconnect the brake and continue along the Danube.

The river meanders along lazily through pear and apricot orchards, surrounded by rolling green hills and small towns with Benedictine abbeys. Swarms of Dutch and German bike tourists surround me, and although it is nice to see so many families bicycling, the restaurants and guesthouses (aptly named "Velohotels") set up for the touring hordes are hopelessly crowded.

At a campsite near Linz, a woman tells me that "the chef will return in ten minutes," which has me musing on culinary possibilities until I realize that she means the manager, or chief. She directs me to a small patch of grass on the lawn, next to a group of orderly and well-man-nered teenagers. I fear that they will keep me up half the night, but they merely sit around their campfire and sing "Jesus Christ is Lord of All," and other similar numbers. I drift off in my tent thinking about how incredibly varied the human species is.

I arise before any morning prayers can begin, and get a head start on the day. It is funny that although my bicycle gives me a way to be different than the average tourist, I probably see far fewer sights and do far fewer activities than that average tourist does. All my hours are spent cycling, and then recovering from cycling. Even with an early start, by the time I roll into the charming streets of old-town Linz, I must trade an afternoon swim and stroll for washing clothes and dinner shopping.

One thing I do accomplish in Linz is to pick up a new rim after cycling several hundred kilometers on the broken one. After my two-week wait for a rim in Uzbekistan, it is amazing to walk into a bike shop, put money on the counter, and walk out with a new wheel minutes later. On the other hand, the cost of labor is so high in Austria that it is actually cheaper to buy a brand new wheel than to have one rebuilt. I recall India, where every little bit and piece of anything was recycled and reused; here I am, tossing 100 dollars worth of perfectly good parts into the rubbish bin.

The Danube continues out of Linz into Germany, but I turn away from it and follow a different *radweg*, as the bike paths are called, into the Alps and on to Salzburg, the city where Mozart was born. I want to linger in the quaint streetside cafés that play odes to the great composer, but my plan is to escape Europe before the cold weather arrives, and there is a lot of land left ahead. Maybe it is just that I no longer know how to sit still.

Then again, I am moving at a snail's pace compared to some of the tourists that I meet in town. Two American women gravitate towards me in a bar, hearing an accent they find familiar, and buy me a beer after learning how long and far I have travelled. Monique and Linda are in Europe for a month. They were in Zurich yesterday, Paris the day before, and Amsterdam two days before that. Tomorrow they will be in Vienna, and plan to head to Prague the following day. This morning they took a Sound of Music tour, and plan to go on a jet skiing trip to the lakes I have just come from tomorrow, before their train leaves.

They tell me that the French and Austrians are rude and snobbish, the Dutch mellow, and that I mustn't miss the glacier train in Switzerland, which goes up to the "top of Europe," adding that Europe is pretty affordable on a budget. When I start adding up the costs of their daily tours, train tickets, and accommodations, I begin to wonder just what kind of a budget they are on.

I follow the Inn River through long, narrow valleys, hemmed in by dark peaks that cast shadows on the valley floor. I reach the city of Innsbruck in several days, and stay for a week in the apartment of Jurgen Pollheimer and his partner Sylvie.

My stay in Innsbruck is marred by the first incidence of vandalism that has occurred in my seven years out in the world. Jurgen and I return from a climbing outing to find Odysseus, secured in a basement bike lockup, with his new rear rim kicked in. Jurgen is horrified and apologetic, immediately writing a nasty note to post on all the mailboxes downstairs, and offering to buy me a new rim. I laugh it off, telling him it is just rim number four, and that at this point in the journey, it will take far more than a broken rim to stop me now.

I tell Jurgen that even if my bicycle were stolen, I wouldn't be deterred. He sees the determination on my face, and replies, "I know."

Hitomi and I begin to get in touch, now that I am in Europe with easy access to mail and the Internet. Time has healed most of the wounds, and I am surprised at the depth of our newfound communication, and at our mutual willingness to take responsibility for our past actions.

Every mountain pass reminds me of another one somewhere in the world, with the two of us struggling up it. A curve in a river valley reminds of a day we spent somewhere else; a flat tire recalls the day we spent patching tubes in some exotic place. All the whooping descents, roadside adventures, and spontaneous encounters that only happen via bicycle travel serve to remind me that we will never travel on two wheels again without each other's spirit. We may never be interested in—or capable of—becoming a couple ever again, but we feel a kinship like brother and sister.

Issues of dependency were serious ones in our relationship, and Hitomi often told me that she feared she would not be able to make a journey like this one on her own. I shared the same fear, and often thought sadly to myself after we parted, that she would return home and probably never tour again. So it is with great relief and tremendous happiness that I receive a letter from Dharmsala, where Hitomi has recently arrived, saying that she plans to cycle solo to Ladakh and Kashmir! I relate this information to friends of ours, and realize from their amazed responses how much I, too, underestimated her.

As the summer goes by and I wander through Europe, I come to relish her dispatches from the roof of the world. I read of her climbing the Barralacha La and the Taglang La, encountering her own version of the struggles I had. And despite the daily news bulletins that report instability along the line of control on the route to Srinagar, I recall my own journey through that harrowing passage, and have faith that she is making her own sound decisions.

Leaving Vienna, I get a card saying she has made it to Kashmir, and is resting on a houseboat in Dal Lake. I fold my hands together in prayer, her spirit carrying with me on another road, thousands of miles away.

It is not easy to leave Austria's forests, valleys, and mountains, to say nothing of its fantastic bicycle paths and campgrounds. The food may not be Thai or Indian, but the giant breakfasts of hearty breads with meats and cheese make me forget the spices of the Orient, and keep me well fueled for the mountain cycling.

As I continue to follow the Inn River, I come across several groups on guided raft tours. The Inn has challenging whitewater, and several of the campsites I stay in are packed with kayakers and rafters, who nod at me in salutation for sharing in an outdoor pursuit. I watch in disbelief as one rafting group heads into a rapid with several members talking away on their cell phones, while their guide screams at them to paddle.

One of the campgrounds has a very fancy set of toilets, with seats that revolve automatically after flushing, circling under a brush that pops out to disinfect and clean everything. I think of how this might go down in China. There are days, back in this world of comfort and convenience, when I swear I am on a different planet.

I spend all of twenty minutes cycling through the tiny Federation of Liechtenstein, where roadside kiosks try to capitalize on the diminutive country's merits by selling Liechtenstein kitsch. I forego the keychains, coffee mugs, and placemats, and cross the mighty Rhine River into Switzerland.

I know Switzerland is noted for its precision. Trains run exactly on time, cuckoo clocks cuckoo exactly on the hour; and watches and army knives function precisely and unerringly. So, it seems strange that on my second day in the country, the bike path disintegrates into a confusing, rough wooded trail.

I discover a different Switzerland in the Graubunden and Surselva regions, where the inhabitants live on Romanian time rather than follow the cuckoo clocks. Locals sit stone-faced in cafés sipping schnapps, and elderly farmers pause to check me out as I pass by, saluting me with a *"buna sera"* (good evening).

After this encounter, Switzerland more or less picks up where Austria left off, and everything functions again like clockwork. Mountain travel is well-organized and convenient, with inns, lodges, and huts everywhere. Bike routes are well laid out, and the roads quiet and peaceful, save for the cute yellow post buses, which toot melodious horns as they ease around steep switchbacks.

Homes are tidy and picturesque, with boxes of geraniums perched on every windowsill beneath freshly painted shutters. Each home seems an exact replica of the one beside it, and I wonder if it is illegal to have a planter full of anything other than geraniums, or if a less-than-immaculate garden is considered a public menace.

The country is connected by a series of narrow valleys, through which rivers including the Rhine and Rhone flow. From the Surselva, I cross the OberAlp and Furka Passes, zigzagging into the clouds and looking out at endless mountain summits. I marvel at Mount Rosa, the Matterhorn, and the mighty Eiger, as impressive as anything in the Himalayas; then I descend into the Valais and along the Rhone into Martigny.

Backereis become *boulangeries*, and grapevines begin to fill the landscape, signs that I am nearing the French border. I continue to climb to passes, only to descend into new valleys, and prepare to go up and down once again. Occasionally, I wonder if I will ever run out of mountains to climb and roads to ride, yet as the land stretches out in front of me, I find this unimaginable.

The Col de Montets appears in afternoon mist, and suddenly I am looking at the highest peak in Europe, the Mont Blanc Massif, dominating the skyline over the Chamonix valley. Just like that, I am in another country, another culture. A sign reads "Bienvenue a France," and I glance down in time to see my odometer register 35,000 kilometers.

France passes by in a blur, much of this due to the availability of excellent wine, which costs less than water or soda. I buy a bottle of red table wine to go with every meal. I start out thinking I will not be able to finish it, but halfway through cooking, I am giddy and thinking of purchasing a second bottle. Staying with friends in various towns, I notice that the locals drink even more than I do, and come to the conclusion that if I cycle too long in France, I will soon become an alcoholic.

In Annecy, Mark and Kim from New Zealand show up, out on a

short tandem tour of the Alps. We sit in sunny plazas next to the lazy city canals, eating *chevre*, fresh goat cheese, with long fresh-baked baguettes, sipping café lattés and watching old men play bocce ball. Back in New Zealand, Mark asked me if I ever tired of the nomadic life; here, however, sitting leisurely in the sun, he asks if I have been leading this life throughout the mountains of Europe all summer, then says, "I could get into doing this, big time!"

Outside of my meetings with friends, I have little human contact in France. People are not unfriendly, but are isolated and rushed. France has more automobiles and one-per-car drivers than I have seen in ages, as well as huge shopping malls and multilane roads and expressways. Also, as my high-school French is limited to a severe butchering of the language, my own efforts to be personal are few. However, the French passion for food and drink overcomes other barriers, and though I am usually ignored when I sit in a park or on a bench, whenever I have any kind of food or beverage laid out in front of me, people go out of their way to come over and wish me *"bon appétit."*

I no longer cycle to see, to learn, or even to travel—or, at least, this is how it feels. I ride solely to ride, because I know nothing else. My legs pump endlessly, calves powering me through the hills of the Jura, body bathed in sweat in the heat of Indian summer. The leaves on the trees have changed color, but otherwise it feels like the middle of August, and the waves of steam off the tarmac make me nauseous.

I pass through the Haute Saone, a region of vineyards, traditional basket makers, and reed plantations. The wine business is thriving, but other crafts have sadly fallen by the wayside, and the small villages appear to be dying out. Only a few old folks and stone farmhouses remain. The small-town bakeries are still operating, as are a few corner cafés, but for the most part, life and amenities have moved to the malls, located on highways out of town. Change comes to every area of the planet, and nothing can stop it.

I pass through Champagne, the Ardennes, and into the valley of the Meuse River, which leads into Belgium, and is full of kayakers. I shop in Profoundville, and while contemplating this name, pass through the nearby Forest of Dave, where I am sorely tempted to spend an evening, but I decide to put in the miles instead, an all-too-common decision as of late.

My Belgian cycling pals Patrick and Hadewych told me that they left Belgium to escape the weather. True to form, the skies turn gray and rain pisses down shortly after I cross the border. Wet spray accompanies me north past fields of mustard greens and small towns that look exactly alike.

Belgium is very cycle-friendly, with bike paths running the length of the small country, though my usually infallible inner compass fails me despite the well-marked lanes. Near the ancient cathedral town of Mechelen, I somehow get turned around and end up cycling twenty kilometers back along a river. I do not discover my mistake until I stop for lunch at a roadside table, which I realize is the same one I stopped at in mid-morning!

To make matters worse, I find that a bottle of soy sauce has leaked all through my pannier, staining my gear and drenching my food. I sit silently in the rain, munching a saturated, salty cheese sandwich, and try to figure out how many miles I must ride to reach the Atlantic.

In Antwerp, I meet Hadewych's sister and father, and they treat me to a delicious home-cooked meal, plying me with questions about Patrick and Hadewych, and asking about my own journey. They ask me what is next, but I cannot answer most of their queries about work, settling down, and returning to a more humdrum existence. I feel like a soldier returning from a war, alienated and out of touch, unable to comprehend the priorities and concerns of everyday life.

Volunteers, foreign aid workers, and attachés who have served in war zones and far-off places for years are often debriefed upon coming home, as they may have trouble adjusting to their old surroundings, and it occurs to me that I may need one of these debriefings. After cycling through much of the world, a distraught reaction to missing a bus or getting a parking ticket seems utterly trivial. After enough time in the developing world, a flush toilet or washing machine no longer appears a luxury, but an absurd waste of water. Though I relish the time spent off my bike, I notice that after a few days in the city, I feel boxed in, surrounded by the meaningless chatter of urban life, and I long for the solitude of the open road, and to be spinning my wheels out in the countryside.

I cross the Dutch border to find polluted ports, freeway congestion, and replicated shopping plazas and chain stores. The population density is high, and I feel a lack of breathing space, surrounded by a sea of people and machines moving at a tempo that suggests a life out of balance. It is strange to think that in the Orient, I was often caught in the crush of a far greater mass of humanity, yet it never filled me with these feelings of contempt and weariness.

I am gawked at in almost all the towns I pass through, often by groups of schoolchildren who all wear the same uniform. My loaded, well-worn bicycle, as well as my gaunt and weary frame, both draw stares of interest and incomprehension whenever I stop. In Asia, I received the same stares, but they were always followed up by the onlookers approaching and making contact. I long for someone to offer tea, to pull on my arm hairs, or just to smile, and my own usually big grin has dwindled after so few people return it.

Holland is graced by an extensive series of bikepaths, which connect every inch of the tiny country from city to village to dyke. Well-signed lanes cross from the canals of Amsterdam, alongside tulip fields and windmills, and even into Schipol International Airport. The alternative transport structure is impressive, but for the moment, I can only meditate gloomily on how much Europe has come to resemble North America, or for that matter, the new global landscape. The 7-11's, Burger Kings, and other faceless landmarks can be found from Bangkok to Bali, Sydney to San Francisco.

I reach the Atlantic after several gray, windy, and depressing October days. A thick cloud lingers above the ocean as if it has rented space for the oncoming winter. After more than 35,000 kilometers, my cycle journey across Asia and Europe has come to an end.

I have roughly 3000 miles left to ride from the Atlantic to the Pacific. I don't want to get caught out in another winter. I have one more country to cross to get back where I started from, and I hope I am saving the best for last.

"America," so many people have said to me, with looks of wonder or disdain on their faces, in so many places in the world. It is time to see it for myself.

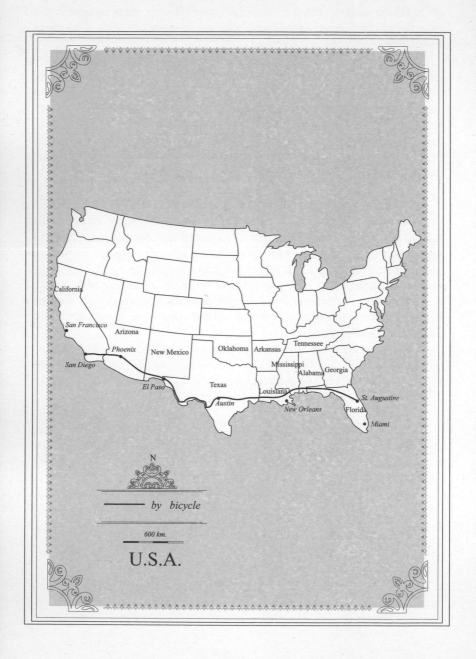

N

by bicycle

600 km.

U.S.A.

Part Five

The Journey Home:
Across America

The American mind resembles a glove compartment, jammed tight with useless junk that no one pays any attention to until we consider cleaning it out; and even then, even as we wonder why we so needlessly clog up our lives, unable to part with it all, we just jam it back in its place.

Brian Swimmer

I am not much an advocate for travelling, and I observe that men run away to other countries because they are not good at their own, and run back to their own because they pass for nothing in the new places. For the most part, only light characters travel. Who are you that have no task to keep you at home?

Ralph Waldo Emerson, *The Conduct of Life*

The whole object of travel is not to set foot on foreign land; it is at last to set foot in one's own country as a foreign land.

G.K. Chesterton

Chapter Twenty-Two
U.S.A.-South

*He that travels in theory has no
inconveniences; he has shade and sunshine at his
disposal, and wherever he alights finds tables of
plenty and looks of gaiety. These ideas are indulged
till the day of departure arrives, the chaise is called,
and the progress of happiness begins. A few miles
teach him the fallacies of imagination. The road is
dusty, the air is sultry, the horses are sluggish, and
the postilion brutal. He longs for the time of dinner
that he may eat and rest. The inn is crowded, his
orders are neglected, and nothing remains but that
he devour in haste what the cook has spoiled, and
drive on in quest of better entertainment. He finds at
night a more commodious house, but the best is
always worse than he expected.*

Samuel Johnson, *The Idler*

I n Amsterdam, I ride an immaculate bicycle track all the way
to Schipol Airport, and straight into the terminal, where there
is a lane just for bicyclists. At the KLM desk, I am given a gigantic bike box for all my belongings, asked if I have enjoyed my stay in
Holland, and given a cheery sendoff.

In the U.S., I arrive in an airport without a Tourist Information desk.
When I ask some police officers about the best route to take into town as
a bicyclist, they tell me that there is no route, and that it is illegal to cycle
on the freeway. Welcome home.

Like Odysseus, I return to a land that I no longer know. The speed of daily life is terrifying. People sprint everywhere as if they are late for important meetings, gabbing on cell phones, punching numbers into Palm Pilots, doing everything except sitting still. Maybe it isn't that I no longer recognize home—it is that what once was familiar no longer recognizes me.

People are friendly, prattling off "how ya doin'" as they whiz by, but when I begin to answer, they are already gone. I am relieved that I do not have to ask people if they can speak English, or struggle with a strange language to do basic things like shopping or banking, yet I feel tongue-tied in my mother tongue, so used to explaining things by pantomime and body language.

I encounter a pair of Mongolians on a street corner, playing a traditional harp and cello-like instrument, engaging in a round of throat singing. Enraptured, I stand and watch them, and they seem surprised to see someone who lingers. I am transported to a windswept plain in Mongolia, where there is little needless chatter and lots of open sky, and I wonder if someday I will go there just because of this moment.

Saint Augustine, Florida, will be the starting point for my journey west. The shortest and fastest route across the country goes from Florida to the California coast, and rather like the rest of my countrymen, I am pressed for time.

The highways into Saint Augustine are a never-ending stream of cars, speeding past an unceasing lineup of fast food, fast gas, and other conveniences. The service stops promise speed, but certainly not service. In most of the places I stop, people are rude and impatient, greeting me with leers that seem to ask, "What do you want?" Motorists stop for gas, soda, and potato chips, complaining about the heat and traffic, and yelling at their kids to shut up. Almost everyone is extremely large and very loud. I gaze on in a daze, surrounded by sickness: overeating, overspeeding, life completely out of balance.

Saint Augustine is something of a change of scenery, as the old town is replete with reconstructed buildings that retain a Spanish and tropical feel. Saint Augustine was "found" by Ponce de Leon in 1513, when he claimed the area for Spain, attacking a French fort to gain control of the town. In 1763, the British took Cuba hostage, and traded her for Florida, bringing thousands of Italians and Greeks over to work on the plantations, where many died in the humid and overcrowded working conditions. After the Revolutionary War, the Spanish took control again, and the United States was ceded control in 1821 after the Spanish-American war. Signs all over town proudly claim, "The Oldest Town in America."

I head in the direction of the Golf World complex, where an IMAX cinema is showing a documentary on Mount Everest, which I heard about overseas and am looking forward to seeing. The theatre is located in a confusing maze of malls, and I end up arriving ten minutes late, rushing to the front door out of breath. As I fumble with my money, a security guard tells me that the cashier is closed.

"That's okay," I tell him. "Here's some cash and just keep the change."

"Sorry," he replies. "There is no late seating allowed."

I plead my case, telling him I have lived in Nepal and have come all the way here just to see this film, and surely he can make an exception.

"No," he retorts sternly. "It is steep and dark in the theatre."

I inform him that I have been in plenty of places that are steep and dark, and that I can manage my way just fine, but he says that liability makes it impossible. I offer to sign a waiver relieving the theatre of liability if I should stumble, but he refuses to budge.

"I don't make the rules," is his final comment, and I wish I was back in India, China, or Uzbekistan, where a straightforward smile or a five in the palm would have me through the door in a flash.

As I sit in a café scribbling copious notes into my journal, a young woman wanders over to my table to ask what I am writing about. She is a philosophy student at the local university, and is flabbergasted to learn that I have bicycled here. She screams at her friends, "This guy just rode his bike all the way here from California! Can you believe it?!"

I try to tell her that I have ridden from California to here *westward*, making a complete circle of the globe, but for some reason she cannot understand, and mutters over and over how far it is from California to Florida. I don't dare mention Turkmenistan.

I spend a week on the coast, cycling out to the long sandy beaches in the sultry October weather, and spending hours gazing at the thunderhead-laden skies. Swollen clouds are hastened along by gale force winds, as heavy as the thick air.

People continue to approach me wherever I go. Perhaps my smile and relaxed demeanor are an open invitation to converse, or maybe most folks just need someone to talk to. They often don't listen, and have plenty to say, but are good at heart. A woman on the beach comes over and gives me a slice of pizza for no apparent reason, and when I try to strike up a conversation, she just smiles and walks away.

In a park in town, I meet Maria Sasso. She and her husband work for a cruise ship company, and are tied to mortgage payments on a new house, a truck, and a few other gadgets. Yet she remembers fondly the days when she got out and saw some of the world, and though she says she enjoys her job, she admits that the protocol of corporate employment is horrible.

"So little vacation time," she complains, "and all we seem to do is work. It makes everyone selfish and unfriendly, and we don't even have much time to spend with our friends. I know from my travelling that we have the highest quality of life around, but lately I have been thinking that the cost is pretty high."

I agree with Maria, but think that the *quality* of life here really isn't all that high. If nobody has time for kids, family, or friends, and if quality is measured by the number of expensive goods rather than health care or education, then perhaps we are living in an illusion. The more I talk to people, the more I sense helplessness and despair. Times are good economically, and restaurants, theaters, and shops everywhere are packed. Yet many folks seem demoralized and overwhelmed in so many ways. They buy a car, buy a house, go into debt, work, work, work, come home, and find themselves there in a chair with a clicker in their hand.

Maria tells me not to be dismayed by it all. "You still have your bike ride ahead of you," she says. "Promise me you won't sell out. It is so refreshing to see what you are doing. Keep your lifestyle and your way, okay?"

I grin, and tell her that there is little danger that I will change now.

The whole state of Florida appears to be on an animated roll. A man approaches as I wheel out of St. Augustine and comments, "Ya shore got that thang rigged up fo' the long haul." In Palatka (which means "tent" in Russian, though there is no camping to be had), a woman saunters up as I fill my water bottles and bellows out, "Hot 'nuff fo' ya? Heck, I done me some cyclin,' but ain't nothin' the likes of what yer doin'!"

The country roads have little traffic, but are strewn with Budweiser cans, disposable diapers, and runover armadillos, tributes to the American motorist. There are supermarkets in the towns I pass through, but they are often lacking fresh fruit and vegetables. Then again, who needs these products? A glance at shoppers' carts reveals piles of canned products, frozen dinners, and multiple six-packs of soda.

Outside, the humid conditions are far more akin to Thailand than to my image of fall in the U.S.A. At six p.m., extremely hot and sweaty, I roll into Cross Creek, a tiny intersection with a gas pump, a convenience store, and a rundown fishing camp. I knock on the manager's rickety trailer, and a woman weighing at least 250 pounds rolls out and chimes, "You done look plumb wore out."

She slaps me on the back, tells me to pay her in the morning, and shows me a spot to pitch my tent. The campground is full of mosquitoes and hellacious fire ants, which bite me as if they haven't eaten in years. Mercifully, there is a small shelter with a mesh screen on it, which even has a fan, where I can at least sit and write in peace and comfort. A fellow who lives in a trailer wanders in soon after I do, though, and my quiet is broken while he tells me his story.

Bob came here fifteen years ago from California, mainly for the fishing, which he says has dried up. He says he prefers the peace and quiet out here to the insanity of California, and loves listening to the owls hoot, but no sooner does he tell me this than he retreats to his trailer and turns on his television. A ghostly blue light flickers from his dark trailer, and I resume my writing.

The weather has turned to a fine drizzle, but the humidity makes me feel as if I am in a bathhouse. It is pointless to put on rainwear, and I remain sticky whichever option I choose. Hurricane Irene has just struck Cuba, and is making her way up the Florida coast; while reports show no danger of a direct strike, it does look like I am in for a deluge.

I make my way to the Suwanee River, immortalized by John Foster's famous song, in which he took out the *u* so the name wouldn't be mispronounced. The river itself is murky, dark, and infested with alligators, and doesn't appear worthy of a song. However, the State Park along its banks is pleasant.

Hurricane Irene is sitting somewhere on my tail, and huge black clouds hover nearby, while to the west, the horizon looks clear. The air is still sultry, but riding across the bug-infested swampland is smooth and easy, as Irene's breath blows me across the land at over thirty miles an hour. I pass through pine forests where the Seminole Indians were slaughtered in days gone by, and then across the Florida Trail, where Hernando De Soto massacred the Apalachees on his conquest of Florida.

Why did these people commit such atrocities to take control of a swampy and hostile terrain, which they had little idea how to manage? Evidently it was all worthwhile; bug-free, gator-free Texacos and Dunkin Donuts now dot the land.

As I move towards the Apalachicola River, small hills begin to replace swampland, and the humidity lessens. Tired of lugging my useless winter gear around, I stop at the post office in Chatahoochee to get rid of as much of it as possible, sending it to friends up ahead in New Mexico. I have been carrying around several international postal reply coupons, which I try to use, but the clerk has never seen such things and has no idea how they work. She glances from the coupons to me, and says, "You must be from way out west somewhere, way *way* out west."

Chatahoochee lies near the border with southern Georgia, just before the passage from Eastern to Central Standard Time. This area is the beginning of the Bible Belt, a region known for its religious fervor, stretching on through the South across Alabama and Mississippi. Baptist churches appear every mile or so, often just small prefab structures in the woods. The Gospel must be going strong, but so are Burger King, McDonald's, Jack in the Box, Taco Bell, Arby's, Kentucky Fried Chicken, and Wendy's, to name but a few.

Forsaking the burger and grease establishments, I buy some lentils in a market and head out to find a campground. On my way, I run into two touring cyclists, the first I have seen in the U.S. They are an older couple, missionaries from Nebraska, and have stickers on their bikes that read "Pray for the Peace of Jerusalem" and "God Loves Israel." They have come 3000 miles, and are looking forward to finishing. They tell me that they sleep in motels every night, and tend to eat in McDonald's every chance they get. Theirs is a different style of travel than my own, yet I admire them for being over sixty-five and out there in the elements, pedalling every day.

Near the Blackwater River, I find a private campground with signs all over the lawn that say "Jesus is the Reason." The manager asks me where I have been cycling, then drops his jaw halfway over his belly when I tell him, and drawls, "Good grief, ah jest can't buh-leeeve that."

I set up my tent and look at the signboards that surround me, wondering if Jesus is the reason for all the fire ants that attack me throughout dinner.

I spend my last night in Florida in the Big Lagoon State Park, a serene spot on the Intercoastal Waterway, just off the Gulf of Mexico. The lovely beaches are empty, just out of tourist season, with seventy-five-degree water, and palm trees to sleep under. The lagoon is home to salt marshes, which provide a haven for large populations of herons and thrushes, as well as alligators, raccoons, possums, and the omnipresent and irritating noseeum (the local version of a biting midge).

When I reach the park entrance, the ranger at the gate asks, "Whadda's this?" at my camp registration form, where I have written "my bicycle" in the space for address.

"Ain't you gotta address?" he demands, glaring at me. He doesn't listen when I tell him that my bike has been my home for the past years.

"How about a driver's license?" he tries. I inform him that I don't have one of these either, it not being required to operate a bicycle, and tell him that if he needs identification, I have a passport.

He glares back, looking rather befuddled, and says, "Whadda's dat?"

Under a full moon, I wander along the murky lagoon, trying to spot herons and alligators. I reflect on all the moons behind me, from the first one on the Yangtze River to ones over Mount Everest and Ayers Rock, and I consider the passage of time that has brought me here. The spaces between the moons: what do they mean? What have I learned, and how have I grown? There are many questions, yet never enough answers.

Three young boys appear, also out looking for gators. My silent presence frightens them at first, but then, with the irresistible curiosity of young boys out for an adventure, they come over to chat. They ask if I have an RV or mobile home, and look confused when I tell them that I only have a bicycle. They ask where I have come from, and listen attentively as I talk about my travels.

One of the boys looks at me, and in a southern drawl, gushes the last words I will hear before leaving Florida: "Why, gosh darn, Mister, yer just like Forrest Gump on a bicycle!"

The Heart of Dixie, as they call Alabama, looks like anywhere else as I pedal along her southern coast. Monstrous hotels and high-rise condominiums are going up along the beach, turning the open space into yet another urban sprawl.

Sandwiched between all the buildings, the Perdido Key Reserve is a bastion against the onslaught, a tranquil stretch of sand dunes covered with sea oats. Clouds of Monarch butterflies descend upon me, attach-

ing themselves to my handlebars and mirror, cruising along for the ride until I close in on the condos again. As if on cue, they rise and depart into the wind.

I run into a retired couple named Charles and Didi touring on their bicycles, and it strikes me that all the long-distance cyclists I have met thus far in the United States are seniors. Everybody else seems to be too busy working.

The developments disappear as I ride through pine forests to Fort Morgan, site of the Battle of Mobile Bay in 1864. Homes along the ocean-front here are fragile-looking structures, built on thin stilts to ensure that they stay above water. One hurricane would be enough to wash them all out to sea, and perhaps this explains why most of them have "For Sale" signs plopped in the sand. The entire area has a ghostly feel to it.

As I leave Alabama for Mississippi, the road becomes a minefield of broken glass, scrap metal, and strewn garbage. On the outskirts of Biloxi, which is one endless strip mall, it worsens, with drivers honking impatiently at me, flipping me off, and yelling profanities. Feeling extremely uncomfortable, I take the next side road and leave the coast for a hillier route through the De Soto National Forest.

The southern states are narrow, and pass quickly as I cross them east to west, which makes it easy to shrug off any gripes I may have about the places. I only spend a few nights in Mississippi. Road blues aside, I am not thrilled by the characters I run into on her backroads.

In the National Forest, I come to Airey Camp, a free "primitive" camp-site set on a small lake in a clearing. The site is far more inviting than the trailer parks I have shelled out for in the last nights, but my plans for a quiet evening along the lake are dashed by the blare of heavy metal tunes thundering from speakers in the bed of a rusty pickup truck. Two fat tattooed men stand around spitting out obscenities and chucking empty Budweiser cans on the forest floor. They glower menacingly at me. Wanting no contact with them whatsoever, I make my way closer to the lake, where a lone truck is parked and it seems quieter.

As I restake my tent, a small muscular fellow emerges from the truck and wanders over, hauling a wild mongrel of a dog, which fortunately is on a leash. He announces, "Git yer kit all set up, and come over to smoke a bowl."

Watching him stumble away, I figure he is a better choice than the drunken hillbillies—who have been looking over at my tent as well—so I walk to the truck and am soon introduced to Howard Castanelli and his tales of woe.

Howard has bone marrow cancer, which he claims was caused by his former employment at some sort of chemical plant. He says that he had been documenting it for six years, but that no one would believe him. With no job or money, he lived in a chicken coop until he finally found a sympathetic attorney who was willing to help him. Now he has received some sort of settlement, with medical treatment and back pay. He bought this truck, which he has outfitted with a gas cooker, television, CD deck, binoculars, a sleeping bag, a lot of marijuana, and other essentials.

Howard lives in state forests year round, telling me he has a list of favorites where the rangers know him and won't disturb his solitude. He says he can no longer go into cities, as all the time in the woods makes it "plumb imposserble ta live normal."

Howard appears to be a real survivor, but there is a sense of tragedy about him. His bottles of medication are numerous, and he says it has become much harder for him to walk as of late. On his dash is a picture of his son, whom he tells me he never sees. His ex-wife in California left him when he became ill. He tells me how he fought the system, and how long he lived on nothing before receiving any kind of aid, saying that he feels free out here now, but that he shouldn't have gone through what he did to get here.

Years ago, when I was hitchhiking across the country, reading Jack Kerouac, and living on the cheap, I would have been *awed* by this character, for lack of a better word, but today I feel really sorry for him.

I ask Howard about safety in the forests, and he grimaces wickedly and pulls a set of sharpened knives from a container. He tells me that he has been studying a martial art called Follow the Dragon for fourteen years, and that nobody will even think about messing with him. He also nods at Butch, his mongrel dog, who at thirteen months is already the size of a bear cub. Howard says he has been training Butch to kill.

Another pickup truck rolls up, and a large man stumbles out and banters drunkenly with Howard. He is obviously an acquaintance, though no introductions are made. Howard gives the fellow a couple of tokes on his pipe, then says, "Ya wanna see ma new toy?" and whips out a 357 Magnum.

The pair dicker over the gun for a time, and then the man drives off. Howard again tells me how no one will mess with him. It is time for me to leave. As I climb into my sleeping bag, I can only think of leaving these woods, and these men whose talk is so full of anger and violence. They

live on some sort of jagged edge, and I am not sure how to tread on it.

In the morning, Howard comes by with Butch, asking me if I'd like a pipeload before hitting the road. I refuse the offer, but do stop by to take his photo. He has the television on in his truck, and is watching cartoons quite avidly. He tells me that he watches cartoons to understand how young kids are being programmed these days, so he can know how they think. While he tells me this, he brandishes his knives, and reassures me that no one will mess with him. I hope for their sake that he is right.

I get on the road again, cycling on back roads inhabited only by signboards advertising the upcoming local elections. Danny Joe Slade and Robert "Slick" Lee are running for Sheriff, while Ronald McDonald is contesting the District Attorney spot.

The Louisiana border appears shortly, where elections are also happening. David Duke, the former Grand Dragon of the Ku Klux Klan, is running for Senator, and his face and name appear everywhere. The political face of the South stands in such contrast to the everyday hospitality and friendliness I tend to come across.

Mahatma Gandhi said, "Politics begins with the person next to you." As if to prove his point, the first time I stop in Louisiana, a mini-mart clerk comes rushing out with a deli sandwich and Coke, which she forces on me in spite of my protests, and wishes me good luck.

There is a stillness on the backroads of Louisiana, and often, I do not even hear leaves rustling or trees swaying in the breeze. This total silence prevails even while I stop for lunch under a tree next to a school, which is amazing, considering that school is in session. The weather has cooled considerably, and is somewhere in that transition zone between fall and winter, when cool and misty mornings are followed by warm and languid afternoons. I ride dreamily along the empty roads, the silence broken only by the creak of rockers on well-worn porches, where women sit knitting and gossiping.

Every day brings some sort of surprise, usually some scene or event that defies my stereotypes of the rural South. In the town of Bogalusa, I take a motel for the night, managed by an elderly Indian couple. They are flabbergasted when I communicate in basic Hindi, and even more shocked when I tell them that I have bicycled across India. My room costs thirty dollars, but not wanting to bother with my fifty-dollar traveller's check, they settle for twenty dollars in cash, and wish me well.

I find a Chinese restaurant for dinner, where the staff are yelling at each other in Mandarin in the kitchen, but when the cute waitress comes out to take my order, she speaks to me in fluent southern drawl. The menu offers specialties such as "sweet and sour collard greens" and "black-eyed peas in bean sauce," about as regional as one can get anywhere on the planet.

A day later I am back in the sticks, again running into the characters who are becoming an all-too-common occurrence in my daily ride. I camp at a private campground full of abandoned trailers, run by a woman with four children. As I set up my tent, I am startled by a man who appears out of the woods, decked out in camouflage and brandishing a large rifle. He has a bad case of psoriasis, and gives me quite a fright, but it turns out that he is the woman's husband, and the owner of this lot.

His name is Mitch, and he has been trying to bag a deer for dinner. Eyeing my spinach and sweet potato meal and probably wondering where I am getting any protein, he asks me what I am doing. When I tell him of my travels, he replies, "Ain't nothin' wrong with dat."

Mitch's son comes by as we sit and gab, asking his dad if he can go to the "sto." Mitch yells at him that it is "store," not "sto," but he pronounces the words the same way. He then launches into a tirade against the schools, saying that there are too many black kids, and complaining about the "niggers fighting all over the cities." I sit silently, not knowing how to respond to his prejudices.

It would be easy to dismiss Mitch as an ignorant racist, yet as I listen to his complaints, I see that he is just another victim of tragic circumstances, and it is not my place to do anything but be a good listener. Mitch lost his job in Baton Rouge, had his house and everything he owned repossessed, and has been forced to move out here. He doesn't like it much, but reckons it could be worse.

"At least it's quiet here in these woods," he says, "and if I ain't got no money fer food, I can always bag myself some meat."

America is supposed to be the land of milk and honey. If you don't like it, change it—or move on to something better. Out in the hinterlands, though, I am not running into many folks who claim to be moving on to bigger and better things.

A day later I reach the Mississippi River, where a young kid on his small bike chases after me, crying, "Hey, bike bro, where ya goin'?" The

Mississippi, just like the Yangtze, is somewhat more impressive in name and history than in action. Murky and wide, she cuts a slow swath through the swamplands on her way to New Orleans and the Gulf of Mexico.

I pass through St. Francisville, where turn-of-the-century homes have been protected from the wrath of the river by a series of levees, built by the U.S. Army Corp of Engineers. The town was initially settled as a burial ground by Spanish Capuchin monks, who chose its higher ground to escape their often flooded homes across the river. The monks named the town after their patron saint, Francis.

As I ride down to the ferry that crosses the river, a man in a car pulls up alongside to chat, telling me that he had a bicycle many years ago. "Purty good ridah, too," he states.

"But now you have a car," I say.

"Yup," he replies, "a big car and a big belly too!"

He guffaws, slaps his ample midsection, and roars off, giving me the thumbs up.

I wonder why Americans are so talkative, why so many people come up unannounced and begin telling you all the details of their lives. Interestingly, nobody here ever says anything about me travelling alone. In most of the rest of the world, people would ask if I was married, if it was hard going solo, or if I wouldn't prefer riding with a partner.

Leaving the Mississippi behind, I enter Cajun country, cycling across the bayou into Opelousas. The French settled this area in 1720, naming the town after the Opelousa Indians who were native to the region. By 1750, Acadiens began making their way here from Canada. Acadie was a French area of the province of Nova Scotia, and despite declaring themselves neutral, Acadiens were shipped to new American colonies by the British. Most ended up in Louisiana, and as the settlements grew, the Acadiens became Cadien, and eventually Cajun.

Today, Opelousas city is home to famous Cajun chefs, who whip up such seafood delights as gumbo, jambalaya, etouffée, and boudin, a spiced sausage. Opelousas is also the birthplace of zydeco music, and is a pleasant enough place to take a much needed day off.

A local directs me to the best seafood joint in town, the seventy-year-old Palace Café, where I sit and gnaw away at the Crawfish Platter, a whopping serving of fried catfish, fried crawfish, crawfish etouffee, and bisque, a spicy gumbo-like concoction served over rice. It's a good thing I need the calories.

In the next several days, the terrain and culture change rapidly. I whiz through Evangeline Parish, where locals speak French in a Southern drawl, and the names on mailboxes reflect the ancestry of the region: Fontaine, DesHotels, and LeBeau. In DeRidder, I come across an inordinate amount of roadkill. Frogs, badgers, dogs, cats, possums, hedgehogs, armadillos, and even a magnificent owl all lie mangled and flattened on the asphalt.

I cross the border into Texas, where the swamps disappear, replaced by forested roads. Despite the serene appearance of the area, it is frequented by an onslaught of pickup trucks, all driving at ridiculously high speeds. Roadside stalls begin to spring up, offering headstones, gems, trinkets, and Rudolph the Reindeer's Xmas Trees; anything to make a buck. I stop to take a photo at one particularly gaudy spot, and a man comes out and warns me, "Betta stay off these narrow roads. They'z rednecks out heah like nuthin' betta then ta run ya ass down! Mah blessin's to ya, and best a luck!"

Nobody tries to run me off the road, but I do travel the most rubbish-strewn stretch of terrain I have ever encountered. The bitumen is covered with cans, cups, disposable diapers, and gay porn magazines, which has me reflecting on how difficult it must be to be gay in rural east Texas.

I run into another bicyclist along road 1416 (the four-digit road numbers an indication of just how incredibly huge this state is). Her name is Melinda, and she is making her way across the country. Her fiancée bailed out of an impending marriage, and after going through some deep depression, Melinda tried therapy; when it didn't seem to help, she took the rest of her therapy money and bought a bicycle.

Melinda tells me she has a whole new lease on life, and after two months on the bicycle, is once again marveling at the world. I tell her that "cyclotherapy" will cure just about anything, and she agrees, though she says that it certainly won't help clean up the roads. She quips that cycle touring is supposed to be about smelling the roses, but here in Texas, the reality is more like smelling the endless array of roadkill and dirty diapers.

Across the Texas border, the definition of space changes, perhaps an indication that I have reached the west. In Louisiana, Mississippi, Alabama, and Florida, houses defined properties, their shapes, structures, and styles forming impressions on the surrounding land, and giving each plot a personality. Here, homes look like they have been dropped at random on plots of land, and it is the space that defines. Fortunately, this reduces the eyesores, as the houses are truly ghastly, mostly prefab boxes.

There are a lot of junctions through the countryside, and routefinding is difficult, though the locals prove a valuable source of information, if a bit hard to understand. One fellow instructs me to "tek a raht on da ferst dat (dirt) rud, den left at da mailbox post up en der hill."

I pass through Kirbyville, former home of the Texas Rangers. During the 1870s, this area was known as the Scrapping Valley because family feuds caused an absurdly high number of killings and bloodletting. The Rangers, formed in 1820 to defend Texas settlers from Indian raids, were called in to settle the disputes and make peace. They did, helped by their fearsome reputation; one writer described them as "able to ride like Mexicans, shoot like Tennesseeans, and fight like the devil."

Today's Texas Rangers are a baseball team, and the Scrapping Valley might only be worthy of its name for all the scrap that litters its roads. I come to the conclusion that the byways out here should be named by their debris: Diaper Alley, Styrofoam Expressway, and Coke Can Parkway might be appropriate. I wonder if the garbage is more evident because there is less urban and more open space. The sad fact hits me that the U.S. might be the filthiest country in the developed world.

A monstrous wind tears across the Livingstone Dam, where I am camped, in the middle of the night, moving my tent—which isn't anchored—with me in it. I get up many times to re-anchor things, and when I do sleep, I dream of being blown away in a tornado.

By morning, the gusts have not abated, and ripping winds shriek down from the north, indicating the arrival of a cold spell. The crosswinds make riding almost impossible, but once I get into the heart of the Big Thicket Forest, I can make some progress.

People continue to be friendly. Near a grocery store in Coldspring, a man approaches my bike, looks it over, and then asks some questions about my journey. He says to me, "I'll tell ya what. You come home with me. I'll give ya yer own bed, TV, groceries, and it won't cost ya nuttin'!"

The offer is sweet. Here I am, on the eve of the twenty-first century, and a total stranger is inviting me to his home. I have a lot of miles to cover, however, so I thank him for his kindness and move on.

As I move down the road, I wonder about this. Years ago I would have been at his house in a flash, but now I am too jaded, and too jealous of my privacy. Perhaps my territorial boundaries have reverted back to

American style, and I now need as much space as everyone else here, a space as wide as the sky under which I ride.

Farther along the road, I meet a cyclist named Chris, who sits in disbelief for several minutes after I have filled him in on my journey. He asks if he can take a few photos of Odysseus and me, and happy to oblige, I chuckle to myself over a memory. Years before, when I went on bike tours, I always came back with slides of zany characters I had met. "This guy lived on his bike," I would tell my friends, or "Can you believe that this fellow has ridden so many miles?" It occurs to me that now, I have become that character in the picture.

At seven a.m., the first frost of the season is on my tent, and as I start out, the thermometer on my pannier reads twenty-eight degrees Fahrenheit. The roads become hillier, a sign that I am entering the Texan Hill Country and nearing the state capital, Austin. The small towns through here become much more scenic, as I ride past old wooden homes with spacious verandahs. I even see old-fashioned soda fountains in corner drugstores, serving thick milkshakes in silver decanters, a nice change from the fast food outlets that have become the norm.

It turns out that this area is of German descent, and communities have names like Oldenburg, Rutersville, and Althaus. German settlers came here in the 1850s, starting cotton gins and prospering, and the families never left. Mailboxes read *Offerman*, *Mueller*, *Zbranek*, and *Maurkiewicz*, and the groceries in the tiny communities are some of the best I have come across since leaving Amsterdam. A shop in Roundtop has German wheat beer, dense brown bread, thick and hearty sausages and cheese, as well as gourmet chocolate, and I waste no time depleting the shelves of various goodies.

Camping at a spotless RV park, I savor my Weizenbier and think of all the vignettes of life I have seen since Florida. Kids looking for alligators; Laotian shrimpers; rednecks; hillbillies; jovial southerners; and now the German communities of hilly central Texas. For all her woes, America never ceases to be interesting.

The following morning I am in Bastrop, a town on the outskirts of Austin, back in the land of shopping malls and mini-markets. A woman named Ann approaches as I park in front of a supermarket and informs me that Bastrop used to be a small place with "people-sized" shops, but that now it is just an extension of Austin, full of monstrosities. "It's all

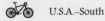

gone down the tubes if you ask me, but hey, here I still am," she smiles.

She asks about my travels, then says, "I've always wanted to go to Peru, to see the mountains and of course Macchu Pichu. Australia, too. I was going to do it ten years ago, but then I had a son, and...here I am."

I continue to be amazed by how many people share my feelings about "progress." It doesn't take travelling to see it—the madness of a fast and furious life, a life out of balance.

Ann wishes me luck, and I tell her that I hope she makes that trip to Peru. As I ride into Austin, it occurs to me that I am halfway across the country, and that the land under my wheels is running out.

Chapter Twenty-Three
U.S.A. West:
Running Out of Road

*From the time I was nine until I was
seventeen, I spent most of my holidays bicycling on
the Continent. This was the best education I ever
had, far better than schools. The more one circulates
in his travels, the better citizen he becomes, not only
of his own country, but of the world.*

Franklin D. Roosevelt

*We shall not cease from exploration, and
the end of all our exploring will be to arrive where
we started and know the place for the first time. A
condition of complete simplicity. And all shall be
well and all manner of things shall be well, when
the tongues of flame are in-folded into the crowned
knot of fire, and the fire and the rose are one.*

T.S. Eliot

Austin, the capital of Texas, is an anomaly in the middle of the
Lone Star State. Surrounded by the Bible Belt, the oil barons,
cowboys, and cheap beer, Austin is a rocking university city,
more recently home to many high-tech computer firms, which pour steady
income into the upscale restaurants, shops, and colorful plazas.

With 50,000 university students at the University of Texas, Austin
has a ripe audience for music and merrymaking. Hundreds of bars line
downtown streets, each belting out blues, jazz, and rock. After months of

Coors and Bud towns, it is wonderful to wander into pubs offering selections from Dunkelweizen to Hoegarden, beers I had been drinking overseas all summer.

I do some pub crawling to blow off steam after the past month's riding, and soon encounter several foreigners. I meet Luis, a Spaniard, and Mike and Richard, two Brits, all of whom have also been doing some bike touring. Their opinions of the country parallel my own, reminding me that I am looking at my home with foreign eyes.

Richard tells me, "There are so many *damaged* people here in America. We've got them too, but nowhere near as many as here."

Mike agrees, observing, "The ignorance of the rest of the world is mind-boggling—and virtually no one really listens when you talk to them."

Luis is a bit more positive. "I love the pioneer spirit," he says, "the fact that in America you can do what you want, invent and reinvent yourself, and create any kind of life." After some consideration, he adds, "At moments, this aspect is beautiful, but from an overall perspective, the inventions are often dismal, and the pioneering uninspiring."

Out of Austin, Texas resumes; open space, southern drawl, and huge ranches. Juniper bushes dot the landscape, signs that the high deserts of New Mexico and Arizona are not that far away.

I follow the Guadalupe River through the territory of Texas' most noted denizen, Lyndon Baines Johnson. LBJ was born in Stonewall, lived in Johnson City, and had a ranch among the rolling peach orchards, which are now out of season. The closest thing to a peach I can get is a scoop of peach ice cream in Kerrsville.

I continue along the Guadalupe, which flows toward the Mexican border and the Rio Grande. In the morning sun, I come across Utopia. It took seven years of cycling, but here I am. Utopia is a small town at the end of the hill country, at the foot of the Sabinal Canyon. The local postmaster named it not for its charm or beauty, but for its weather. I shudder, imagining what it would be like to ride through here in August, and decide that Hell might be a more appropriate name.

The Mexican border and the Rio Grande are not far off my path, and sombreros and cowboy hats have become the headgear of choice. All the frontier towns here have gun shops and U.S. Border Patrol offices. The parched earth is dominated by prickly pear and juniper, buried under blue skies that stretch on forever. Huge ranchlands bar entrance to most of the land, sealed off by barbed wire and electric fences—even this empty and inhospitable land has been parceled up.

It is fifty miles between gas pumps, and one day the only sign of life is a group of Border Patrol vehicles escorting an apprehended group of illegal entrants through the desert. They eye me as I pass, but going at a snail's pace across the hot and barren sands, figure I am not worth a second glance, and continue their march south.

I wheel into Del Rio just after dusk, the largest outpost of life along the Rio Grande until El Paso. As I eat supper at the Jatra Thai restaurant, a man approaches and asks if the big bike rig parked outside is mine. He turns out to be a newspaper reporter, and when I awake the next morning, I am surprised to see myself splashed across the front page of the local daily, next to an article announcing that over forty percent of the local population is transient.

My fifteen minutes of fame occur in the local supermarket, when a little girl in the produce section exclaims loudly to her mother, "Isn't that man the one in the newspaper?" An older man claps me on the back and barks, "God bless you son," while other bystanders stare at me as if a Martian has landed.

I grab some grapes and carrots and make a beeline for the checkout stand.

Out of Del Rio, the road is cut through limestone cliffs, rolling up onto the high desert plateau. Not a tree is in sight, though every piece of local flora has needles. Sotol, prickly pear, and lechaguilla are thorny and resilient enough to survive the barren and harsh landscape that surrounds.

This area used to be the center of the Chihuahua Trail, a wagon route from Chihuahua to New Orleans, and later from San Antonio to California. The route was unclear, and parties often ran out of food and supplies. The Southern Pacific Railway was built in the 1860s, mostly by Chinese slave laborers living in abysmal tent cities thrown up in the sands. Today's outposts don't look as if they have improved much on the past; I ride past ramshackle trailers, broken-down buses, rinky-dink shops, and the ubiquitous Border Patrol offices.

Inhabitants of these places look as if they have been around for ages; grizzled, wrinkled, wind-whipped, and sun-drenched, they bear the scars of this harsh land. Days are long and slow in the desert, and people appear to have plenty of time to chat. They leave as much space between their words as there is space between fences, towns, and cacti.

My existence out here revolves around water. I pedal, drink, pedal, drink. By midday, I am so parched that I feel dizzy. The mountains across the Rio Grande in Mexico shimmer in the haze like a hallucination.

The town of Langtry consists of a gas pump and café, an opportunity to guzzle and refill bottles. It is hard to imagine this place as a bustling rail camp, full of workers, gamblers, prostitutes, and outlaws. The term *godforsaken* seems to fit.

The legendary Judge Roy Bean lived in Langtry, running a joint that was part billiard hall, part saloon, and part courtroom. Bean, who was *the* law west of the Pecos River, used one law book to administer justice, asking customers to serve as jurors. When this didn't work, a six-shooter on his desk always did.

History aside, desolate Langtry becomes a spot of significance for me when I pass the 40,000 kilometer mark here. 40,000 kilometres is more or less the distance around the equator, and a milestone I had dreamed of reaching. I celebrate with a double swig of water.

Two hours later, I am out of water again, and this time it is a road crew that helps me out. They have iced water tanks on their work truck, and a cooler full of soft drinks, which they insist I drink. The foreman asks if I am out to break some kind of record, and when I say no, he responds, "Just for fun, eh?"

His crewmates look at him, then at me. Glancing at my dehydrated frame and wild-eyed look, one tells the foreman, "It shore ain't fun."

In the Sanderson Canyon, the tailwinds that have been accompanying me almost all the way across the south do a full turn and hammer me relentlessly. I need every ounce of energy to propel myself forward. Deer bound along the roadside, and the scenery is spectacular, with vast mesas and multi-colored cliffs stretching across the skyline, yet I have little time to appreciate any of it. I can only put my head down and concentrate on each pedal stroke.

There are no services until the town of Marathon, over fifty miles away, and the two liters of water I am carrying begin to look very inadequate. Dehydrated and anxious, I stop to investigate a couple of discarded drink containers at the roadside. One contains a foul-smelling yellow mystery liquid, and the other is full of old Gatorade with big globules growing in it. I push on, sipping my remaining water in tiny increments.

Wind is tremendously physically punishing for a cyclist. It dries out the nose and mouth, and stings the eyes. Skin becomes sunburned, yet the body often remains chilled. There is no relief from the tedious drumming in the ears, or from the burning pain in the calves, hands, and fingers as one pedals seemingly in place.

However, the worst part of cycling in windy conditions is the mental strain. One begins to play games of comparison: how bad is this gust compared with the last one? One worries about running out of water, about being unable to reach the next safe haven, about having a breakdown out in the squall. Most worries are irrational and exaggerated, yet they play havoc with the riding.

I spend hours counting to ten in different languages; trying to remember the words to Elton John songs; recalling the starting lineup of the Oakland A's championship teams of the seventies. I focus on my breath, remembering the *vipassana* training I have received. Most of my coping techniques, though, fall prey to the infernal gale whistling through my wheels.

At my lowest point of despair, I wish that I could share this misery with someone else, drafting behind them and trading stories. And just like that, along comes Cyril.

At first, I think the figure in my rear view mirror is a figment of my frazzled imagination. Yet as it approaches, and the minutes drag on, I realize that there is indeed a bicyclist coming up behind me. Shaking my head in disbelief, I stop, and a breathless rider arrives, pulling a trailer behind his mount. He asks if I am the guy who has ridden around the world, and when I answer in the affirmative, he breaks into a grin and tells me that he has been trying to catch me since Tallahassee.

Cyril is on a tour of discovery, and we soon discover that we share much in common. We spent formative years in the same town, frequented the same haunts, and of course, share a passion for cycling. He first heard of me from other cyclists he encountered in Florida, and was intrigued by my pilgrimage. The rumors and legends around my story ("he's been travelling twenty years, for a hundred thousand kilometers!") only served to fuel his desire for an encounter.

Cyril is younger, stronger, and far less world weary than I am, but he is just as thrilled to share the misery of riding in these insane conditions. He slows his pace to mine, and we draft in and out, yelling tales of our lives above the roaring gale. The distances shrink, our throats feel less parched, and we arrive in Marathon with light to spare.

Relieved to be out of the wind for at least a few hours, Cyril and I set up camp, shower, and head out to the Oasis Café. Over Mexican food and beer, Cyril tells me about his solo journey across the country and about the kindness he has been shown in so many places. He wondered, early on, about his decision to travel solo, but says he has found that the bicycle as a mode of travel only serves to increase contact with people.

The conversation turns to women, and Cyril tells me that he has been with a girlfriend on and off for seven years, a CEO wannabe at an investment firm in San Francisco. She enjoys outdoor pursuits, but "only on weekends," as he puts it, while for him it is so much more. Remembering some of my own past entanglements, I understand him completely. As a sticker on my old road bike said, "We live, love, eat, drink, and sleep bicycles."

I tell Cyril, "I guess that's why you are here and she is there," and he smiles.

We arise to more wind and prepare to roll out, only to be thwarted when I discover that I have broken yet another rim! This time, a deep gash has appeared under a spoke in my rear wheel. It is my fifth blown rim of the trip. Not to be deterred, I patch it up with duct tape, and Cyril and I hammer out the thirty odd miles to the town of Alpine.

Alpine does not have a bike shop, but there is a hardware store that sells heavy wheels that won't fit my steed. The staff looks at my already out-of-date seven-speed sprocket as if it is an invention of the future. They do assist in removing the freewheel, led by a spiky-haired man who mutters "ye-ah" in a baritone voice over and over.

I call a bike catalog sales outlet, which promises overnight delivery of a new rim, but when I tell them where I am, they inform me that Alpine is "way, way out there." I will have to wait four days, which I figure is better than two weeks in Uzbekistan. Alpine is a more than decent place to spend some time off. It is an artist's community, with several authors in residence and dozens of painters who display their wares in the many galleries that line Main Street.

The days drift by, and my rim still doesn't arrive. In the hardware store, I inquire about its whereabouts, but the smiling clerk just performs different renditions of "ye-ah, ye-ah," in response to every question I ask. I give up and go to the library.

After a mutually hearty goodbye, Cyril pushes off, hoping to reach El Paso by Thanksgiving. I finally receive my wheel just as a "norther" (as the winter storm bringers are called) whips down from Minnesota, and as I head out into the dawn air at seven a.m., I see that the temperature stands at eighteen degrees. I shudder to imagine what it was like three hours earlier.

It is Thanksgiving Day, but no holiday for me, nor for the Border Patrol, the only other people out in the bitter cold with me. The temperature is extreme, but mercifully, the winds are minimal, and in all my gear, I am up to the task. I manage the first thirty miles to Valentine, a dot on the map with a few closed buildings, set under the Fort Davis peaks off to the east. The mountains rise brown and barren, like a chocolate block above golden hayfields and expansive ranches.

My water bottles start icing up, the gusts of wind increase, and by late afternoon I have slowed to a crawl. Tossed by the wind, eyes filled with grit, I make out the snakelike specter of Interstate Ten in the distance, with huge trucks winding their way through the desert canyons. After what seems like light years, I fight my way into the town of Van Horn. Frozen and dehydrated, I am in no condition to camp, cook, or think, but when I check into the local campground, it is as if the gods of cycle touring are reading my mind.

The owner takes one look at me and says that she has one heated cabin that she will give me at a discount. I nod meekly in approval and say I'll take it, to which she replies, "Now, it is Thanksgiving, you know. Come on over to the big house after you've showered, and join the feast."

An hour later I am sitting in a warm room with a motley collection of locals and winter sunbirds, gorging myself silly with turkey, stuffing, cranberry sauce, and pumpkin pie, again thinking how a little human kindness can carry one to the ends of the earth.

As I descend into the Rio Grande Valley, the pecan orchards and cotton fields buffer the wind. In the warm winter sun, which has made a much-appreciated return, I am reminded of Uzbekistan, and I reflect on how this immense world, filled with such myriad differences, is also home to so many spots that look exactly alike.

I pass through communities like Sierra Blanca and Fort Hancock, quiet places with dusty collections of ramshackle trailers. Boys and girls with slicked-back coifs of jet-black hair and immaculately polished shoes emerge with their parents from small eateries, stuffed on *carnitas, gorditos, menudo, caldo rez,* and other entrees displayed on large roadside signboards. Mexico is a stone's throw away.

I use Border Patrol checkpoints as water filling stations, and the usually suspicious wardens become quite friendly once I tell them what I am doing, often inviting me in to chat. In one spot, the head honcho gives me a lecture on how their presence is stopping the highway from being "one continuous stream of wets" ("wetbacks" is a derogatory term describing those who cross illegally). He asks about my travels and tells me I am lucky to travel here, as it must be easier than in Red China.

Not wanting to talk politics, I mosey on, stopping several hours later in a forlorn Chinese restaurant for lunch, where five dollars gets me a greasy all-you-can-eat meal and a chance to practice my Spanish with the waiters. The proprietress wanders over to ask if I like the food, and it turns out that she is from north-eastern China. When I ask how she likes living in the southwest, she replies, "Hate much much. No tree, no green, too hot, no speak English." She stalks off to count her receipts, but manages to crack a smile when I recite all of the twenty-odd words I know in Mandarin.

Sated, I continue across the desert past junkyards and scrap heaps, full of rusted auto hulks, tires, and cracked glass panels that obscure the view of the Franklin Mountains. It is with great joy and relief that I reach the Texas State line, 1200 miles and one month after entering from the other side. My energy level soars briefly as I leave the glass- and debris-strewn pavement of Texas behind, only to plummet as I enter New Mexico and begin battling an unpaved washboard road, deeply rutted and scoured with sand.

I reach Las Cruces in a bad mood, tired and cold, and opt for another Gujarati-run motel. The rooms have been maintained like the ones I frequented in India and China: the carpets are full of cigarette burns and semen stains, the light fixtures are coated with dust, and the tables are sticky. The kitchen area has a musty refrigerator full of moldy food, cockroaches the size of small mice, and a rusted pot that sits on an equally grimy burner.

Thoroughly disgusted, I consider checking out, but the sound of angry men yelling and pounding at the neighbor's door makes me think twice about venturing outside. I settle in and listen to the security dog, a large German Shepherd, as it strains its chain across the yard and growls menacingly into the coming night.

I recognize that I am coming unglued, reaching the end of my tether. This journey should have been laid to rest ages ago, perhaps on European shores, or after 40,000 kilometers, or maybe on that day when I first refused an offer of taking tea.

Yet I persist. I dream of the Pacific each night, of seeing that long swath of blue as I finish the last pedal strokes, of tossing my bike into the

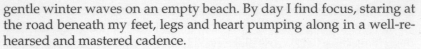

gentle winter waves on an empty beach. By day I find focus, staring at the road beneath my feet, legs and heart pumping along in a well-rehearsed and mastered cadence.

A friend once told me what a great dreamer I was. She commented that I was an endless source of energy, drive, and ideas, but that I never completed anything. While I didn't want to agree with her wholeheartedly, I had to admit that she had a point.

I had often told myself that when the journey was no longer here and now, it would be time to do something else. Now, however, all that matters is that the Pacific Ocean is two and a half weeks away.

A much-needed break in Silver City restores my energy and cheers me up. Cyril is relaxing in the local youth hostel when I arrive, and my friend Phil Tierney (who I last saw in Crete) has come from Albuquerque to catch up on stories. Jim and Tori, a couple I met in Turkey, live nearby, and I also see Elke, who I left on a road full of drunken motorists in Tbilisi over a year earlier.

It is a welcome break to be surrounded by friends and travellers, with their keen interests and open minds, and I enjoy my stay. Unfortunately, I suffer a debilitating back injury lifting my bike into Phil's truck one afternoon. Although we spend a week soaking in hot springs and living a life of leisure, by the time it comes to say goodbye, my back is still spasming, and I am in constant agony.

I lighten my load by mailing off every unessential bit of gear, filling my bags with Tiger Balm, painkillers, muscle relaxants, and a heating pad. Feeling like a mobile infirmary, I leave Silver City with a grim laugh at how ugly and pathetic my last steps have become. My journey is no longer about the beauty of the landscape, the thrills of bicycling, or the characters I meet, but is focused instead on avoiding pain and further injury, fleeing the cold, and laying the beast to rest.

I cross the Arizona state line, wobbling past creosote, sage, and juniper. From the maroon and cinnamon mountains come herds of wild pigs, scampering across the highway and nearly getting embedded in my spokes.

As I pass over the Piloncillo Mountains, the wind and cold grow relentless, and only ten days ride from the end of my journey, I pass one of the most exhausting days in seven years. Outside of Globe, my fingers feel like wood inside my gloves, and my face feels raw. When I stop at a roadside gas station, immersing my hands in hot water produces so much agony that I forget about the pain in my back.

At last, crossing the Gonzales Pass, I leave the cold behind, descending into the Sonoran Desert, a garden of cacti of every shape, size, and color. The winds remain, and the traffic becomes heavier as the city of Apache Junction materializes. I am suddenly surrounded by golf courses, condominiums, and people in shorts and t-shirts. Trailer park retirement communities are crammed all over the valley, with names like Citrus Grove and Desert Breeze, part of a sprawl of bone ugliness set under a backdrop of a sunny desert paradise.

Despite the urban chaos, tacky development, and heavy traffic, I am in a good mood. It is warm, the mountains have receded, and my back is enjoying the benefits of the heat and lack of hills. I escape the city as quickly as possible, stopping only to chat with a man named Carl, who tells me that by living on a bicycle, I am truly a *no-mad*, or "not mad."

The following day, my spirits sag again. It is Christmas, and as I make my way across a landscape of sage, ocotillo, saguaro, and creosote, I reflect that I should be at home with friends, feasting, giving presents, and making merry. Instead, as usual, I am fighting the wind under a big empty sky, with only the persistent gusts as company. Four drunks sitting outside a mini-market look at my bike and ask how many bridges I have slept under.

Despondent, I forge ahead, wondering if any stores will be open, and where I will spend the night. The open space may be unending, but much of it is private property, sealed with barbed wire and electric fences.

In the late afternoon, I come across an RV Park, the Ramblin' Roads, where once again, American friendliness comes shining through. Upon my arrival, the manager tells me to hurry in for Christmas dinner, and within minutes I am seated in a large hall filled with retirees and sun birds, folks from Minnesota, Maine, and other northern climes who drive their mobile homes down here to spend the winter. I am plied with turkey, yams, and pumpkin and pecan pie, and hundreds of people introduce themselves, wish me Merry Christmas, and offer good cheer.

As dinner winds down, women disappear into the laundry room and their RVs. Televisions are turned on, and the men, in their Stetsons, suspenders, and cowboy boots, light fat cigars and settle in for rounds of poker. Stuffed, clean, and warm, I retire to my sleeping bag, reflecting on how, world over, we are all alike.

I awaken to howling northeastern winds, which have me up and packing quickly. Back in Texas, I had given up on the idea of reaching the Pacific on New Year's Day of the new millennium, but if I can get two days with tailwinds like this, I will be able to double my mileage and do it.

The card players are up already, coffee mugs in hand—if they ever really went to bed. They are talking about how much they won and lost the previous evening, and discuss going out and blasting quail for today's entertainment. I scramble to get on the road before they can start displaying their weapons.

It takes little time to be blown into Quartzsite on Interstate Ten. Quartzite is possibly the world's largest RV gathering, and looks like an outdoor circus. Thousands of RVs, trailers, and tents sprawl across the desert, and a giant swap meet is taking place in the center of it all, with vendors hawking beads, spices, porn videos, homemade bread, solar panels, dolls, and bric-a-brac and curios piled high enough to fill a football stadium.

Gazing across the wide expanse of tents under a warm winter sun, I figure that this wouldn't be a bad place to be homeless, as there certainly are no bills or rent to pay out here. As I cycle through, it occurs to me that perhaps many of the vendors are here for this precise reason.

Even a set of flat tires cannot stop me today, and in the early afternoon, I cross my last border, the Colorado River, and enter California. Everything becoming a set of "lasts:" last mountain, last state, last river crossing, and soon, last mile.

The California side of the Colorado is lush and green, courtesy of the state's agrotechnology and hydroponic wonders. Avocados grow beside tomatoes and brussel sprouts, and even the tiniest of towns have shops stocked with abundant and cheap produce.

I finally call it quits in the tiny hamlet of Palo Verde, which is composed of two bars, a store, and a run-down trailer park where the manager informs me that there is no need to pay, as I am riding a bicycle. At the local bar, a place full of grumpy and crotchety old men, the owner, Jack, apologizes for their "country boy manners," and asks what brings me to this part of the world. Weary, I tell him that I'm just cycling across the state on a short ride that will have me home in a few days.

People the world over have their own image of California. The Golden Gate Bridge welcoming immigrants and gold seekers through her gates. The high technology of Silicon Valley. Hippies in hot tubs. The glitzy streets of Hollywood.

The state is indeed a mecca of diversity. I start the morning breezing along next to sheep in green pastures, moving within hours into the rock formations of the aptly named Chocolate Mountains. Another hour finds me surrounded by seemingly endless sand dunes, and finally, I pass into the agricultural belt of the Imperial Valley, surrounded by Mexican laborers hauling produce from irrigated and verdant fields.

Water is a valuable commodity in the desert, and in Glamis, the entrance to the Imperial Sand Dunes, the one and only shop is selling gallon jugs for four dollars. When I ask the surly owners if I can fill my water bottles, they wave dollar bills at me.

The dunes roll like a set of waves across the horizon, and remind me of the Thar Desert in Rajasthan. Yet the beauty of the area is destroyed by armies of all-terrain vehicles, which scream up and down the dunes, crushing and obliterating their beautiful contours. The jovial riders make wisecracks as I ride by: "Looks like yours is the quietest buggy here." "Bet it don't ride too good on the dunes."

I avoid their banter and pump harder, closing in on the In-Ko-Pah summit and Cleveland National Forest, rising out of the haze thirty miles away. It is the last hurdle that separates me from the Pacific.

San Diego lies only a little over 100 miles away, yet I could be thousands of miles away in another country. The Evan Hewes Highway out of El Centro is the worst road I have ridden in the U.S., potholed and rutted with nary a smooth stretch of tarmac anywhere. Bouncing along and swerving around piles of broken glass, I come into Plaster City, basically a single hideous plastic factory, belching noxious fumes.

Stopping to refill my water bottles, I meet a fellow cyclist, a tall and scrawny fellow named Gordon. He tells me that he bought his old mountain bike in Flagstaff, Arizona, rode it to Florida and back, and is now en route to Los Angeles. He rides mostly on the interstate highways, sleeps in rest areas, truck stops, and the occasional campground, and finds food in dumpsters. He has been hit by cars twice, escaping without serious injury each time, but his bike now bears a steel rim, a repair made after the last knock.

Gordon is a Vietnam veteran, and tells me that he has had problems with alcohol over the years. As we cycle on together, he talks about locating places with Alcoholics Anonymous groups, and of finding day labor for six dollars an hour. He smells of smoke and drink, has not bathed in ages, and travels with nothing but a light blanket, a wrench, and an extra shirt strapped to his bike. We are as different as they come, yet I am touched by how much we understand each other through living on bicycles.

Gordon says that he started cycling because he got tired of waiting for rides as a hitchhiker. He had been living in a veteran's home in Hattiesburg, Mississippi, which took care of all his needs, but he got fed up with sitting around and watching television every night. He figured most of the people's mental and medical problems there were furthered by staying in the home like robots, rather than getting up and doing something. He loves the simplicity, freedom, and affordability of cycle travel, and has learned that cycling is one addiction that keeps him healthy and out of trouble. I agree with him wholeheartedly.

As we ride along, chatting amiably, I think of the characters I have met on the American road. In Europe, most cyclists are middle class, with top-notch bikes and Gore-Tex gear. Yet here in America, as in the developing world, it seems that the poor and the homeless resort to a life on a bike as a last resort.

In Ocotillo, I stop at a trailer park for the evening, while Gordon continues up the mountain into nightfall. His choice turns out to be better than mine, as the trailer park is another gem, imbued with a pervading odor of feces and urine.

The most happening place in town is, of course, the Lazy Lizard Saloon. Fourteen barstools cradle the bottoms of eleven men and three women, who are busy drinking cans of Budweiser and discussing the recent karaoke contest. I scribble notes, trying not to drown in the cloud of cigarette smoke, receiving strange looks from the crowd.

I leave in the morning, whizzing past large men with pants hanging halfway off their asses. The mountains in front of me, which represent the last challenge of my journey, are not the Alps or the Himalayas, but the boulder-strewn canyons of the In-Ko-Pa summit.

The climb out of Ocotillo is quite easy, not really a true summit or mountain pass at all, but a series of winding hills that don't want to peter out. The road rises through a maze of canyons bordered by jumbled boulders, then descends into strands of manzanita, chaparral, oak, and eucalyptus, signs of the California coastal environment I know so well.

There is little traffic on the road, which still feels wild despite being quite near San Diego, and as I descend, I imagine that I am riding some path deep in the heart of South America. I catch myself in this daydream and realize that I am right here, right now, in this beautiful place, my home, seeing home like I have never seen it before, and loving every minute.

The road hugs the border, with canyons and mountains twisting off far into Baja California, never ending. I descend, ascend, descend again, and repeat the entire ritual over and over, a mantra that has become a part of me. As I pass through Potrero, a man waves me over to ask where I am headed. "To the ocean," I tell him, and he looks at me disappointedly.

"Oh, is that all?" he chirps. "It looked like you might be going for a longer ride."

I can only smile.

The canyons and mountains begin to slip away, replaced by the malls and usual ugliness of urban America. I wait for a dramatic and sweeping view of the Pacific, but there isn't one, only the haze and barrios of National City. Yet as I cross Interstate Five, I know that I have almost run out of land.

There is one more hill to ride over, and as I crest it, I breathe deeply and wait to exalt as I catch sight of the ocean. But it still isn't there; it lies out of my sight, blocked by the huge naval port that sits on the coast. I laugh at the absurdity of it all. Life never quite works out the way we expect.

Turning onto Harbor Boulevard, I make my way past glass and debris into downtown San Diego. An Asian woman steps off the curb at a light to become the millionth person to ask where I am going. I tell her that I am not going anywhere, which piques her interest, and she pursues her line of questioning.

Her name is Kar Yai, and is an exchange student from Hong Kong. Upon learning of my travels, she offers to buy me lunch, and we step into a sushi bar in the heart of the city, where we share a moment. It is another of those billions of precious moments that have made up this journey. There have been moments of faces, ideas, magnificent vistas, and caring souls, as well as all the garbage dumps, neon lights, and shantytowns.

It is New Year's Day, the dawning of a new century, and there is a sleepy and relaxed atmosphere everywhere. Part of it is likely due to the heavy celebrating of the night before, but perhaps this is also a time for everyone to reflect on where they are, at a moment they will probably always remember.

Kar Yai gives me an impulsive embrace, kissing me and whispering,

"Congratulations, and welcome home." I wonder if she sees my gaunt and exhausted figure as a remnant of the American cowboy, roaming freely across the land that perhaps was once the America of her dreams. I hug her back, and say goodbye, perhaps the thousandth goodbye in a tale of a thousand and one nights.

Then I wheel out toward the ocean.

I step off a boardwalk onto a beach where small waves lap up against sand occupied only by driftwood and seaweed. I recall the day I left home, unable to steer Odysseus because of all the weight piled on, and I remember my first day riding with Hitomi, struggling to climb out of the Japan Alps.

I remember the rise of the Himalayas, the monsoon forests of Southeast Asia, the cathedrals of Europe, and the thousand kind spirits who gave me tea and shelter. I see my mother's smiling face, her spirit and ashes scattered into the very waves I now stand before.

I expected to be overwhelmed by a maelstrom of emotions today, but at the moment, the emotional fireworks seem to be over. I shed no tears, dance no jig of wild jubilation. I just feel very, very tired.

I strip Odysseus of all his gear and carry the bike out into the waves, dipping both wheels into the salty froth that surrounds me. I gaze across the endless blue expanse ahead and remember the words on the gravestone of the Greek writer Nikos Kazantzakis:

"I hope for nothing. I fear nothing. I am free."

As I make my way out of the water, a piece of paper blows by. It is a flyer, advertising a New Year's century ride offered by a local bicycling association. I figure I am in decent enough shape.

Epilogue

I should have known better than to think that my journey would ever really end. After all, are not our external explorations just physical manifestations of our inner travels, which go on throughout our lifetimes?

I expected to go through great difficulties during my first year back home, settling down, reacquainting with friends, and fitting into what others tend to term a *normal* life. Surprisingly, the initial transition was easy. I moved to the Pacific Northwest, discovered that I was just as passionate about mountaineering as I was about bicycle travel, and created a comfortable niche for myself in a warm community while I set about writing these memoirs.

However, a pilgrimage this far and wide couldn't help but bring about some sweeping changes in my worldview, and I noticed after about a year that I had not recovered from culture shock. Little things got under my skin. I was irritated that people would not linger over slow cups of tea, that children were taught to beware of strangers, that people always seemed to have something to *d o*, rather than just *b e*. I found myself slipping back into the old pattern of addiction to possessions, an epidemic in my country that exists on a level beyond comprehension, causing great spiritual suffering in peoples' lives. I often felt sickened by the sheer amount of material wealth I confronted every day, yet I was constantly reminded by advertisers and others that I did not have nearly enough.

I felt hemmed in. No matter how full of wonder I tried to be, no matter how vibrant my community was, nothing could quite replace the colors, sights, smells, and teeming life I had seen in the developing world from the seat of my bicycle. I missed outdoor markets. I was given odd stares when I tried to bargain in department stores. Worst of all, my manageable material life of four panniers and a backpack quickly mushroomed into a closet full of outdoor gear, CDs, and books.

Sitting on the corner with a cup of tea in hand did bring a host of interesting characters into my life, but let's face it: when you sit with a cup of tea on the corner in America, you are a bum with no job and no place to go.

After a year, I bought a funky second-hand cruiser bike and went to Vietnam, Laos, and Cambodia, spending three heavenly months with only a towel, toothbrush, camera, and repair kit.

As I bounced along dusty Highway One just north of Saigon, lathered in sweat induced by Vietnam's afternoon heat, it occurred to me that there were not even any mad dogs or Englishmen on my road. It also hit me that nothing had changed.

Yet change appears to be the only thing permanent in our lives—at least, other than our breath, as the monks at Wat Suan Mok believe. I remain the eternal Odysseus, constantly perusing maps, scouting exotic locales, and planning new adventures.

The new journeys, however, are not dreams. A friend inquired whether I wanted to bicycle to South America with him, asking, "Wouldn't it be a dream come true?" I had to disagree—we would certainly have our share of adventures, but it most definitely was no dream. I knew that I would be able to accomplish such a ride, something I had no idea of when I first set out for the high roads of Asia. Travel is no longer my dream, but my waking life.

If I have learned anything in all my wanderings, it is that I am a lucky man. I have seen more castles, dragons, princesses, and enchanted forests than most, and I have made enough memories to enjoy for several lifetimes. I look forward to more, but if someone told me I had a week left to live, I think I could bow my head in thanks and hang up my boots with grace.

I think often about places and faces around the planet. What became of the little girl selling custard apples on a Thai street corner, who smiled at me as if I was a long lost relative? How is life for the Afghan trader from Kandahar, who bought me dinner in the desolate wilds of Turkmenistan? Have he and his family survived the latest war in his country?

Mr. Suzuki still is the salaryman of a small company. Coleman Johnson still works the grape harvest in France each season and then makes his way to Asia, armed only with a good book or two and a deck of cards for cribbage. Tara Sundas met an Australian trekker, fell in love, and is now married, living in Sydney with her husband and new baby.

Hitomi and I talk or write whenever we can. She has returned to Japan and is saving up for another trip to India. She cycles a lot around the small island where she lives, often stopping to brew coffee on her camp stove. She tells me that during these times, she often remembers a high pass, mountain vista, or zany character we encountered on our road of dreams.

We talk sometimes of having another adventure, but time, money, and other commitments always manage to curtail these plans. As the days pass, I realize how seldom we find windows of opportunity to follow our dreams. We must be ready to jump at these opportunities.

My stories, photos, and memories make it possible for me to recall each day of the journey in vivid detail; in this manner, I will carry its length and breadth with me to my grave. It is not dead, yet it will certainly never be repeated. And writing these words, I put my "last stand" to rest, hoping that the wind will carry my words to some heart or soul fluttering with aspiration like a Tibetan prayer flag—a heart or soul just waiting for the right breeze to carry it forth.

Acknowledgements

No man is an island. If you don't believe this, just try riding a bicycle around the world. My journey and subsequent book would never have been planned, made, nor completed without the invaluable help, love, and inspiration of countless numbers of people.

First and foremost, thanks to my editor, Curtis Foreman, who got my manuscript off its dusty position on a shelf, and breathed a life into it. To Craig, Janey, Cyril, and others who read some early drafts and made critical comments. To Dave Halbakken for computer wizardry, and to Judy for her scrutiny in the final copy edit. Thanks especially to Aim Forward in Bangkok; Eag, Ping, Tuan, and Sombat, for helping me to see things through. An extra special thanks to Sombat Somkiatcharoen, who patiently worked through the night on maps, cover design, and layout, never complaining about my finicky *farang* needs.

In Japan, thanks to Eep and Michiko Luiken and to Koichi and Miki Minemura, who were steadfast friends, and helped me finance my dream.

In Nepal, thanks to PT Sherpa for his long explanations of all things Nepali, to Rajiv Shrestha, for being the best travel agent in the universe, to the Sundas family, for letting us into their lives.

In India, thanks to Tajinder Pal Singh, for opening his home and family to me in a time when I most needed a brother.

In Thailand and Malaysia, thanks to Prem Thawat and Gary Yip for being bike wizards.

In New Zealand, to Mark Bachels and Kim Moreland, for a home away from home.

In Australia, to Alex Edwards, for inspiration in the rainforest.

In Pakistan, to all the hotel managers who always had a cup of tea, and never a bad word, even on the worst of days, and to Coleman, Audrey and Craig for their companionship.

In Central Asia, to Zaina Beshekeyova, Sergei Mamantov, Elena Ivanova, and countless others for their Silk Road hospitality and care, and to US Aid and Peace Corps offices for their invaluable assistance. To Sonja Raub and John McGown, for understanding a bike traveller's needs, and paving the way for me.

In Europe, to Patrik, Hadewych, Jurgen, Phil, and Elke, who rode, visited, or travelled with me, and gave a much-needed respite from seeing different faces every day.

In the U.S., to Elle, Cyril, my Uncle Bill, and old friends in New Mexico who made the landing a bit softer.

This book is dedicated to my mother, who never fully knew how perfectly she passed the gift of excitement and wonder about the world on to her son.

To my oldest friends, Craig and Chris, who have relished my stories and always been supportive of my endeavors and interested in my adventures, for being there for me, even if I have often not been there for them. Your spirits are carried in the top of my panniers.

To Pred, Janiene, Sally, Morgan, Dan, Victoria, Craig, and all my climbing and drinking friends in Bellingham, for teaching me that there is life after bicycle touring, and still a few dreams left to pursue.

Most of all, this is for Hitomi Sumita, for being the best friend and bicycle travel partner a person could ever ask for.

Finally, to Jom. For love, and for showing me how to be completely still.

Bangkok, Thailand, October, 2004

Odysseus' Last Stand

Copies of this book may be ordered from the publisher. Standard library and wholesale discounts are available.

Odysseus' Last Stand	$16.95
Shipping and handling	$2.00
WA residents add 8% sales tax	$1.35
	$20.30

Please send check or money order to:

1321 King St. Suite 1 , #337
Bellingham, WA 98229

Also available online at www.odysseuslaststand.com